Managing Media Companies

Second Edition

Managing Media Companies
Harnessing Creative Value

Second Edition

Annet Aris
Jacques Bughin

WILEY

A John Wiley and Sons, Ltd, Publication

Other Wiley Editorial Offices

John Wiley & Sons Inc., 111 River Street, Hoboken, NJ 07030, USA

Jossey-Bass, 989 Market Street, San Francisco, CA 94103-1741, USA

Wiley-VCH Verlag GmbH, Boschstr. 12, D-69469 Weinheim, Germany

John Wiley & Sons Australia Ltd, 42 McDougall Street, Milton, Queensland 4064, Australia

John Wiley & Sons (Asia) Pte Ltd, 2 Clementi Loop #02-01, Jin Xing Distripark, Singapore 129809

John Wiley & Sons Canada Ltd, 6045 Freemont Blvd. Mississauga, Ontario, L5R 4J3 Canada

Wiley also publishes its books in a variety of electronic formats. Some content that appears in print
may not be available in electronic books.

Library of Congress Cataloging-in-Publication Data
Aris, Annet.
   Managing media companies : harnessing creative values / Annet Aris. – 2nd ed.
      p. cm.
   Includes bibliographical references and index.
   ISBN 978-0-470-71395-2 (pbk.)
   1.   Mass media–Management.   I. Title.
   P96.M34A75 2009
   302.23068–dc22

                                                                2008044728

British Library Cataloguing in Publication Data
A catalogue record for this book is available from the British Library

ISBN 978-0-470-71395-2

Typeset in 10/12 pt Goudy by Thomson Digital, India
Printed and bound in Great Britain by Bell and Bain Ltd, Glasgow.

To Helen and Louise   A.A.

To Noémie and Florent   J.B.

TABLE OF CONTENTS

ADVISORY BOARD xi
ABOUT THE AUTHORS xii
PREFACE xiii
ACKNOWLEDGEMENTS xv

CHAPTER 1
Introduction 1
Media: One or Many Industries? 1
Current State of the Industry 5
Focus and Scope of the Book 11

CHAPTER 2
Rebalancing the Media Value Chain 13
Current Practices Mostly Historically Grown 13
Fundamental Changes Still Ahead 20
Consequences for the Management of Media Companies 29
Is a Fundamental Rethink of Future Business Models Needed? 34
Key Takeaways 36
Case Study: The Welt Group: Creating New Business Models For
News Provision 38
Case Study: Hubert Burda Media: In Search of New Digital Business Models 57
Case Study: Mediaset: From Focused Broadcaster to Value Chain Operator 69

CHAPTER 3
Creating and Leveraging Innovative Content 83
Future Role of (Blockbuster) Content 83
Should Content be Redefined? 89
Management of the Content Generation Process 92
Peer Production, User-generated Content and Co-creation 101
Key Takeaways 102
Case Study: Endemol: Diversifying the Content Portfolio 104
Case Study: OhmyNews: Creating a Sustainable Model for Content
Co-creation 112

CHAPTER 4

**The Fight for Customer Attention: Intelligent Mass Marketing
and Cautious Niche Strategy** 121
The Increasing Need to Understand Customers 121
Strategic Brand Management 128
Fine-Tune the Marketing Strategy to Revenue Model 133
Marketing Strategies for Subscription-based Players 136
Marketing Strategy for Niche and Thematic Offerings 141
Key Takeaways 143
*Case Study: Canal+: Keeping Consumer Loyality in the Face of Platform
Competition* 144
Case Study: EMI: Developing New Marketing Models for the Digital Age . 156
Case Study: Telenet: Leveraging Digital Segmentation 167

CHAPTER 5

End-to-end Supply Chain Management 179
Achieving Operational Excellence in Supply Chain Management 179
Enhancing the Effectiveness of Standardized Media Supply
Chain Processes 181
Improvement Levers for Non-standardized Processes in the
Media Industry 189
Managing the Transition to Digital Platforms 192
Key Takeaways 197
Case Study: RTL Group: Creating a Digital Value Chain 198

CHAPTER 6

Ways Out of the Advertising Commodity Trap 211
Traditional Advertising Under Increasing Pressure 211
The First Wave of Advertising Spending Shift: Direct
Marketing and Below the Line 213
Digital Technology at the Core of the Second Wave 214
Reaching New Capabilities in Advertising 226
Key Takeaways 247
Case Study: Schibsted: Diversifying the Advertising Source 248

CHAPTER 7

Corporate Strategy in Media 259
Current Media Landscape 259
Future Portfolio Logic 266
Key Takeaways 276
Case Study: Liberty Global: Multichannel Portfolio Play 277
Case Study: Lagardère Active: Restoring Growth Through Operations ... 284
Case Study: Sanoma Group: Restructuring the Portfolio for Growth 293

CHAPTER 8

The Future Role of Online Media   303
Online Start 1995–2001: 'Overestimate in the Short Term'   303
Period of Consolidation 2002 to 2008: Building the Digital Platform   306
Online Media Business Models   312
Key Takeaways   321
Case Study: Second Life: Peer Production Through Co-creation   322
Case Study: YouTube: Building Social Media   330

CHAPTER 9

**People Management in Media Companies: Creative Managers or
Managed Creativity?**   339
Current People Management Practices in the Media Industry   339
Current Challenge: Embrace 'Creators' Yet Do Not Understate 'Transformers'   341
Common Principles of People Management Processes for 'Creators' and
'Transformers'   342
Management of 'Transformers'   345
Management of 'Creatives'   346
People Management in the Digital Media Era   356
Outlook and Open Questions   364
Key Takeaways   364
Case Study: BBC: Adapting the Organization to the Digital World   366

INDEX   375

ADVISORY BOARD

A theory is only as good as the real-life practice turns out to be. The case studies play a crucial role in the book, as they illustrate and bring alive the outlined management theory. For most of the case studies, we have asked those companies that are at the frontline of working through the management issues discussed in the book to share their experiences with us. Key managers of these companies are members of our advisory board; they have been selected as managers who changed or are in the process of changing the face of the media industry. It is not only through the case studies that they have been crucial in shaping this book: they have been sparring partners in our advisory practice and have contributed either as guest lecturers at INSEAD, where they shared many valuable experiences and insights, or as project coaches for students. Others, such as Robin Harper of Second Life, have kindly, and enthusiastically, agreed to cowrite the case studies of their companies. The YouTube case study was inspired by conversations between Chad Hurley and one of the authors at the Aspen Institute workshop on distributed co-creation in July 2007. Needless to say, we owe all of these media personalities a great debt of gratitude for their contribution. The current advisory board consists of:

Eija Ailasmaa, President and CEO, Sanoma Magazines and Board Member, Sanoma Group
Carolyn Fairbairn, Director of Group Development and Strategy, ITV plc
Marco Giordani, CFO and Board Member, Mediaset
Immanuel Hermreck, Executive Vice President, Human Resources, Bertelsmann AG
Paul-Bernhard Kallen, Member of the Board, Hubert Burda Media
Birger Magnus, Executive Vice President Norway, Schibsted ASA
Steffen Naumann, CFO and Member of the Board, Axel Springer AG
Shane O'Neill, Chief Strategy Officer, Liberty Global and President, Chellomedia UK
Miguel Paes do Amaral, Media entrepreneur and investor, former Chairman and CEO, Grupo Media Capital CEO Quifel Holdings SGPS, S.A
Guillaume de Posch, former CEO, ProSiebenSat1 AG
Maxime Saada, Managing Director CanalSat, Director of Strategy, Groupe Canal+
Philip Schindler, Managing Director Google, Northern Europe
Duco Sickinghe, CEO, Telenet, Belgium
Hannu Syrjaenen, President, Sanoma Group
Peter Wuertenberger, Chief Marketing Officer, Axel Springer AG
Alison Young, Management Development Director, Pearson PLC

Our thanks also go to previous members of the advisory board, whose insights still form an important contribution to the book:

Rodolphe Belmer, Managing Director, Groupe Canal+
Humphrey Cobbold, former Director of Strategic Development, Trinity Mirror plc, Director at Candover
Detlef Hunsdiek, former Executive Vice President, Human Resources, Bertelsmann AG, Executive Vice President Corporate Management Development ThyssenKrupp AG
Andreas Kindt, former CIO and Board Member, T-Home (Deutsche Telekom AG), CEO of Loyalty Partners Solutions, Munich
Hans Mahr, former Executive Coordinator, RTL Group, currently CEO of Mahrmedia
Hubertus Meyer-Burckhardt, former Board Member, Pro7Sat1 AG, CEO Polyphon (TV Production), talkshow moderator NDR, Germany
Marc Olivier Sommer, former Board Member, Direct Group, Bertelsmann AG, Board Member Arcando AG

We want to express our gratitude for their commitment to this project and for sharing their passion for managing media companies.

ABOUT THE AUTHORS

Annet Aris is a Dutch native and Adjunct Professor of Strategy at INSEAD at Fontainebleau, France, where she initiated and teaches courses on media management to MBA students and media executives. Annet is also a member of the board of the OPTA, the Dutch regulatory authority for telecoms, cable and postal services. Before that, she was a partner at McKinsey & Company and the co-leader of the firm's German Media Practice. She holds an MSc in engineering and an MBA from INSEAD, has written numerous articles on media management and is a frequent speaker at media seminars around the world. She is an independent board member of the Sanoma Group in Finland and Hans-Heemann AG in Germany. She chairs the International Advisory Board of the Faculty of Economics and Business Management of the University of Maastricht and is a board member of the foundation Beeld & Geluid in the Netherlands.

Dr Jacques Bughin is a Belgian native and a senior partner and director at McKinsey & Company. He is a core leader of the firm's Global Media and Entertainment Practice and has conducted numerous client engagements across all major media sectors and continents. His work extends to high-tech, telecoms and cable companies, as well as to Internet companies. He currently co-leads the McKinsey Technology Initiative, which is aimed at understanding new business and strategy models to best leverage digital technologies. He is a core leader of the firm's marketing practice, where he co-leads the digital marketing initiative. Jacques holds a BA, MA and PhD in economics. He is a Fellow of the Free University of Brussels (ULB), ECORE, and of the University of Leuven (KUL). Jacques has written numerous academic papers in leading management and economic journals, such as the *Journal of Economic Behavior and Organization*, the *European Economic Review* and *Management Science and Electronic Markets*, and frequently contributes articles related to digital and traditional media to the *McKinsey Quarterly*. He has been a contributor to many books. He is a frequent speaker at media and Internet conferences, such as NAB, MIDEM, INMA, Cable Europe, Internet World, Broadband Summit and the Marketing Science Institute.

PREFACE TO SECOND EDITION

The first edition of this book, written in 2004, was originally meant as teaching material for MBA students at INSEAD. However, it quickly turned out that its scope was much wider than that. It was not only read by students from all over the world, from Hunan to Moscow and Boston, as part of their media courses but also became very popular among a wide range of media managers. The book found a prominent place on the bookshelves of managers in the print, TV and Internet industries, coming from a variety of functional backgrounds, such as finance, human resource, advertising sales and general management; more importantly, it was actually read. The feedback we got was that the focus on the skills needed to manage media companies combined with a large number of real-life case studies in the context of a fast-changing industry environment was very helpful.

In the meantime, however, many developments that were described in the first edition have actually taken place, often at a much faster pace than originally expected. New challenges are emerging, such as the fast rise of Web 2.0 and social networks and a fundamentally changing advertising landscape. Although the skills described in the first edition are still valid, we wanted to 'stress test' them in the context of the recent acceleration of digital transformation. While revising the text and updating the cases, we finally ended up rewriting more than half the book, hence we even contemplated publishing it as an entirely new title. However, as many of the basic principles and core competencies described in the book still hold – some stronger, others slightly de-emphasized, or fine-tuned – we finally decided that it is still the same book, but enriched with new, more relevant case studies, such as YouTube, Second Life and many others. It has again been an exciting journey to which many parties have contributed, especially the media practice of McKinsey & Company, Inc., and our advisory board.

ACKNOWLEDGEMENTS

For the second edition, special thanks go to **Angelique Mannella**, INSEAD MBA student 2008 and **Stephanie Nols**, a business analyst at McKinsey & Company Brussels. Angelique played an instrumental role in the rewriting of the case studies on the BBC, Hubert Burda Media, Canal+, EMI, Mediaset and RTL as well as the writing of the new case on the Welt Group. Stephanie contributed to the writing of the OhMyNews and YouTube case as well as the rewriting of the Telenet case.

The authors are also indebted to and grateful for the ongoing help of current and former colleagues at McKinsey & Company, McKinsey media clients around the world and many other experts who have readily offered their support and insights throughout the process of preparing the materials and conducting the first round of the course. For their support with the first edition, special thanks go to:

Cornelius Grupen, former consultant at McKinsey & Company's Hamburg office. He co-authored Chapters 1, 3 and 4 as well as the Lagardère Media, RTL Group, Canal+ and Schibsted case studies.

Timo Voswinckel, former consultant at McKinsey & Company's Munich office. He co-authored Chapters 5 and 8 as well as EMI case studies.

Kirsten Weerda, Associate Principal at McKinsey & Company's Munich office. She co-authored Chapter 9.

Sir John Birt, former CEO, BBC (Chapter 9).

Matthew Brittin, former Associate Principal, McKinsey & Company, London, Managing Director Google UK.

Menno van Dijk, Director, McKinsey & Company, Amsterdam.

Sandrine Devillard, Principal, McKinsey & Company, Paris (Chapter 5, Lagardère and Canal+ case studies).

Alexandra Dmitrieva, former Senior Information Analyst, McKinsey & Company, Paris (Lagardère and Canal+ case studies).

Thomas Farstad, former consultant, McKinsey & Company, Oslo (Schibsted case study).

Lutz Finger, INSEAD MBA 2004 (Mediaset and Sanoma case studies).

Philip Graf, former CEO, Trinity Mirror Group.

Alexander Guntram, Knowledge Expert – Media, McKinsey & Company, Munich (all chapters).

Huan Hoang, former Media Research Analyst, McKinsey & Company, Munich (all chapters).

Michael Icent, INSEAD MBA 2004 (BBC case study).

Mirjam Laux, Wharton MBA 2004 (Liberty Global and BBC case studies).

Nick Lovegrove, Director, McKinsey & Company, London (Chapter 5).

Sam Marwaha, Principal, McKinsey & Company, BTO New York (Chapter 5).

Robert Musslewhite, former Associate Principal, McKinsey & Company, Washington DC (Chapter 4).

Henrik Poppe, former Associate Principal, McKinsey & Company, Oslo (Schibsted case study).

Max Ringlstetter, Professor at the University of Ingolstadt/Eichstatt (Chapter 4).

Friedrich Rojahn, INSEAD MBA 2004 (Hubert Burda Media case study).

John Rose, former Executive Vice President, EMI Group, director at BCG (EMI case study).

Trude Sleire, former Engagement Manager, McKinsey & Company, Oslo (Schibsted case study).

Gert Stuerzebecher, former Vice President, Management Development, Bertelsmann AG.

Peter de Wit, Principal, McKinsey & Company, Amsterdam (Chapter 4).

Catherine Witter, former consultant, McKinsey & Company, London (BBC case study).

Michael Wolf, former Director, McKinsey & Company, New York.

The authors wish to thank the staff of John Wiley & Sons, Ltd, Chichester, especially Georgia King, Nicole Burnett and Céline Durand. Without the high quality and remarkable flexibility of your support, it would not have been possible to write this book. You have set a fine example for many media companies!

January 2009

INTRODUCTION

1

What is generally spoken of as 'the media industry' covers in reality a range of businesses, which differ not only in the type of media produced but also in their revenue models. Before discussing how 'the media' should be managed, it is important to understand what is behind this general term. This introductory chapter specifically aims to answer the following questions:

1. *What is the media industry? What are key differentiating factors and commonalities within the media industry?*
2. *What is the current state of the industry? What key challenges have to be faced?*
3. *How will these challenges be addressed in this book?*

Media: One or Many Industries?

Few industries are as diverse, shifting and high-paced as the media industry. The industry is a unique crossbreed of creativity and business, comprising a wide array of segments, enterprises and players – some of them dedicated strictly to economic value creation, others bordering on eccentricity.

The core element which ties all these businesses together is content, that is creations people want to spend time looking at, listening and/or contributing to as a goal in itself (this excludes activities such as e-commerce, search, outdoor advertising and direct mail, whose main purpose is to facilitate a next action). The most traditional way to look at the media industry is by type of media used (media sector): printed products, such as books, newspapers and magazines; and electronic products, such as films, TV, radio, games, music and, more recently, Internet and mobile content. However, to understand the business dynamics within each sector, it is important to distinguish along a number of other dimensions. For example, some of the media sectors have a number of distinct sub-segments, employing very different business models. Take television, for example: there is free (commercial) TV, public service broadcasting and various types of pay TV. What's more, they can all be broadcast using terrestrial, satellite or cable infrastructure or be streamed via the Internet. Overall, several key factors cut across the different media sectors that we must become familiar with in order to understand the dynamics of individual businesses.

Revenue model

Many media businesses are at least partly financed by advertising. In particular, advertising plays a central role in free TV, Internet, some newspapers (depending on the country) and certain types of magazines, such as high-end fashion magazines.

Other media businesses are mostly financed through consumer revenues. Consumer revenues can be either subscription-based or single-copy-based. 'Single-copy'-based businesses are strongly 'hit'-driven. Sales and profits can vary greatly depending on whether the company produces a blockbuster or not. Modern music and films, but also consumer books, and yellow press newspapers are typical examples of hit-driven industries. On the other hand, there are sectors characterized by a strong emphasis on subscription, such as national quality newspapers or weekly magazines and pay television. Of course, the business dynamics vary greatly for each of the three revenue models. In advertising-financed businesses the key factor of success is the 'reach' (the number of consumers who are exposed to the media product) within the target group of the advertiser. In a 'single-copy'-sales driven business the focus is above all on 'real option' management. Subscription-based businesses are managed to optimize the customer lifetime value with overall customer satisfaction as a key parameter.

Customer intimacy

Several sectors are typical mass media oriented, in which revenue models are based on maximizing audience reach – that is the number of consumers within a broadly defined target segment (e.g. population between 14 and 49 in the TV industry) – without knowing the individuals. Typical examples are free TV and single-copy newspapers or magazines. Key skills are to understand mass audience needs through market research, creating content with wide appeal, adequate aggregation/packaging of the content and mass-marketing the products.

Other sectors focus on building an individual relationship with their audience, whom they know by name and address. The focus of these sectors – typically subscription print products, pay-TV cable operators or Internet service providers – is on acquiring the most profitable consumers, optimizing the ARPU (average revenue per user) and reducing 'churn' (loss of subscribers). A special group within these businesses is made up of those media companies that target businesses or institutions dealing with education, or academic, financial or business information rather than individual end consumers. This category requires a business-to-business approach for its content, sales and marketing strategies.

Type of content

Some media are mostly news- and information-focused; some focus on entertainment; some offer a mix. The news-focused businesses (daily broadsheets, news channels, business magazines) will have to cope with political sensitivities and have to be much more stringent in guaranteeing objectivity, for example by installing Chinese walls between the editors and the business side.

Position in value chain

Only a few media businesses, such as newspapers, magazines, movie and game producers, actually generate content themselves. Most media companies are in the business of identifying attractive content, packaging it, for example in the form of CDs, TV schedules, newspaper and magazine layout – and marketing it. Finally, there are the distributors, those companies that operate distribution platforms and infrastructure – such as cable, copper and wireless networks and Internet servers. These companies have to manage the infrastructure, develop a relationship with individual end consumers and ensure that there is attractive content on the platform.

Common challenges

Despite all the differences, there are also significant commonalities in the media industry. Almost all media businesses face five main challenges: continually developing new content offerings, addressing a triple market interface, coping with volatility, dealing with multiple local, rather than truly international, markets and balancing economic with more social objectives.

First, at the heart of every media business there is a *perishable commodity*: content. Whether it is news or entertainment, reports or stories, fact or fiction, content is essentially intangible and depends on fashion, trends and inspiration. Often, it has to be created anew every day and it is – apart from a few evergreens – mostly short-lived. The extreme cases are, of course, the live transmission of sports or news. In general, a TV channel's content portfolio has a lifespan of three to five years, except for a few blockbuster formats such as *The Wheel of Fortune, Seinfeld*, or cult programmes such as the RTL Group's *Gute Zeiten, schlechte Zeiten*. Core print titles, such as the Lagardère-owned *Paris Match* or *Elle* magazines, have led their markets for decades, but only the formula and positioning have remained the same – the actual content has always changed to reflect the latest news and trends. As a consequence, today's media winners are much more likely to be tomorrow's losers than is the case in most other industries. The challenge to stay on top of a creative process, which is subject to quick and frequent changes, has made the media a 'people business'.

Second, the media industry is facing a particularly *complex market structure* (Figure 1.1). Media companies generally compete on three fronts: for compelling content (authors market), then for end-consumer attention and spending (consumer market) and also for corporate marketing budgets (advertisers and sponsors market). Publishers trying to be equally attractive to audiences as diverse as writers, readers and advertisers must balance their efforts very carefully and often still run into conflicts of interest.

Third, the media industry is, on average, *very volatile in comparison to other industries*. Industry revenues tend to be cyclical; advertising spend, especially, is strongly correlated to GDP (Figure 1.2).

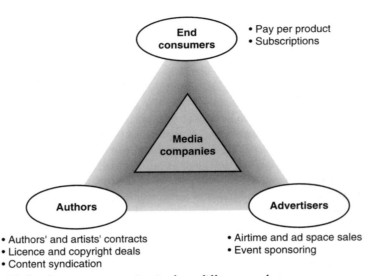

Figure 1.1 Media players are competing in three different markets

Revenues are in general also very dependent on single hits. In many cases, creating and marketing new products such as TV shows, CDs or films involve great uncertainty as to consumer acceptance, for instance 80% of the new prime-time shows on TV in the United States are not renewed for a second season on the air. This high level of uncertainty, combined with the industry's high production costs, presents very high risk. As a result,

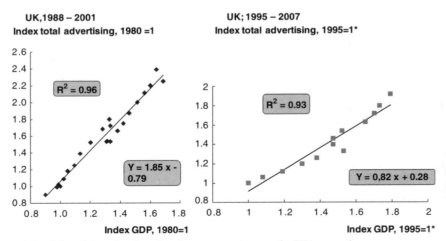

Figure 1.2 Advertising closely related to economic growth, UK example

*First quarter only
Source: Quarterly Survey of Advertising Expenditure 2002 (Advertising Association, AC Nielsen MMS, and WARC), Economic Trends/ONS

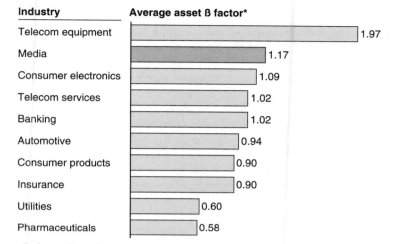

Figure 1.3   Industry beta factors

*Regressed at a monthly frequency for five years against Financial Times World Actuaries Index
Source: McKinsey analyses based on data from Bloomberg

the systematic risk component of the cost of capital in the media industry (called 'beta' in the financial jargon) is significantly above average (Figure 1.3).

Fourth, the media industry is still very much characterized by *local, rather than global, content markets*. Only a few characters and artists have global appeal. Of the 20 best-rated TV shows in Europe, it is common that 80–90% are local. Global magazine brands are adapted to local content tastes and even Internet sites are much more successful when they have country-specific sites.

Finally, media companies play an important role in society as they filter and comment on information and determine the 'quality' of the entertainment offered. This gives them a social responsibility, which they have to balance with profit-maximizing objectives. This means they often have to cope with political pressure and power plays. It is not uncommon for media companies – especially those that are privately owned, but also some publicly listed companies such as Axel Springer in Germany – to have objectives which go beyond economic value creation and have a vision on how they should contribute to society.

Current State of the Industry

The media industry is currently going through a major transition and traditional media companies are fundamentally rethinking their business models. The main driver of this change is the digitization of media and the platforms through which it is distributed. What has happened?

The second half of the last century was a story of unique growth for the traditional media companies. Media products such as books, magazines and TV may, at first sight, seem to be competing for a share of the same consumer market. Although this is technically true, overall media usage and spending have, in fact, grown steadily over the past decades in real terms and the different media, in relation to each other, have experienced very little cannibalization. The same is true for advertising spending, an important source of revenue for media companies, which has been growing as a percentage of GDP in most countries.

This growth was mostly fuelled by innovations in technology, such as printing, radio broadcasting or TV. For example, small-screen film revenues have been sustained over a long time with the consecutive introduction and promotion of (terrestrial) TV, video, cable/satellite, VHS, DVD and home cinema technology. New products, additional channels and technical innovations have rarely substituted for, but rather have supplemented, existing offerings. Although considered revolutionary at the time, radio has not displaced print, and nor has TV superseded films. The strategy most media companies followed was to keep the old medium and invest in the new medium as it came to market. As the narrowband Internet started to emerge in the late 1990s, media companies initially treated it as the next new medium and invested in it, hype was created with overinflated prices for Internet advertising and astronomical prices for Internet start-ups. As the bubble burst in early 2000, many of the traditional companies got very weary and discontinued their Internet activities to a major extent. This was also driven by the fact that they started noticing that Internet offerings were cannibalizing their traditional offerings – which were much more profitable than the initial Internet websites – so they preferred to ignore the emerging Internet models. The slow transition from paper-based to online classifieds advertisement offerings by most newspaper groups is a good example of this behaviour. Meanwhile, Internet usage grew faster than predicted and a large share of the online market was taken by the new start-ups, such as Yahoo!, eBay, Amazon, Monster and, later on, Google. Once the incumbent media companies started to reinvest in online offerings, they were often too late to catch up with the market entrants.

If by neglecting the Internet the traditional media would have just missed out on a new media channel, the impact would have been limited. The Internet, however, is just one element of a much more fundamental change: the shift from analogue to digital media. Although the ability to produce digital media has been around for a long time, the combination of three factors has resulted in the unprecedented speed of market penetration by digital media and with that a fundamental change in the rules of the game.

The first factor is the fast roll-out of high-capacity digital platforms, starting with broadband Internet. The speed of penetration in northern Europe and the United States even exceeded the speed of penetration of the mobile phone and the PC. Especially in those countries where there were seriously competing cable and telephony infrastructures, such as the Netherlands, Belgium and Scandinavia, the penetration was very fast (Figure 1.4). The second wave is the roll-out of digital TV, which after a hesitant start is now in full flight, greatly increasing the number of channels people have access to. With the penetration of digital technology, not only a major shift in the use of media is visible but also a significant increase in alternative delivery mechanisms will arise, such as downloading or streaming for all electronic media, be it films, TV programmes, games or news.

Much less talked about, but with a similar potential impact, is the fast progression in compression and storage technologies. During the first decade of the twenty-first century,

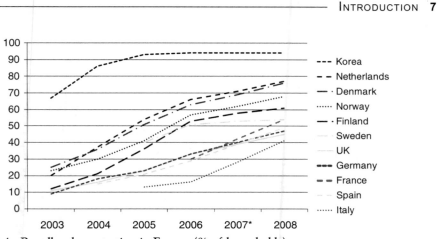

Figure 1.4   Broadband penetration in Europe (% of households)

*Data for 2007 interpolation between 2006 and 2008
Source: McKinsey Analyses based on data from OECD, ITIF

there has been an 85% annual improvement in storage capacity thanks to a combination of improvement in physical storage (i.e. improvement in physical storage capacity for the same price) and a decrease in memory needed because of better compression technologies. This means that, if this speed is kept up, by 2013 a DVD recorder, which can currently store 50 films, could store 650 000 films for the same storage cost. Furthermore, compression has an effect not only on storage but also on the ability to support robust media streams with lower bit rates. MPEG-4 is now the buzz, after MPEG-2, for video delivery services, making an improvement of 50% on the coding rate to deliver high-quality video, opening the door for affordable high-definition TV and other applications.

Finally, the fast development in digital appliances will not only mean a significant decrease in cost for digital receivers such as set-top boxes but will also create new forms of media access. This includes the personal video recorder (PVR), the emergence of PC-TV media centres and mobile phones that are turning into intuitive, personal, mobile media and communication centres.

The combined effect of these three factors is that content, once digitized, can be distributed and stored at almost zero marginal cost. The implications of this are significant and result in a fundamental shift of paradigms between the analogue and digital world.

- *From the management of scarcity to fight for attention:* in the analogue world, a main role of media companies was to make best use of limited available media space: the evening programming on television, the 30 pages of the newspaper and the music slots on the radio. In the digital world hundreds of TV channels, video-on-demand offerings and countless websites offer almost limitless content, and the main challenge of a media company is to get its offering noticed. At the same time, analogue offerings will lose significant market share as people spend more time with digital offerings and increasingly start to use media in parallel (Figures 1.5, 1.6 and 1.7).
- *From content consumption to interaction:* in the analogue world, media consumption is mostly passive and the content creator has a rather incomplete and vague idea of how

Minutes/day

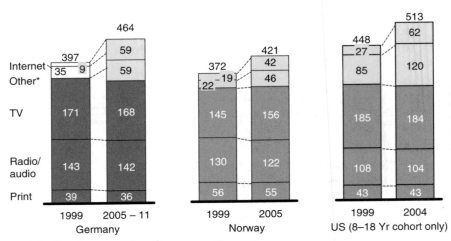

Figure 1.5 Development of media consumption patterns

*For example, videos, DVDs, games, includes computer usage other than Internet
Source: McKinsey analyses based on data from SevenOne Media; Norge Statistics Sentralbyrĺ; the Kayser Foundation

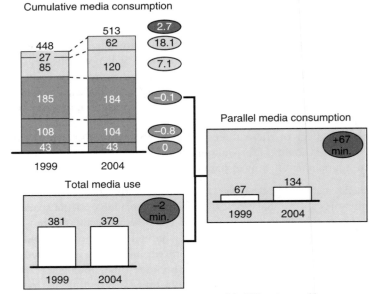

Figure 1.6 Media consumption patterns 8–18 years old, US, minutes/day

*For example, videos, DVDs, games, includes computer usage other than Internet
Source: McKinsey analyses based on data from the Kayser Foundation

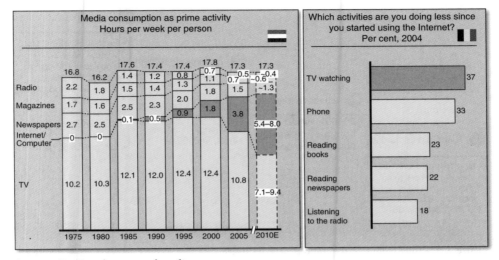

Figure 1.7 Development of media usage

Source: McKinsey analyses based on data from Sociaal Cultureel Planbureau, Statbel, VSS; EIAA (Netherlands) – European Media Consumption Study 2004 (Belgian figures)

individual readers/viewers react to content. In the digital world the consumers cannot only give direct feedback but also (co)create content, often with surprising success (Figure 1.8).

- *From paid to free content:* most content on the Internet is free or much cheaper than analogue content. In order to stay competitive, media companies are increasingly shifting their offerings to free, advertising-financed content (e.g. the commuter newspapers and video on demand). This results in an increased demand for advertising in a market which is growing only slightly above GDP.

- *From advertising reach to advertising impact:* in the analogue world media companies are paid by advertisers based on the number of people (within the demographic target group of the advertiser) who are exposed to the media product (reach). The target groups can only be based on broad demographic terms as it is not possible to measure individuals' exposure to the media. In the digital world, a much more precise targeting is possible, for example one based on search behaviour or detailed TV watching patterns. In addition payment models can be based on actions (e.g. clicks) rather than supposed exposure. The greater measurability of digital media will make it more attractive for advertisers once they have figured out how to measure and use these new media. This effect, combined with the increase in supply of advertising inventory, owing to free content, and the loss of reach, owing to increased competition in offering, will make it increasingly difficult for analogue media to generate sufficient advertising revenues (Figure 1.9).

Traditional media companies are thus faced with a double challenge. On the one hand, their analogue business is clearly maturing in most Western countries, or in some cases already declining, and they will have to manage this to maintain profitability. As the industry historically is geared to growth, this will mean a significant change in

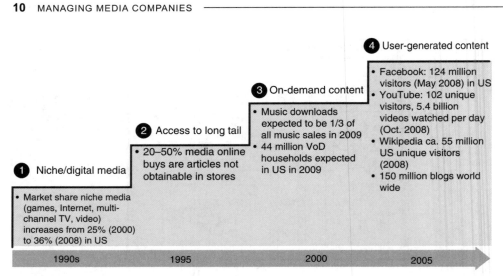

Figure 1.8 **Shift from passive to active media usage**

Source: Mckinsey analyses based on data from Comscore, Nielsen Online, TechCrunch, Technocrati

management practices. Industry consolidation, vertical integration, more refined segmentation and pricing and the avoidance of fierce competition will be the main challenges. At the same time the companies will have to build their digital businesses using a whole new set of rules and compete with new entrants who are already fully geared to the digital world.

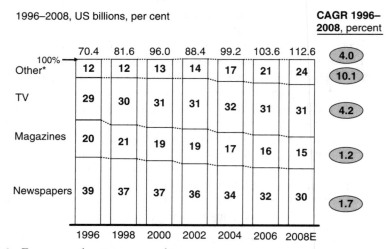

Figure 1.9 **European advertising expenditure**

*Includes cinema, Internet, radio and outdoor
Source: McKinsey analyses based on data from ZenithOptimedia March 2008

Focus and Scope of the Book

Most of the challenges described above apply to all media sectors, albeit in different ways. They will require fundamentally new skills and new ways of managing the business, while at the same time preserving core skills around content generation. The focus of the book will be on what skills media companies will need to be successful in the future and what they can do to build these skills. Although most skills are closely interconnected, the discussion will be structured along four core processes, which characterize most media businesses: the content generation process, the content delivery process, advertising sales and end-customer interaction (Figure 1.10).

Of course, the implications will vary significantly depending on the type of media business and will be illustrated by concrete examples and case studies. The main focus will be on newspapers, magazines, TV/cable, music and the Internet. The examples will be based mostly on the European media industry as, on the one hand, there is currently a strong bias towards the United States in most literature on the media industry and little is available on Europe and, on the other hand, the European situation poses some additional complexities (multiple, smaller local markets, significant presence of public service broadcasters, regulatory environment), which make it an even more interesting environment to discuss.

The following chapters will give first an overview of current practices in the industry and how they are likely to be affected by the 'digital disruption' (Chapter 2, 'Rebalancing the media value chain'). Then each of the core processes will be discussed in more detail, with a special focus on the future skills needed to manage these processes, from content generation (Chapter 3, 'Creating and leveraging innovative content'), consumer

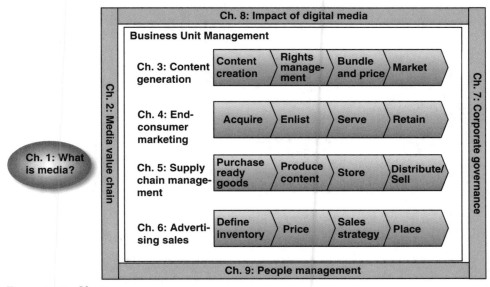

Figure 1.10   Chapter structure

marketing (Chapter 4, 'The fight for customer attention: intelligent mass marketing and cautious niche strategy') and content delivery (Chapter 5, 'End-to-end supply chain management') to advertising sales (Chapter 6, 'Ways out of the advertising commodity trap'). As most media companies are conglomerates of multiple media activities, Chapter 7, 'Corporate strategy in media', will discuss the implications for corporate strategy of media companies. Chapter 8, 'The future role of digital media', will then give an outlook on new digital businesses and the role they will play in the industry. Last but not least Chapter 9, 'People management in media companies: creative managers or managed creativity?', discusses how the media industry manages its most important resource – namely people – and the challenges the industry is facing to build the skills and motivation required to face the new digital era.

For each chapter, one or more case studies will be presented to illustrate the issues discussed. These case studies have been written in cooperation with the media companies concerned. They thus represent the real managerial issues that the book aims to tackle.

REBALANCING THE MEDIA VALUE CHAIN

As media products are invented anew every day, day-to-day management practices are the key to success. However, as in many other industries, most of these practices have grown historically. Given the major changes the industry is currently undergoing, it is very uncertain to what extent these practices still apply. This chapter will answer three major questions:

1. *What are the core processes in traditional media and what are the current strengths and weaknesses in the way they are managed?*
2. *What are the major disruptions the media industry will be facing in the coming years and what are the consequences for the way the core processes should be adapted?*
3. *Will there be a significant shift in the future business models of media companies?*

Current Practices Mostly Historically Grown

As we have seen, the media industry is managed along four relatively distinct core processes, that is: content generation, content delivery, advertising sales and end-consumer interaction. The concrete activities however can vary significantly by media sector (Figure 2.1).

The processes are, as in most industries, characterized by historically grown practices. In general, the more mature media sectors – such as magazine and newspaper publishing – tend to have fine-tuned and optimized these processes more tightly than younger media sectors – such as TV and music.

Content generation process: the heart of the media industry

The content generation process (Figure 2.2) is considered the heart of the media business. In this process, the most important step is ensuring the generation of content and their translation into rights. Here, rights are defined in the extended sense, that is not only the

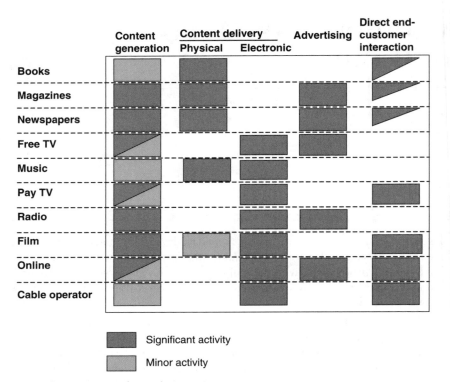

Figure 2.1 Core processes by media sector

Source: Author analyses

legal piece of paper defining who owns what content but also the concrete output resulting from a creative process, such as a book or script, a song take, an article, a film tape/digital file, etc. Rights are generated partly in the media company itself (e.g. newspaper and magazine articles, in-house TV production) and partly by a large number of mostly independent creatives (e.g. musicians, authors, script/song writers, independent producers) who are often represented by agents. Identifying the high-potential creatives and binding them to the company is still regarded as *the* make-or-break factor for a media company's success. The cost of producing the content is monitored, but, when push comes to shove, costs are generally subordinated to (perceived) revenue potential.

How the value is divided between the creatives, their agents and media companies is determined in the second step, when the rights are bought and sold. A wide variety of deals exists. The most common are deals where the creator gets a fixed sum or a share of revenues every time his/her product is broadcast or sold. A whole industry with a wide array of collection agencies has evolved around the management of these rights. Another model is the 'cost-plus' deal, which is very common in the European TV production industry, where the producer gets paid for the cost of its production plus a prefixed profit margin. Other deals are output deals, where TV channels buy packages of content mostly from US production studios, where they agree to buy all the output from the studio (good and bad products) for a predefined period and have the right to broadcast this output for a

	Create rights	Buy/sell rights	Package	Price	Marketing to Distributors / End consumers

	Rights creators	Type of deals	Packaged end-product	Pricing principle	Marketing instruments	
Books	• Independent authors	• Upfront fee* • Share of revenue	• Book	• Fixed cover price in Germany and France	• Book store visits/promotions • Fairs	• Advertisements • Book reviews • Awards
Newspapers/ magazines	• Journalists – Employees – Freelance	• Licence fee	• Magazine/ newspaper	• Fixed cover price		• Direct mail • Friendship actions • Advertisement
TV	• Producers – Own – Movie majors – Independent	• Cost-plus • Revenue share • Output deals	• TV programme grid	• Free TV: No fees • PSB: Regulatory fees • Pay: Subscription		• Advertisements
Music	• Musicians	• Revenue share	• CD	• Fixed cover price • Promotions	• Radio/TV promotion • Store promotion	• Promotion by scene leaders

Figure 2.2 Content generation process by media sector

*Bestselling authors
Source: Author analyses

limited number of times. There are also 'revenue sharing' deals, where the creator and the media company agree to share the (advertising) revenues generated by the content. The type of deal has, of course, an enormous influence on the economics of a media company. For example, in the case of an output deal, once the right is purchased, it becomes a sunk cost to the media company and, given the comparatively low marginal costs of delivering the actual products, the top priority for media companies is to generate as much revenue as possible from the rights they own. With variable revenue sharing, the emphasis will be less on revenue maximization and more on finding the point where marginal profits (variable revenues minus variable costs) are maximized.

Selecting and packaging the individual pieces of content into an integrated offering is historically the core competence of most media companies. Best practice companies package content in such a way that the packaged product (e.g. magazine, CD, evening TV programme) as a whole is more attractive than the sum of its parts and thus retains customer attention. Weaker elements of the offering are sandwiched between the popular products in such a way that they do not distract from them.

Pricing the products for end consumers, although an important driver of revenues, has received relatively little industry attention. Very often, prices follow historical patterns and are mostly a result of a comparison with those of competitors, rather than a careful analysis of the willingness to pay of individual consumers.

Price changes are infrequent, and there is limited price differentiation. Often, price differences between products have no strategic rationale, for instance one would expect some correlation between sales volume and price of books, but usually this is hard to find (Figure 2.3).

Top US bestsellers

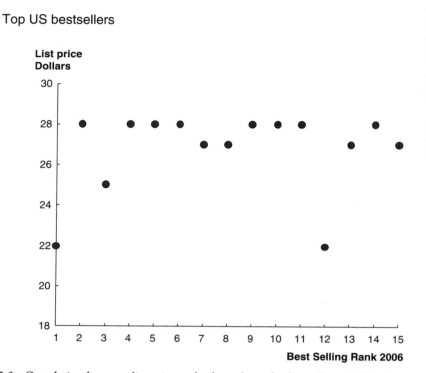

Figure 2.3 Correlation between list price and sales volume for bestsellers, US book example

Source: McKinsey analyses based on data from *Publisher's Weekly*

Marketing the products is the last step in the content generation process, in which marketers 'place' the product into the market with the help of advertising campaigns, promotions and below-the-line marketing, addressing both end consumers and distribution channels (e.g. shops, music radio stations). Traditionally, this is mostly a 'B2B' (business-to-business) process; marketing efforts are, besides a few mass-market campaigns and promotion through own media channels, mostly directed at powerful opinion shapers, such as radio DJs for music or distributors such as cinemas (movies), bookstores, supermarkets (magazines, music, newspapers) and kiosk chains.

Content delivery: a necessary but burdensome task

The content delivery process is especially important for those sectors that deliver physical products (e.g. books, magazines, newspapers, videos, CDs, DVDs; Figure 2.4).

Content delivery – the process of turning a right into a product and ensuring the product's distribution – is usually looked upon as a cost, and not as a value-creating activity, and is often handled in a separate area of the organization. The focus is very much

Purchase ready goods/services	Produce	Store	Distribute		
			Wholesale	Retail	End consumer
Main goods purchased	Production facility	Storage facility	Main channel	Main channel	Main direct channel
Books • Paper • Printing	• Third-party, (own) printing facility	• Book ware-house	• Specialized national wholesalers	• Book retailers • Warehouses, supermarkets	• Book clubs
Newspapers/ magazines • Paper • Printing	• Own (third-party) printing facilities		• Regional print distributors	• Newspaper stands • General outlets	• Own home delivery crew • Mail
TV • Equipment • Production services	• Studio and outdoor production (own/third party)	• Programme tapes warehouse	• Cable, satellite, terrestrial	• Electronic stores (pay TV) • General outlets	
Music • Discs	• CD production facilities	• Music warehouse	• Specialized wholesalers	• Music stores, general outlets, supermarkets	• Music clubs

Figure 2.4 Content delivery process by media sector

Source: Author analyses

on optimizing efficiency and effectiveness, while remaining within the quality boundaries set by the content departments.

For the purchasing function of print companies, the most important product categories are paper and printing services (the latter only when outsourced). For electronic media, the purchase or leasing of technical equipment and facilities is the main focus. In both cases, quality – as defined by the creative people – plays a very important role (e.g. wood content and bulk for paper, technical specifications for cameras, etc.), and, as the technicians themselves also tend to have a preference for sophisticated solutions, this can result in an eclectic and overqualified range of goods and equipment being purchased.

In the print and music businesses, efficiently printing the products is a highly industrialized and optimized process geared to maximizing utilization, while still allowing for the necessary flexibility. In TV and film production, the more project-based character of individual productions, combined with requests for special equipment/layout from the producers, consequently makes it more difficult to optimize utilization, often resulting in significant slack in these processes.

Warehousing and defining optimal order quantities are particularly important issues in the book industry: in some countries, the share of unsold books returned to the publisher accounts for as much as 30% of the total printed.

Efficient distribution is, again, above all an issue for print. Here, the key step is disposition (sending the correct number of products to each outlet). Often this is a lower-level activity within the organization, so the quality of disposition varies greatly among companies.

	Define advertising inventory	List price	Sell	Revenue management	Copy production	Incorporation in content
	Type of inventory:	General trade terms:	Type of sales force:	Customer-specific trade terms:	Key actor	Key actor
Newspapers	• Open-end inventory – Classifieds – Display	• Size/location based prices • Volume discounts	• Own sales force, often regional	• Customer-specific rebates (often volume-related)		
Magazines	• Open-end inventory	• Size/location based prices • Volume discounts	• Own sales force, often regional • Strong role media agencies	• Customer-specific rebates (often volume-related)	Ad agency	In-house department media company
Free TV	• Limited number of minutes per hour (due to regulation)	• Reach-based prices • Volume discounts	• Own sales force, often regional • Strong role media agencies	• Share deals with agencies • Customer-specific rebates (often volume-related)		

Figure 2.5 Advertising sales process by media sector

Source: Author analyses

Advertising sales: sell rather than shape

For magazines and newspapers, as well as free TV and radio, selling advertising space effectively is a high priority, as advertising revenues are often a large share of overall revenues. Here, as well, the process differs between sectors (Figure 2.5).

While print products have a large advertising inventory flexibility, TV channels in Europe must systematically optimize scarce resources, as usually only a limited number of minutes of advertising are allowed per hour of programming. Only a few TV channels apply sophisticated yield management techniques for the sale of these scarce places, similar to the techniques used by airlines when selling airline seats. Most European TV channels, however, still adhere to the first-come, first-served principle, with large but mostly low-margin accounts getting the first pick. Discounts officially published on rate cards are often volume-based; the real net prices are, however, not always directly linked to the attractiveness/importance of the advertiser. Most advertising sales forces are managed traditionally, that is they are often organized by customer size and region and selling only one type of media. The regional aspect is driven by the desire to better interact with the media agencies, which play an important intermediary role in all media sectors. The sales approach is mostly push, that is the sales force tries to sell the available advertising inventory as effectively as possible, with little room left for the advertiser to shape the inventory.

Production of the ads is done by third parties with little involvement of the media companies. The process of the physical incorporation of the advertisement into the media product used to be quite cumbersome, with ad copy delays or last-minute changes upsetting the relatively inflexible production process. However, since the advent of electronic data transfer, this has become much less of an issue.

The allocation of advertisements to time slots or print pages is, in most cases, related to the target audiences of the advertiser. However, the sophistication of this matching process and, therefore, the monetization of the audience vary greatly by media company.

End-customer interaction: slow transition from 'administering' to customer relationship management

Efficiently acquiring, developing and retaining end consumers is a core activity for subscription-based businesses such as pay TV, cable operators, book clubs and (to a lesser extent) newspapers and magazines, which is also reflected in the sophistication of the processes (Figure 2.6).

The most sophisticated customer acquisition approaches are found at book clubs, cable companies, pay-TV operators and, lately, Internet Service Providers (ISPs) who often apply state-of-the-art database marketing approaches. For magazines and newspapers, for which subscription plays a less prominent role and the interaction with the subscriber is much less frequent, the approaches tend to be broader.

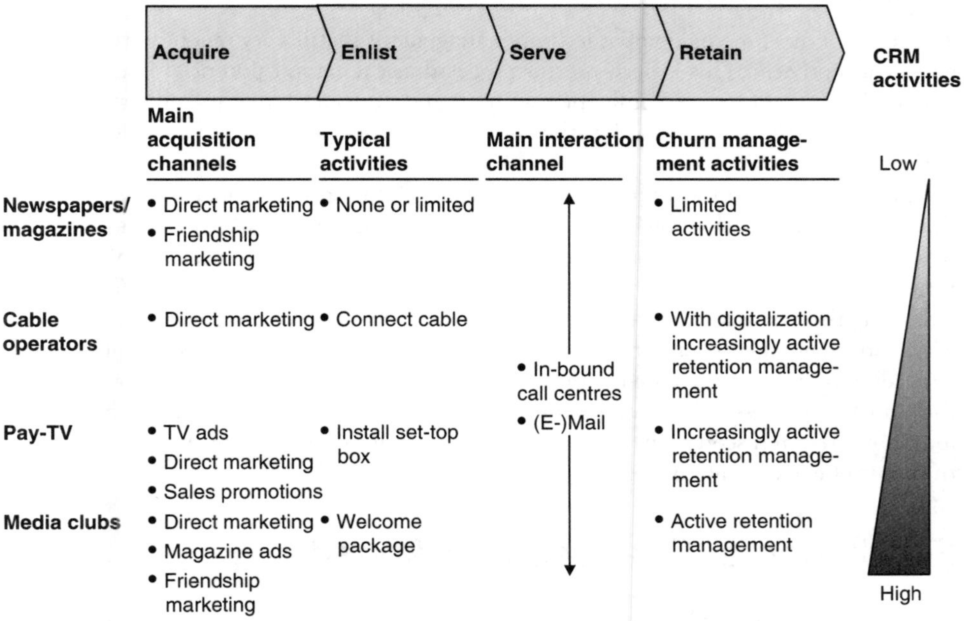

	Acquire	Enlist	Serve	Retain	CRM activities
	Main acquisition channels	**Typical activities**	**Main interaction channel**	**Churn management activities**	Low
Newspapers/ magazines	• Direct marketing • Friendship marketing	• None or limited		• Limited activities	
Cable operators	• Direct marketing	• Connect cable	• In-bound call centres • (E-)Mail	• With digitalization increasingly active retention management	
Pay-TV	• TV ads • Direct marketing • Sales promotions	• Install set-top box		• Increasingly active retention management	
Media clubs	• Direct marketing • Magazine ads • Friendship marketing	• Welcome package		• Active retention management	High

Figure 2.6   End-customer interaction process by media sector

Source: Author analyses

Customer service and up-selling customers to higher-value offerings are especially important for pay TV, cable and ISP. Best practices can be found mainly in Anglo-Saxon countries, which have a long tradition of direct marketing and less restrictive privacy laws than Continental Europe. However, most other European countries have made a quantum leap in quality over the past few years.

The quality of churn management (preventing consumers from cancelling their subscription) still varies among companies. Newspapers and magazines, especially, are traditionally less aggressive in this field. Lately, print companies are becoming more focused on churn management as a key lever to stabilize volume. Media companies who do not sell directly to consumers tend to follow a very generic marketing approach. They often divide the market into only a few segments, along either demographic or 'media taste' lines. They carefully track the actual viewer numbers (ratings), mainly in order to correctly bill the advertisers. Market research is done on the individual segments; however, the depth of the research and the extent to which the insights are actually used in the company vary greatly. There is still great scepticism amongst content creators as to the value of market research for the content creation process. An exception here are magazine publishers, who have often a much more intimate knowledge of their readers as their products are much more finely segmented and closer to the target groups.

Focus of media companies: above all on the content generation process

The focus of most media companies' top management is still very much on the content generation process. This is because this process has the largest potential impact on the bottom line, given its great influence on both end-customer sales and advertising sales (which are strongly driven by the number of viewers/readers) and year-to-year variability.

The content generation process is very much a 'real option' management challenge, that is investing in a large number of potential future hits (options) and knowing when to invest further or to discontinue investing in the options. This requires an analytical and intuitive ability to recognize option potential. Managing this process is very different from managing the other core processes, which are much more geared to system optimization. This can create significant stress within a media company, resulting in a large divide between functions and a tense relationship between the creative part of the company and the 'support' processes (e.g. marketing, ad sales, production) (Figure 2.7). The support functions are often seen as an execution machine that drives content into the market in the most effective way possible.

Fundamental Changes Still Ahead

The digital transition will greatly affect the way media businesses are run. This will above all be caused by the fundamental changes which drive the paradigm shifts described in Chapter 1.

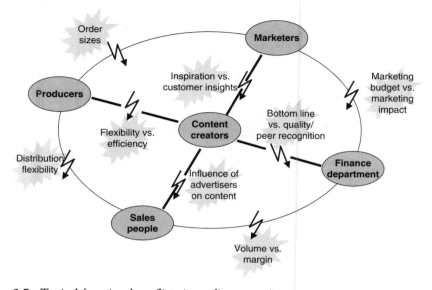

Figure 2.7 **Typical functional conflicts in media companies**

Source: Author analyses

From the management of scarcity to the fight for attention

The replacement of the scarcely available analogue channels/products by 'ubiquitously available' digital products affects both the type of content people consume and the way they consume it. With regard to type of content, one of the most important changes is the accessibility of the famous long tail (as identified by Chris Anderson in his book *The Long Tail: How Endless Choice is Creating Unlimited Demand* (Hyperion, 2006)). Through e-commerce, download or streaming, consumers suddenly have access to media products they could not even buy in the largest media stores, as the demand per product is too low to justify the allocation of physical shelf space. That there is a large aggregate appetite for these types of low-volume products shows up in the sales figures of e-media stores, where often 20–30% of sales are made up of long tail products (Figure 2.8). For media companies this opens up unexpected new perspectives; they can now not only exploit their archives (once they are digitized) but also create and sell products to niche audiences. However, this requires a deep understanding of these micro-segments in order to cater to this group profitably.

Also there are now multiple distribution ways by which consumers can access content. This gives the consumer much greater freedom and choice. Rather than be told by the media industry what to consume when, they now have the freedom to access individual products (single songs, particular news articles, video on demand, etc.) rather than 'push' packages (CD albums, newspapers, pay-TV channels) at flexible and tailored prices rather than fixed average prices. Furthermore, digital media consumers will increasingly have access to content when they want it, rather than having to wait for the release schedule of the film majors, TV channels or book publishers. Overall, this implies that media

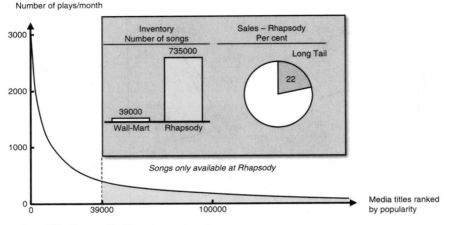

Figure 2.8 The long tail effect in music sales

Source: McKinsey analysis based on data from *Wired* magazine

companies will have to start thinking about completely different business models when offering their content to their consumers. Many old industry practices (pre-packaging, fixed prices, release windows) will be turned upside down and completely new approaches will have to be found.

From content consumption to interaction

The emergence of the active media consumer will affect media businesses in several ways. First, consumers will become much more vocal in their judgement of media offerings through rankings, ratings, voting and comments. The role of the 'experts' will diminish. Second, consumers will want to contribute: the fast rise of Web 2.0 websites, such as Facebook, YouTube and blogs, clearly shows that this latent need can finally be fulfilled as the restrictions of the analogue world are lifted. Media companies will have not only to enlarge their offerings to incorporate communication elements but also to think through strategies on how they can incorporate consumer feedback and contributions ('user-generated content', or UGC) into their programmes and product design.

From paid to free content

The shift to more advertising-financed media can have major ramifications for media businesses. First of all, there will be a shift in the type of target audiences, as media companies will have to adapt themselves more to the targets of the advertisers. The focus will be on maximizing reach within this audience. At the same time there will be increased revenue pressures as more parties are competing for the advertising money and pressure will be to reduce content cost and to shift to lower risk and cheaper content. The importance of advertising sales skills will increase significantly.

From advertising reach to advertising impact

Traditional media will increasingly come under pressure from advertisers as their reach will decline owing to the competition between digital offerings, and there will be increased demand on much better information concerning who has been reached, what the impact was and performance-related payment models. Traditional media companies will have to come up with new targeting and measurement models as well as attractive payment models to stay competitive in the long run with the pure digital players.

Need for change varies by industry sector

The implications of all these developments obviously vary in their extent by media sub-sector, requiring some sectors to prepare already in the very short term for a major change in business model and giving others more leeway to develop new strategies (Figure 2.9).

Music industry leading the pack

The impact of the digital disruption has been most clearly noticeable in the music industry. Global recorded music sales fell by 45% between 1997 and 2007. The main drivers for this enormous drop were the fast growth in piracy and a shift from CD sales to paid digital downloads. Piracy is both physical (with the PC as hub for copying pre-recorded CDs or burning blank CDs) and digital (mostly through peer-to-peer sites). The shift from CD to

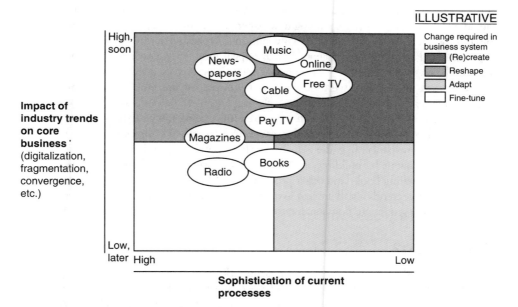

Figure 2.9 Impact of industry trends by media sector

Source: Author analyses

paid download is disadvantageous for music companies, in spite of higher margins per track for downloaded songs, because the number of tracks bought declines sharply when consumers are not 'forced' any more to buy the whole CD. An additional effect which drives down music sales is that large specialist music retail chains are driven into bankruptcy by the fast decline in sales. The initial reaction of the industry was highly defensive: much energy was spent on 'defending' the industry against online offerings, through legal suing, development of sophisticated digital right management (DRM) systems and the search for better technological protection against piracy. The industry made some half-hearted efforts to build its own online offering; however, the results were not very convincing. However, with the advent of Apple's iPod and iTunes offering, the industry realized that online was there to stay and finally started to seriously develop new offerings: different price tiers were introduced for CDs, depending on the product version (simple CD, CD with textbook, DVD); contracts were made with serious online music stores; and marketing approaches and artist contracts were fundamentally rethought. In addition the music industry tried to maintain profits through radical restructuring and portfolio pruning as well as further industry consolidation (Sony/BMG merger) and more focused marketing budgets in order to get its cost structures under control. Whether these efforts will prove sufficient remains to be seen.

Newspapers increasingly under pressure

In spite of being one of the oldest, most established media forms, newspapers are also significantly under pressure. Most 'newspaper-heavy' countries, such as those in northern Europe and the United States, are witnessing a continuous decline in readership (mostly caused by fewer younger people reading newspapers). The shift of classified advertisements to the Internet has especially affected daily national broadsheets. So far, the industry has responded by launching new formats, which appeal more to younger readers, such as free commuter newspapers like the *Metro* and *20 Minutes* brands, or a shift from broadsheet to tabloid format. Also, after a very hesitant start, newspapers are now seriously investing in building up an attractive, online classified offering. Extensive news sites are being developed and the online and print editorial staff are increasingly being integrated. In addition several newspapers are seriously trying to get their readers to pay for their online content – with mixed success. Some newspapers (e.g. die *Zeit* the *Sueddeutsche Zeitung* and *Bild* in Germany) have started to experiment by building on their trusted relationship with their readers, and are publishing and selling books and other products. Whether these measures will be enough to offset the negative trends is still unclear as market values of newspaper groups are plummeting. Many newspaper groups are now starting to fundamentally rethink their business proposition.

Free TV next?

The free-TV landscape in Europe and the United States is also increasingly under pressure. First of all, with the roll-out of digital broadcasting platforms, digital niche TV channels are taking a significant market share. In 2002 in countries like France, the United Kingdom and Italy, 50–80% of the TV households only received between five and eight channels; in 2008 this changed dramatically: 30–40% of households received 25–30 channels, either

TV households, per cent

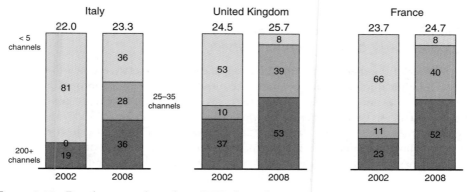

Figure 2.10 Development of number of TV channels on offer

Source: Author analyses based on data from *Screen Digest*

through analogue cable or digital terrestrial broadcasting platforms, and 30–50% of the households received 200+ channels either through digital satellite, digital cable or DSL/ glass fibre networks (Figure 2.10). By 2012, when analogue terrestrial broadcasting will be switched off in most EU countries, the expectation is that all TV households will receive at least 30 channels and a majority of households 200+ channels (the exact percentage will vary by country, depending on the available infrastructure and marketing strategy of the digital platform operators). The increase in the number of channels will have a significant impact on the market share of the original free-TV channels. In the United Kingdom the market share of the main networks (BBC, ITV, Channel 4 and Five) declines from 100% in the analogue terrestrial world to 70% market share in the digital terrestrial environment (25–30 channels) and to around 50% in the 200+ channel environment. In addition it is expected that with the roll-out of digital platforms viewers will increasingly turn to video-on-demand (VoD) offerings. The rise of the digital personal video recorder (PVR) is also a cause for concern as penetration is growing fast and a large share of PVR users do blend out advertising. This is partly compensated by longer viewing and more time spent on catching up on programmes from the major channels; however, the jury is still out.

So far the major channels have reacted by integrating vertically with production companies (e.g. the RTL Group and Fremantle, the acquisition of Endemol by Mediaset, the acquisition of independent content producers by ITV) to ensure a steady flow of content and full rights ownership. Several channels have aggressively diversified to non-advertising revenues, such as own CD sales, TV shopping, call-in, etc. (French channels TF1 and M6 being prime examples). They are also actively launching digital offerings – such as own niche channels, VoD offerings (free catch-up services or partly paid video download services and long-form video download offerings such as Hulu.com by NBC Universal and Newscorp) or pay-per-view offerings, such as Mediaset's pre-paid TV-cards for football matches. Interactive applications are being developed but no silver bullet has been found yet. It is still unclear whether the economics of these activities will be attractive enough to compensate for the threat to the traditional free-TV model.

Platform operators: transformation from infrastructure provider to content and communication service provider

The roll-out of the digital platforms drives significant vertical convergence in the value chain. Traditional infrastructure operators are turning more and more into media players. Cable companies and, to a lesser extent, telecoms operators are starting to compete with media companies. Besides offering a 'triple play' access bundle to TV, Internet and telephony, they are signing for own sports and Hollywood VoD rights, and have developed their own bundled content offerings, including games, VoD and music downloads/streaming. Equipment manufacturers such as Apple, Sony and Nokia are transforming mobile phones, mp3 players and game consoles into media centres with own content offerings. For the media industry, this means a significant increase in competition, often by players who may have a strong financial backing and direct access to consumers (Figure 2.11).

Which platform operators will win the race for the access to the home will vary greatly by country. Some countries, such as the Netherlands and Belgium, have historically very strong analogue cable platforms and here the cable operators are competing head on with the telecoms operators. In other countries, cable has always played a minor role and telecoms traditional operators are increasingly competing against new entrants, such as Free in France and Fastweb in Italy, which partly build their own (glass fibre) infrastructure and partly use the infrastructure of the telecoms operator, especially the final

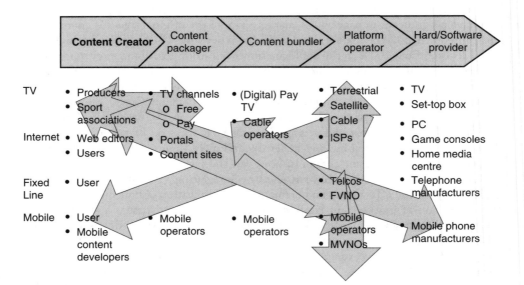

Figure 2.11 Convergence in media and telecoms

Source: Author analyses

connection to the homes ('last mile to the home'). Regulators play an important role in ensuring access to the telecoms networks for these new entrants.

The dynamics of cable companies and telecoms operators (telcos) are quite different. Historically, the cable operators in most European countries were owned by the state, municipalities or the national, state-owned telephone operator. The cable was mostly about providing a cable infrastructure ('pipe') to homes at a fixed monthly fee and delivering through this pipe an analogue TV package of approximately 30 channels. The end of the last century and the beginning of this one saw the privatization of most cable companies and their new owners aggressively investing in upgrading the cable networks to digital standards. This entailed significant investments, which the cable companies hoped to earn back through additional revenue from the sale of digital services. Unfortunately, the early take-up by the end consumers was lower than expected and many of the cable companies got into serious financial problems. After a phase of drastic restructuring, most cable companies are now back to a much sounder financial footing and are aggressively rolling out a multiservice strategy head-on with the telcos, including a digital TV bouquet with interactive offerings, a broadband ISP and 'voice-over-Internet protocol' (VoIP) telephony and increasingly also wireless access and applications.

Telecoms companies used to be state-owned, too, but most have now been privatized. With deregulation, in most countries third parties (virtual network operators) have gained access to the telco network to offer alternative telephony services. This has led to a decline in market share for the incumbent telcos, which was exacerbated by a shift away from fixed-line to mobile telephony. Although incumbents do have their own mobile operators, the market share of these operators is significantly smaller in the mobile world than the market share in the fixed-line world. Most incumbent telcos have been early movers in offering Internet access in addition to telephony and have been able to become (one of) the market leaders in most countries in Europe. With the rise of triple play offerings, many telcos found that their copper lines were not able to deliver high-quality TV, especially not to large audiences at once, and they were faced with the decision of having to significantly invest in their networks in order to compete with the cable companies. At the same time cable companies and third parties started to offer telephony over the Internet (VoIP) at a much lower cost than traditional telephony, forcing the telcos to also shift to this type of offering. Many telcos are therefore now at a critical cross-road where they, on the one hand, have to invest significantly to be competitive in the long term in triple (or quadruple if mobile phones are included) play offerings and, on the other hand, are at the same time faced with significant losses and a slowly emptying copper network in their core, fixed-line telephony business. As the mobile markets are also maturing in Western Europe and the United States, it will be increasingly difficult to offset this with profits from this sector.

Pay TV: the jury is out

In most Continental European countries the pay-TV players offering premium content through satellite and cable had a rough start. In the analogue world they had to compete with a very strong free-TV offering (especially in countries such as Germany and the Netherlands with a strong analogue cable penetration, offering a 'basic package' of 30 channels) or there was head-on competition between two pay-TV players (Spain, Italy,

France). The introduction of digital satellite was only of limited help, as the transition from the subscribers from analogue to digital turned out to be very cumbersome. Only BSkyB, in the United Kingdom, which was a very early mover and was prepared to invest significantly in rolling out the digital set-top boxes, succeeded in building a leading market share of almost 30%. The pay-TV players in other countries only slowly improved their position as the industry consolidated to one player per country (Spain, Italy, France). With the rise of the digital, cable and telco platforms they are now, however, faced with serious new competition. Not only do these platforms have a product advantage as they offer much more services than satellite (triple play, interactivity), they also have more financial power and strong end-consumer relationships on multiple fronts. They lack, however, the content creation and branding skills as well as the relationships with the content providers, which the traditional pay-TV players have. Competition for exclusive blockbuster content such as football championships is, however, increasing and overall it is still unclear how competition will play out.

Magazines: their own worst enemy?

The magazine industry is less affected overall by digitization and other technological changes than the other sectors; however, the impact will vary greatly genre by genre. Overall, the magazine industry is facing slowing growth or in some countries even decline in both readership and advertising sales, and, as usual in maturing markets, demand is fragmenting greatly. In this environment the players run the risk of becoming their own worst enemies, as competition for a market share increases. The number of magazine launches has been rising steadily, with only limited success. The moment a successful format is launched, competition follows within weeks with the perfect copycat. The fight for advertising share is fierce in many countries. The industry has reacted so far by selectively raising cover prices and by trying to diversify revenue sources, for example in Italy, where the distribution structure allows for profitable add-ons, such as CDs or DVDs, being folded with the magazine sales. However, after initial success, this revenue source is on the wane. Also there has been an increasing focus on launching niche magazines and exploiting the magazine brand in many dimensions (e.g. the sale of branded merchandise such as diaries or bed linen, or the organization of summer fairs or conferences). Magazine websites are being developed actively, however, as they are mostly financed by banner ads – the lowest growth type of Internet advertisements – and have a limited number of visitors; magazines have found it difficult to generate significant contributions with these sites.

Books: finally moving to electronic formats?

The book industry is also starting to be affected by digitization. Academic books are increasingly sold in electronic formats, giving professors the opportunity to mix and match their 'own' books. The initiative of Google to digitize all the books in the world is continuing steadily, and, by 2007, Amazon was selling 6% of its book titles electronically through its Kindle offering, and the number is rising fast. The physical-book market is characterized by stagnating demand (although significant annual fluctuations are possible) on the one hand and an increase in the number of titles published, especially in the area of fiction and on-demand books. Also there is a continuous shift away from high-margin hardbacks to lower-margin paperbacks. The industry itself is consolidating, both on the side of the publishers and on the side of the retailers. The cost of the authors is polarizing between a few, very expensive, best-seller authors and many unknown writers, who get paid minimal fees but are also difficult to market. The industry is coping by trying to professionalize its practices, for example through more sophisticated pricing approaches, more effective allocation of marketing money and by introducing better forecasting methods. The consolidation is likely to continue.

Other sectors are also facing significant changes

Other sectors, although not discussed extensively here, are also facing significant changes. In the games industry a shift to multiplayer online games is clearly visible. In the professional information industry, there has already been a major transition to online platforms and databases – especially in the areas of science, medical, legal, business and financial information – and new revenue models have been developed. Also in business-to-business (B2B) magazine sector major changes are expected as the offering and advertisements will increasingly move online. The radio industry was relatively stable; however, it is now also experiencing the impact of increased mp3 listening and competition from powerful online offerings, such as Last.fm, which can cater much better to the listener's individual taste.

Consequences for the Management of Media Companies

The above-mentioned developments greatly increase the complexity of managing a media business. A new set of skills will be needed to play in this new environment. For each of the core processes, this implies that long-standing practices must be challenged, as the new playing field will require companies to act along multiple dimensions in a much more interactive way. A few media companies, which will be described in the case studies in this book, are already aggressively going down this road and have been achieving good results. By learning from their experiences but also from other parallel industries, which are going through similar major transitions (e.g. the mobile telephony industry, retail), managers can adopt best practices for coping with the new environment.

Fundamental changes needed in the management of core processes in the short term

In the short term, media companies will have no choice but to fundamentally rethink the way they manage their core processes in order to develop new practices which fit the digital environment.

The main changes to each process are highlighted below. A more detailed discussion of these changes, specific best practice examples and possible approaches for implementing the changes are provided in Chapters 3, 4, 5 and 6.

Change content creation from a one-way to an interactive process

Traditionally, mass-market content generation tended to focus on finding blockbuster content/formats and marketing them as aggressively as possible to a broad audience. Although this strategy will remain an important backbone of the media industry, its overall contribution will decrease, as costs for blockbusters continue to rise and audiences fragment and start spending more and more time on media where they actively select or even create their own content. To offset this trend and capture the opportunities which digitization and new market forces offer, media companies will have to approach content creation more interactively:

- *Better understand and respond to customer needs:* Market research, although necessary to convince advertisers and pre-test new concepts, is traditionally looked upon with great scepticism by many creatives, as it is difficult to measure new concepts and uncover hidden needs. However, fragmentation of the market has made it increasingly important to identify and understand different segments in order to tailor products effectively, especially as most segments tend to like multiple types of content rather than just one genre. At the same time, mass-market players will need to fine-tune their offerings continually to defend their audience share against niche players. This will also require sophisticated consumer insight. As it becomes more and more difficult to identify (and pay for) original blockbuster artists and formats, more media companies are turning to 'test-tube' concepts, such as commercially created boy and girl bands and reality-show heroes. Designing these concepts requires a deep understanding of consumer preferences. Besides understanding the content preferences, media companies will also have to develop a deep understanding of how and when people would like to access content, as there are many more channels to access the same content and consumers have much more freedom to determine the timing. Another very important element is the individual willingness to pay for content, especially in the light of the fast growth of piracy opportunities and the rise of free media. Finally, media companies will be expected to react to the feedback that consumers give them in the form of SMS voting, e-mails and call-ins, and adapt their offerings accordingly. All these factors mean that content creators will have to become more open to consumers' wishes. Those companies that manage to balance creative new impulses with a deep understanding of the end-consumer market will be the winners in the content game.
- *Include user-generated content (UGC):* Successful news websites already leverage extensively user-generated content, an extreme form of this is OhmyNews in Korea, a quality newspaper whose content is almost exclusively user-generated. Also in other areas, UGC is playing an increasingly important role: YouTube and other portals have become the latest way of scouting for talent and testing new artists. Publishing UGC is a powerful way to bind consumers. Understanding the dynamics and leveraging the potential of UGC will become an important new skill for media companies.
- *Cascade rights to multiple platforms:* As content costs increase, media companies will need to look for ways to monetize branded content across different media products/channels and through merchandising, resulting in much closer cooperation between the different

types of media than has traditionally been the case, potentially transforming the organization from a product-specific to a consumer segment oriented organization.

- *Develop value-based end-user pricing strategies and tactics:* Although, overall, the media market is tending towards more free content, a fragmenting market can also give media companies some great opportunities. For instance, they could introduce a more sophisticated pricing approach, both for intermediaries/retailers and for end consumers, by differentiating prices per segment based on segment-specific price elasticity and the relative price/benefit ratio of the specific offering.

- *Develop strong brands for packagers:* An enlarged variety of product offerings makes it increasingly difficult for end consumers to orient themselves and choose the right TV programme, book or song. Although new roadmaps, such as EPGs (electronic programme guides), search engines and social network websites will facilitate the search process, consumers can also simplify the search process by orienting their choices to the brand position of the strong media brands, that is the umbrella brand of the TV channels, record labels, magazines or newspapers (e.g. RTL, Virgin, *Brigitte* or *Bild*) and, in some cases, book publishing houses. Research shows that channels that seem similar at first sight can have very different positions in the mind of the consumer. Building and positioning a brand with a clear offering will become a key skill in the future.

The consequence of these trends is that the marketing function will have to take on a much more strategic role. Traditionally, the marketing department was mostly a communications department, focusing on advertising and promotion and measuring audience ratings. In the future, marketers will need to take the lead in identifying attractive customer segments, uncovering their needs, realistically testing new concepts (especially the 'test-tube' formats) and developing sophisticated pricing strategies. Chapter 3 discusses the content generation process in more detail, while Chapter 4 covers the topic of effective content marketing.

Develop the content delivery process into a key strategic differentiating factor

As discussed above, it will become more risky and difficult in the future for media companies to build a sustainable competitive advantage solely based on a superior product/content offering. At the same time, digitization will offer many new opportunities for consumer interaction. This means that companies will have to differentiate themselves not only in the content they deliver but also *in the way it is delivered*. In other words, media companies will need to extend the definition of their value proposition beyond pure content benefits. As examples from other industries show, process and relationship benefits should become equally important (Figures 2.12 and 2.13).

For media companies, process benefits might consist of ease-of-access, multiple-distribution channels and convenient transactions. Relationship benefits cover such elements as personalized services, two-way communication with the consumer, emotional attachment to the brand, loyalty rewards, etc. While relationship benefits are usually

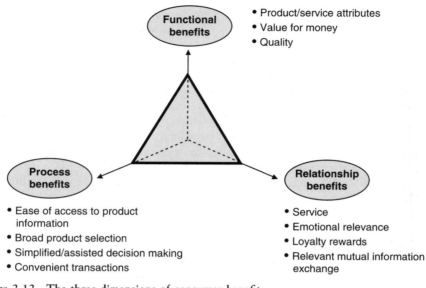

Figure 2.12   The three dimensions of consumer benefit

Source: McKinsey analyses

created by the end-consumer interaction process (discussed below), process benefits are driven mainly by the content delivery process. Both leveraging digitization to develop multiple-distribution channels and payment forms and enabling two-way communication through a variety of analogue and digital channels can therefore become key differentiating factors, as recent developments in the music industry have shown. This implies that

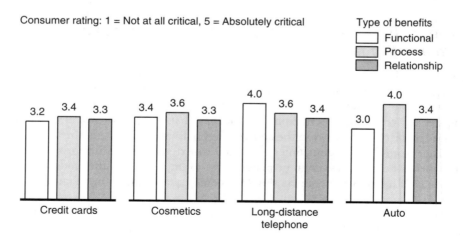

Figure 2.13   Relevance of benefits by industry

Source: McKinsey consumer research

content delivery will have to change from an enabling process to a strategic process: shaping the delivery of content will become an important determinant of the offering's overall value proposition. The future of content delivery processes is discussed in detail in Chapter 5.

Replace advertising sales with (digital) marketing concepts

Although the advertising ecosystem (consisting of advertisers, media buying agencies, media companies) has a natural tendency to lag behind changes in consumer behaviour, there are clear signs that a larger-scale shift of advertisements to digital media will happen in the coming years. This, combined with the expected overall increase in supply of advertising inventory by the media, will mean that traditional media companies will have to fundamentally revise their approach to advertising sales in order not to lose out to new media companies and other players, such as platform operators (cable, telco) and appliance manufacturers (mobile phone, home media centres, set-top boxes), who have also mass access to consumers and often a deeper knowledge of the individual consumer. Advertisers will require a much better targeting to the consumers according to the advertisers' specific needs/marketing strategy; they will expect a much more precise feedback as to the effectiveness of the campaign and they will push for performance-based payment models. Advertisers will increasingly want to use digital-marketing techniques across multiple platforms, and media companies will have to be able to come up with cross-media offerings. Finally, the quality of the advertising copy will become increasingly important, as people get more freedom to decide what they watch, and so media companies might decide to start to play a role in this field too, by creating attractive multimedia stories around the advertised products, stories which go beyond a 30-second spot or a one-page advertisement. All this requires a professional business-to-business (B2B) marketing organization capable of developing and implementing sophisticated B2B marketing strategies. An aggressive advertising sales force on its own will not suffice. How to transform the sales function into a more sophisticated B2B (digital) marketing organization is discussed in detail in Chapter 6.

Rebalance the end-customer interaction process from focusing on acquisition to optimizing the complete 'customer lifetime funnel'

As mentioned above, the customer interaction process will be responsible for developing relationship benefits. To do so successfully, it will have to change from a support service into a strategy shaper. As the digital market matures, the overall emphasis of the process will shift from being focused on customer acquisition to a better balance between acquisition *and* retention. Understanding when and why people value the media or why they do not, why they leave and which levers are the most effective to retain them is key in a low-growth environment. Among mobile operators, who faced the challenge of a saturated market earlier than expected, those with superior retention skills and better understanding of customer value are the most successful in defending market share and upgrading their customers. How to optimize the end-customer interaction process is the main topic of Chapter 4.

Closely integrate and rebalance the core processes

The consequence of the above developments is that the four core processes can no longer be managed as distinct, mostly sequential, activities. Both in developing the offering and in bringing it to market, content generators must work closely with marketers, content deliverers, ad salespeople and end-customer interaction departments to incorporate their input into the product design and expand the product definition to multiple dimensions. The traditional hegemony of the content generators will become less pronounced, and the role and quality of the other processes will need to be strengthened to capture the new opportunities.

Management of media organizations needs to be adapted to the new requirements

Reshaping the core processes will have significant consequences for the way media companies are managed. The traditional functional organization that has developed around the four core media processes and in which content generation (e.g. editors/ programmers), marketing, production and advertising sales functions work as autonomous units must be replaced by a much more hybrid organization, in which the different functions work together intensively along the value chain. Depending on the intensity of cooperation needed, this can take the form of intelligent coordination processes, matrix organizations or, in its most extreme form (multimedia) consumer segment-oriented profit centres, in which all functions are decentralized.

At the same time, the organization will have to become much more disciplined in the way it manages its processes. With digitization, information technology will no longer be a support tool but an intrinsic part of the value creation. This will be possible, however, only when IT processes and business processes are aligned, and the organization adheres to the defined processes. Culturally, media organizations should ensure that the traditional boundaries between 'suits' and 'ponytails' disappear. This transition must begin at the top, with the board itself setting the example. Recruitment, training and incentives will have to be adapted to this new organization. Very importantly, companies must give the same priority to the management quality of content delivery, ad sales and the end-customer interaction process as they now give to the creative process. This requires hiring and developing the same type of heavyweights with deep functional experience in these areas as is currently the case for the creative tasks. Further investments in professionalizing these processes are needed so they become best practice, not only within the media industry but also in comparison with other industries. Chapter 9 outlines the organizational challenges in more detail.

Is a Fundamental Rethink of Future Business Models Needed?

Redesigning their value chain and actively gearing their offers to digital consumer needs, while leveraging all revenue-generating opportunities, will help media companies to cope with disruptions. The fundamental question remains, however, as to whether the traditional media business model – which is based on the generation of content, reaching large attractive target groups with this content and earning money through the sale of content and/or advertising – will survive in the medium term. Other business models, built on completely different premises, might be needed to ensure long-term profitable growth. Media companies might think of different roles they can play, based on core competencies they already own. Thinking beyond the current boundaries, a number of possible strategic plays can be considered, for example:

- *The branded pre-selector:* The enlarged content offering will increasingly confuse consumers. Some will enjoy the freedom and use the opportunity to select what they want when they want it. However, based on the experience of the music industry, this segment tends to be only 15% of the total population. There will still be a large segment that will appreciate guidance, either from friends or trusted sources. There is an attractive opportunity for media companies to fill this gap. To the extent that they own brands, which have a trust-based relationship with the audience, the brand could take over the role of a 'trusted adviser', that is a guarantee that the scarce resource 'free disposable time' is spent well. This can be done through mass offerings, which are likely to fit the taste of the specific audience, and through individually tailored programmes. Revenues will be made through either subscription, payments for certain pieces of content or tailored advertising.
- *The 'ultimate marketing machine':* In this case, the media company defines itself as matchmaker between the consumer and the content. Through a very deep and intimate knowledge of the consumer, it not only knows what type of content the consumer likes but also knows how and when he or she would like to access it. The company has access to a large depository of content, either own or through third parties. At the same time the company has deep advertiser relationships and is able to place the right type of advertisement with the right type of consumer. The marketing skills required for this go significantly beyond what fast-moving consumer-goods companies possess, as the multitude of products and channels is much higher and support from sophisticated database marketing and smart algorithms is needed. Customer relationship management (CRM) skills will be key. Google would be an emerging example of this model; however, Google is a limited marketing tool, because while it can analyse and record, to a degree, a person's Web-browsing behaviour, the results of such analysis cannot be transformed into personalized data with which to make sophisticated judgements with regard to individual consumer attitudes and preferences.
- *The 'hit' exploiter:* This media company concentrates fully on generating hits, ideally mass-market (as consumers will always want to have something they can talk about with their friends/colleagues the next morning) or possibly also for larger segments. The 'hit' is conceived such that the content is exploited in as many ways as possible: multiple media, merchandise, communication, etc. The media company acts as the orchestrator and earns on every activity. Its key skill is to generate a continuous flow of new hits.

Of course, these strategic plays must be translated into sustainable business models, which might also be applied in conjunction with the traditional model. Also it is still in the stars whether these plays will actually function. The key point is, however, that media companies will have to free themselves from their traditional way of doing business and start thinking along new paths. Radical change must be carefully crafted, given the conservativeness of both consumers and advertisers, and also creatives; yet first movers can gain unexpectedly wide acceptance in media as well, as the inventors of reality TV shows found, and as new online businesses such as online search (Google) or social networking sites (e.g. Facebook, Bebo) have demonstrated.

The coming years will require significant changes from media companies. The companies that have successfully survived the recent downturn, or even benefited from it, are the ones that had their house in order, that is had high-quality processes in all four core areas and ensured that the four areas worked together intensively. How to manage the transition to best-practice processes in the digital world is the topic of the next chapters.

Key Takeaways

1. The current practices of media companies are historically grown and not always state-of-the-art. Especially areas such as pricing, strategic marketing and end-to-end supply chain management can be improved in many media companies.
2. The traditional focus of media companies has very much been on content generation; other processes have often been regarded as subordinate.
3. Major industry disruptions are ahead, owing to the unprecedented speed of digitization of media, resulting in a significant change in consumer behaviour. Consumers spend more time on the Web, they take a more active role in deciding what media they want where and how and they contribute more actively. Advertisers have been slow to follow but are likely to change their behaviour significantly in the coming years. Powerful new players are entering the industry, such as the Internet giants, cable and telecoms platform operators as well as phone and other hardware manufacturers, all fighting for the control of the digital home and advertising money.
4. These disruptions will result in a shift in sources of revenue. This will mean that media companies will have to develop new business models.
5. The extent and cause of disruption will vary between media sectors. In the short term, the sectors most strongly affected, especially by technological developments, will be the music industry, newspapers and free TV. Pay TV and cable will also be greatly affected. In the short term, magazines and books will be affected to a lesser extent by technological changes, but they will run the risk of reduced profitability through destructive industry behaviour in a maturing market.
6. Fundamental changes will be needed in the way media companies manage their value chain:
   - In the content generation process there will be a much larger need to listen to and understand the consumer both with regard to his/her content preferences and to the way he/she consumes and/or contributes to content.

- The content delivery process should enable the media company to deliver the content to consumers on multiple channels and appliances when they want it.
- The advertising sales process should be replaced by (digital) B2B marketing with a focus on targetability and measurability.
- The end-customer interaction process should be strengthened with the help of professional CLM (customer lifetime management).

7. In the medium term, media companies should consider the transition to fundamentally new business models such as 'branded pre-selector', 'content marketing machine' or 'hit exploiter'.

8. Overall, there will be a need for a much more integrated management of all processes.

The Welt Group: Creating New Business Models For News Provision[1]

Peter Wuertenberger, head of the Welt Group, is reflecting on the many changes that have occurred within the newspaper industry and within his organization in recent years. The Welt Group, a wholly owned subsidary of Axel Springer AG, publishes the newspapers *Die Welt*, *Welt am Sonntag*, *Welt Kompakt* and the *Berliner Morgenpost* in addition to the Internet and mobile news outlets Welt Online, Welt TV and Welt Mobil. The Internet posed great challenges to the newspaper industry, and, in 2007, the Welt Group relaunched its brand in response to these challenges.

The newspaper industry worldwide has faced declines in total circulation and revenues. Individuals are increasingly using the Internet as their primary news source, and consumer preferences are shifting away from print subscriptions to free newspapers and free online content. Classifieds such as job-search advertising, which used to be the mainstay of newspapers, are increasingly moving online. And the challenges don't end there. Even obituaries, which used to be the sole domain of newspapers, are moving online, as evidenced by Tributes.com, a new venture launched by Jeff Taylor, the founder of Monster.com.

Although the Internet threat has been looming since the early 2000s, the fact that broadband penetration has reached the 60% threshold in many countries in 2008, combined with the fear of recession, has hit the newspaper industry hard, with many newspaper groups losing up to 90% of their market valuation between mid 2007 and end 2008. Axel Springer, the mother company of the Welt Group, lost around 45% of its value between August 2007 and June 2008 in spite of positive results. Will the new Welt strategy be enough to stem the tide?

Company History

Axel Springer AG

Axel Springer AG, founded after the Second World War by Heinrich Springer and his son Axel, has long been a market leader in the German newspaper business. Starting from the release of its first titles – *Nordwestdeutsche Hefte* and *Horzu* (weekly radio listings, now one of the leading TV guides) – in 1946, Axel Springer AG has launched and acquired many successful newspapers and magazines in Germany and internationally. Currently, it publishes 170 newspapers and magazines. Additionally, it has diversified into online offerings and invested in TV production, IPTV channels and radio companies. In 2008, the company consists of five divisions: newspapers, magazines, digital media, printing and logistics. As of 2007, Axel Springer AG was

---

[1]This case is developed solely as the basis for class discussion. Cases are not intended to serve as endorsements, sources of primary data or illustrations of effective or ineffective management.

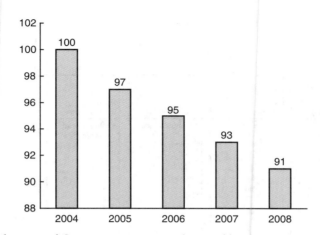

Figure 1   Development of German newspaper market – sold copies, 2004 = 100

Source: McKinsey analysis based on data from IVW

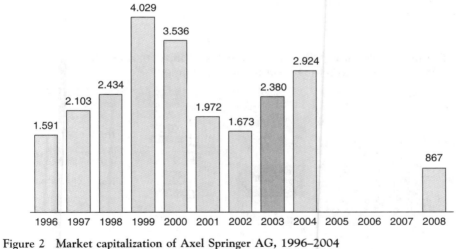

Figure 2   Market capitalization of Axel Springer AG, 1996–2004

Source: McKinsey analyses based on data from Datastream; Bloomberg

estimated to account for 17.2% of the German newspaper market's value.[2] At the core of its many divisions lie Springer's sociopolitical values. The newspaper company has a strong belief in its constitution. Its corporate principles, originally formulated in 1967, serve to define the sociopolitical beliefs with which its publishing operations are run.

---

[2]Datamonitor, July 2007. 'Newspapers in Germany Industry Profile'. Reference Code: 0165-0559.

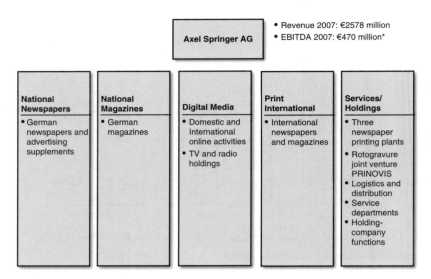

Figure 3   Axel Springer at a glance, 2007

*Adjusted for non-recurring effects of purchase price allocations
Source: McKinsey analyses based on data from Axel Springer AG

Figure 4   Axel Springer AG is the leading newspaper publisher in Germany

1) Except weekly newspapers, based on BDZV/IVW, Q1–3/2008
2) Based on paid circulation Q1–3/2008
3) *Source:* Huegel Statistik 2006. Based on gross advertising volumes amongs all regional newspapers in Hamburg/
Berlin, Q1–3/2008
Source: Axel Springer company data. Reproduced with permission

The Bild brand

The Bild brand is Axel Springer's major brand. In Germany, it reaches 26 million readers,[3] and its newspapers hold an estimated 81% of the market share of German newsstand sales.[4] *Bild-Zeitung*, first released in 1952, is the leading German tabloid to date, and the *Bild am Sonntag*, launched in 1956, is the leading Sunday paper in Germany. Over the course of the 1980s, the company achieved increasing growth through leveraging the Bild brand to launch magazine sub-brands such as *Bild der Frau*, *Bildwoche*, *Auto Bild* and *Sport Bild*. Additionally, through acquisitions and transferring titles such as *Auto Bild* abroad, Axel Springer was able to expand internationally since the late 1980s. Today, *Auto Bild* is present in more than 29 countries. The brand currently consists of newspapers, women's magazines, car and sports magazines, and IT and games magazines. Axel Springer is the German market leader both in circulation and advertising spend.

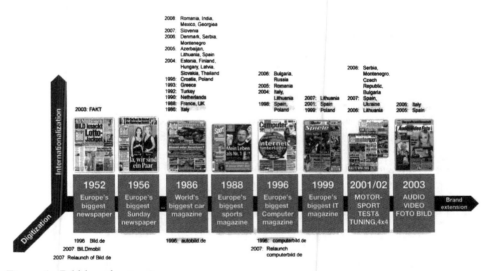

Figure 5   Bild brand extension

Source: Axel Springer AG company presentation. Reproduced with permission

Diversification and international expansion

Through the BILD brand, Axel Springer has been expanding internationally since the 1980s. Early 2000 Springer strongly expanded into Eastern Europe and started businesses in Hungary, Poland, the Czech Republic and Russia. By 2007, it was the second-largest

[3] Axel Springer roadshow presentation 2007. IVW stats as of April 2007.
[4] Axel Springer roadshow presentation 2007.

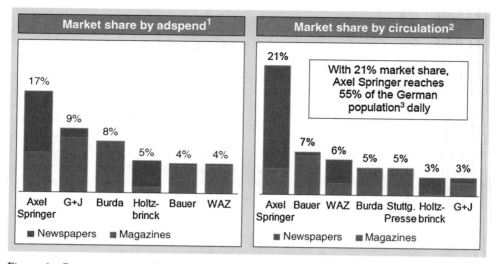

Figure 6 German print market shares

(1) AC Nielsen, gross adspend excluding classified ads, supplements and media advertisement Q1–3/2008
(2) Company estimate based on IVW Q1–3/2008, paid circulation; weighted market share taking into account different title frequencies.
(3) In a 2008 Pressemedien II: combined reads among German 14+year olds of all covered Axel Springer AG newspapers, magazines and 100% owned subsidiaries.
Source: Axel Springer AG, company data. Reproduced with permission

publisher in Hungary and the largest publisher of national daily newspapers in Poland. Axel Springer now publishes 100 titles internationally, and has publishing activities or licences in 31 countries in Europe, Russia and Asia.

Axel Springer also diversified into TV, broadcasting and radio. From 1985 untill 2008 Axel Springer was shareholder of SAT1 later ProsiebenSAT1 Media AG the leading German TV group.

In 2008, Axel Springer has shareholdings in international, regional and IPTV networks and stakes in two broadcasters. Axel Springer owns 25% of the Turkish broadcaster Dogan TV, a 24.7% stake in TV Berlin and a minority stake in Hamburg1, both regional TV stations. In the first quarter of 2007, Axel Springer Digital TV GmbH was launched to produce digital video for the online portals of Axel Springer.

In radio, Axel Springer holds a large portfolio of direct and indirect minority investments in radio stations in Germany, consisting of radio stations such as Radio Hamburg, Radio NRW and Radio PSR and PSR2 among others. Regulatory restrictions prevent the company from taking majority stakes in the stations to consolidate their market position.

The Internet spurred Axel Springer to diversify through a series of online acquisitions and investments, and to date it has more than 50 online assets. Its online portfolio ranges from online accompanying sites of its major print brands such as computerbild.de and autobild.de to sites such as immonet.de, which contains real-estate classifieds and offerings of the association of German real-estate brokers (Ring Deutsche Makler). Springer also has classified sites dedicated to jobs, cars and marketplaces, and news sites such as wallstreet:online, a leading capital markets portal. By 2007 its top acquisitions included Zanox, an online marketing site; auFeminin.com, a leading women's portal in Europe; and idealo.de, a buying/selling marketplace.

Given the volatility of the media sector the company decided to diversify its activities further. The organization entered the mail services market through a majority stake in Pin, one of Germany's largest mail service providers. However by 2007, Axel Springer had up to €620 million of write-downs on its investments in Pin. This was due namely to unexpected political developments, where the government introduced mandatory increases in the minimum wages for postal workers, coupled with a continuation of tax exemptions afforded to Deutsche Post AG, its competitor. As this was the second time the company was prevented from executing its diversification strategy through bold moves into more traditional activities (TV, delivery services) by the regulatory environment, it decided to focus its diversification on digital opportunities and to invest in a series of promising digital business models rather than to make big moves into other sectors.

Through digital diversification and international expansion, Axel Springer is shifting from a print publishing focus to an integrated multimedia focus. And it is with another of Springer's leading brands, Welt, that this shift can clearly be seen.

	Poland	Hungary	Russia	Switzerland	Spain	other		
Print	10 magazines; 4 newspapers Market share 44.6% (circulation national daily newspapers)	30 magazines; 10 newspapers Market share 19%, largest publisher (based on advertising revenues)	4 magazines Market leader weekly people magazines	1 newspaper; 13 magazines (biggest consumer magazine); Market leader TV listings, business/ financial	13 magazines Market leader videogames magazines, computer magazines	France: 4 magazines + AUTO PLUS (50%). Czech Republic: 6 magazines Romania (40%): 12 magazines	€304.3 m Internat. revenues, (Segment Print Internat.)	€43.5m, (Segment Newsp.+ Mag. National) €440.3m Internat. Revenues 22.1% of total revenues
Digital media	News portals: dziennik.pl eFakt.pl newsweek.pl Others: students.pl sports.pl popcorn.pl auto-swiat.pl	Regional news network in 8 countries Women portal nana.hu Economical newsportal vg.hu	ok-magazine.ru computerbild.ru runewsweek.ru	handelszeitung.ch students.ch bilanz.ch partyguide.ch usgang.ch students.ch stocks.ch beobachter.ch tele.ch tvstar.ch	computerhoy.es autobild.es hobbyconsolas.es micromania.es	Czech Republic: Leading car portal, auto.cz; Turkey: Dogan TV (25%)	€81.7m Internat. revenues (Part of segment Digital Media)	
auFeminin.com	Germany, France, Italy, UK, Spain, Belgium, Switzerland, Canada, Morocco							
zanox	Germany, France, Italy, UK, Spain, Benelux, Switzerland, US, China, Sweden, Poland							

Figure 7 **A strong international presence**

Source: Axel Springer AG, Unicredit German Investor Conference, September 25, 2008. Reproduced with permission

The Welt brand

In addition to the BILD brand, Welt is synonymous with Springer's presence in the German newspaper industry. Die Welt Publishing was acquired in 1953, and along with it the daily broadsheet *Die Welt* and the Sunday newspaper *Welt am Sonntag*. The *Die Welt* daily, although well known for its intellectual, conservative position, has for a long time not been profitable since it was originally founded in 1946. However, Axel Springer, and later on his widow Friede Springer, felt that the newspaper was an important addition to the diversity of opinion in Germany, as it was a staunch promoter of the values the company stood for, such as the free market economy, rejection of political totalitarianism, good transatlantic relations, reconciliation with the Jewish people and support of the vital rights of the state of Israel, upholding liberty and law in Germany and the unification of the peoples of Europe (see http://www.axelspringer.de/en/artikel/Corporate-principles-for-a-liberal-world-view_40575.html, corporate principles for a liberal world view).

Welt, and in particular the *Die Welt* daily, has evolved over the years and has often played an innovative role in the newspaper industry: from the *Die Welt* daily being the first national daily newspaper to use colour photos in its editorials in 1968 to establishing its online presence in 1995 and relaunching *Die Welt* as a modern newspaper in 1998. The turn of the century brought tough times to the Welt brand, and in 2002/03 Axel Springer saved more than €135 million through rigorous cost cutting. This cost cutting involved merging *Die Welt* with the regional newspaper *Berliner Morgenpost*, which was acquired along with the B.Z. and the book and newspaper publisher Ullstein AG in 1958.

The Welt brand continued to evolve, and in 2004 it launched the *Welt Kompakt*, a tabloid-format daily newspaper. In contrast to most other European newspaper groups, who also decided to change the format of their newspapers from broadsheet to tabloid in order to save costs and to create a product which, with its shorter and punchier articles, might be more appealing to a younger readership, Welt decided not to do away with the broadsheet format, and instead published both formats in parallel, for different target audiences. The launch of *Welt Kompakt* was a great success: newspaper circulation grew quickly and it reached a much younger, urban audience.

Convergence was at the core of Welt's new strategy. This is seen in the Welt Newsroom, where journalists from the four newspapers and the online portal work side-by-side. Additionally, this convergence can be seen in the content offerings through print/online/mobile/IPTV. Welt has adopted the strategy of releasing news online first, before offering cross-media access to the content. The year 2007 brought a major relaunch of the Welt brand, with 'performance' being placed at the centre of Welt's brand philosophy, reflecting its liberal values, and one that distinguished the newspaper from its main competitors: *Frankfurter Allgemeine*, *Sueddeutsche Zeitung* and *Die Zeit*. This brand promise applies to three Welt newspapers: *Die Welt*, *Welt am Sonntag* (the Sunday newspaper) and *Welt Kompakt*, as well as to the Internet and mobile news outlets Welt Online, Welt TV and Welt Mobil.

This cross-media strategy has also opened up new streams of advertising revenue. New marketing and advertising packages involve all distribution channels (print, online, mobile, IPTV). These packages allow advertisers to combine traditional display

Brand essence	Brand equity	Value proposition
Performance	brave + direct + optimistic	**Self-confidence** **WELT motivates me to have a strong and differentiated point of view.** **WELT gives me strength.** **Advantage** **WELT challenges me to develop new thoughts and to think ahead.** **Inspiration** **WELT moves my spirit and my heart. I enjoy WELT.**

Figure 8   Brand concept of Welt

Source: Axel Springer AG company presentation. Reproduced with permission

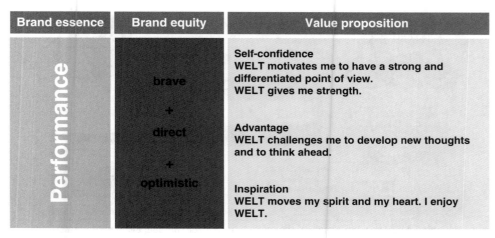

Print		Online	Mobile	IP-TV
DIE WELT aggregated	**WELT am SONNTAG**	**WELT ONLINE**	**WELT MOBILE**	**WELT IP-TV**
Leading quality newspaper in Germany	The strong market leader among Sunday quality newspapers (B2B, B2C)	The sophisticated news and lifestyle portal for a strong target group	Best information and service for the mobile generation	The strong online pictures-update
WELT KOMPAKT	Paid circulation: 404,291	PIs: 137.9 million	609,130 page impressions/month	**WELT-TV-Clips**
First quality newspaper in tabloid format	Reach: 1,166,000 readers	Visits: 20.6 million	www.mobile.welt.de	**Newsflash**
Paid circulation: 278,141		Unique audience: 3.493,46 million	**WAP-Portal**	
Reach: 734,000 readers		(May 2008)	**SMS-Push-Services**	

Figure 9   The Welt Group

Source: Axel Springer based on data from AWA 2007; AGOF 2007-IV; IVW I/2008. Reproduced with permission

advertising with new innovative online methods. Additionally, Welt has introduced Welt Klasse, a premium promotion platform targeted at leading industry brands that offers a full service package, for 'consumer-oriented multi-channel communication', including store promotions, advertorials and editorial design, which are all used to involve readers more closely with the brand.

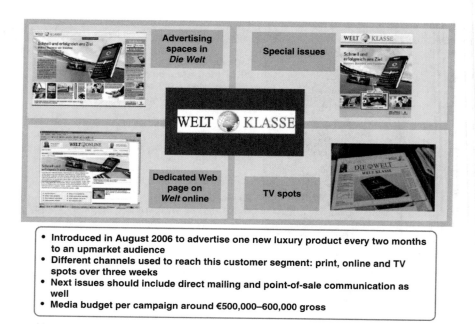

- Introduced in August 2006 to advertise one new luxury product every two months to an upmarket audience
- Different channels used to reach this customer segment: print, online and TV spots over three weeks
- Next issues should include direct mailing and point-of-sale communication as well
- Media budget per campaign around €500,000–600,000 gross

Figure 10   Welt cross-media premium-bundled advertising offer: WeltKlasse

Source: WeltKlasse; Ihr Sprungbrett zu neuen; Premium Zielgruppen; Axel Springer Summer 2007. Reproduced with permission

The Welt website was completely rejuvenated and, taking into consideration the direction in which the market was going, optimized so that its articles came out on top of Google search results. This resulted in a 450% increase of page visits in the first year alone (March 2007 to March 2008). These changes were fruitful, and the Welt/Berliner Morgenpost group recorded a profit for the first time in 2007.

Figure 11   Number of observed updates of websites in an hour

Source: McKinsey analyses based on news websites

Current Situation

Industry dynamics

Advertising and readership

Historically, copy sales and classified and display advertising have been the primary revenue streams of the newspaper industry. The Internet has threatened all of these revenue streams, especially in advertising, for example, as online classified advertisements for real estate, cars and jobs are more attractive and cheaper than their paper counterparts are.

CAGR 2002–2006, per cent

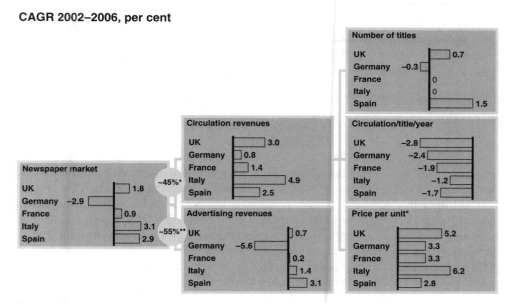

Figure 12   Drivers of newspaper revenue growth

*Including newspapers purchased through subscription
**Except for France, where the share of circulation in revenues is 60% and the share of advertising is 40%
Source: McKinsey analyses based on data from world press trends 2007 reports; PwC global entertainment report, 2006–10, team analysis

Newspaper readership is declining steadily in both the United States and Europe, not only because younger people read less but also because readers read less as they grow older. For print newspapers, reader loyalty tends to be quite high, as consumers are unlikely to change their reading preferences and so will stick with the same publication year after year. However, this loyalty is not necessarily transferred to the online environment. For advertisers, loyalty to the same publication is not generally high. As the numbers for 2007

UK example, GBP million

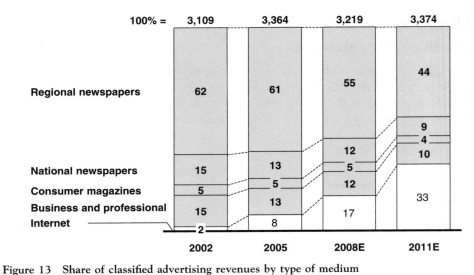

Figure 13 **Share of classified advertising revenues by type of medium**

Source: McKinsey analysis based on data from Advertising Association and Enders Analysis; comScore

and early 2008 show, advertisers are rapidly moving to online alternatives such as Google and Monster. Online classified players are even gaining marketshare in the offline world.

The Interactive Advertising Bureau indicates that, for example, in the United States annual revenues for 2007 for online advertising have exceeded US$21 billion, and have increased by 25.6% from 2006. Furthermore, consumer advertisers represent the largest proportion of Internet ad spending, and accounted for 55% of the 2007 annual revenues.[5] This trend towards consumer advertisers moving to online classifieds continued into early 2008. The *New York Times* witnessed a decline of 22.6% in classified advertising for jobs, real estate and autos during the first half of 2008. In July of 2008, industry analysts predicted that newspaper advertising would fall 8% over 2008 amid significant declines in classified advertising.[6]

Early missteps

Although the benefit of hindsight makes it easy to say now, early on in the Internet era there were several missteps taken by many in the newspaper industry. These missteps have contributed to independent online sites gaining readerships and advertising revenue from the industry's traditional leaders. From the late 1990s until around 2002, the strategy of many newspaper companies was to simply replicate their print editions online. This, in

[5]IAB report published in conjunction with PricewaterhouseCoopers.
[6]Chaffin Joshua, (2008) 'Key US ad spending forecast cut by half'. *Financial Times*, 8 July 2008.

combination with the move to not use their best journalists for the online edition, resulted in online editions being of poor quality compared to print. The brand prestige stayed with the print edition, and allowed new entrants to gain online readerships. The proliferation of high-quality and highly specialized information and entertainment websites resulted in fewer visits to newspaper sites, and to diminishing brand loyalty. Furthermore, the newspaper industry did not enter the online classified market aggressively for fear of cannibalization with their print advertising business. They lost out early on in job-search classifieds to new entrants such as Monster.com.

Challenges of the transition to online

Newspapers now have greater insight into what is required to be competitive online. The rules are often different online, and do not always involve traditional journalism as taught in journalism school. Traditional newspaper journalists tended to save up the news story for the next day's newspaper rather than pass it on to the online editorial staff; however, given the growing competition from the online media, more and more journalists are beginning to realize that stories should be broken online first, and so there is a growing belief that online editorial staff should include the best journalists. Many companies are putting print journalists in the same room as those who work online, so that writers are working for the website *and* the print edition. This requires a significant cultural change.

Another debate concerns the influence advertisers have on editorial content. New ways of advertising are blurring the traditional separation of content and advertising that existed in the print media. In the past there was a strict code of conduct and often regulation determining what constituted content and what constituted advertising. The Internet is opening up areas of content production that are directly financed by advertisers and designed for marketing. It is no longer easy to discern advertising from content, something which goes against a key tenet of traditional journalism.

Additionally, newspapers are investing in new ventures that are only peripherally related to journalism. Schibsted, for instance, has started an online slimming club, called Viktklubben.se, and, as indicated above, Axel Springer acquired auFeminin, the popular online portal for women.

Yet, there are many threats to the industry as it gains greater online presence. Not only is there competition from online-only sites, there is also competition for news sites from all around the world. Aggregator sites such as Google have facilitated this competition. On the one hand, this increases readership, as shown with the UK's *Guardian* online site, where it has a significant number of readers from America. On the other hand, people no longer have to turn to the national or local newspaper to receive their news. Online, newspaper brands must compete against local, national, international and online-only rivals. Often, it is not the newspaper sites which have the leading position in online news.

Additionally, greater online presence and online advertising revenue does not even come close to replacing the revenue received from print advertising revenue. A significant portion of online advertising revenue goes on searching advertising sites such as Google, and to classified sites such as Yellow Pages, and online job listing sites like Monster.com.

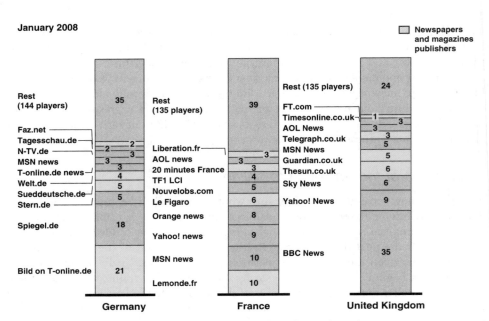

Figure 14 Market share news websites, per cent of total visits/month

Source: McKinsey analyses based on data from comScore

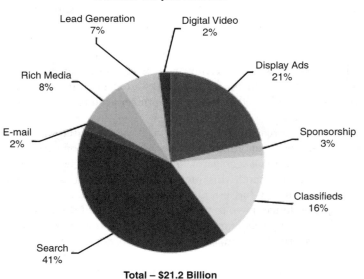

Figure 15 Internet advertising revenues by advertising type, US

Source: IAB Internet Advertising Revenue Report, 2007. Reproduced by permission of IAB

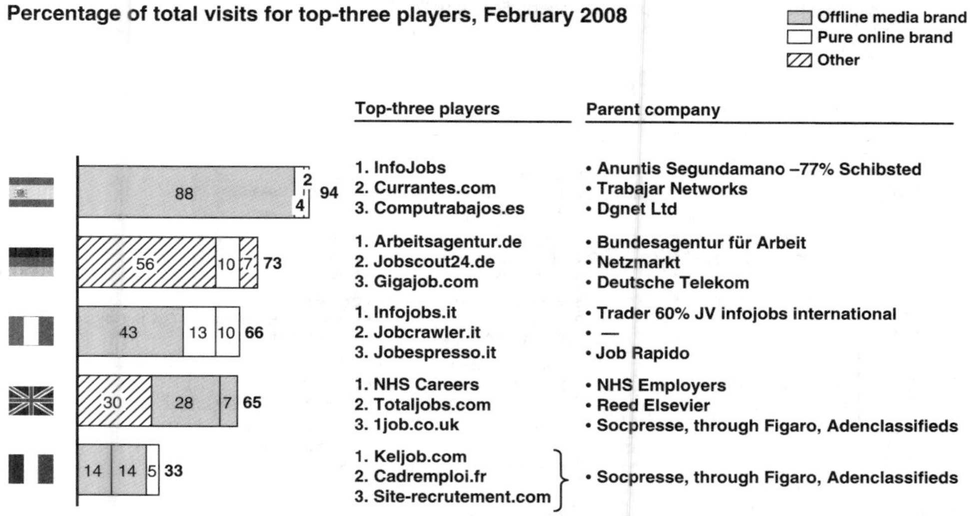

Percentage of total visits for top-three players, February 2008

- Offline media brand
- Pure online brand
- Other

	Top-three players	Parent company
	1. InfoJobs 2. Currantes.com 3. Computrabajos.es	• Anuntis Segundamano –77% Schibsted • Trabajar Networks • Dgnet Ltd
	1. Arbeitsagentur.de 2. Jobscout24.de 3. Gigajob.com	• Bundesagentur für Arbeit • Netzmarkt • Deutsche Telekom
	1. Infojobs.it 2. Jobcrawler.it 3. Jobespresso.it	• Trader 60% JV infojobs international • — • Job Rapido
	1. NHS Careers 2. Totaljobs.com 3. 1job.co.uk	• NHS Employers • Reed Elsevier • Socpresse, through Figaro, Adenclassifieds
	1. Keljob.com 2. Cadremploi.fr 3. Site-recrutement.com	• Socpresse, through Figaro, Adenclassifieds

Figure 16 Online job classified market

Source: McKinsey analyses based on data from comScore

Percentage of total visits of top-three players, February 2008

- Offline media brand
- Pure online brand
- Other

	Top-three players	Parent company
	1. Immobilien Scout 24 2. Immonet.de 3. Immowelt.de	• Deutsche Telekom AG • Axel Springer –100% • Holtbrink/Ippen/WAZ Medien gruppe (75%)
	1. Casa.it 2. Immobiliare.it 3. Eurekasa.it	• Gruppo Rea, Real Estate, Newscorp • Eurekasa srl • Eurekasa srl
	1. Seloger.com 2. Pap.fr 3. Acheter-louer.fr	• Groupe Se Loger • Groupe particulier a particulier • Groupe Adomos
	1. Fotocases.es 2. Idealista 3. Grupo Facilisimo.com	• Anuntis Segundamano –77% Schibsted • Private • —
	1. Rightmove.co.uk 2. Vebra 3. Findaproperty.com	• Publicly listed • Guardian Media Group • Associated Newspapers Ltd

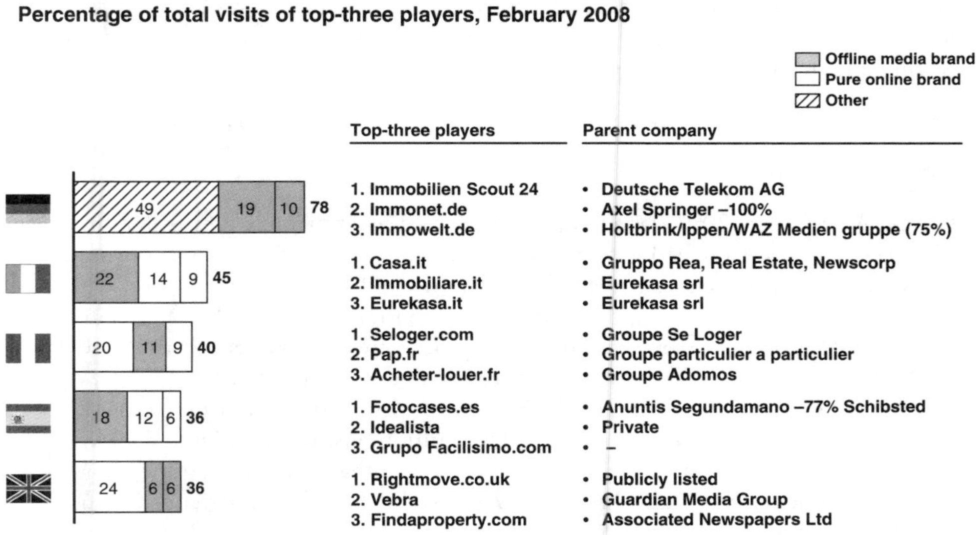

Figure 17 Online real-estate classified market

Source: McKinsey analyses based on data from comScore

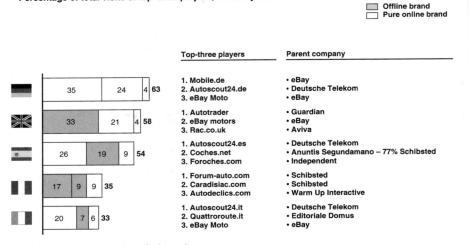

Percentage of total visits of top-three players, February 2008

□ Offline brand
□ Pure online brand

	Top-three players	Parent company
35 | 24 |4| 63	1. Mobile.de 2. Autoscout24.de 3. eBay Moto	• eBay • Deutsche Telekom • eBay
33 | 21 |4| 58	1. Autotrader 2. eBay motors 3. Rac.co.uk	• Guardian • eBay • Aviva
26 | 19 | 9 | 54	1. Autoscout24.es 2. Coches.net 3. Foroches.com	• Deutsche Telekom • Anuntis Segundamano – 77% Schibsted • Independent
17 | 9 | 9 | 35	1. Forum-auto.com 2. Caradisiac.com 3. Autodeclics.com	• Schibsted • Schibsted • Warm Up Interactive
20 | 7 | 6 | 33	1. Autoscout24.it 2. Quattroroute.it 3. eBay Moto	• Deutsche Telekom • Editoriale Domus • eBay

Figure 18 Automobile classified market

Source: McKinsey analyses based on data from comScore

Search advertising and classified advertising represent the greatest proportion of online advertising revenue.

In order to recover lost revenues caused by the shift to online advertising, many newspaper groups have implemented cost-cutting measures. The third-largest newspaper group in the United States, McClatchy, announced drastic measures for 2008, including reducing its workforce by 10%, and outsourcing tasks such as advertisement production, editing and even some journalistic work to India.

The Welt Group

For the Welt Group, 2007 was a landmark year, as it was profitable for the first time since the newspaper was launched. As well as gaining more readers, the Welt Group enjoyed a strong financial performance; profits broke the ten-million-euro mark.

It is estimated that through its various distribution channels the Welt Group has reached 3.4 million readers and online users. Despite the market trend of decreasing readership, the *Die Welt/Welt Kompakt* has increased in circulation by 11% between the first quarters of 2007 and 2008. Welt Online also witnessed strong growth in its readership in 2007, resulting in over 163 million visitors in March 2008. It also assumed a leading position online compared to other German online newspapers such as Sueddeutsche.de and FAZ.net. Welt Mobil has also experienced a sustained increase in usage over 2007. Additionally, based on analysis by Ulrich & Partners, the Welt Group reached a leadership position among quality newspapers for the display advertising market.

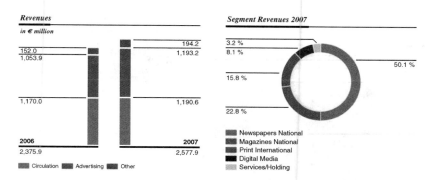

Figure 19　Financial performance of Axel Springer AG, 2007, in Euro million

Source: Axel Springer AG, annual report 2007. Reproduced with permission

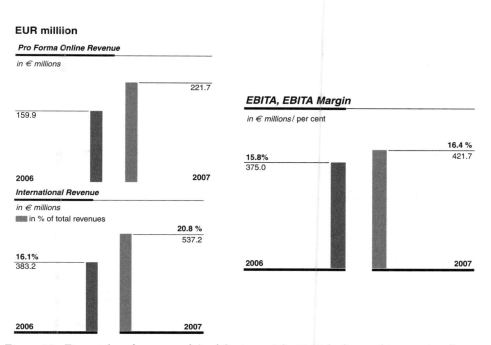

Figure 20　Financial performance of Axel Springer AG, 2007 (online and international)

Note: Pro Forma Online includes revenue from the Digital Media business unit and online revenues of major print brands (i.e. bildonline.de)

Source: Axel Springer AG, annual report 2007. Reproduced with permission

Profits of the Welt Group have increased to a high seven-figure euro sum during the last three years

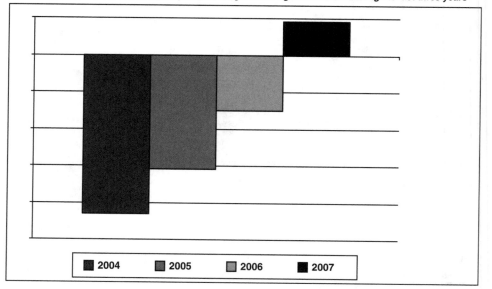

Figure 21   The Welt Group's profitability

Source: Axel Springer AG. Reproduced with permission

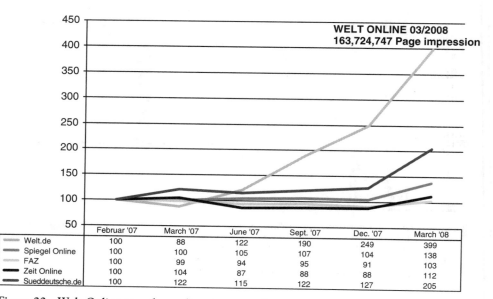

Figure 22   Welt Online vs. other online news portals

Source: IVW, February 2007 to April 2008; index-linked illustration. Reproduced with permission

Strategic Challenges

The Welt Group seems to be a prime example of a successful new 'cross-media' strategy for newspapers. Yet, it still faces many challenges as the group's business moves from a print and publishing focus to a multimedia one.

Future revenue model

One of the greatest dilemmas facing the Welt Group, and many in this industry, is how to recoup lost advertising revenues as print subscribers and advertisers move online. Estimates for the United States suggest that a print subscriber generates about $500–900 a year from advertising. Online, the estimates are as low as $5.50 per reader.[7]

Increased competition from Web 2.0

With the fast rise of 'social network' websites and consumers spending almost 30% of their online time on these type of sites and increasingly using RSS feeds, traditional news sites are under pressure.

Competition for a share of online advertising

The market size of online advertising is expected to grow substantially in the coming years. However, industry estimates are that 50% of the global online advertising revenues are shared between Google and Yahoo!. Growth in online advertising revenues is above all in search advertising and rich media offerings (Web video clips). Internet 'display' advertising (banners etc.) is increasingly losing its market share. Can a news site compete with these global giants in the long run?

Attracting visitors

An increasing number of visitors to news websites, in many cases more than half, ends up at the website because of a search query rather than because users have typed in a specific URL (website address). *Die Welt*'s website currently profits greatly from this as it frequently comes at the top of Web search results. As other websites, however, are getting more and more sophisticated, competition for the top spot will increase. Will it be possible to increase the direct attraction of the online brand again or should other strategies be adopted to retain the number of visitors?

Convergence

One of the core beliefs of the media industry is that 'content is king'. Those who own it will need to increasingly innovate on content-delivery platforms and advertising

---

[7]Hussman, W., Jr. (2007) 'How to Sink a Newspaper', Wall Street Journal Online, 7 May 2007.

methods to ensure their content reaches the intended target groups through optimal platforms. But maintaining a multitude of platforms (online, mobile, radio, TV, IPTV) may prove to be challenging and costly. Can enough additional revenue be generated to offset these costs?

* * *

As there are few other newspaper groups which are as far down the road as the Welt Group, the management cannot look to others for answers to these questions. Will there be a long-term cross-media business model for news providers, which is economically sustainable and appealing to journalists? How important will branding be in the future or will content be the major differentiator? Should *Die Welt* try to become as widely distributed as possible or should it target a specific community?

Hubert Burda Media: In Search of New Digital Business Models[1]

Hubert Burda Media (HBM), one of Germany's leading magazine publishers, is a company which embraces change. Hubert Burda himself is often one of the first in his industry to detect new tailwinds, such as the opening of Eastern Europe, to strengthen his publications' position. Yet 2008 brought a new set of challenges that could fundamentally change the focus of the organization: the domestic German readership market for magazines continues to decline, while high-quality online content has significantly boosted its presence. Furthermore, online advertising, and in particular the dominance of online search engines, is increasingly affecting print advertising. HBM is investigating new ways to stay competitive in the face of online competition.

Company History

HBM is an innovative German media organization with diverse operations consisting of magazine printing and publishing, investments in Internet projects, Internet Web services, radio and some digital television channels. And at the heart of this organization is a family-owned printing and publishing business.

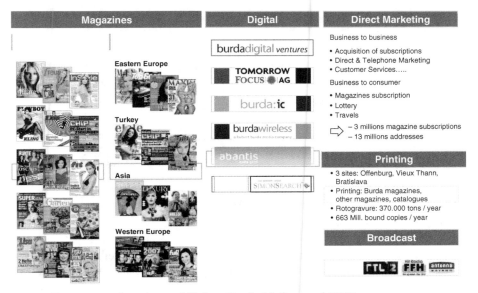

Figure 1   Divisions and products of Hubert Burda Media, as of 2008

Source: Hubert Burda Media company data. Reproduced with permission

---

[1]This case is developed solely as the basis for class discussion. Cases are not intended to serve as endorsements, sources of primary data or illustrations of effective or ineffective management.

Burda's beginnings date back to the late 1890s, when a printer, Franz Burda, took over his employer's business. During the following decades, Burda became a major player in printing and publishing within Germany. One of Burda's early successes was a weekly radio listings guide, *Bild & Funk* (which roughly translates as *Sight and Sound* or *TV and Radio*). This magazine became the company's backbone in its early years. In the ensuing decades, Burda's magazine-publishing business continued to gain momentum and launched many innovative formats, such as the *Bunte Illustrierte* (a leading weekly celebrity magazine to this day) and a fashion magazine, *Burda Moden*, launched by Anne Burda, the wife of Franz Burda junior, the son and successor of the founder, which offers patterns for homemade clothes. Almost from its inception, was exported to many countries, catering to the need of post-war women to be dressed fashionably at affordable prices.

From the 1960s to the 1990s, the company launched and/or acquired a large number of successful, mostly weekly, magazines, building new brands, which were then in turn extended into new thematic sub-brands. In 1993, Burda solidified its place as a major player within the publishing industry in Germany with the launch of *Focus*. *Focus*, a news magazine, was positioned to compete directly with the well-established German news magazine *Der Spiegel*. The magazine was a resounding success, as it took a very refreshing approach to news journalism, with short, punchy articles, an appealing and colourful layout and innovative, service-orientated topics, such as rankings of Germany's best doctors, lawyers and universities. Subsequently, the *Focus* brand was extended both within and beyond magazine publishing.

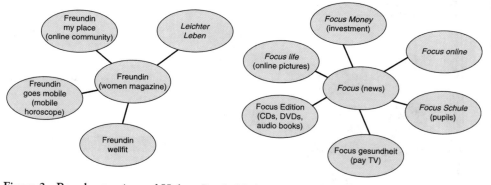

Figure 2 Brand extensions of Hubert Burda Media

Source: Hubert Burda Media company data. Reproduced with permission

During the mid-1990s, the company was a highly successful and well-respected German magazine publisher, ranked second in the market (just behind Gruner + Jahr), publishing over 40 national titles. However, by then the board predicted that the market had peaked and saw the potential impact of the Internet on the media industry, and so it pursued a three-pronged diversification strategy: further internationalization, expansion into other media, especially the Internet, and the development of service businesses based on its back-office activities. To reflect this change in scope, the name of the company was changed to HBM in 1999.

Internationalization

By the late 1980s, Burda had started to expand its readership to other European countries, and also brought foreign magazine titles to the German market. Burda's move to publish a Western magazine in the USSR spearheaded its decade's long expansion into foreign markets, and its collaboration with foreign publishers. *Burda Moden* was the first Western magazine to be published in the USSR. Soon after expanding into the USSR, Burda entered into a joint venture with French publisher Hachette to launch a licensed German version of *Elle*. After the fall of the Berlin Wall, the company acquired several East German newspapers to establish a presence there. (These papers were sold off again in 2007 as part of an overall consolidation strategy.)

By the mid-1990s, Burda decided to step up its efforts and actively pushed its international expansion. It started publishing magazines in Asia, and entered into joint ventures in China, South Korea, Thailand and Indonesia, part of which had to be discontinued later following regulatory changes. The late 1990s brought several acquisitions in Turkey, Greece, Italy, Spain and Mexico. In 1998, Burda and Rizzoli, an Italian publisher with whom Burda had a strategic alliance, jointly acquired a stake in the Turkish publisher Huerguec. They then created the group Dogan Burda Rizzoli. Further acquisitions were made by this group in Greece, Italy and France. In July 2004, the partnership with Rizzoli was finished when Burda acquired the shares from Rizzoli. By 2008, more than 40% of its magazine revenues came from abroad, up from under 10% in 1995 (around 24% of total revenue).

Figure 3   Leading magazine publisher in six countries abroad

Source: Hubert Burda Media company presentation. Reproduced with permission

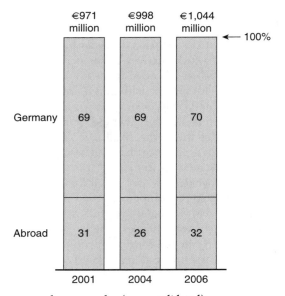

Figure 4   Magazine revenue by geography (unconsolidated)

Source: Hubert Burda Media company data; Media Perspektiven. Reproduced with permission

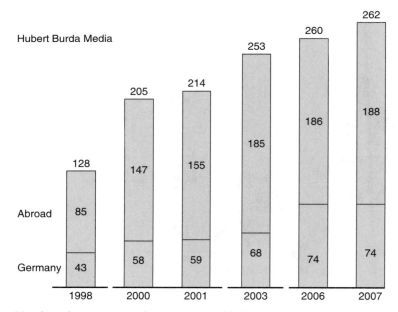

Figure 5   Number of magazines and newspapers published

Source: Hubert Burda Media company data. Reproduced with permission

Diversification into other media and the Internet

Although Burda focused a great deal of attention on expanding into foreign markets in the late 1990s, it also had ambitious plans for the domestic German market. During this period, Burda also started to diversify more actively into different media, such as radio and television activities and, above all, the Internet. Over the years Burda has systematically invested in regional and local radio stations, such as the highly successful popular Bavarian music station Antenne Bayern, BBradio, Donau 3FM and Radio 107.7 in Stuttgart. However, owing to regulations, it was not possible to take majority stakes in this highly fragmented market. On the TV side Burda picked up on the success of *Focus*, and launched *Focus TV* (an infotainment show on free-to-air broadcaster Pro7) in 1996 followed by a number of other TV productions for a variety of German free-TV channels. In 2006, it launched Focus Gesundheit, a digital TV channel. By 2008, the company had over 30 direct and indirect stakes in radio and TV activities.

Burda picked up on the importance of the Internet early on. The company was well positioned to enjoy the Internet boom following its Internet launch of *Focus Online* in 1996, and with its subsequent investments in Internet publishing through Focus Digital AG, to eventually creating one of Germany's largest Internet companies through the acquisition of the Tomorrow group, the Tomorrow Focus AG. Additionally, in the 1990s, Burda took on the role of a venture capitalist and began to invest in various Internet ventures, mostly technology-based start-ups and growing businesses that were already successful. Most of these companies lived through the Internet collapse in early 2000 and are now thriving. Some of them have been sold and others still make up part of the company's portfolio.

The digital activities of the company have been concentrated in either Burda Digital or Tomorrow Focus AG. Burda Digital comprises an IT division, an internet division – which contains the internet start-up's Burda has invested in, and which developed into a holding of internet companies with a turnover of ca. Euro 300 million in 2008 – division and a wireless division. Tomorrow Focus AG includes the following business divisions: portal services (Tomorrow Focus, Cellular), an e-commerce branch (Holidaycheck, Elitemedianet, Playboy) and a technology branch (Tomorrow Focus technologies). The portal services offer an expansive marketing portfolio of HBM-owned offers and partner brand platforms. Portal offerings include: Focus Online, TV Spielfilm Online, plus many partner brand platforms such as Antenne Bayern, Bunte Online, Chip and Sevenload. The company also manages databases of editorial content available for a multitude of online services, and produces content and technology for interactive TV, Web TV and mobile technology. Additionally, it is involved in the marketing of editorial content and advertising space and provides consulting services to companies for e-commerce and content-management solutions. It also plays a role in the mediation of alliances between suppliers of online services and other companies. In 2007, Tomorrow Focus intended to focus increasingly on its e-commerce business, which it anticipated would augment the existing advertising-financed portal division. This strategy led to the acquisition of a majority shareholding in Elitemedianet GmbH in July 2007 and increased shareholding (to 80%) in HolidayCheck AG in August 2007. Like all other divisions in HBM, Tomorrow Focus functions as an independent profit centre.

By 2008, digital revenues for HBM were approximately 19% of total revenue for the organization.

Service businesses

In 1995, the company was comprehensively reorganized into profit centres, not only the magazine publishing groups but also the supporting and administrative services. In this new structure, 'office services', such as printing, advertising sales, purchasing and HR, were centralized and sold their services to the magazine groups and third parties.

In this way, scale effects could be utilized and third-party revenues for these services generated. From these profit centres, two developed into significant contributors to the company's revenues. The printing group became one of Germany's leading rotogravure printers with significant third-party business. This group makes up about 10% of total external revenue.

Publishing groups

Support profit centres	Super	Arabella Strasse	Mediapark	Burda People Group	Milch Strasse	Chip Holding	Burda Eastern Europe	Focus Magazine, Focus TV	Etc.
Services (F&A, HR)									
Procurement Centre									
Internet/(IT Tomorrow Focus/Burda Digital)									
IT (digital systems)									
Print									
Publishing centre									
Direct (direct marketing/CRM)									
Media Distribution									
Community Network (ad sales)									

Figure 6   ECC Hubert Burda Media profit centre organization: combination of publishing group and service centres

Source: McKinsey analyses based on data from Hubert Burda Media

Another division that showed significant growth was the direct services business. Originally, a small department for subscriber services it now offers a wide array of B2B (dialogue marketing, CRM services, community marketing) and B2C (lotto services, product marketing, etc.) services, making up approximately 10% of total revenue.

In March 2003, the BurdaYukom GmbH was created, bundling all existing publishing services for third parties (B2B and B2C magazines for corporations).

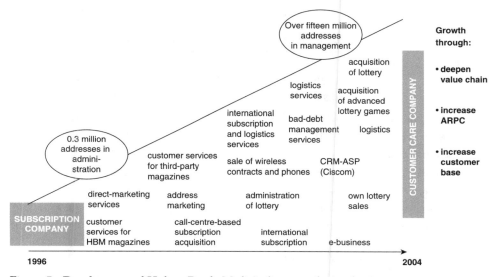

Figure 7   Development of Hubert Burda Media's direct-marketing business

Source: Hubert Burda Media company presentation. Reproduced with permission

HBM distinguishes itself within the magazine industry because of its strong portfolio of magazines, high-quality printing facilities, international expansion into Europe and Asia, diversification into radio and television and strong stake in Internet offerings and technology.

Current Position

As described above, a significant part of Burda's portfolio consists of other activities, such as direct-marketing services, Web and radio content, television productions, advertising sales services and investments in online companies such as Tomorrow Focus. These have all contributed to its strong position today.

Burda was able to increase revenue in 2008 despite the difficult domestic market and in spite of continued cost cutting and restructuring measures in the declining printing business and domestic magazine-publishing houses. Above-average investments in emerging markets, the Internet and foreign publishing houses helped to offset the revenue impact of these cost-saving measures. Operating performance increased by 2.9% from €2.15 billion to €2.21 billion and consolidated (external) sales grew by 5.3% from €1.6 billion to €1.69 billion. Magazine sales were stable, with international growth compensating for domestic market decline, making up 64.3% (2006: 65.1%) in external sales; the digital area grew quickly to make up 16.3% of sales (2006: 14.4%), dialogue marketing stabilized at 9.8% (2006: 9.8%) after years of fast growth, printing revenues declined slightly and made up 9.3% (2006: 10.4%). Clearly, the digital area experienced the greatest growth contribution during 2007, with an increase in sales of 19% to €274.5 billion. International sales of the publishing houses also experienced significant growth with an increase of 11.3% to €374 billion.

EUR million

	2001	2002	2003	2004	2005	2006	2007
• Revenues							
– Gross	1,840	1,857	2,004	1964	2062	2151	2214
– Net	1,396	1,404	1,526	1477	1525	1603	1687
• Publishing	1,124	1,144	1,120	998	1015	1044	1085
• Printing	201	191	179	479	510	559	602
• Balance sheet total	873	827	845	845	894	958	1026
• Investments*	176	121	114	154	200	142	223
• Depreciation	47	43	42	38	39	46	49
• Personnel costs	349	357	374	365	372	367	381
• Number of employees at year-end	5,717	7,051	7,388	7909	7644	7817	7991

Figure 8   Financial results for Hubert Burda Media

*Including investments in new magazines
Source: Hubert Burda Media company data. Reproduced with permission

EUR million

	2005	2006	2007	2005–07 CAGR
• Magazines	1003.8	1084.6	1084.6	+4
• Digital	174.3	230.7	274.5	+25.5
• Direct marketing	158.6	157.5	166.2	+2.4
• Print	173.8	166.3	156.9	–5
• Other	3.3	4.4	5.1	+24
• **Total**				**+5.6**

Figure 9   Consolidated revenues for Hubert Burda Media

Source: Hubert Burda Media company data. Reproduced with permission

Strategic Challenges and Opportunities

The German magazine market is in decline, mostly driven by a reduction in advertising revenue but also by a slow but steady decline in circulation. This is only partly compensated by increases in copy price and number of titles.

Acknowledging that profitable growth will have to come from the other areas, HBM's strategy for 2008 and 2009 focuses on consolidating its printing operations, and placing

2002–06 CAGR, per cent

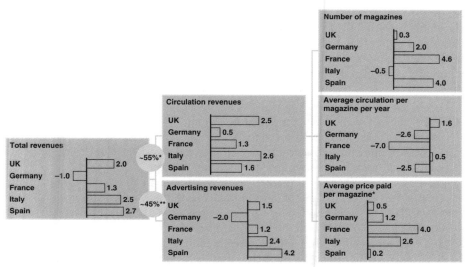

Figure 10   Consumer magazines market development by revenue driver

*Including magazines purchased through subscription
**Except for Germany, where the share of circulation in revenues is 40% and the share of advertising is 60%
Source: McKinsey analyses based on data from PwC global entertainment report, 2006–10, team analysis; Noticas de la comunicacion; IVW; Tableaux Statistiques de la presse, 2007; Prima Comunicazione; ABC

EUR million

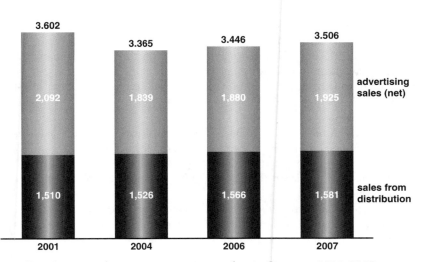

Figure 11   Development of consumer magazine market in Germany 2001–2007

Source: Hubert Burda Media company data based on VDZ; PwC; German Entertainment and Media Outlook 2006–2010. Reproduced with permission

even greater emphasis on foreign magazines, direct marketing but mostly digital opportunities.

Looking forward, HBM has the objective of obtaining one-third of its revenue from digital markets by 2011 (2007: 16%). In order to accomplish this, it decided to further strengthen its cross-media strategy, which leverages Burda Digital and Tomorrow Focus AG, along with several other digital initiatives. Its cross-media strategy involves the following:

Online Content Presence: Hubert Burda Media already owned over 40 internet companies in 2008. Through the acquisition of the American company Glam Media, HBM will gain further access to an extensive network of more than 500 online publishers, lifestyle websites and online communities.

Vertical Markets: To improve market reach, vertical markets, such as travel; will be created by bundling Burda brands and marketing them with partner brands.

Cross-media Marketing: The focus of the cross-media marketing is to aggregate HBM content and market it collectively. Burda brands, vertical partners, website, video and e-commerce offerings will be integrated across different media platforms and forms of revenue. Initially, 40 Burda brands, communities, video formats and e-commerce sites will be aggregated.

Central Online Content Pool: The creation of the Burda Community Network for content will involve marketing content on the Internet, in addition to marketing content to external partners.

Collaboration with Tomorrow Focus AG: Tomorrow Focus will be responsible for the online marketing of the new aggregated content. To gain greater presence in online marketing, Tomorrow Focus AG acquired a stake in Adjug, which operates an online marketplace where advertisers can buy and sell advertising content.

Online Advertising and E-commerce: Newly created vertical markets will be monetized through online marketing and e-commerce, which by 2008 already generated a turnover of ca. Euro 200 million. Intelligent targeting and marketing of customer profiles may also provide additional revenue.

Video: To address the anticipated growth in digital and mobile video, HBM plans to produce video content for multi-platforms: IPTV, mobile video, analogue and digital TV channels.

Investments and Acquisitions: Similar to the acquisition of Glam Media, more fast-growing online companies are being considered for acquisition.

To enable the cross-media strategy the company was restructured and a new cross-media division introduced.

In addition to the cross-media initiative, the company decided to continue to invest in digital ventures, but it will no longer invest in start-ups. The focus will be on successful digital companies that are not far from an IPO or trade sale. As the investments required are significantly higher, it was decided to delegate the management of the digital participations to a company called Action Capital Partners, which will also launch a new fund, Heureka Growth, into which not only HBM but also selected third parties can invest.

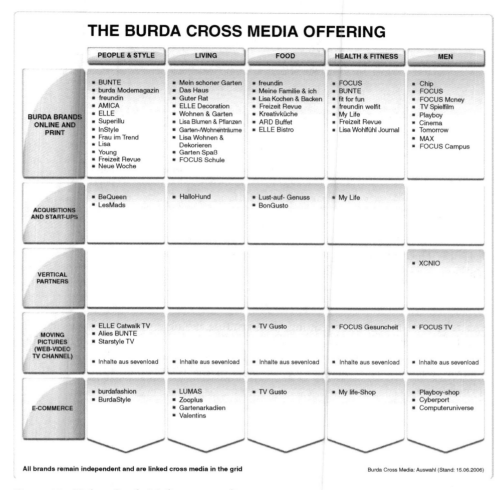

Figure 12   Hubert Burda Media cross-media strategy

Source: Hubert Burda Media company data. Reproduced with permission

∗   ∗   ∗

Looking forward HBM realizes it has to perform across all its divisions in order to achieve growth. There are many fundamental questions to address. For the German magazine business cross media offerings will become increasingly important, however new skills and approaches are needed to get it off the ground. The Direct Marketing business will have to decide how the next wave of direct marketing will look like: will there be a structural shift

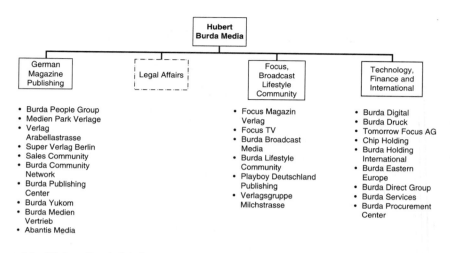

Figure 13   Hubert Burda Media organization 2008

Source: McKinsey analyses based on Hubert Burda Media Company data

from telephone-to online marketing. The printing business will have to decide on a consolidation strategy given the over capacity in Europe. And last but not the least, HBM will have to decide on its international growth strategy. How fast should it grow? Should it move actively outside Europe, e.g. to some of the BRIC countries (Brazil, Russia, India, China)?

Mediaset: From Focused Broadcaster to Value Chain Operator[1]

Gruppo Mediaset, Italy's largest broadcaster and market leader in TV services, has enjoyed strong performance for many years. It controls more than half of Italy's TV advertising market, and has only one main competitor, RAI, a state-run broadcaster. But in 2007, Marco Giordani, the CFO of Mediaset, was faced with a 7% drop in advertising prices, proposed legislation that will make it easier for competitors to enter the market and a falling stock price.

Mediaset's stronghold is in Italy, and although it does own Spanish broadcaster Telecinco, until recently its international presence was limited. The company just completed a bold strategic move as it took a 33% share in Endemol, a TV content production company present in 25 countries, and with hits such as *Big Brother*, *Deal or No Deal* and *Who Wants to be a Millionaire?*. Mediaset, along with Cyrte Investments and Goldman Sachs Capital Partners, acquired Endemol from Spanish Telefonica in late 2007. Marco wonders whether Mediaset, although a very profitable company, needs even greater diversification, especially given that the Italian TV advertising market is getting closer to maturity. Additionally, he questions how strong Mediaset's position is against the threat of new entrants, particularly from Internet companies.

Company History

The origins of Mediaset date back to 1978, when Silvio Berlusconi started Telemilano, a local TV network. Two years later, Telemilano became part of Canale 5, a network of local channels owned by Mr Berlusconi's company Fininvest. Over the course of the 1980s, Fininvest acquired and enhanced two other networks, Italia 1 (1982) and Rete 4 (1984). In the early 1990s, the channels officially obtained national broadcasting licences, and gained market share against the public service broadcaster RAI. At the same time, Fininvest also took over the major Italian publisher, Mondadori.

Between 1993 and 1995, Fininvest's television activities – then including the three broadcasting networks, TV rights management, production, film distribution and advertising sales – were consolidated into Gruppo Mediaset. The objective of this consolidation was to form an integrated TV and communication group, with the ability to grow through investments from strategic and financial partners. With his entry into politics and election as prime minister in 1994, Silvio Berlusconi handed over operational control of Fininvest to his long-time partner, Fedele Confalonieri. Berlusconi remained politically active and was prime minister from 1994 to 1995, 2001 to 2006 and was again re-elected in 2008. In 1996, Mediaset went public with Mr Confalonieri as its chairman, and over the next three years the group started to diversify and expand internationally.

---

[1]This case is developed solely as the basis for class discussion. Cases are not intended to serve as endorsements, sources of primary data or illustration of effective and ineffective management.

International expansion

Although Mediaset has attempted to expand its operations throughout Europe, with its acquisition of the telecoms operator Albacom in 1996, and its joint venture with Germany's Kirch Media Group in 1999, it has not been that successful. Albacom was written off and the Kirch Media Group became insolvent in 2002. Its first real international success came with the acquisition of Telecinco.

Telecinco

Mediaset has been a majority shareholder of Telecinco since 2003. Telecinco is one of Spain's leading TV networks, and has the largest audience share. Mediaset entered the Spanish market with a minority interest and worked with local partners to raise its stake to 50.1% in 2003. In 2004 Mediaset went public with Telecinco and experienced one of its most successful years. Telecinco's success is in part due to the fact that its organizational structure and management approach were modelled after Mediaset. Today, it contains an advertising and sales division, a press agency, a film co-production division, free-to-air (FTA) digital terrestrial TV (DTT) channels, analogue TV channels, and Internet and teleshopping divisions.

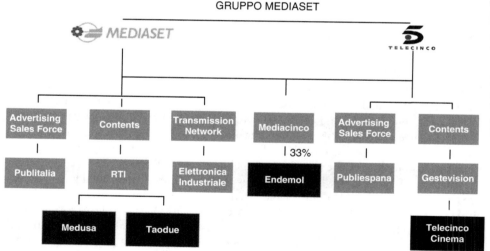

Figure 1   Mediaset's organizational structure

Source: Mediaset Company Presentation, 2008. Reproduced by permission

Internet and digital age

At the height of the Internet boom in 1999 Mediaset launched Mediaset Online, a portal for news and sports bulletins, weather reports and cinema information, however overall its online offerings have remained limited; this is mainly because online penetration in Italy was slow in comparison to other northern European countries. The recent formation of RTI

Interactive Media is intended to improve its online offering. RTI Interactive Media is a new division within Mediaset responsible for several websites focused on news, sports and community events. Additionally, through the teletext service MediaVideo, RTI provides a multimedia news service available on DTT (a digital TV broadcast platform that transmits the signal to an antenna attached to the TV which uses the digital instead of the traditional analogue technique, thus increasing the number of channels that can be transmitted from 4–5 to 25–30), and through Rivideo it provides a site to download films, TV series and sports.

Mediaset was initially producing channels to be broadcasted via the Sky platform; however with the introduction of DTT in 2003, Mediaset fully dedicated itself to the production of channels to be broadcasted on its DTT platform and expanded this offering to include Boing, a children's channel, and a shopping channel in 2004. Since 2004, Mediaset has continued to expand its DTT packages.

Recent years

In recent years Mediaset has enriched its DTT pay-TV services, launched a mobile TV initiative and continued to build its offerings in advertising and sales, its free-to-air (FTA) channels, digital antennae broadcast infrastructure, TV drama and film production, online shopping and the Internet. Furthermore, Mediaset has also enhanced its presence on the DTT TV platform through digital offerings such as the Disney Channel.

Although traditionally a FTA broadcaster, Mediaset expanded into DTT pay-TV in 2005. Acquiring the rights to broadcast First League soccer matches in 2005 was pivotal to expanding these services. Prior to 2005, the satellite provider Sky Italia had exclusive rights to broadcasting live First League soccer matches. With the DTT rights to First League soccer matches, Mediaset became the first broadcaster in the world to offer live pay-per-view soccer on DTT. In contrast to Sky Italia, a subscription was not required to view the soccer matches, as Mediaset launched a DTT pay-per-view service similar to that used for pre-paid mobile phone cards.

In addition to expanding its DTT offering, Mediaset has also invested in mobile-TV capabilities. In 2006, Mediaset launched Europe's first digital terrestrial mobile TV network using DVB-H technology. This service was launched in conjunction with the mobile operator Vodafone, TIM and H3G. There has not been a huge uptake in mobile TV in Italy – which is also due to relatively high prices – however a 2008 ruling to make DVB-H an official standard for the EU is expected to generate some momentum.

Although the company developed a wide range of digital activities, it has found it hard so far to generate significant positive contribution with these initiatives.

Current Situation

Industry dynamics

The Italian TV market was estimated to be worth €9.5 billion for 2007, with €2.9 billion generated from subscriptions, €1.6 billion from public funding and €5 billion from advertising. For 2008, the market size is expected to reach €10 billion. In addition to a substantial market size, Italy boasts one of the highest daily TV consumption rates in Europe, ahead of Spain, the United Kingdom, Germany and France. Given these market conditions, one might assume there would be myriad TV viewing platforms and content packages for the viewer to choose from. Yet the Italian TV market is highly concentrated, in part because of regulation that has made it difficult for new competitors to enter the market. Currently, the two largest broadcasting operations RAI and Mediaset hold 85% of both audience and TV advertising.

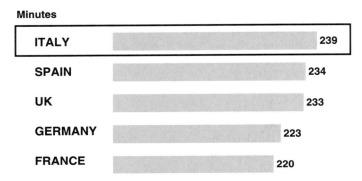

Figure 2   Daily TV consumption in Europe

Source: Mediaset company presentation based on data from GFK; Auditel; Sofres; Mediametrie; BARB. Reproduced by permission

Advertising

Although the advertising market in Italy generated sales of just under €9 billion in 2007, it is not as developed as other European markets, and has some of the lowest relative advertising spending in Europe. In 2007, Italy had, with 0.58%, a lower advertising spend/GDP ratio than several other European markets, such as Germany, where the ratio was closer to 0.73%, and the United Kingdom, with 1.08%. Furthermore, the total advertising spend per head in Italy is €151 compared to €216 in Germany and €359 in the United Kingdom. Not surprisingly, the advertising market is growing, and from 1998 to 2007 it experienced a compound annual growth rate (CAGR) of 4.8%. This growth rate is higher than that experienced in the United Kingdom, Germany and France.

Mediaset and RAI have the greatest share of both the total advertising market in Italy and the TV advertising market. The Italian market is quite unique in that television accounts for more than half of the national advertising spend, while print (which usually dominates) and the Internet take some of the lowest market shares in Europe. In 2007, Mediaset claimed 34.5% of the total advertising market and 64.2% of the TV advertising market. RAI claimed 15.6% of the total advertising market and 29% of the TV market. The lower share of RAI is partly due to regulations which limit the amount of advertising RAI can broadcast.

Although still representing a small percentage of the total advertising market, Internet advertising experienced huge growth. It is estimated that it grew 42.7% over 2006. Although occupying only around 3% of the total advertising market in 2007, with its significant growth potential, Internet advertising may occupy a larger portion of the market in the future.

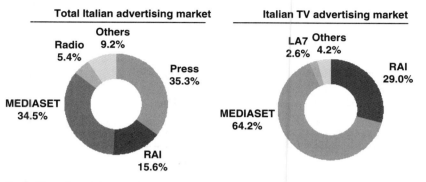

Figure 3   Italian advertising market

Source: Mediaset company presentation based on data from Adex Nielsen, 2007. Reproduced by permission

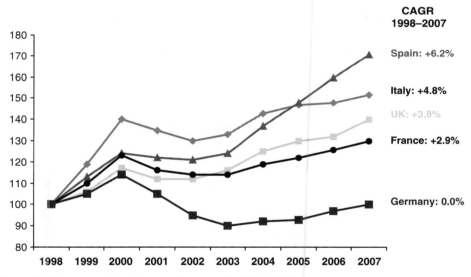

Figure 4   European advertising market: trends 1998–2007

Source: Mediaset company presentation based on data from European Advertising and Media Forecast. Reproduced by permission

Impact of regulation

In 2004 a new media law (*Legge Gasparri*) was passed to respond to the lack of diversity and pluralism in broadcasting in Italy. The law was intended to encourage the TV market to fully switch to DTT, provide anti-trust reforms and allow companies to diversify into more than one media category. The law also suggested that RAI, the publicly owned broadcaster, might be privatized. The anti-trust reforms limited a single company to hold 20% of the total share of the media market revenue (*sistema integrato delle communicazioni*). This 20% does not only include advertising revenue but also other kinds of revenue, such as

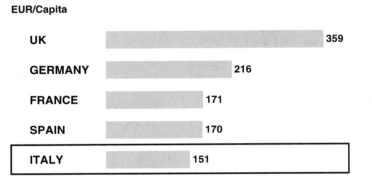

EUR/Capita

Figure 5   Advertising spending per capita

Source: Mediaset company presentation, 2008. Reproduced by permission

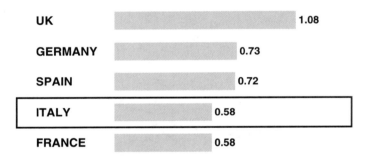

Figure 6   Advertising/GDP ratio

Source: Mediaset company presentation, 2008. Reproduced by permission

licence fees, pay-TV fees and newspaper and magazine revenues. The law also relaxed the limits on media ownership, so broadcasters could also own newspapers, for example.

Yet the law was not that effective, and a year after its adoption RAI and Mediaset continued to control over 90% of all television revenue and audiences. Thus, amendments were made to the law under the Prodi government (2006–2007). Once again, an attempt was made to create a more competitive and pluralistic market and to guarantee the greater independence and efficiency of RAI. But the provisions proved ineffective, as RAI was not privatized, and it became even more difficult for newcomers to enter the digital market.

Further provisions suggested by the Prodi government involved putting 40% of transmission capacity on the DTT multiplex broadcasting capacity owned by RAI, Mediaset and Telecom Italia Media up for tender. Provisions also involved restricting any broadcaster from having more than 45% of the advertising market. The implications of these regulations were that advertising limits would be placed on Mediaset's domestic channels, and one of the channels, Rete 4, had to move away from analogue to digital. These provisions, however, have not been implemented yet and the new government has just proposed that Mediaset be allowed to keep the analogue frequencies for Rete 4 until the completion of the digital switchover in 2012.

Regulation also had an impact on soccer rights in Italy. In 2007, the Italian government introduced changes to the way in which soccer rights are negotiated. For the 2010/11 season, the sale of rights will involve collective bargaining. Additionally, the new regulation puts the negotiation of secondary rights at the discretion of individual clubs. This implies companies could win the rights to broadcast the games but must negotiate separately the rights to place television and studio equipment in the stadiums.

The Italian government is also very active in another aspect of the TV industry. With the EU-imposed deadline of 2012 to switch to digital TV, and with Italy behind schedule, the Italian government decided to heavily subsidize the set-top boxes required for DTT viewing. By mid-2004, fewer than 6 000 Italian households possessed digital TV set-top boxes. The slow adoption rate was in part due to the DTT technology implemented in Italy. Italian DTT is more sophisticated than that used in other European countries, as it allows for interactivity and conditional access. Italian households therefore need specialized and more costly set-top boxes than required in other European countries. In 2004, the government initiated a programme to provide a €150 subsidy for each set-top box.

Platforms

As described above, Italy and the rest of the EU must switch to digital TV by 2012. With analogue TV on its way out and with only one major satellite provider and limited uptake of IPTV, DTT dominates as the digital TV viewing platform in Italy. As of 2007, more than half of Italian households (54.3%) were equipped to receive digital TV (satellite and terrestrial) and an estimated 6 million households currently have set-top boxes to receive digital TV. RAI, Mediaset and Telecom Italia all provide DTT transmission platforms, with RAI and Mediaset dominating the market share. Currently, 28 channels are available in free digital terrestrial mode with national coverage, nine of which are the same as the

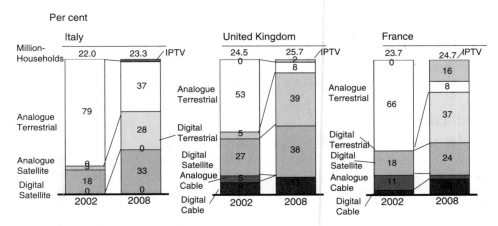

Figure 7   Development of TV platforms

Source: McKinsey analysis based on data from *Screen Digest*

Million households, per cent

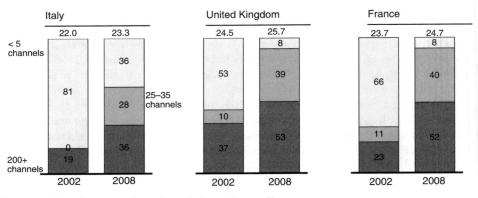

Figure 8   Development of number of channels on offer

Source: McKinsey analyses based on data from *Screen Digest*

analogue offer (simulcast) and 19 are new channels, with more expected in the coming years.

Both publicly owned RAI and Sky Italia, which is controlled by Rupert Murdoch's News Corp, provide satellite TV in Italy. Yet RAI's stake of the market is insignificant, and thus Sky Italia enjoys a monopoly in satellite TV coverage. However, Mediaset delivers pay TV packages through its DTT platform, serving an unanswered demand for premium content. Mediaset recently expanded its satellite broadcast service to include the Disney Channel and the all-sports channel Premium Calcio. Despite the significant uptake in Mediaset's DTT package, and Sky Italia's higher-priced packages, Sky Italia's satellite subscriber base (4.4 million in 2008) is still significantly larger than Mediaset's (2.7 million in 2008).

Both Internet and mobile TV have a small presence in Italy. Mediaset dominates the mobile TV platform, with an estimated 850 000 subscribers in 2007. FastWeb (bought by Swisscom in 2007) dominates the IPTV market in Italy, with an estimated 350 000 subscribers in 2007. Although IPTV currently has limited uptake, FastWeb's investment in fibre to the home (FTTH) will increase IPTV's market share in the future.

Mediaset

Mediaset's revenues depended almost entirely (95%) on advertising. The group is perceived to be very good at selling advertising; its ad agency, Publitalia, sells advertising for its channels and is considered the dominant ad sales force in the country; Publitalia enjoys an excellent reputation for its professionalism. Due to the digital roll-out in Italy, Mediaset is focused on generating revenue from a wider range of sources, including operations abroad. Its strategy still involves maintaining a leadership position on FTA generalist TV as it continues to provide the largest share of advertising revenue. However, it is also focused on becoming a multichannel, multiplatform service. Through expanding its offerings on the DTT platform, it has found a new market for premium content, particularly for football matches. Additionally, Mediaset is concentrating on becoming a leader in the content market, and gaining a greater international presence. The acquisition of Endemol, in addition to several other activities abroad, reinforces this focus.

International expansion

In 2007 and 2008 Mediaset expanded both into Asia and Africa. In 2007 Mediaset entered into China through a joint venture with a local partner. There, it will be selling advertising for a new sports channel that currently broadcasts in seven regions and reaches more than 400 million people. In 2008 Mediaset collaborated with Quinta Communication to relaunch Nessma TV, a satellite channel in north Africa, with an estimated audience base of 90 million.

Diversification through content production

Mediaset recently expanded its content production capabilities in Italy. In 2007 Mediaset bought Medusa Film, a leading Italian film production and distribution company, and in 2008 acquired Taodue. Taodue has been a leader in producing Italian TV drama since the 1960s. During 2008, a joint venture will be created between these two companies to establish a new Italian production company.

The acquisition of Endemol

The acquisition of a 33% stake in Endemol, a Dutch TV production house, from Telefonica was pivotal for Mediaset in many ways. It substantially increased its international presence, as Endemol is present in 25 countries, and significantly increased its content production activities. Although the acquisitions of Medusa and Taodue also contribute to Mediaset's content production operations, they are nowhere near the scale of Endemol's activities.

Given the differences in activities and geographic scope of both companies, Mediaset plans to keep an arm's-length approach to management, and anticipates that Endemol will remain independent from Mediaset.

Mediaset, Cytre Investments, a company controlled by John de Mol, the founder of Endemol, and Goldman Sachs created a consortium to acquire Endemol. And after acquiring Endemol, John de Mol brought back Aat Schouwenaar as an interim CEO. Schouwenaar had quit from Endemol three years earlier. He was succeeded in 2008 by Ynon Kreiz.

Mediaset is implementing a strong incentive programme for management in an effort to continue to build on the success of Endemol. Mediaset is faced with the challenge of maintaining the success of a company whose foundation is based on a network of local creative entrepreneurs with a strong track record in the TV industry. This represents a first for Mediaset, as its portfolio has not previously involved such an extensive network of creative talent.

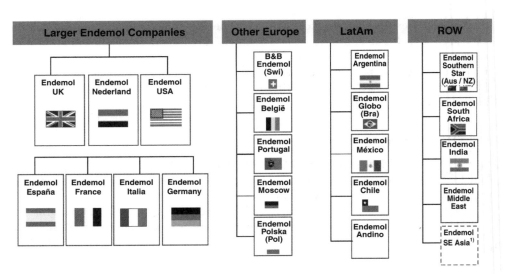

Figure 9 Endemol's international presence

1) In the process of setting up
Source: Mediaset company presentation, 2008. Reproduced by permission

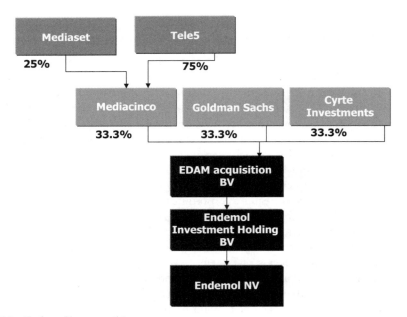

Figure 10 Endemol's ownership structure

Source: Mediaset company presentation, 2008. Reproduced by permission

Financial performance in 2007

Mediaset's share price was affected greatly in 2007. It closed the year at €6.9, substantially below its initial price of €9.2 at the beginning of the year. Although not its best year on record, which was most likely due in part to the volatile advertising market, Mediaset did perform fairly well. Consolidated net revenue grew by 8.9% to reach €4 billion, compared with €3.7 billion in 2006. Additionally, the group's EBIT rose to €1.15 billion, an increase of 10.8% compared with the €1.04 billion of the previous year. Furthermore, operating profitability rose to 28.1% from the 27.7% of 2006.

On 1 July 2008, the share price reached a further low as it dropped to €3.98 after reports of sluggish ad sales, concerns around the company's efforts to recast itself as a content provider and the release by ISTAT, the Italian government's statistic office, showing weak economic growth. Restoring investor confidence is a key priority for the company.

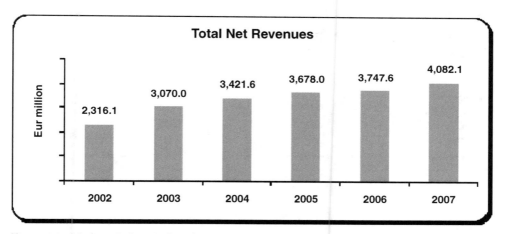

Figure 11   Mediaset's financial performance

Source: Mediaset financial report, 2007. Reproduced by permission

Strategic Challenges

In 2007 Mediaset moved into new markets, and new countries. It changed from a company present in two countries to a company present in at least 25. But did it get too big too fast?

International expansion and diversification

In light of declining advertising sales and regulatory threats, Mediaset started to look elsewhere for new revenue streams. The acquisition of Endemol represents a move into content production, and a means to gain international presence. But if one compares Endemol with Telecinco, Mediaset's only other international operation, one sees little commonality. Telecinco's success is in part due to the fact that its organizational structure

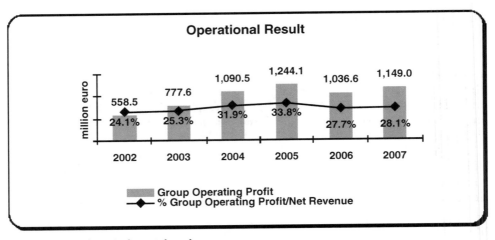

Figure 12 Mediaset's financial performance

Source: Mediaset financial report, 2007. Reproduced by permission

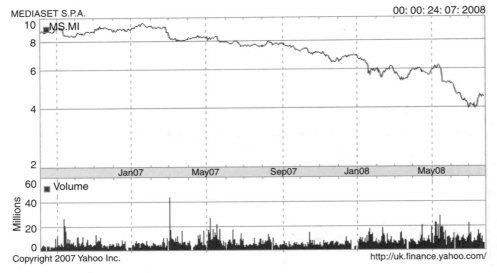

Figure 13 Mediaset's stock price

Source: Yahoo! Financial

and management are modelled on Mediaset. But managing Endemol, a company driven by creative talent and one consisting of a large-scale content production operation, will be new to Mediaset. Furthermore, the challenge of successfully integrating a Dutch company with its strong-willed founder, John de Mol, as co-owner, into a long-standing Italian family-run business may prove challenging.

In 2007 Mediaset also expanded its digital TV offerings, in particular its pay TV service, targeting an unaddressed segment of the premium content market, thus expanding the FTA DTT offering in an effort to become 'multichannel and multiplatform', but does it have sufficient online presence to do this?

Digital threats and opportunities

Although the advertising market in Italy lags behind other markets, there's a trend worldwide where online advertising is taking market share from television advertising. Some estimates suggest that in 2009 Internet advertising will overtake TV as the leading advertising medium worldwide. Although Mediaset is not as reliant on advertising revenue as it was in the past, it still represents a significant proportion of its income.

IPTV, as a new distribution platform for TV distribution, does not currently have significant uptake in the Italy. However, the June 2008 agreement between Telecom Italia and rival FastWeb to facilitate the roll-out of a new glas fibre optics network to the home (FTTH) may spur greater competition from IPTV, and with that, an increase in market-share of digital niche channels and on demand offerings.

Overall, contrasting Mediaset with the United Kingdom broadcaster ITV, which already has a substantial Web-based TV platform, and a goal of generating €150 million in digital revenue by 2010, one wonders whether Mediaset is well positioned for online competition.

*   *   *

Having lived for some time on the leeside of the digital revolution, Mediaset is now facing many challenges in a fast-changing industry beset by highly uncertain regulatory conditions. The company has been very successful in the traditional FTA business and has fine-tuned and optimized its organization to become one of the best-run FTA companies in its industry. Will it be able to transform itself into a vertically integrated, multiplatform company? How fast should it move? Will it be enough to build new businesses on top of the traditional FTA business or will there be too little critical mass, and so is a fundamental reorganization needed? What will be the best approach to avoid rejection of new 'body parts' such as Endemol? Will the arm's-length approach be enough to create shareholder value?

CREATING AND LEVERAGING INNOVATIVE CONTENT

Generating successful new content is the core of any media company. Especially the company's ability to create (new) blockbusters is seen as the ultimate test of the company's ability to compete.

Historically, content creation has been considered more an art than a science, best left to the creatives. This chapter discusses how recent developments challenge this belief and how the content generation process could be better managed in the face of new market developments, including the rise of peer content production. Four key questions will in particular be addressed:

1. *What will be the future role of (blockbuster) content?*
2. *Should content be redefined in the wake of new market developments?*
3. *How can the content generation process be best managed?*
4. *How does user-generated content fit in, and what is the value of peer content production for media in general?*

Future Role of (Blockbuster) Content

The coming years will see an increasing need for new content. The roll-out of digital platforms and fragmenting consumer taste will lead to an explosion of demand. Not only will traditional players try to fill this gap but also new players such as platform operators (cable, ISPs, mobile) will start to offer content, as their original services turn increasingly into commodities.

In a world that will be flooded by content, the consumption of media is likely to polarize further with, on the one hand, the increased focus on blockbuster formats and, on the other, the exploitation of the so-called 'long tail', that is the content which is only sporadically consumed but that cumulatively can still deliver a significant amount of content consumption.

The market is clearly segmented by these patterns of consumer behaviour within the different media: several established content production companies, such as Endemol, HBO and Pixar, have managed to create a consistent stream of new blockbuster content and are the current winners in the industry, growing at double the rate of other content producers. But also there is a set of companies which have been highly successful by leveraging the peer production of content to be exploited in the long tail, including OhmyNews, a South Korean online news company which publishes user-generated articles, or TheNerve, a content production media company leveraging creators from all over the Web to develop new content.

Both developments are challenging. Peer content production profits from the fact that traditional content production is usually a high fixed-cost business with low marginal cost of distribution and reproduction (hence the high level of successful piracy); peer production enables a significant reduction of fixed costs, while using the Web as a low-cost, as well as a widely used, global platform. The downside of this model is that it is often difficult to guarantee sufficient quality control in face of such a decentralized creative process – who can guarantee that a voluntary contributor on a site like OhmyNews is as fact-based as the professional journalist of high-profile newspapers such as the *Financial Times* or the *Wall Street Journal*? This is essentially the criticism put forward by the publishers of any traditional encyclopedia versus Wikipedia, the well-known user-generated encyclopedia on the Web.

Traditional centralized content production companies have their own challenges too. Generating blockbusters, in itself already a difficult task, is especially difficult in the media, as it is a typical 'hit and run' industry. While in other blockbuster-driven industries (e.g. pharmaceuticals) the copyright laws protect the innovation from copycats, imitation in the media industry is easy, as its products are largely intangible (e.g. a format concept such as reality TV). This limits the incentive to innovate too quickly and radically. Furthermore, owing to digitization, most of the media products can be distributed virtually, and be reproduced instantly, facilitating piracy or the bypassing of copyright laws. The music industry is the most well-known example of this but this is also starting to happen in the news area, with the distribution of information feeds, or the distribution of videos on many Internet video platforms, without the agreement of major television networks.

Traditional media: blockbusters!

In many businesses the 80/20 rule applies, that is 20% of products make 80% of sales. In media this is typically even more skewed: on average, the rule tends more towards 90/10. The 10% includes the blockbusters. At Endemol, the largest independent video production house in the word, in 2006 its top ten formats out of its current library of more than 1 200 titles (i.e. 1% of formats) generate over 50% of its average revenue, going up to 80% in some countries. Prominent examples of these blockbusters include *Big Brother*, *Deal or No Deal* and *Fear Factor*. Examples of 'mega blockbusters' brands in other media sectors are Madonna, Robbie Williams or Coldplay (recorded music), Stephen King and John Grisham (book publishing; Figure 3.1); *Vogue* and *Elle* (magazine publishing) and the *Terminator* series or *Titanic* (movies).

When considering not only the yearly revenue but the lifetime value of blockbuster content, the picture becomes even more dramatic. Not only does a blockbuster capture a

☐ **Significant change**

Largest U.S. consumer book publishers ranked by bestseller share

Publisher	Publisher's share of bestsellers 2006* per cent	Change in share from 2005 per cent
Random House Inc.	28.4	+26
Penguin USA	15.8	+15
HarperCollins	15.0	+28
Simon & Schuster	14.3	-16
Hachette Book Group	9.1	−45**
Holtzbrinck	6.2	−10
Hyperion	3.3	−11
Houghton Mifflin Trade & Reference	0.9	+13
Kensington	0.8	n.a.
Harlequin	0.3	−63
Rodale	<0.3	n.a.

Figure 3.1 Books are a hit-driven business with substantial changes from one year to another

*Share of the 1530 hard cover bestseller positions during the year
**In 2005, Time Warner books were not part of Hachette yet, sales volume has been included for comparison reasons
Source: McKinsey analysis based on data from Publishers weekly

disproportionate share of current revenues, but also it is much longer-lived than any other content. For example, European TV broadcasters' programming is often dominated by seasoned blockbuster formats. Usually 40% of the shows are at least three seasons old and another 30% are at least two seasons. In effect, only a third of the network's programming is typically based on new shows. To take again the case of Endemol, a blockbuster like *Big Brother* has been on air since 1999, and was still, a decade later, broadcast in 19 countries, *Deal or No Deal* started in 2002, and owing to Endemol's major global network doubled its coverage every two years, from being on air in fewer than ten countries in 2003 to 25 in 2005 and 46 in 2007 (Figure 3.2).

The dominance of seasoned blockbuster content is continuing to increase. While the number of new releases is still growing in areas such as book and music publishing, the success of new titles is declining across the board. Compared to 1999, less than half the new releases make it to the best-seller lists, reach the top of audience rankings or win a platinum disc.

Future skills for tomorrow's blockbuster

For media companies that want to be successful at playing tomorrow's blockbuster game, it will be important that they not only become better generators of truly innovative blockbuster content but also become better at managing the blockbusters through their lifecycle.

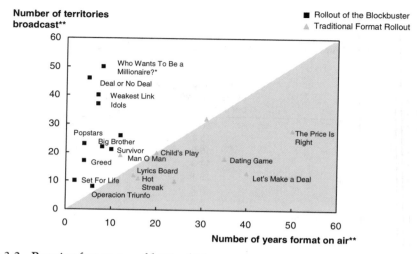

Figure 3.2 **Running fast on top of hitting high**

*Format licensed by Endemol for select markets
**Endemol show information from 2006; Fremantle shows from 2004
Source: McKinsey analysis

Innovate rather than imitate to create tomorrow's blockbusters

Arguably, the most promising path to generating new content with blockbuster potential is innovation rather than imitation. The media industry has seen an almost unhindered inflation of similar titles, formats and products in recent years. The trend of replicating successful products has been helped by limited (international) copyright protection and comparatively short production lead times. For example, a successful TV show format observed in one country or market can fairly easily be reproduced, with slight adaptations, in another market. However, the viability of replication as a product development strategy for media companies is rapidly decreasing. In a national market replicas are mostly significantly less successful than the first. For example, the RTL Group was the first in Europe to revitalize the family quiz show with a big budget when it aired *Who Wants to be a Millionaire?* in 1999. Today, the show has a greater audience share than the four most successful copycat formats combined (Figure 3.3).

International copying has also become more difficult as many large TV production companies such as FremantleMedia and Endemol have built up efficient global distribution processes to make sure that they are the first ones to roll out their successful formats internationally while at the same time adapting them to local tastes.

Recent blockbuster successes show that innovation is critical. It can be seen on television with the advent of reality TV (*Big Brother*), casting shows (*Pop Idol*) and premium TV formats with film appeal (*Sex and the City* or *The Sopranos*).

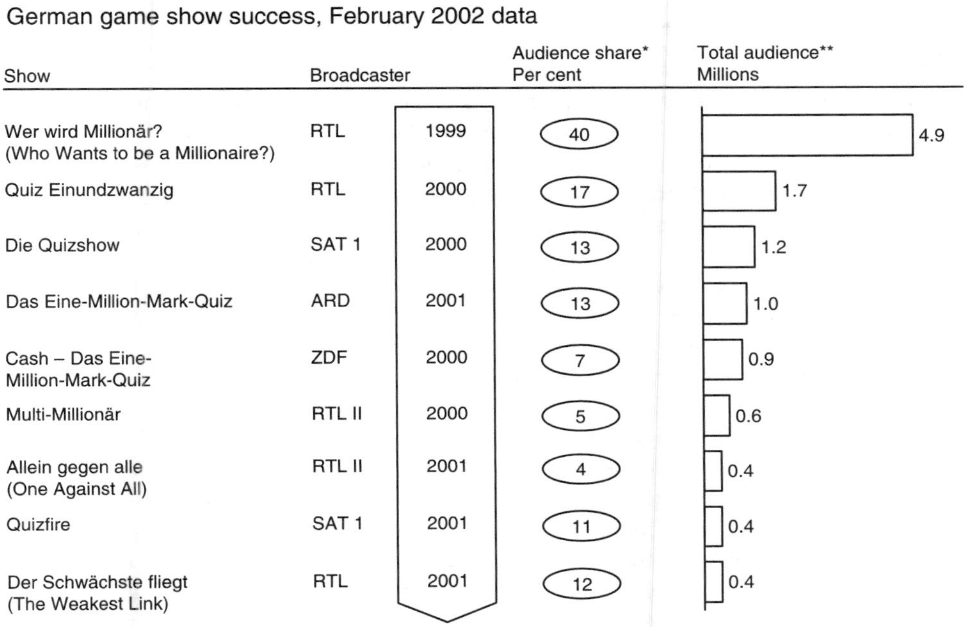

German game show success, February 2002 data

Show	Broadcaster		Audience share* Per cent	Total audience** Millions
Wer wird Millionär? (Who Wants to be a Millionaire?)	RTL	1999	40	4.9
Quiz Einundzwanzig	RTL	2000	17	1.7
Die Quizshow	SAT 1	2000	13	1.2
Das Eine-Million-Mark-Quiz	ARD	2001	13	1.0
Cash – Das Eine- Million-Mark-Quiz	ZDF	2000	7	0.9
Multi-Millionär	RTL II	2000	5	0.6
Allein gegen alle (One Against All)	RTL II	2001	4	0.4
Quizfire	SAT 1	2001	11	0.4
Der Schwächste fliegt (The Weakest Link)	RTL	2001	12	0.4

Figure 3.3   First-mover advantage exists in format innovation

*Adults aged 14–49
**Weighted to account for time of broadcast
Source: McKinsey analysis

Proactively plan the blockbuster's lifecycle

In a fragmenting digital media world it will become increasingly difficult to create new mega blockbusters, and so it will become increasingly important to manage the existing stock of blockbuster content and rights aggressively to achieve maximum revenue over a blockbuster's lifetime. More than ever before, media companies will have to ensure that they have the rights and ability to exploit the full commercial potential of existing popular formats and brands. There are many opportunities to do this, depending on the media segment. For example, in the case of TV shows, reruns, relaunches and spin-offs; in recorded music, the release of 'best of' albums and backlist compilations; and, in all sectors, vertical and horizontal brand extension and leverage for non-advertising revenues, such as content-branded merchandising. Although most media companies are already active in this field, the approach is often opportunistic and roll-out strategies are developed only after the offering has become a success. Successful companies face these challenges by considering the commercial potential and secondary revenue opportunities very early on during the development process. For example, recent TV blockbuster formats such as *Big Brother* and *Pop Idol* were designed, tested and produced for extended international cross-media revenue from the start.

To effect leverage through blockbusters, companies should address multiple dimensions in parallel:

- *Merchandising original content:* Media companies have the opportunity to draw revenues out of content that they have already generated or for which they have acquired the rights. This can include ongoing revenues generated from sales of videos and DVDs, video on demand (TV) and the rebundling/packaging of anthologies and compilations (music and print publishing). The key here is to include these rights in the package deal with the artist up front.

- *Content/brand leveraging and extension:* Well-known products can be leveraged and optimized with audiences to help create additional revenues. Companies can use their popularity to extend the reach by creating sub-brands or spin-offs that reflect the popularity of the original products. This allows companies to take advantage of having a 'captive' audience that is favourable towards the new products, based on their loyalty to the original. Also, branding certain events or holidays which are targeted at the same audience, such as, for example, the Discovery Tours (co-branded with the Discovery channel), can yield attractive results, for example through commissions from the travel company. Licensed products are also key, as they provide revenue-generating opportunities without having to invest upfront. There are multiple champions of this strategy in many media sectors—take, for example, blockbuster magazines: *National Geographic* has extensively diversified to television shows, *Elle* has developed special magazines such as *Elle Decoration* and Sanoma's highly successful Dutch women's magazine *Libelle* has developed special events etc.

- *Ancillary revenues:* Additional revenue growth can be captured through ancillary actions based on existing products. These can comprise a number of examples, including generating revenues from TV shows using call-ins, SMS-based participation, voting or betting.

- *Syndication of content for other distribution platforms:* Although market demand was smaller than expected during the dial-up Internet boom years, leveraging existing content through syndication will soon become an additional source of revenue for companies, as the investments for developing these products have already been made. The development and success of broadband together with the first evidence of convergence (PC-TV, mobile TV, etc.) suggests that the market is poised to grow. Disney has been powering this strategy extensively, with blockbuster programmes such as *Desperate Housewives* available on-demand on many interactive television and Internet platforms, or even as download on the video iPod from Apple.

- *Extensions along the value chain:* Finally, other stretching examples are starting to see the light, in the form of business development in other parts of the value chain. Martha Stewart, with her company OmniMedia, which specializes in lifestyle content origination, is known for developing content for multiple media. Now her company is developing a specific online advertising network for third-party lifestyle blogs and sites, with some early success (Figure 3.4).

The key challenges to overcome are organizational barriers and rights. As most content leverage initiatives involve multiple parts of the organization, progress is often delayed by unclear responsibilities (problems are shifted around the company) and power struggles. The projects also run the risk of becoming very cost- and time-intensive, as there is little

Martha's Circle
- Launched November 2007
- Ad network for 20–30 third-party lifestyle blogs and sites
- To preserve premium ad rates, OmniMedia editors approve all affiliates for editorial quality and screen for inappropriate content
- Advertisers choose from four content areas: food, kids, home and entertaining
- Adify is technology provider
- Network sites drew 3.9 million visitors and 25 million impressions in February 2008

'Publishers are brand stewards. The folks ... who are assembling these massive networks, most come out of the technology sector. Some of them are good business models, but they are not about protecting brands.'
Wenda Harris Millard, MSO President for Media

Selected affiliate sites	Selected advertisers
BenjaminChristie.com	Levi's
The Bridal Bar	Ace Hardware
Charles & Hudson	Bank of America
Desire To Inspire	Bertolli
DIY Bride	Hidden Valley Ranch
Style Me Pretty	Macy's

Figure 3.4   Martha Stewart OmniMedia extension to online ad network

Source: McKinsey analysis based on company website; *USA Today*

standardization and the wheel is reinvented many times. Putting in place efficient project structures and clarifying responsibilities upfront are key to ensuring that the additional revenues generated are larger than the additional costs. When media companies negotiate rights, they have to make sure that they include the rights for ancillary activities upfront, when the artist is still relatively unknown.

Should Content be Redefined?

Although blockbusters will keep on generating a large share of revenue in the media industry, they also pose some serious risks, especially those blockbusters that depend on creative talent. New, talent-driven content production has become more and more costly over the past years. For example, the money spent by TV companies on sports rights has been growing over the past decade, with annual growth rates ranging from 9% to 14%. This cost increase, combined with the lower hit rates of new product launches, means that content costs of most media companies have risen significantly. Not surprisingly, media companies are looking for other ways to generate new content profitably. At the same time current trends create new degrees of freedom for media companies to try new ways to make money.

Diversify to non-blockbuster segments: bread and butter

Very often so-called bread-and-butter products or artists generate a significant share of a media company's profit. This group is vitally important, although often neglected. Its artists and formats are low-profile, but achieve considerable cumulated volume.

Examples include initially less widely known but high-rolling recording artists, often from genre niches, such as Faith Hill or Garth Brooks; advisory books (e.g. Dale Carnegie) and genre fiction (crime, mystery) in publishing; and documentaries, folk music or cookery shows on TV.

Some media companies focus almost exclusively on this segment and do very well, for example the Bauer Magazine Group in Germany. In higher-profile media companies these products are in constant danger of receiving insufficient management and creative attention because they lack glamour. Identifying and developing these bread-and-butter products may require very different skill sets, depending on genre, thematic niche or target audience. Also in the digital world this content will have to be marketed more carefully. As non-blockbuster content it will be more and more difficult to draw attention to these products and more effort has to be put into creating a loyal community which will stay with the content over time and can be addressed actively.

Shift away from talent-driven to other forms of content: media artefacts

Blockbusters very often rely on specific creative talents, such as Elvis Presley, Steven Spielberg or Thomas Gottschalk. These are rare talents and spotting them is not easy. It requires, among other things, an extensive network of experienced scouts. Once recruited, these stars and/or their products need to be developed through aggressive marketing and managed for quick pay-offs to cash in on the development expenditure before they go looking for new contracts. The key to success lies in the spotting and development of this talent. Finding enough of them in the first place to feed into the content generation process is the key challenge. As this 'true' talent is becoming more expensive and harder to promote, media companies are increasingly looking to other forms of content.

From these, media artefacts are the most promising. Media artefacts' success is marketing-driven, typically short-lived and depends, to a large extent, on casting and promotion expertise, often involving audience participation at an early stage of the development process. Examples include the TV industry's more interchangeable stars, such as winners and runners-up of casting shows. For media artefacts, innovation is in the format and in the marketing rather than in the actors. The key challenge is to find out how many of them and which types the market can accommodate.

Deciding on the right portfolio mix between 'true talent', 'marketing artefacts', and 'bread and butter' types of format is an important first step of every content strategy, as it has significant consequences for how the company is managed and resources are allocated.

In itself it is not a bad thing when media companies have multiple types of products, both with regard to market scope (blockbuster vs. bread-and-butter) and content scope (talent-driven vs. marketing artefact). Artists and formats are not necessarily destined to remain in the same product category for ever. Both marketing clones and bread-and-butter products may eventually turn out to be – or be developed to become – true talents

Importance of Balanced Repertoire Mix in Content Generation/ Sourcing: Recorded Music Mail-Order Example

In the case of one European recorded music mail-order business, looking at the repertoire from a portfolio mix perspective yielded substantial upside potential, in terms of both management efficiency and profitability. The company's sales mix essentially consisted of three products: current top 100 albums, standard/backlist repertoire and exclusive in-house compilations featuring multiple artists. While the top 100 and backlist products are indispensable in attracting new customers' attention and retaining current customers (who would otherwise turn elsewhere for the 'standards'), the real value was in the exclusive compilations. First, they are much more profitable than other items in the repertoire (up to twice the contribution margin) because the content is purchased as licences rather than as finished CDs, allowing for cheaper in-house manufacturing. Second, these compilations are exclusive to the mail-order company and not available anywhere else. And third, the company's true sourcing, production and marketing expertise is built around compilations, while its sourcing of up-to-date/ standard products is not exceptional. By focusing its in-house efforts on exclusive compilations of available backlist content and partnering with third-party suppliers of top 100 and standard repertoire, the company eventually managed to improve its music return on sales (ROS) from −2% to 6%.

(Figure 3.5). Take, for example, Robbie Williams, who started out as part of a marketing-driven boy band but has emerged as a major best-selling recording artist, with a popularity and lifecycle far exceeding that of other marketing-driven artists. Similarly, today's true talents may become a media company's bread-and-butter repertoire for the 'oldie' segment

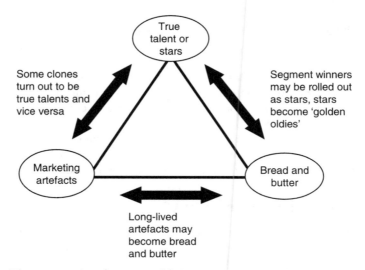

Figure 3.5 **Three categories of content with inter-category transitions**

Source: McKinsey analyses

sooner or later. Former best-selling top stars such as Elvis Presley, the Beatles or the Rolling Stones continue to generate steady revenue streams in sizeable music market sub-segments for their respective rights owners.

Media companies will, therefore, be well advised to remain flexible with regard to the innovation approach they take, as products and the rate of artists moving from one category to another will, arguably, increase. However, at the same time, they should be clear about their strategy in these areas and make sure that the organization is aligned in such a way that it can cater to the specific needs of particular segments.

Management of the Content Generation Process

Generating a continuous flow of new content will become even more important and complex for media companies in the future. However, the innovation machine is apparently malfunctioning for many media companies. In a McKinsey survey, among a large sample of European traditional media companies, the findings were very clear on this matter: while innovation was ranked a top priority by more than two-thirds of the survey respondents, slightly less than 15% considered themselves good at innovation.

Innovation obviously can be managed in part, and media companies can learn a lot from other industries such as pharmaceuticals or even the car industry, both of which have been investing quite significantly in developing core process management around innovation and new products. However, it should be taken into account that the media industry will face many types of innovation beyond just content: typical product innovation (such as launching a compact newspaper format or video adds to newspaper), process innovation (such as developing play-out automation in television), and also the development of business models that are needed to cope with industry disruptions caused by new digital offerings, such as search advertising, PVRs, online classifieds, etc. In addition, media companies will have to invest in innovating their brands, for instance MTV expanded its music brand to a teen brand, leveraging new TV formats such as *Jackass* and The *Ozzy Osbournes*.

In so doing the media industry cannot just rely on its talents. First of all, the scope of innovation will go far beyond content creation. Also media companies have an inherent difficulty in separating talents from innovations: while talented people are usually creative, they are not necessarily key innovators.

In thinking about their innovation strategy, media companies must first decide how much content they want to generate in-house versus sourcing externally and, second, how they can best manage their innovation processes for content and beyond.

Content generation: make or buy?

There are large differences between media sectors, with respect to the extent that they create their own content or source it externally. Newspapers and magazines are typical content creators; key editors are all part of the staff. Historically, TV channels relied strongly on bought content, be it Hollywood films and series or sports events. However, with the rise in popularity of local content, they have increasingly shifted to own production. The music industry is on the other end of the scale, relying almost exclusively on external content creators.

Given the future importance of key content and the importance of owning all the rights, media companies, especially electronic media, are increasingly considering more and more integrating backwards and building or diversifying to buy their own production companies.

The arguments for vertical integration are clear: an own content producer will allow, for example, TV networks a much better execution of their content strategy both with regard to viewers and advertising. Also it will be much easier to create products that go beyond a single medium and cover multiple channels and allow for brand leverage. The drawbacks are, however, still there: too much dependence on one source of content is dangerous and, given the fact that content generation is about the generation of many options, media companies could miss out on the blockbusters of tomorrow. In general this is why companies such as RTL, which acquired Fremantle, or Mediaset, which recently took a major stake in Endemol, continue to have the content business on arm's length, in order to spread risk.

Managing the content innovation process

The McKinsey survey of leading media companies in Europe on innovation showed that successful innovators have three characteristics in common: they have a clear sense of direction, they are open to new ideas and they have a rigorous approach to execution. Creating a strong direction is closely related to having a clear content strategy, as discussed above. Openness to new ideas and rigorous execution depends very much on the way the innovation process is managed (Figure 3.6).

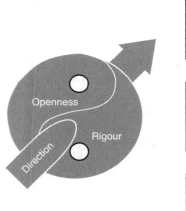

Strong direction

- Clear overall growth direction, translated into targets for the divisions of the organization
- Top management focuses on realizing high growth ambitions as no. 1 priority
- Clear lines of responsibility and accountability exist; success is recognized and rewarded

Openness to new ideas

- Open eyes/ears to external via MTV lab, research departments, market surveys, licensing of concepts and alliances with leading companies (e.g. MS, Philips, Intel)
- Viewers involved in all stages of new product development
- Strong brand and talent proposition attract top talent

Rigour and speed of execution

- Ideas quickly developed into pilots that are tested and further developed to meet viewer preferences
- Selection between ideas based on high-quality business plans and valuation framework
- Timely and within-budget execution of projects, owing to clear process with milestones/criteria

Figure 3.6 Example of a media growth company with all elements in place: MTV

Source: McKinsey: Innovation and growth: being more than creative, November 2003

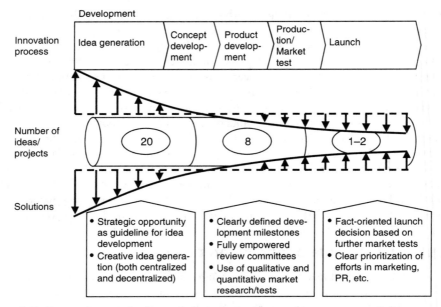

Figure 3.7 Innovation can be fostered through the improved management of the programme pipeline: a 'funnel', not a 'tunnel'

Source: McKinsey analyses

As in other industries, innovation success is about establishing a process that ensures the right ideas get the right attention to help guarantee success. Some product developers, however, say that the more you structure the process, the higher the risk of killing creativity. The trade-off between risk of missing out on killer ideas on the one hand and potential audience impact and commercial return on the other will have to be carefully balanced throughout the process of innovation. What our experience demonstrates, however, is that this balance is usually more critical in media than any other industry. This reflects the fact that creative ideas have more intangible components than product features in contrast to, say, a new pharmaceutical blockbuster. In the same way, basic innovation management principles are rarely applied in media, yet obvious steps can be taken to improve the management of innovation.

Content generation can be thought of as a three-stage funnel, going from idea generation – via development – to product launch (Figure 3.7). Key success factors along this funnel include: generating breakthrough ideas, focusing on the most promising ideas, testing pilots/ prototypes extensively and rigidly monitoring and managing new products' success.

Idea generation: open up to new ideas

As far as initial idea generation is concerned, media product developers should aim for a funnel rather than a tunnel, that is they should ensure sufficient openness and management attention on extensive original idea generation. With a business as dependent on a

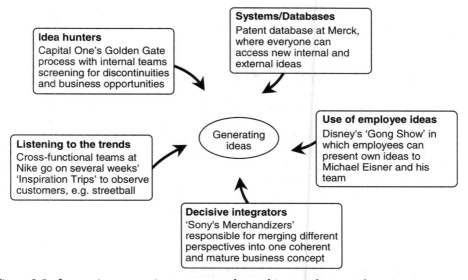

Figure 3.8 Innovative companies are constantly reaching out for new ideas

Source: McKinsey analyses

limited number of hits as the media, allowing as many ideas as possible during the initial brainstorming stage is vital. Media players can learn from successful developers in other industries that have similar dynamics, such as fashion producers or venture capitalists (Figure 3.8).

This stage of the innovation funnel is the bottleneck for 'true talent' content as described in the previous section. The challenge for media developers is to find enough true talent initially to feed into the innovation funnel, as there is a limited pool available in terms of both artists and concepts/plots for shows, films and magazines. For more marketing-driven products, innovation at this stage can, paradoxically, mean clever replication or adaptation, as they are differentiated through packaging rather than substance.

The first step of an innovative idea generation process is to define white spots in the product portfolio or the market. Taking into account relevant discontinuities in society, technology and fashion can help broaden the innovative space. Successful players leverage creative talents and experts both within and outside the company; some even partner with other consumer industries, such as retail or consumer goods.

The main challenge is to make sure that potential new projects receive enough thought and attention before they are actually developed. For example, TV broadcasters traditionally pay producers on a cost-plus basis for the production only, thereby discouraging production houses from investing sufficiently in new idea generation. As a result, many producers, especially the smaller ones, are very short-term-focused and replication of successful existing formats has become more common, effectively shortening product lifecycles and thwarting innovation. The solution is to invest more in product development, that is by co-financing script development, thus ensuring that dedicated idea generation is rewarded.

Innovative Idea Generation Example: Researching White Spots

To create new production ideas, a leading US TV network did extensive research to understand which viewer segments were underserved during various time slots, ultimately to engage in counter-production and programming. For example, the network looked at neglected topics for these underserved segments, such as information, documentaries and family content. By developing competitive content for individual time slots/customer segments, the network managed to increase its audience share significantly and was also able to test new content for future broad roll-out.

Creative market research approaches needed

Traditional market research approaches are not adequate to identify and test new concepts. Unusual tools, such as open brainstorming sessions or field trips to encourage innovation across the entire organization, should supplement them; examples include Disney's 'Gong Show' and Nike's 'Inspiration Trips'. Experience from magazine publishing shows that innovation based on external insights can be as effective as classic research-driven efforts (Figure 3.9).

In general, market research pertaining to media users is much more an art than a science. While consumer preferences in the area of consumer goods' product properties can be fairly easily researched and implemented, media users are not necessarily

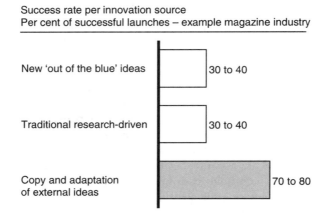

Success rate per innovation source
Per cent of successful launches – example magazine industry

New 'out of the blue' ideas — 30 to 40

Traditional research-driven — 30 to 40

Copy and adaptation of external ideas — 70 to 80

Figure 3.9 Innovation based on external insights compared with classic research-driven efforts

Source: McKinsey analyses

dependable in communicating their preferences for content, scheduling and packaging accurately and exhaustively. Media usage behaviour is often driven by minuscule factors of which users themselves are sometimes unaware. For example, female executive magazine readers in a recent survey said they were looking for more career and stock market information in combination with lifestyle features. When the new magazine was introduced, it did not take off. A survey subsequently showed that this reader group was willing to deal with business topics only during business hours and not in their leisure time. The magazine was discontinued.

Consequently, setting up media-based market research requires much more care, experience, psychological refinement and sophistication than almost any other industry. As one publishing executive put it: 'Women may say that they like a magazine's baking section, but I only believe it if test people actually start eating the cookies on offer while they are discussing it.' Working with external experts becomes increasingly important to achieve this level of sophistication.

Development: filtering/portfolio management

Initially creating and allowing for as many ideas as possible is vital to a company for it eventually to produce a few stars. However, it is crucial that robust filtering processes are in place both before and during the development stage. This is very important to ensure that product ideas, format innovations or new talents receive the appropriate attention and budget required to exploit their full market potential when they are eventually launched or released. Attempting to simultaneously develop too many products to market maturity will result in diluted support resources for each product and will compromise chances for success in the market. Companies that neglect portfolio and forced-ranking approaches find themselves with a large number of barely profitable titles (Figures 3.10 and 3.11).

Focus is also key because markets will typically be able to accommodate only a limited number of products in any given category. This particularly applies to the 'marketing artefacts' described in the previous section, as consumers will support only a limited number of similar marketing-driven formats at any given time and will also tire of them in case of oversupply. While true talents are input-constrained, owing to their scarcity, marketing clones are conversely output-constrained because of these saturation effects.

It is vital, therefore, to evaluate ideas based on a transparent process that can be applied across markets/countries, business units and departments. The governing objective is to ensure that filtering/development decisions are not just based on the personal judgements of production staff but instead reflect a multitude of perspectives, dimensions and interested parties in a structured and transparent approach (e.g. creative aspects, financial planning, ad sales, marketing). A leading European magazine publisher is, for example, seriously considering introducing what it calls 'moderators'. Its main task will be to accompany the whole development process, making sure that results are challenged across departments and asking editors critical questions, without making them feel threatened.

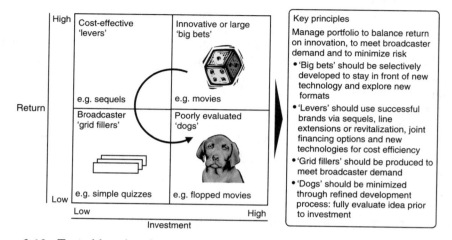

Figure 3.10 **Typical brand evolution to maintain a balanced risk–return portfolio**

Source: McKinsey analyses

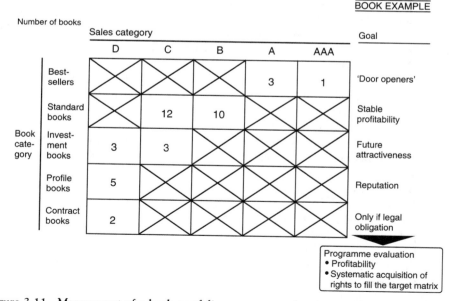

Figure 3.11 **Management of a book portfolio: programme planning matrix**

Source: McKinsey analyses

Even before the first product tests/pilots, media developers can get substantial market feedback from both end consumers and advertisers, for example by using focus groups (as exemplified by Reed Elsevier's in-house consumer panel testing centre) or by pitching new products with potential advertisers and partners (e.g. mobile operators in the case of dial-in TV shows). One very successful German publishing house works closely with a cutting-edge market researcher focusing on actual audience behaviour, rather than on declared preferences, to assess the true market potential of its development projects. This ensures that a sophisticated market research perspective is properly reflected in a process traditionally dominated by the artistic ambitions of creative staff and producers. In another case, a magazine publisher worked closely with its key advertising clients before relaunching its job-search magazine. Advertising sales increased substantially after the relaunch, as advertisers' placement needs had been uncovered and addressed during product development. Often, however, developers fail to fully leverage market research and consumer insight. This happens partly because market researchers are often not taken seriously by creative managers (editors, producers) and partly because most market research is tactical rather than strategic.

When production begins, less is more: media players should focus rigorously on a few high-potential innovations to ensure there are sufficient means available for (pre-) production, marketing and concept refinement during early release stages. Risks can be further hedged by producing pilot shows, episodes, records, releases or editions, and letting market decisions drive further production/roll-out (Figure 3.12). As discussed above, in TV broadcasting only about one-third of new launches are still on air after one year. Experience shows that the vast majority of these will be NPV-positive investments (NPV stands for 'net present value').

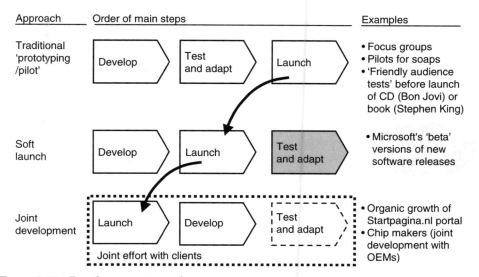

Figure 3.12 Rapid prototyping and testing

Source: McKinsey analyses

Consequently, the challenge will be to combine the funnel – initially as many original ideas as possible – with real-market testing of the most promising. Endemol has very successfully applied this approach by testing its innovations in the Dutch market, where a pilot's market potential can be tested at a very moderate cost prior to international roll-out. The Dutch market has various advantages as a testing ground, ranging from manageable size to above-average international orientation and few linguistic/cultural constraints.

Once a new product has hit the market, it is critical that the company closely monitors its success to enable decisions about further development, adaptations/fine-tuning and discontinuation. RTL TV and FremantleMedia managed to maintain, and even increase, audience share of one of its long-running daily soaps, *Gute Zeiten, schlechte Zeiten*, from 24% in November 2000 to 27.6% in May 2001, by monitoring audience satisfaction and fine-tuning the show accordingly. Endemol also proactively manages its library to extend the lifetime of its blockbusters – they go through a continuous creativity cycle to keep formats fresh and appealing to audiences and they have periodic exchange meetings among their country subsidiaries to share revenue and rating-improving best practices, etc.

Continuously measuring the quality of the innovation process is an important success factor. Key performance indicators, such as number of new titles launched, readership distribution and revenue split by 'age' of product, should be applied to a company's entire portfolio to ensure sufficient innovation and fine-tuning. More specific metrics apply to individual products, such as development costs and speed to prototype/first pilot, relative audience/market share, (new) subscriptions and churn reduction (Figure 3.13).

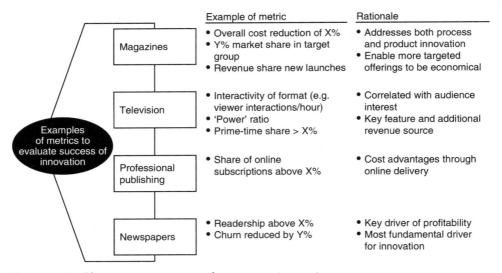

Figure 3.13 Clear metrics are required to measure innovation success

Source: McKinsey analyses

Integrated players, operating both production and broadcasting/publishing businesses, have the added benefit of being able to recognize the distributors' perspective, even before production, and to engage in real-market testing in-house, for example in smaller markets with limited risk to get audience/advertisers' feedback and use the input to improve the product. Some production houses have even been known to forward-integrate towards broadcasting/publishing to gain privileged access to real-market audience feedback.

Peer Production, User-generated Content and Co-creation

As discussed earlier, concentration of revenue on a few products/content brands is usually high – and is likely to increase with digitization. This is because, on one hand, digitization can extend the potential revenue of products/content blockbusters. On the other hand, digitization enables the distribution of content and products to micro-audiences. This extension is usually referred to as the 'long tail', well advertised by Chris Anderson in his recent book of the same name.

Usually, the examples of long tail concern the tail of content *distribution*, such as extra book sales on Amazon versus Wal-Mart, CD sales on CDnow versus other major music stores, etc. Yet, the long tail phenomenon is also happening in content *creation*, and a new paradigm is emerging, called by some 'peer production'.[1] This phenomenon appeared first in the software industry, in particular in the open source movement with its communities of people working together to develop copyleft products such as Linux and others.

In the case of digital media, 'peer production' is the combination of user-generated content, organized as a model of distribution, such as YouTube for video distribution, or of production such as TheNerve for video content production, or a model of both, such as OhmyNews, an online news company in South Korea which both harnesses citizen journalism and aggregates articles for a compelling news offering to the public.

Generally speaking, most peer production has taken place in information and media services. This is because traditional information and media have high fixed costs and relatively low marginal costs to distribute or reproduce. Peer production therefore offers the potential of reducing creation costs.

In recent years, user-generated content platforms enhanced by social media have demonstrated impressive traction, as witnessed by the exponential growth of websites such as YouTube, Wikipedia and many others. However, those examples must not be entirely taken as proof that social media and user-generated content will be replacing the old traditional way of media content *generation*. First of all, in most user-generated content platforms, there are more people viewing the content than 'creating' it; barely 10% of YouTube visitors contribute to video creation. The same goes for Wikipedia, and many other platforms. Second, the long tail principle also applies to content created by the users, with 10% producing 90% of the new content. Combining these two tails' effects, 1% of

---

[1]See Yochai Benkler's seminal article 'Coase's Penguin, or Linus and the nature of the Firm', *Yale Law Journal* (2002) vol. 112, pp. 369–446.

video platform *users* create 90% of the content. The actual number of relevant 'peer' producers is thus much smaller than the *audience* of those sites. Also platforms such as YouTube are well designed for short-form video, but it may be a very different ball game to produce long-form video formats for TV or the big screen. Companies trying the long-form peer production content are still very much experimental, and have yet to launch valuable, let alone blockbuster, products. For example, the 'audience-owned' film project *A Swarm of Angels*, which has assembled up to 50 000 members who have agreed to fund movie productions in return for collective creative influence on script development, has still not emerged with a project with a qualified output.

In general, user-generated content can likely be seen as a complementary form of content generation, possibly as a way for amateurs to signal their capabilities to professional content creators.

Another interesting development in the digital world is the advent of branded co-creation, that is users are not only generating content per se, but do so in the context of co-creation with brands. Maxis, a well-known game producer, for instance, published *The Sims*, a true blockbuster which was developed to a major extent by the users of the game. Maxis, as the owner of the game's copyright, has benefited significantly from this co-creation phenomenon. Another well-known example is Second Life, a grid platform, where users can develop their own social virtual world; the platform has not only been built by members of Second Life as a 3D virtual environment but also, more and more, is used by companies to co-create new products and designs with Second Life members.

The jury is still out on those phenomena, but the Web offers a clear potential for peer production and co-creation that content creation companies must experiment with in the near future if they are to succeed, as a way of complementing their skills and creating new venues for monetization potential.

Key Takeaways

1. The importance of content, as well as content process management, will increase with the roll-out of digitization and further demand fragmentation.
2. Blockbusters will remain key to the success of media companies; however, it will become increasingly difficult and expensive to create blockbuster content.
3. True blockbusters can only be created through innovation, not imitation.
4. Planning and managing the blockbuster over its lifecycle and leveraging all secondary revenue opportunities will become critical for tomorrow's blockbuster's profitability.
5. Media companies should consciously develop a diversified content strategy that extends and hedges against blockbusters.
6. Portfolio strategies must be a mix of three key valuables:
   - market scope: blockbuster and bread-and-butter
   - content scope: talent-driven and marketing artefact
   - product scope: content, distribution, customer service and more.

7. Each different strategy mix will require very different organizational skills.

8. The content generation process can be systematically managed; however, the specifics of the media industry should be carefully considered.

9. Successful innovators in the media industry have a strong sense of direction, are open to new ideas and execute rigorously.

10. Idea generation is a combination of the creative search of unorthodox areas and professional market research.

11. Chances of success for new ideas are greatly increased by systematic portfolio evaluation, rapid prototyping and systemic measuring, even in the media industry.

12. With the Web, models of peer production, user-generated content and co-creation will develop; while likely to be more complementary than substitutes, they point towards the socialization of content creation and the potential to develop new integrated platform and brand affinity.

Endemol: Diversifying the Content Portfolio[1]

Endemol has just announced the hiring of a new CEO, Ynon Kreiz. He will be replacing Aat Schouwenaar, who was operating as ad interim CEO since the company was bought out of telecoms company Telefonica in 2007. The new shareholders stand for a consortium led by Goldman Sachs and private broadcasters Tele 5 in Spain and Mediaset in Italy.

The company is seeking a new curve of growth, following its strong historical revenue growth in the past, and it must successfully manage the transition in order to become a strong contender in the digital media industry. Fortunately, Endemol lacks neither the assets nor the competence to succeed.

Endemol is a global leader in television and other audiovisual entertainment and is active in 24 countries, generating revenue of above US$1.5 billion, with an EBITDA of 18%, and taking an ever-increasing portion of the broadcast market worldwide.

EUR million

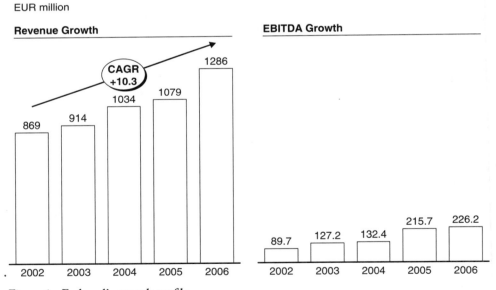

Figure 1   Endemol's growth profile

Source: McKinsey analyses based on data from Endemol

---

[1]This case is developed solely as the basis for class discussion. Cases are not intended to serve as endorsements, sources of primary data or illustrations of effective or ineffective management.

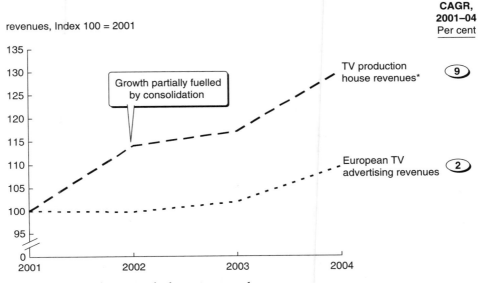

revenues, Index 100 = 2001

CAGR,
2001–04
Per cent

Growth partially fuelled
by consolidation

TV production
house revenues*

9

European TV
advertising revenues

2

Figure 2   TV production and advertising growth

*For 24 companies with revenue > €35 million
Source: McKinsey analysis based on data from Zenith; European Audiovisual Observatory; JPM

For years, the company has created innovative and sometimes provocative, mostly non-scripted, entertainment ideas, like *Big Brother*, a programme where strangers are put together in a house which they are not allowed to leave and where they are filmed 24 hours a day. It has consistently developed one or two global hits per year, from *Fear Factor* to *Deal or No Deal*, the *Star Academy*, *Home Edition* and many others. Over the last five years, the company has managed to create an average of more than 100 new formats each year, producing more than 500 shows, with a current library of more than 1 200 formats.

Out of its top 10 formats being produced by this year, nine were created and designed in-house. Endemol had set up an extensive network of companies in 24 countries, allowing it to quickly develop and roll out its hits, through co-development and the sharing of new formats and other intellectual property.

Company History

Joop van den Ende and John de Mol founded Endemol in 1994, through the merger of their two major television production companies in the Netherlands. Using mostly its capabilities in non-fiction, but also taking the risk of testing new fiction formats as part of its global output deal with RTL in the Netherlands, Endemol rapidly evolved to become a leading format-creation and production company. This rapid growth was further reinforced through acquisitions of other independent production companies.

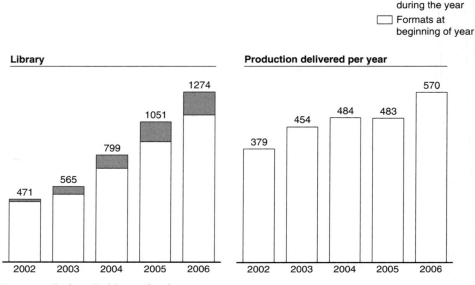

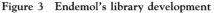

Figure 3   Endemol's library development

Source: McKinsey analyses based on data from Endemol

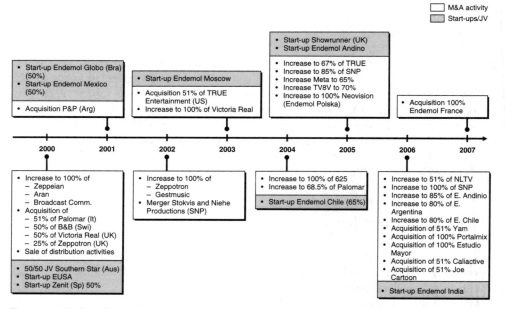

Figure 4   Endemol's acquisition developments, 2000–2007

Source: McKinsey analyses based on data from Endemol

Endemol Entertainment Holding NV was listed on the Amsterdam stock exchange in 1996. With the advent of the first wave of the Internet, convergence was believed to be a major source of value creation for platform operators such as cable, telecoms and satellite. Vivendi in France, the owner of Canal+ and CanalSat, started the diversification with buying Universal, a Hollywood studio. Telefonica, the Spanish telecoms operator that up until then had diversified its operations in South America, followed Vivendi's lead and made a public offer for Endemol in 2000.

Following completion of the acquisition, Endemol was delisted. From mid-2000 until mid-2007, Endemol has been part of Telefonica S.A. In 2005, Endemol France separated itself from the group through an IPO but was reintegrated in February 2007. On 3 July 2007, Endemol's major shareholder Telefonica sold its 75% stake in Endemol to Edam Acquisition. Edam Acquisition is jointly and equally owned by Cyrte Investments, an investment vehicle of John de Mol; Mediacinco, a joint venture of Italian Mediaset and Spanish Telecinco; as well as Goldman Sachs Capital Partners.

Challenges

Endemol shareholders' natural ambition is to continue the pace of growth of the recent past. Non-scripted content is still a very important revenue generator, as it makes up a significant part of the programme of leading free-TV channels in Europe. In addition,

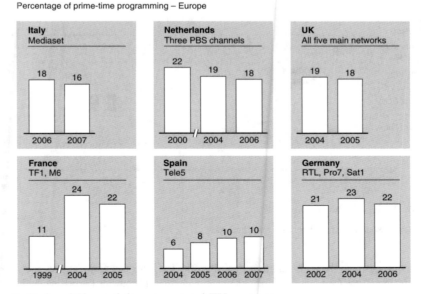

Figure 5 Endemol Share of the non-scripted TV content

Source: McKinsey based on data from European Audiovisual Observatory; TNS Sofres; Bilans CSA; Informa Media; IP; Kagan

Endemol had been one of the first companies to exploit a diversification of its revenue source in the form of call-TV, etc. Yet this source of revenue is flattening and being challenged by the various regulations that have been enforced following several scandals involving the abuse of some telephone voting systems that were used for call-TV programmes.

Looking forward, three key levers will create the bulk of value for content-production companies. First, a continued stream of new format successes is necessary; second, hits should be replicated and possibly adapted to meet local tastes on a global scale. Finally, it is clearer and clearer that revenues from digital media are becoming very sizeable and creating opportunities for new alternative revenue models, such as sponsorship and paid digital content.

Endemol's current stream of programmes is largely successful, with many key formats being broadcast in a large number of countries, up to 46 countries for a key format such as *Deal or No Deal*. On average, Endemol has been able to generate 1.3 new successful global shows a year, enough to sustain revenue growth.

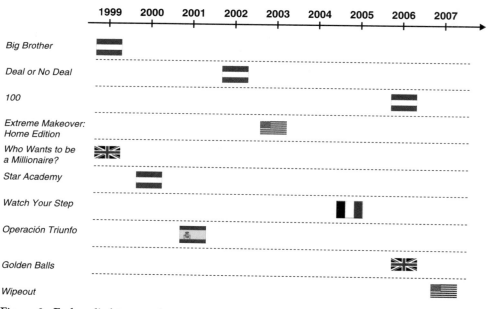

Figure 6   Endemol's hit examples

Source: McKinsey analysis based on data from Endemol

Several upcoming shows hold great promise. *Golden Balls* is a game show created in the UK in 2006; *Wipe Out*, created in 2007, is a reality TV show based around physical challenges and is a successor to *Fear Factor*, and will be aired on ABC.

In general, however, the programme library of Endemol is affordable for only major free-to-air broadcasters, who are, increasingly under pressure as advertising spending is migrating to the Internet and the economic cycle is in a downturn. This makes it less likely that these broadcasters will invest in costly non-scripted formats of Endemol, except when a programme is a real brand killer. In some markets Endemol sells its programmes on a cost-plus basis (i.e. the broadcaster has to pay the production costs as they occur plus a profit margin). In addition, the broadcaster is obliged to engage Endemol's production division – while this guarantees Endemol's margin and amortization of the technical facilities, it has a downside as Endemol has under this deal no access to the other revenues generated by the programme (e.g. through digital revenue diversification).

The development of call-in and SMS television revenue, once a significant source of income, is dwindling after the introduction of the new regulations which may prompt Endemol to invest in it less and less as time goes on. Digital diversification is starting to take off. It includes the 'Virtual Me' partnership in online games with Electronic Arts and the development of *Deal or No Deal* casting websites etc., but success is still uncertain.

However, a few digital trends might open up new opportunities:

1. Digital markets are growing at 30–50% a year in most of Endemol's core markets. In the United States and United Kingdom, digital revenues are predicted to surpass those of TV advertising in the coming years.

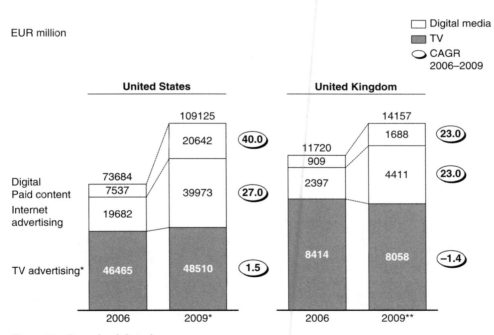

Figure 7   Growth of digital revenues

*TV advertising includes Public Broadcaster licence fee where applicable. Paid content includes Internet and mobile
**Forecast
Source: McKinsey analyses based on data from Kagan; PricewaterhouseCoopers

2. Many advertisers currently spending money on the television spot market are shifting their budgets towards digital sponsoring and are experimenting with direct branded content – although still small, expectations are that investments in these types of activities are going to double as a share of advertising spend in the next five to seven years. A few digital creative companies such as Radical Media has reached notoriety by producing the *Gamekillers* dating reality show on MTV directly sponsored by Unilever, in exchange of Axe Dry deodorant placement in the show. Not only did the show do well – it drew an audience of more than 10 million viewers in three months – but it also directly influenced sales, with Axe Dry estimated to be boosted by as much as 60%.

3. Online games and gambling are a major revenue source in the making. Endemol's new venture, Virtual Me, with Electronic Arts is part of that attempt at finding a new revenue stream. However, it remains to be seen whether it will create a major stake in this new online area. Gambling is also a major opportunity in Europe with the possible opening of the markets against the local state monopolies: it could replace the declining call-TV market. There are large developments in the areas of social networks and user-generated content platforms, Endemol, as a production company, however, does not seem to be the natural owner and/or consolidator of this market, although it

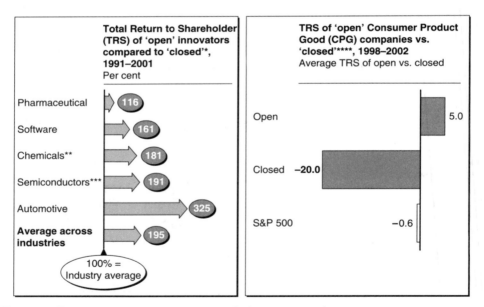

Figure 8   Open companies in comparison with their more insular peers

*Based on practices reported in innovation survey of global companies; calculated as unweighted average
**Only European and American companies
***1990–2000
****Based on number of alliances announced by 77 global Consumer Product Good (CPG) companies, 1998–2002
Source: McKinsey analyses based on data from Datastream

should take care that it leverages those new models to promote its content. Rather, other digital developments, such as co-creation and open innovation, seem intriguing.

Companies opening their innovation processes and R&D, such as Procter & Gamble with Connect and Develop, or Sermo in the pharmaceuticals industry, among many others, seem to deliver larger returns to their shareholders. Owning creatives is key, but is there a way to leverage co-creation with digital platforms as done internally by game publishers (like Maxis blockbuster's *The Sims*) or externally by others?

OhmyNews: Creating a Sustainable Model for Content Co-creation[1]

Oh Yeon Ho should be proud. He had just received the Missouri School of Journalism's Honor Medal for Distinguished Service in Journalism in 2007 for having opened the way to 'citizen journalism'. Also, he recently opened the OhmyNews School of Participatory Journalism. To teach best practice of citizen journalism and user-generated content (UGC), US$400 000 were invested in the school, which has a daily capacity of 300 students and overnight facilities for 50 students. Diverse courses will be offered, ranging from digital camera workshops to video news gathering.

OhmyNews is one of the new breed of media companies that use social-networking sites on the Web to develop new forms of participatory journalism. As one of the first in this field, the company quickly gained widespread, even international, recognition and established a strong platform from which to grow.

2000–2001 Beginning	2002–2003 The successful years	2004–2007 Branching out

• Launch of OhmyNews by Oh Yeon Ho, February 2000	• 2002
	– Launch of weekly print edition
	– Peak in traffic during presidential elections
	– First positive monthly profit in October
	• 2003
	– First interview from president Roh Moo-hyun granted to OhmyNews
	– First yearly positive profit
		• 2004: launch of OhmyNews International, an English website for citizen journalists from all countries
		• 2006
		– Launch of OhmyNews Japan
		– End of participatory aspect of OhmyNews Japan owing to lack of success
		• 2007
		– Cost-reduction measures
		  • Reduction of staff
		  • Reduction of payments to citizen journalists through new payment policy
		– Opening of OhmyNews Citizen Journalism School

Figure 1 OhmyNews's growth platform

Source: McKinsey analyses based on press search; Company website

Yet even as visitor traffic kept growing, the revenue model and scalability still had to be demonstrated.

---

[1]This case is developed solely as the basis for class discussion. Cases are not intended to serve as endorsements, sources of primary data or illustrations of effective or ineffective management.

Company History

Launch of a new concept: 2000–2002

OhmyNews is coined from the expression 'Oh my God!' and the first name of its founder. The concept dates back to February 2000, when Oh Yeon Ho, a journalist aged 36, decided to launch a news website with a budget of US$85 000. Oh was a big proponent of freedom of speech and had already been imprisoned for one year in 1986 after he took part in a student demonstration against the South Korean government.

The idea was that the traditional model of closed-form journalism would be opened up to UGC, with 'every citizen as a reporter'.

In reality, the OhmyNews concept is more 'semi-closed' in comparison to other UGC news sites, as the news reporting is fully edited. The idea of a broad platform of opinions, however, was still of great interest to a market like South Korea, where the political line of newspapers was mostly conservative.

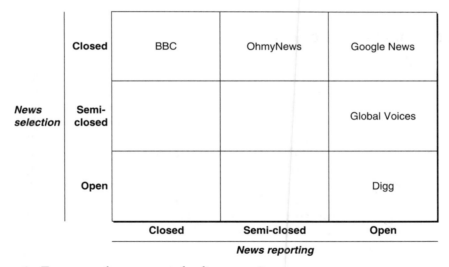

Figure 2   Taxonomy of user-generated online news sites

Source: McKinsey analyses based on data from Wolf Richter; Oxford Internet Institute; Mimeo drat

In terms of content, the news website covers the same subjects as traditional newspapers (i.e. from sport to international news). However, it fundamentally differs in its approach from traditional newspapers as most articles are written by website visitors and it puts these contributions on top of the editorial news reporting.

The editorial process, which has been subsequently replicated by many others, is very straightforward. Visitors post an article, which then gets published on the website after a filtering performed by the OhmyNews professional board of editors to remove incorrect information and to ensure compliance with the style and value guidelines of the news site. The best articles go on top of the front page, and the less interesting below.

To incentivize participation, citizen journalists receive feedback from other users as well as from OhmyNews professional journalists. They also receive some financial compensation. First of all, they receive a fee from OhmyNews, depending on the quality of the article, ranging from $20 for top stories (published at the top of the front page) to $2 for less interesting stories (published at the bottom). Secondly, and a major innovation, writers receive tips from other users if they like the article, through a credit card or a mobile payment system. This part can be significant: allegedly, one citizen reporter received $22,000 dollars in barely three days from readers in response to an article challenging a conservative group. Another contributor managed to raise a similar amount with tips to help immigrants.[2]

The first edition of the news launches at 9.30 a.m. (so that people can read it when they arrive at work), a second one at 1 p.m. after the lunch break and the last one at 5 p.m., just before people leave the office.

Success: the 2002 elections

Initially, the company made losses and was recording on average a monthly deficit of $17,000. The success arrived with an important event in 2002: the Korean presidential elections. OhmyNews helped Roh Moo-hyun, a progressive candidate, to become the new president by influencing its readers to vote for him in December 2002. Indeed, many articles from partisans of the youth political movement were published on the website. This is probably why the *Guardian* cites OhmyNews as being 'arguably the world's most domestically powerful news site'. As recognition, President Roh Moo-hyun granted his first interview as president to OhmyNews.

All this generated a lot of traffic: by 2003, the number of average daily users grew to 1.2 million peaking during the 2002 election at 6.2 million, and 19.1 million page views. This was also visible in the number of citizen reporters: starting from about 15 000 by late 2001, it had about 60 000 citizen journalists registered by 2007.

By 2003 it had achieved €9 million revenue and reached break-even with a posted profit of €0.2 million.

Expansion: 2003–2006

Comforted by his success, Oh decided to diversify. Diversification included branching out to offline and international online development.

---

[2]See www.prwatch.org for more details.

December each year

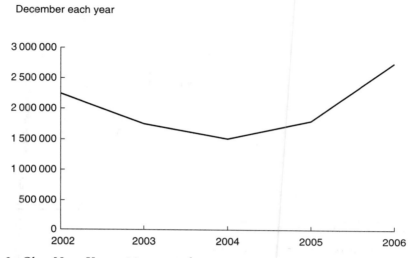

Figure 3   **OhmyNews Korea visitors growth**

Source: McKinsey analyses based on data from press dipping and OhmyNews public releases Media Today

Oh launched a complement to the website, a weekly paper version of OhmyNews, in 2003. By doing so, he was aiming to attract advertisers interested in online advertising, and to reach the portion of the Korean population that did not have access to the Internet. He was soon selling content for mobile devices as well.

In parallel with this diversification, Oh expanded the geographical focus of Ohmy-News to other countries. The first step was the launch in 2003 of the website OhmyNews International (OMNI), a website in English allowing citizen journalists from all countries to send international news. The business model of this website was the same as its parent website, except that news was almost wholly contributed by citizen journalists, which was very different from the Korean version, where still 20–30% of the articles were written by the staff. This international version is supported by about 2 500 citizen journalists reporting from as many as 100 countries today. The second step was the creation of a Japanese version of OhmyNews in 2006, through a joint venture with Softbank.

Current Position

The Korean website currently employs 90 people (2007), of which 65 are professional journalists writing articles, and 25 filter the articles received from the citizen journalists by checking the information provided. Among the employees, 80% were previously talented citizen journalists. The Japanese version occupies about 40 journalists full time.

Staff evolution

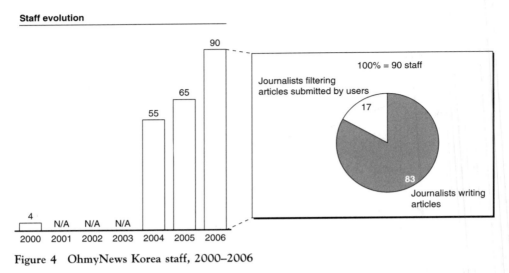

Figure 4 OhmyNews Korea staff, 2000–2006

Source: McKinsey analysis

Today, the number of citizen reporters amounts to approximately 80 000 altogether, including the international versions. Citizen reporters tend to be young men aged between 21 and 35, writing up to 70% to 80% of the articles published.

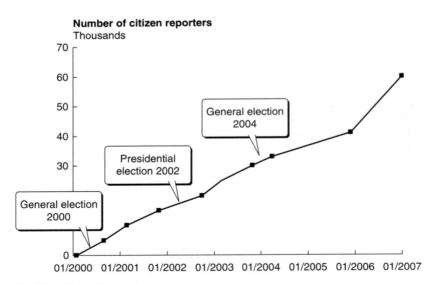

Figure 5 OhmyNews Korea citizen reporters

Source: McKinsey analyses based on data from Sixth International Symposium on Online Journalism, University of Texas at Austin (2005); Press search

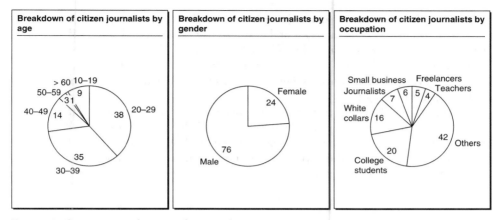

Figure 6   Citizen journalist sociodemographics

Source: McKinsey analyses based on data from Sixth International Symposium on Online Journalism; University of Texas at Austin (2005)

Still, approximately 30% of the articles submitted by citizen journalists are rejected by the editors, because of non-compliance with editorial standards or because they possess incorrect information.

Although the company is still doing well in terms of traffic and contributors, it has never reached its 2002 peak level again. Also revenues did not grow significantly beyond the 2003 level of €9 million. The company posted revenues of roughly €5 million in 2005, and €6 million in 2006, and up to €10 million by late 2007. The sources of revenue are split between advertising (70%), sale of content to third parties, including mobile services (20%), and other miscellaneous sources, including voluntary subscription fees (e.g. donations) (10%). Due to the increase in personel costs however profits dropped.

This resulted in an announcement by OhmyNews that it planned to reduce staff in 2007. The second measure taken by the company was a change to the payment system for citizen journalists: when the article was not published on the main page, they no longer received a payment from OhmyNews. Now, only the best articles are published on the front page and receive a 20 000 won payment. Other articles will still get published on the website subsections but will no longer be subject to editorial control.

In Japan, the operations, from the start, did not run very well. The Japanese website faced a lot of criticism and, in November 2007, only a couple of months after its launch, the participatory concept was discontinued; all articles are now written by professional journalists. In mid-2008, the site was finally discontinued.

Strategic challenges

A key challenge for OhmyNews is to remain profitable as it increases its scope of activities. Although Oh's ambition was to spread citizen journalism around the world, the company now has to focus on sustaining funding for its ongoing concerns.

What is the best way to monetize this website? How can advertising revenue be increased: by further traffic increases and/or price (cost per thousand, or CPM) increases? Typically, participatory websites always have had a lower CPM, so Oh was not really sure whether an increase would be feasible. Maybe he could help journalists from other countries develop similar concepts, but with licensing agreements rather than for free, as he had done in the past?

In terms of cost, the company had already reduced its personnel and payments to citizen journalists. He would see the results by the end of 2007. How could costs be reduced even further without compromising too much on quality? Would there still be enough contributors if he reduced the payments to citizen journalists even more? Some recently launched websites were not giving any compensation to their users, such as LePost.fr in France.

	LePost.fr	Rue 89	Now Public	About.com
Launch date	September 2007	May 2007	2005	1996
Revenue 2006				US$80 million*
Revenue growth 2005–2006				100%
Unique visitors (million)	0.5 (in 1 month)	0.3 (in 5 months)	1	47
Monthly growth			35%	
Initial investment			1.4 million USD	
Page views/visitors		10		
FTE	9	8	20	
Citizen journalists			132,000	
Population (million)	60	60		

Figure 7   **Participatory journalism sites' benchmarks**

Source: McKinsey analyses based on websites

In terms of geographical expansion, is the concept exportable or limited to South Korea? Is the concept dependent on major events, such as elections? A similar French company, Rue89.com, also recorded large traffic streams in the beginning thanks to the French elections: the site was the first to report that Cecilia Sarkozy hadn't voted although her then husband, the future president, Nicolas Sarkozy, was the candidate. The Japanese experience had shown that the concept does not work all the time and the company had to be careful with the quality of the content published. However, the quandary still remains the same: how to find the right balance between the quality of content (i.e. supervision of articles received) and the freedom of citizens to express what they want in their own words. On top of that, some countries had already developed their version of participatory journalism websites. Where are the biggest remaining opportunities? How to deal with competition from new big names such as NowPublic in Canada and About.com in the United States? Even the BBC is launching a UGC part on its news websites. And then there is the competition from the individual bloggers, which were recording a strong growth . . . Should OhmyNews consider them a threat, even though blogs have no professional journalists checking their overall quality?

THE FIGHT FOR CUSTOMER ATTENTION: INTELLIGENT MASS MARKETING AND CAUTIOUS NICHE STRATEGY

The forces at work in the media industry will increase the fight for customer attention. Effective marketing will become a key asset in an industry that is traditionally content-focused. This chapter discusses what marketing skills media companies will need to acquire and master in order to be successful. Key questions addressed are:

1. *Why will consumer marketing become more important in the media industry?*
2. *What type of marketing strategy will fit what media revenue model (advertising-based versus subscription-based, etc.)?*
3. *What are the key elements of successful marketing strategies in media?*
4. *How does digitization affect the answers to the questions above?*

The Increasing Need to Understand Customers

By nature media companies tend to be content-focused. Marketing is often, just focused on marketing communication – market research on measuring audiences. Indeed, paying too much attention to consumer desires is often seen as a risk, as it could lead to middle-of-the-road products and too many compromises.

However, several trends will force media companies to listen more closely to their consumers. For advertising based businesses, a shift from talent-driven to format-driven content (see Chapter 3) will increase the need for a much deeper understanding of what triggers a consumer to watch, read or listen. Second, with interactive offerings and the recent rise of online social media facilitated by Web 2.0 developments, consumer preferences and opinions will have a direct influence on media brands and content.

For subscription businesses, the same trends hold. The importance of subscription businesses will grow as many video access platform operators such as cable and telecoms companies may become media service players themselves. For example, cable operators, like Telenet in Belgium, have developed their own media services offerings, with some noticeable success. For example Telenet launched the second-largest Internet portal in Belgium and is the domestic leader in casual games and user-generated video content. As cable is also branching out to offering telephony, telecoms operators have recently launched their own IPTV offerings, as have mobile operators, like Orange TV in a multitude of countries.

Impact of fragmentation

Fragmentation of supply is a critical trend that has been affecting most media consumer markets since the early 1990s, especially in maturing industries.

In the music industry the number of genres and 'scenes' has been developing rapidly in the past decades, for example the number of rock styles increased from eight in the 1950s to over 150 in 2008 (Figure 4.1).

Similarly, the European media industry has experienced an inflation of television channels and magazine titles since the 1990s (Figure 4.2).

With the roll-out of digital TV broadcast platforms, the number of channels viewed is increasing rapidly in most Western European countries (Figures 4.3 and 4.4).

The causes for this trend vary by media sector. Fragmentation in the magazine industry is mainly driven by changing consumer taste: readers increasingly appreciate focused magazines. This applies especially to men, who in general tend to read more newspapers

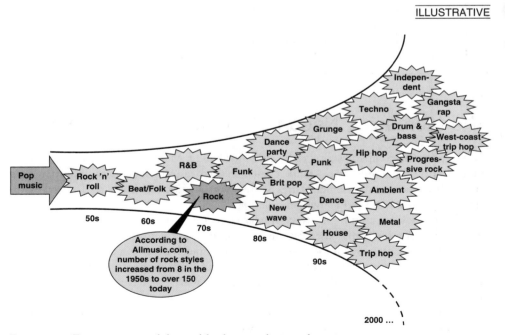

Figure 4.1 **Fragmentation of demand leads to explosion of music genres**

Source: McKinsey analysis

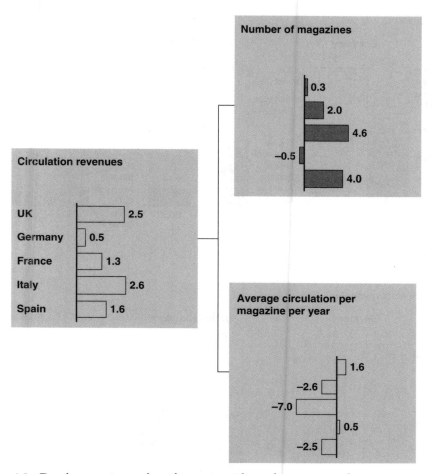

Figure 4.2   Development in number of magazine titles and average circulation

Source: McKinsey analyses based on data from World press trends 2007 reports, PWC global entertainment report, 2006–10, Noticias de la comunicación, IVW, Tableaux Statistiques de la presse, 2007, Prima Comunicazione, ABC

than magazines but prefer special interest magazines, such as sports, news or men's health. As magazines typically have low capital intensity, special interest magazines can already break even at circulation levels of 50 000 or below.

On the other hand, fragmentation in television is mostly driven by technological changes. At the beginning of this century, more than 50% of households in large European countries such as France, Italy and the United Kingdom were still using the analogue terrestrial television broadcasting platform and could choose from only five to eight channels, while the average viewer would prefer to watch at least 15 channels. The fast penetration of digital content delivery technologies like cable, satellite, digital terrestrial TV and, latterly, TV over DSL, changed all this.

TV households, per cent

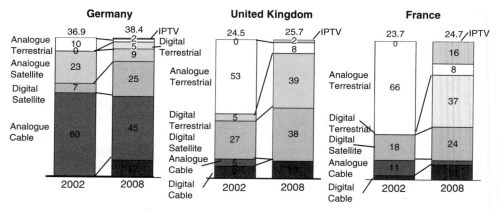

Figure 4.3 Development of TV platforms

Source: McKinsey analyses based on data from *Screen Digest*

TV households, per cent

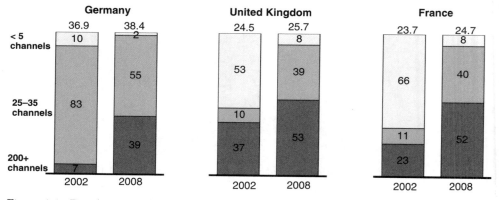

Figure 4.4 Development of number of channels on offer

Source: McKinsey analyses based on data from *Screen Digest*

Internet television will be the next stage in television's development, where viewers will be able to watch 'non-linear content', that is programmes and video clips they select themselves. This gives them access to the long tail of video content, for example through sites such as YouTube, or from country-specific video download sites such as French DailyMotion, German MyVideo and Belgian-based Garage TV. This long tail of video content was initially complementary to mainstream TV viewing, but is transitioning to mainstream itself as it starts to offer programmes from major broadcasters, thus further fragmenting access to TV/video distribution in the medium term. In Japan and South Korea, countries with a very high penetration of high-capacity broadband access (in Korea in 2008, 93% of households had access to an average download speed of 49.5 Mbps and in

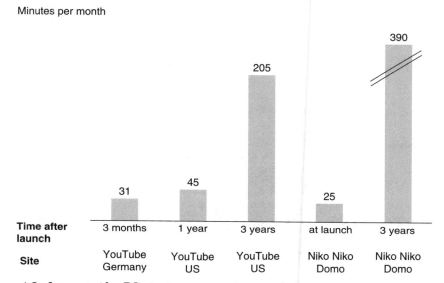

Minutes per month

Figure 4.5 **Internet video PC viewing: average time watched**

Source: McKinsey analyses

Japan 55% of households have broadband access with an average speed of 64 Mbps, according to IFTA broadband rankings), the time spent online on Internet TV is more than four hours a month for a service like Niko Niko Domo, versus one to two and a half hours a month in the United States on YouTube in early 2007 (Figure 4.5).[1] The market is moving fast however, in the US, Hulu, a venture of NBC Universal and Newscorp launched in early 2008 which provides, long form video, boosted its video views from 5 million in April 2008 to more than 140 million 6 months later. This evolution is still underway as high-capacity broadband roll-out is progressing fast and television sets increasingly offer a direct Internet link.

Audiences have reacted to the increased variety of offerings and have begun migrating from a limited number of general interest offerings to a growing array of specialized media products and services. In contrast, some specialized companies have chosen the reverse strategy, with TV channels like MTV becoming mainstream, for example with its European radio channels, such as the teen-focused NRJ, expanding to become mass market. Also, many niche magazines for cooking, gaming, etc. have become established global brands.

Are traditional media businesses seriously threatened?

Are traditional mass-media players threatened by this development? They are to the extent that media cost structure has a high proportion of sunk or fixed content costs that require substantial customer numbers to ensure profitability. For TV players content and

---

[1]The estimates for the time spent on YouTube vary greatly by country and also by provider of ratings; in particular, comScore numbers are higher than NetRating for YouTube.

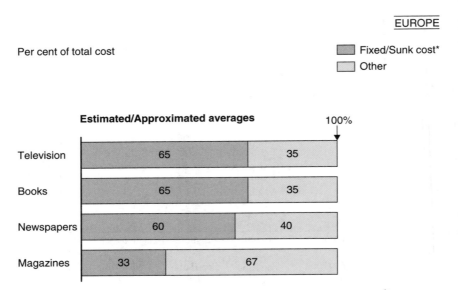

Figure 4.6 **High fixed/sunk cost of many media businesses requires mass audiences**

*Content and production cost, including relevant personnel cost
Source: McKinsey analyses

production costs account for up to 65% of total cost, while for print content and production costs amount to between 33% and 65% of total cost (Figure 4.6). Successful mass offerings must therefore remain the backbone of most media businesses for now, especially for business models relying on advertising revenue, as this revenue is usually closely tied to audience share. Product and brand extensions of ad-based media are also dependent on the number of consumers reached by the original programme/product, as the value of extension is directly linked to the size of the audience which is likely to buy the brand-related merchandise (magazines, etc.). Fragmentation can hurt traditional media significantly as it can draw away a significant number of viewers and/or readers. Since the launch of thematic channels in France, the set of newly launched thematic channels have accumulated more than 40% of audience share, even if individual channels have a relatively low reach. On the Internet, targeted communities, such as auFeminin (a women's portal) can create attractive platforms and generate good revenues from targeted advertising. Traditional media companies are faced with the challenge of developing robust strategies that both preserve against and build upon fragmentation.

Should media companies shift to niche offerings?

Experience shows that media companies must be careful about heading for niche offerings *indiscriminately*. To date, it appears that the customization of media companies' mass offerings has seldom resulted in enough additional revenue potential to cover the incremental investment in tailored content in the short term. Before media companies act, they need to understand the exact nature of fragmentation, that is how fast and where their core businesses will be affected, and also how they can fight back by improving their core mass offering.

Although fragmentation has increased during the first decade of this century, long-term experience from the United States and the United Kingdom shows that its eroding effects on media players' revenues are not as severe as initially assumed. For instance, even if audience figures decline, advertisers may still take a very long time to shift expenditure from one media channel to another, let alone to entirely different or new means of advertising.

And there may even ultimately be a sociological cap to media fragmentation. In a study, conducted by McKinsey in 2002, German TV viewers ranked 'The programme gives me something to talk about with friends and colleagues' as the most important criterion for choosing TV channels.

The effect that fragmentation has on market structure is even more interesting. The audience and advertising captured by a small number of niche players does somewhat reduce the size of the market for mass players. However, those mass players who succeed in defending their audience from competitors can increase their *relative* market share. Experience has shown that higher relative market share often entails disproportionate price premiums for advertising because of scale effects and better brand leverage. This rebalancing effect is visible even on the Web: in 2006, the top 25 horizontal US sites (sites with a broad portal-like offering) captured 35% more share of display advertising revenue than what their page views share would warrant; in the same way, the top sites in key verticals (sites which focus on specific topics such as news, etc.) commanded an ad premium of slightly above 30% versus their online share; in effect, the rest of the destination sites of the Web, or the long tail, only captured 35% of their aggregate page view share – a major and significant discount, that is stronger than what was observed offline (Figure 4.7).

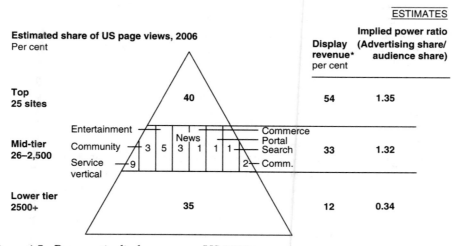

Figure 4.7   Power ratio display revenue, US 2006 >

*Assumes graphical ad split of 60:30:10 and contextual search split of 20:60:20. Based on total display revenue of $7.8b in 2006

Source: McKinsey analyses based on Nielsen Net Ratings Feb 2007

The niche offering can nevertheless be very important to create a strategic *portfolio* of offerings and thus compensate for the market share decline of the original offering. For instance, people who like mass-market sports will watch those in France on lead free channel TF1, but TF1 can guide the same sport addicts to more targeted sport shows, to its cable and satellite audience of Eurosport. Syndicating niche-offering content to create a new mass-market offering can also create attractive additional revenues, such as *Desperate Housewives*, which was syndicated to a highly successful on-demand and iPod download offering. Another example is top video downloads from user-generated content (UGC) platforms that are transferred to mainstream TV channels, for example Current TV in the United States or Pro7Sat1 in Germany, which leverages its own user-platform MyVideo to create to create highly popular programmes for its main television channel.

Strategic Brand Management

Owing to fragmentation, consumers have significantly more choice of media. The more choice consumers have, the easier it is for them to switch, hence the greater the importance of strong brands. This is not only valid for individual programmes, artists or content brands. Recent market research indicates that the drivers of audience loyalty go beyond actual content and include a media channel's overall brand reputation. For instance, TV viewers' channel choice is driven not only by the shows and programming layout but also by the channel's brand attributes. Characteristics such as proven objectivity – for example superior, proprietary news content – can be vitally important to a news network's reputation and, subsequently, drivers of viewer stickiness (continuous time spent on a channel per viewing session) and loyalty.

The importance of brand is underscored with the advent of Web 2.0 and the emergence of major *social network* effects, inducing more and more people to be attracted to a set of specific brands. A destination site like YouTube has witnessed exponential growth to bypass its shareholder company Google in terms of volume of traffic. This exponential growth is being linked to the network nature of the site. On the one hand, more and more viewers are attracted to the sites based on the inventory of video posts, while, on the other hand, video contributors are increasingly prone to contribute to YouTube based on the fame they may derive from the mass of its viewers.

Yet, at the end of the day, all videos posted on YouTube may be posted, and referred to, on other websites. The additional magic of YouTube is its brand attributes: YouTube has built itself as *the reference* pioneer site for Internet video in many countries, and is perceived by its users to be the most innovative site of its kind.

A thorough understanding of current brand position in relation to consumers' preferences is essential to initiating a strategic brand-management process (Figure 4.8). Strong brands differentiate themselves through a clear and relevant brand promise, which builds on two or three core values. These values should be based on the intrinsic strengths of the company and a deep understanding of which factors actually matter in the decision of a viewer or reader to actually move down the 'marketing funnel'.

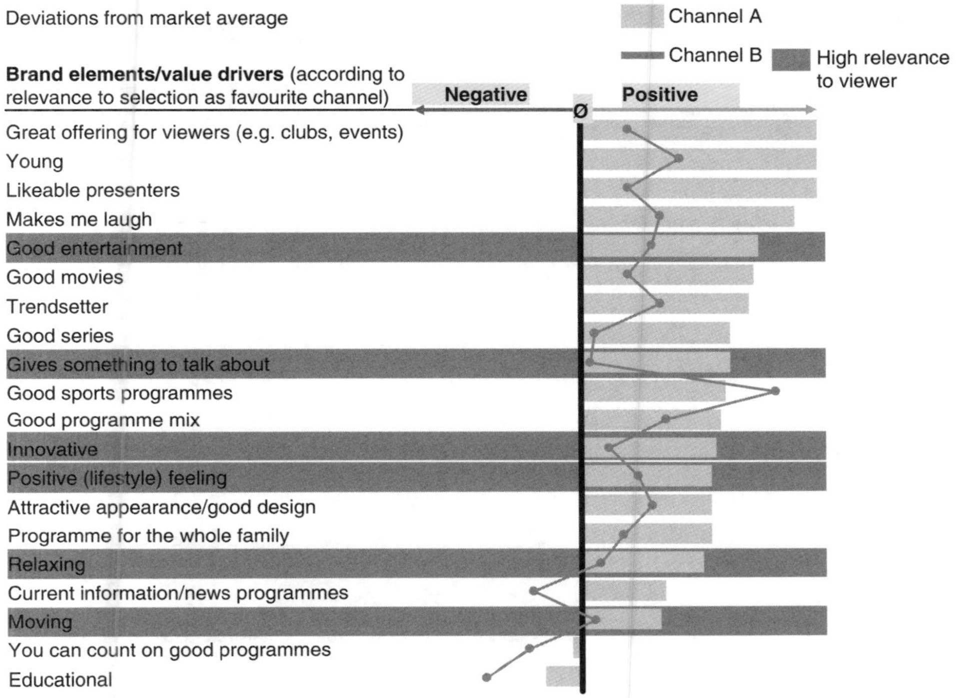

Deviations from market average

Channel A

Channel B   High relevance
to viewer

Brand elements/value drivers (according to
relevance to selection as favourite channel)

| Negative | ∅ | Positive |

Great offering for viewers (e.g. clubs, events)
Young
Likeable presenters
Makes me laugh
Good entertainment
Good movies
Trendsetter
Good series
Gives something to talk about
Good sports programmes
Good programme mix
Innovative
Positive (lifestyle) feeling
Attractive appearance/good design
Programme for the whole family
Relaxing
Current information/news programmes
Moving
You can count on good programmes
Educational

Figure 4.8   Channel A's weaknesses compared to Channel B's

Source: McKinsey analyses

Improving Brand Positioning: Free-to-Air TV Case Example

One of the major European commercial TV channels was puzzled by the fact that its
ratings did not quite match those of its key competitor, although brand awareness was
identical at a very high level (97%). Behavioural audience segmentation revealed that
the channel's weakness was in moving from viewer attraction to viewer retention, rather
than attracting attention in the first place. While the competitor mostly succeeded at
retaining viewers once attracted, the channel itself converted only half of its occasional
viewers to regulars, and only about 20% of these to dedicated viewers ('favourite
channel'). Obviously, creating further attention by investing in brand awareness would
not help to change this. Further market research showed that intangible and/or
emotional brand attributes were the real drivers of the conversion process. The top
five brand attributes driving audiences from occasional to regular viewing were: 'talk of
the town', 'entertaining', 'innovative', 'high-quality' and 'up to date'. Hard factors such
as 'good sports content', 'few re-runs' and 'little advertising', however, made little or no
difference to the decision-making process (Figure 4.9).

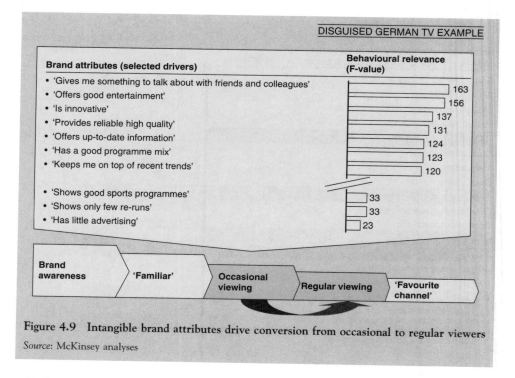

Figure 4.9 Intangible brand attributes drive conversion from occasional to regular viewers
Source: McKinsey analyses

Defining these values and ensuring that the whole organization lives up to them is one of the future key challenges for management. Just investing in pure brand awareness will not make much of a difference except for the smaller players, since brand awareness of most major TV networks in Europe exceeds 95%.

Brand Repositioning: HBO in the Late 1990s

When multiplex cinemas boomed in the mid-1990s and competing pay-TV players upgraded to digital broadcasting via satellite (DBS), the US pay-TV player HBO found itself losing market share. HBO decided to reposition its brand and reshape its offering accordingly. Focusing on premium movies, HBO partnered with theatrical exhibition player Cinemax to create an in-home film offering that goes beyond regular television programming. By transferring attributes from the cinema realm such as 'unique', 'event-driven' and 'innovative' to its pay-TV offering, HBO repositioned its brand as 'the channel that re-invents TV', as summarized in its slogan, 'It's not TV, it's HBO.' Eventually, the company even introduced a separate premium film channel co-branded with Cinemax. To back up the premium promise, HBO engaged in premium programming and tripled its budget for original TV series, producing trend-setting programmes such as *Sex and the City* and *The Sopranos*. Overall, programming expenses increased by 50%, resulting in a 50% revenue increase and a 143% cash-flow increase. This was largely driven by a 100% increase in ancillary revenue, particularly video/DVD sales of its premium content. At the same time, subscription revenue increased by 34%, partly driven by higher average revenue per user (ARPU) generated through additional fees attached to the new film channel.

Strong brands will also increasingly play a role as marketing tools; media consumption and adoption are increasingly influenced by word of mouth. Recent research suggests that 35% of Internet provider choice is linked to word of mouth; in the same vein, a major reason why newspapers are no longer read by teens is not that they do not read. Simply, reading large newspapers is perceived as uncool and old-fashioned. In fact, one major effect of launching compact and colourful free commuter newspapers has been to increase teenager newspaper readership, because the format was closer to the attitudes of the teens – colourful, sharp titles, etc.

Brand Relaunch Process at Welt

In 2005, *Die Welt*, one of Germany's most traditional daily broadsheets, decided to reinvigorate its brand. Known as a conservative and highly reliable newspaper, it felt that a new impulse was needed as part of the overall turn-around programme of the then loss-making newspaper. As a first step, an in-depth analysis was made of the current own and competitive brand positions, and based on this the new brand's essence was defined. Building on its strengths and looking to future trends, the Welt brand was to be focused around 'performance'. This essence was then translated into three brand values: 'brave' (standing by one's convictions, taking responsibility for one's actions and using opportunities to develop things), 'direct' (directly to the point, open for new perceptions, thinking ahead) and 'optimistic' (looking forward to the future, approaching and valuing improvements, being enthusiastic about beautiful things) (Figure 4.10).

Brand essence	Brand equity	Value proposition
Performance	brave + direct + optimistic	**Self-confidence** Welt motivates me to have a strong and differentiated point of view. Welt gives me strength. **Advantage** Welt challenges me to develop new thoughts and to think ahead. **Inspiration** Welt moves my spirit and my heart. I enjoy Welt.

Figure 4.10   Brand concept of Welt

Source: Welt company data. Reproduced with permission

A very important next step was then to bring these brand values alive, both to the readers and advertisers as well as to the organization with the help of a clear value proposition (Figure 4.11).

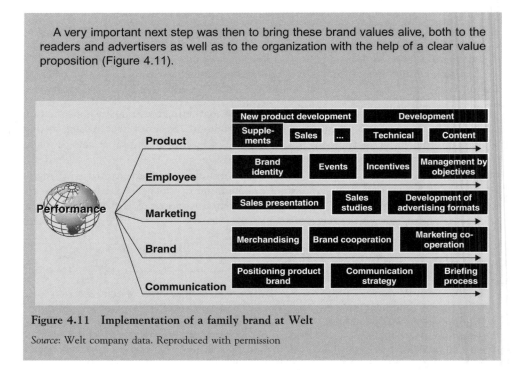

Figure 4.11   Implementation of a family brand at Welt

Source: Welt company data. Reproduced with permission

The rise of Web 2.0 reinforces and extends the word-of-mouth effect. *First*, people use the Web more and more to post comments and recommendations that can not only influence one or two of their close friends but also will be read and viewed much more broadly by all Web visitors. Recent research has demonstrated the so-called effect of 'the strength of weak ties', that is word of mouth is not that effective in influencing your very close friends but much more effective in influencing the weak ties, at three or four degrees of separation.[2] With its global social structure, the Web typically offers these degrees of separation. This potential is harvested extensively by companies such as Amazon to sell more DVDs, music CDs or books.

Second, the Web can really trash brands: Comcast's brand attribute of 'seriousness' was recently challenged when a customer filmed, and posted on YouTube, a company cable installer falling asleep. The video quickly became shared by users of YouTube to top 300 000 views in three days of posting. The damage perceived was large enough for Comcast to fix the problem and fire its technician, but the video kept being shared to top 1 million views within less than one year after the incident.

---

[2]See Sunil Gupta and Thomas Steenburgh, 'Allocating marketing resources', HBS working paper, 08-069, http://www.hbs.edu/research/pdf/08-069.pdf, accessed 24 October 2008.

Fine-Tune the Marketing Strategy to the Revenue Model

In an industry environment of increasing fragmentation and consequently more demanding customers, maximizing customer satisfaction is a top priority for every media player. However, advertising-based and subscription-based businesses face different challenges.

For advertising-based businesses such as free-to-air broadcasting, and to a lesser extent magazines and newspapers, the key challenge is twofold. These businesses need to further maximize audience reach by continually fine-tuning and increasing their understanding of what their audience deems important, and they should optimize monetization of their content through the sophisticated matching of ad-sales strategies to advertisers' needs. Future value creation for subscription-based businesses such as pay/cable TV, book clubs and paid subscription magazines/newspapers depends on a systematic yet cost-conscious monitoring of the drivers of subscriber-lifetime value and the subsequent adaptation of the entire business system to optimize acquisition and minimize churn.

Ad-based models: understand, satisfy and monetize audience *as well as* advertisers

Successful ad-based funded media players have developed a superior and continually adaptive understanding of what (potential) *viewers and advertisers* value. This puts these companies in a position to increase their audience share by fine-tuning their offering. The definition of 'offering' extends in this context beyond content and programming to image and reputation. While short-term audience satisfaction depends primarily on content attractiveness, the overall stickiness and loyalty of consumers are also driven by the brand attributes of channels, magazines and labels.

In addition, it is imperative to understand and exploit in more detail what it is that *advertisers* value. This will enable ad-sales departments to achieve a perfect fit of available ad space or time with advertisers' demands, making sure that the fewest pairs of eyes possible remain not well monetized or undervalued.

Contrary to popular belief, the governing rule on both the consumer and advertising fronts is that it is *not a must* to 'own' the consumer in order to make money. Substantial value can be created without even knowing the consumers' names or by serving them on an individual basis. The overall objective is to continually adapt and fine-tune the media offerings to the preferences that customers and advertisers articulate both directly and indirectly.

Most advertising-based mass media players, especially in mature markets such as the United States, the United Kingdom and northern European countries, are already conducting extensive market research of media audiences. However, audience satisfaction and loyalty remain low in many cases. Going forward, the continuing challenge will be to refine, leverage and synthesize market research to reveal practical insights, and then apply the research in all relevant content generation, programming and marketing processes.

For instance, in the case of free-to-air television – a prime example of capital-intensive, advertising-based mass media – various in-depth analyses of TV audience preferences have shown that it depends on seemingly minuscule factors whether viewers tune in, stay with or return to a specific channel. Media Capital's TVI (the leading TV channel in Portugal) had understood that in the mid-nineties. To maximize audience share, it created a highly systematic understanding of viewer preferences and continually adapted content, programming and marketing accordingly. As a result, TVI managed to grow viewership from a 12% market share to more than 30% in TV prime time in recent years. A large part of this growth is definitely linked to investment in the TV grid, but a significant part is also due to large viewer insights as to what they best prefer and translating this into details such as specific programme timeslot attributes.

Responding to Viewer Preferences: TVI Case Example

In the case of TVI, traditional metrics like GRP (gross rating points) for individual shows or market share of the network were shown to not be a good correlate of TV consumption satisfaction; only four out of ten viewers were 'highly satisfied', with an even lower satisfaction among demographics of younger people. Audience requirements were shown to be much more complex, and included programming preferences and favoured channel layout. For example, according to market research, viewers of the channel's news programme had very specific and strong preferences including: 30 minutes rather than shorter duration, just one news anchor (as opposed to the US model of two anchors jointly hosting the newscast), change of timeslot from 9 p.m. to 6 p.m., more national content than international, shorter features (less than four minutes) and more educational/cultural/social topics than economic/political. By responding to these preferences and monitoring the effects systematically, the network managed to become more distinctive than competitor channels and increased the news programme's audience share from 19% to 35%.

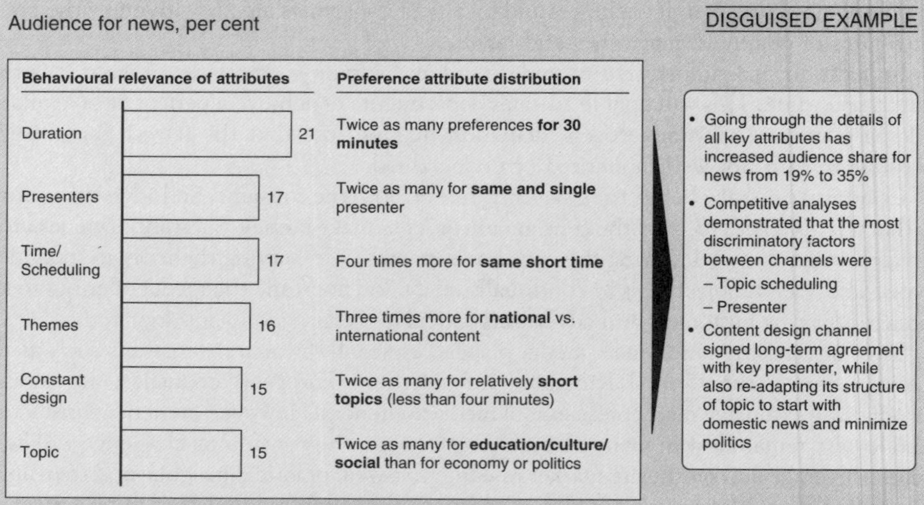

Audience for news, per cent   DISGUISED EXAMPLE

Behavioural relevance of attributes		Preference attribute distribution	
Duration	21	Twice as many preferences **for 30 minutes**	
Presenters	17	Twice as many for **same and single** presenter	
Time/ Scheduling	17	Four times more for **same short time**	
Themes	16	Three times more for **national** vs. international content	
Constant design	15	Twice as many for relatively **short topics** (less than four minutes)	
Topic	15	Twice as many for **education/culture/ social** than for economy or politics	

- Going through the details of all key attributes has increased audience share for news from 19% to 35%
- Competitive analyses demonstrated that the most discriminatory factors between channels were
  - Topic scheduling
  - Presenter
- Content design channel signed long-term agreement with key presenter, while also re-adapting its structure of topic to start with domestic news and minimize politics

Figure 4.12   Improving audience satisfaction for news programmes

Source: McKinsey analysis

In another case, a German free-to-air channel managed to improve its audience share of a daily soap opera by making minor changes to characters and details of the story based on viewers' feedback via SMS. Cases like these show that, in a maturing and fragmenting environment, content attractiveness increasingly depends on incremental adaptations, making the fine-tuning of formats and programming a key success factor (Figure 4.12).

Adapting Offering to Readers' Preferences: Newspaper Example

In 2001, a major European newspaper publisher came under considerable financial pressure because of decreasing reader loyalty. The loyal readers were becoming occasional readers and many occasional readers stopped reading the newspaper altogether. This decreasing loyalty was creating a net annual revenue leakage of more than €5 million. Market research of loyalty drivers showed that the most important reasons cited for decreased readership were 'product and positioning' and 'preferred competitive offer'. To address this decreasing loyalty the publisher subsequently defined four main target groups primarily based on sociodemographic segmentation and prioritized by total size, current loyal reader support and loyalty loss rate. Based on the identified target groups and their declared preferences, the publisher devised a comprehensive retention programme, including promotions, product development and distribution. For example, for 'young mums', subsequent marketing centred on events and activities of relative interest, such as fashion shows and home improvement fairs. As for content, frequency of the parenting section of the paper was increased and more space dedicated to 'health and fitness'. In the area of distribution, pilot programmes and new distribution points such as schools, hospitals and health clubs were tested.

Digitization offers great tools to understand and proactively address audiences even better. Sneak previews of television programmes or movies online have a significant impact on offline viewing; in the same way, people using 'just missed television features' on their interactive digital televisions provide good insights as to what programmes they really want to watch and the best times for scheduling, etc. But another important aspect of digital and the Internet lies in the fact that they can be used as a major audience *attractor back to offline*. In general, media companies have used the Web as a simple online extension of their content offering online, so-called 'companion' websites. In contrast, some media companies have considered this way of using the Web as much too restrictive, and so have developed an entirely new Web offering online. Those 'non-companion' websites typically attract a much larger set of Internet users than what is commanded by the original brand extension of offline to online. Often 80% of their Web visitors – on sites such as MyVideo from television Pro7Sat1SBS provider, or CondeNet from magazine Conde Nast – are new users to the original brand. Using this new pool of new users online to promote an *offline* brand can be a significant factor in driving new audiences towards offline offerings, in some cases reported to represent as high as a 10–15% uplift to the current offline audience.

Optimize responsiveness to advertisers' needs

Provided a free-to-air channel, newspaper or magazine has achieved sufficient content, programming and brand attractiveness, value creation depends to a major extent on intelligent marketing of audiences to advertisers to ensure adequate monetization. Approaches on how to better market to advertisers' needs will be discussed in detail in chapter 6.

Marketing Strategies for Subscription-based Players

Subscription-based businesses such as pay/cable TV, subscription newspapers, and magazine and book clubs to a large extent face the same marketing challenges as mass players; however, in addition they need a refined understanding of the dynamics of acquisition, development and retention of their customers, and about improving entire business systems accordingly. In a world of fragmenting demand, in which mainstream media audiences are tempted by niche and thematic offerings, subscription players who excel at refining their responsiveness to customer (dis)satisfaction will be rewarded by subscriber loyalty.

The business conduct of subscription players is essentially based on the three-stage customer lifetime that determines both growth potential and limits: they attract customers to enrol, develop them for loyalty and maximum revenues and try to retain them for maximum lifetime value (Figure 4.13). Value-based subscription players recognize that:

1. subscription can only be profitable if (discounted) customer lifetime value, on average or, preferably, per segment, exceeds recruitment cost

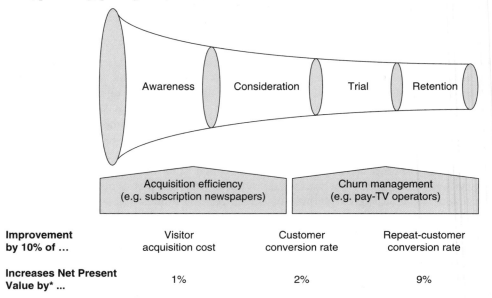

Improvement by 10% of ...	Visitor acquisition cost	Customer conversion rate	Repeat-customer conversion rate
Increases Net Present Value by* ...	1%	2%	9%

Figure 4.13 Maximizing customer lifetime value along funnel

*Online example
Source: McKinsey analysis; e-Performance benchmarking (spring 2000)

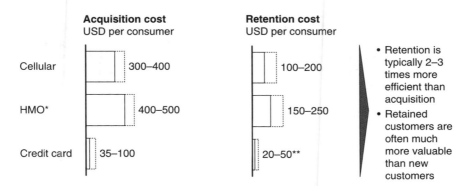

Figure 4.14   The economics of retention are highly attractive across industries

*Health maintenance organization
**Including cost of incentives
Source: McKinsey analysis

2. retaining acquired customers is almost always easier and cheaper than replacing churning subscribers with new acquisition (Figure 4.14)
3. the subscriber base may not grow beyond a certain level, as new acquisitions will eventually level off, continuing to replace churn but not affecting growth – depending on attitudes towards subscription, distribution strategy and relevant brand(s) in the respective markets.

The most important implication of the economics of the customer relationship funnel is that companies should take comprehensive action across the entire subscription business system to improve acquisition efficiency and fight subscriber churn. This is because value-oriented subscriber recruitment and retention are paramount drivers of profit for any subscription-based business. For example, churn management programmes can have up to a 10% profit bottom-line effect, and minimal differences in churn can have disproportionate effects on market share. In particular, the profitability effect of churn increases as businesses or markets approach saturation; the more expensive new subscriber acquisition becomes, the more important it will be to retain existing subscribers.

Increasing Acquisition Efficiency: US Daily Newspaper Example (2002)

In the late 1990s, one US daily newspaper experienced a dramatic profitability downturn, caused by a combination of three factors: a large number of unprofitable or inefficient acquisition sources, a declining base of loyal subscribers and an increasing number of short-term, high-churn subscribers. The publisher thus adapted a radical customer lifetime value (CLV) approach to acquisition channels and target groups, with the overall objective of dropping those with negative NPV (net present value), reducing those with marginal NPV and increasing those with positive NPV. The cornerstone of the subscription efficiency programme was to introduce separate CLV calculations for all acquisition channels, such as billboard advertising, Internet, direct-mail (differentiated by type of promotion) and telemarketing. Next, the publisher created a CLV ranking for 33 recruitment channels as a key tool to use in maximizing the value of future acquisitions. For example, the newspaper found that subscribers acquired through direct mail on a 52-week discount had an average CLV exceeding $200, while subscribers attracted by a one-month free offer that was promoted via a marketing alliance had an average CLV below $50. By continually reallocating marketing spend according to this ranking, the publisher achieved an estimated EBITDA (earnings before interest, taxes, depreciation and amortization) improvement of $35 million over three years. In a similar situation, a Scandinavian newspaper achieved a 10% circulation increase and an EBITDA improvement of 0.7% by segmenting its subscriber base according to lifetime value, focusing on a key segment, rewarding proven loyalty with major rebates as well as by generally monitoring circulation, retention and profitability on a segment basis.

Churn is not a given. A large part of it is both predictable and controllable; in one US pay-TV company, 75% of the causes of churn ultimately were controllable by the operator, for example dissatisfaction with offer/price and promotions or technical reasons. When looking at churn from a subscriber lifetime perspective, a number of retention tools can be applied: recruitment only in core/attractive customer segments, using appropriate offers by monitoring the effect promotions have on subsequent churn, understanding the root causes of (potential) customer dissatisfaction, paying attention to early-warning signs of imminent cancellation, effective treatment of likely churners and improved retention procedures.

The management challenge is to assess a large number of factors that have an impact on churn – structural, such as demographic data characteristics; event-related, such as house move; and behavioural, such as taste – to focus on those with the highest profitability impact.

Successful examples (see below) show that major improvements can be achieved in relatively cost-efficient ways, and large investments in sophisticated customer databases and customer relationship management (CRM) tools are necessary only once a high degree of sophistication has been reached. For example, fully exploring and leveraging in-bound subscriber communication (e.g. phone calls) is often a much more powerful approach than sophisticated database analysis. Better customer service is usually a more effective and quicker way of improving retention than changes to content. For example, a European cable TV company found that up to 60% of cable subscribers who call the operator to cancel their subscription change their mind if their concerns are addressed directly and countered by a targeted offer.

Understanding and Fighting Churn: Pay-TV Analysis Example

In the case of one particular pay-TV operator, a systematic analysis of discriminatory factors yielded the root causes of churn in three categories. In a subsequent comprehensive churn management programme, countermeasures were identified, ranked according to potential and feasibility and implemented accordingly.

The most prominent *structural factors* driving subscriber loyalty were customer tenure and customer segment. Recent subscribers (one year or less tenure) were much more likely to churn than 'old' subscribers were. Young, affluent subscribers were much more likely to churn than unemployed, middle-aged subscribers were. Subsequent value-based segmentation took into account factors ranging from age, sociodemographics and address to rural versus urban environment and household situation. Churn also varied by channels and by type of products bought by the customers, for example top-tier subscribers were much less likely to churn than basic-package subscribers. Once understood, these attractive structural segments could be targeted by adjusting recruitment policies, for example attraction marketing of specific content and events.

Event-related factors relevant to loyalty and churn were promotions, direct customer contact, technical problems and household events. The value-oriented handling of promotional schemes was shown to be particularly important, as it has been proved that some promotions have actually 'created' churn. As more free subscription time or rebate value was offered, churn peaked just before the particular promotion or special offer expired. Paying close attention to in-bound customer communication ˘ especially through call centre contact and, to a lesser extent, mailings ˘ became a key factor for success. Subscriber 'mood' as measured by call centres, for instance, was a valuable predictive indicator of churn and has been used to focus retention measures. To improve retention rates, customer agent effectiveness ˘ rather than operational efficiency ˘ was monitored and developed on an individual basis. In general, increased direct contact with customers (e.g. phone rather than mail) has proved to be a highly effective retention tool. Household events, such as divorce, relocation, children and sudden unemployment, if the operator was aware of them, were addressed with related offers.

Churn management also had to address *behavioural factors* such as declared preferences as well as product and services usage. For example, churn varied with the type of content or programme favoured at the time of subscription. Customers subscribing because of exclusive content (e.g. sports broadcasts) were much less likely to churn than those subscribing because of more interchangeable content, such as movies or news. Behavioural causes of churn were countered by adjusting tiering and package structure to address declared or observed preferences, securing exclusive content and/or building local content.

This pay-TV company's integrated churn reduction programme across all three factors reduced churn from 12% to 10.5% across all platforms, resulting in an increase of 5% in revenue and nearly 2 points in the EBITDA margin.

Ensure efficiency of customer lifetime management (CLM)

When it comes to implementing any concrete CLM measures – for instance in the context of a churn management programme – the key challenge is to be able to proceed strictly on a pilot basis and keep implementation scalable, flexible and lean rather than invest upfront in large-scale IT infrastructure and software (Figure 4.15). Scalability requires any CLM effort to start small and be rolled out on a broader basis only after proven success ('do it, try it, fix it'). For example, in the case of a call centre, pilot-testing a new script for outgoing calls on a sample of 500 contacted subscribers may be enough to derive valuable insights for customer segments up to 100 times that size.

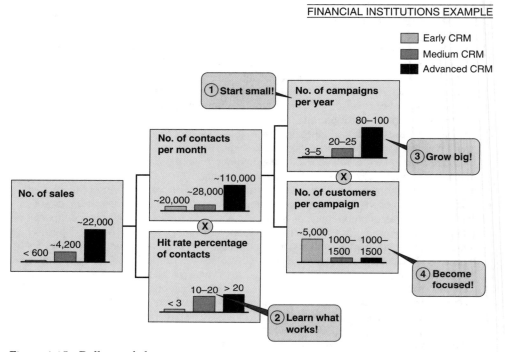

Figure 4.15 Roll-out of churn programmes

Source: McKinsey analysis

The CLM principles above still hold true with the advent of digitization, but become both more powerful as well as more complex. Digitization allows media companies to take tactical CLM actions at a much lower level of granularity, for instance targeting micro-segments of a few hundred customers, rather than in the tens of thousands. With interactive TV, you can not only push more on-demand movie recommendations to on-demand movie users but also go one step further, and micro-segment movie users by type of movies, hours of watching, etc. Netflix, a provider of video-on-demand service by post, even refined a complex micro-segmentation algorithm to predict the best preference and usage of movie ordering of its customers, even opening on the Web its predictive model application, for any user to test and refine, in the hope of even better targeting audience offering.

While many examples can be quoted, the essence of digital CLM is based on capturing all the richness of new data arising from digital touch-points – harnessing those data, deriving adequate campaigns and running them at a much larger scale and velocity is a complex and new capability that needs to be developed by media organizations.

Lastly, with digital, the typical funnel representation of the user – consideration, buy and deepen – suddenly becomes more complex. Online users use a lot more of *third-party* information, from search engines to comparison sites, with online in general adding rather than substituting touch-points for CLM optimization. With Web 2.0, word of mouth online ('word of mouse') is also kicking in, and a set of highly vocal users ('social influencers') will have a greater potential influence on user preferences. These customers' value is thus much more than just their own buying contribution, given the influence they potentially have on total sales and retention. This 'externality' effect may be relatively high – we found it to be in the range of 20% of sales and 10% of churn in cable television.

Marketing Strategy for Niche and Thematic Offerings

Niche and thematic media offerings – especially in the European media market – have faced structural challenges, which is why usually only segment leaders achieve profitability. As discussed above, media businesses that are capital- and fixed-cost-intensive require critical mass, and even a basic sociodemographic targeting of offerings will divide the relevant audience by at least a factor of three (gender, age group, etc.). While thematic offerings may have a higher chance of success in the North American market (which is unique in comprising more than 300 million people who speak the same language), it has been difficult to gather similar critical momentum in Europe, which remains divided along cultural and linguistic lines.

Companies can increase the economic viability of thematic and niche offerings by extending well-established mass brands (e.g. Axel Springer's *Bild*; see Figure 4.16) and

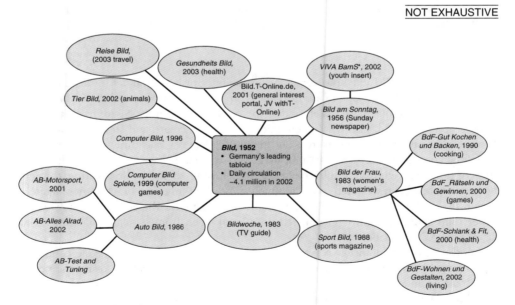

Figure 4.16   Bild brand extension

*BamS = Bild am Sonntag
Source: McKinsey analysis; Axel Springer AG

Hubert Burda in the German publishing market) and by increasing leverage of non-advertising revenues (e.g. the Discovery Channel's subscription-based thematic brand extension, licensing and merchandising strategy; see example in box on the next page).

Brand Expansion Example: The Discovery Channel

In the early 1990s, the Discovery Channel was formed as a single pay-TV channel in the United States, focusing on the then neglected area of high-quality documentaries. Its business was largely subscription-based as part of the most popular cable TV distributors' basic package, but supported by ad revenues. The Discovery Channel has since extended its brand across geographies (11 international sister networks) and into thematic niches. Thematic extension is focused on topics and attributes strongly associated with the brand, such as 'educational', 'wholesome', 'trustworthy' and 'nature/outdoor'. The Discovery Channel's bundle comprises seven thematic channels such as Discovery Health Channel, Discovery Kids, Travel Channel and Animal Planet. All of these are either Discovery-branded or at least have a similar look and feel, for instance through shared type fonts and logos. The channel also leverages its brand outside traditional pay TV to create ancillary revenues, for example through high-definition video-on-demand (Discovery HD Theater), commercial radio (Discovery Radio), in retail (the Discovery Store, with about 200 US outlets) and product licensing (Discovery-branded toys, gadgets and software). While brand extension works well for thematic channels, merchandising profits are lagging behind competitors who can leverage popular characters, for example Disney and Nickelodeon. The Discovery Channel is currently assessing options to leverage its brand for educational products and publishing.

Online and Web 2.0 add, however, some further offering potential, for instance through community-powered media. A case in point is a newborn company called 8020 Publishing, which has been using the Web to develop specific community-based magazines, like photography or travel, and where community users can create and share content. The Web-based community access is free, but in parallel, a glossy magazine is also developed with 'best content' being agreed upon by users, and sold offline from newsstands or through subscription. The current results have been promising so far: offline selling through newsstands has been as much as 70%, much more than any best practice new launch. Given the user-generated nature of the publication's content, the editorial costs are also lower than traditional print media, reducing break-even from typically 50 000 subs to 20 000–30 000 subscribers.

Another case in point is Next New Networks, a new kind of media company, developing UGC micro-television in a form of a network aggregation, using the power of rich media and online video to deliver a platform of interactive television. The success is still to be seen, but 'Triple N' has already managed to become the largest traffic channel generator on YouTube.

To summarize, the overall impact of increasing fragmentation on media companies is twofold: it is a reminder for mass players to continually defend and enrich their traditional offering through more systematic, pragmatic and cost-effective adaptations of their value proposition to an increasingly sophisticated demand from customers/subscribers and advertisers/media planners. At the same time, fragmentation is an opportunity to extend, with care, established brands into thematic niches, or to establish a portfolio of thematic channels, leveraging social media, using the latter for cross-marketing synergies between offline and online.

Key Takeaways

1. There will be an increasing need to truly understand media consumers because of:
   - increasing fragmentation of offering
   - social online media and greater interactivity
   - growth of subscriber-based businesses
   - a shift in consumer taste towards format-driven content.
2. Media companies currently often confine marketing to communication and audience measurement rather than fulfilling and creating new consumer needs.
3. The marketing skills needed differ significantly between mass-market players, subscription-based businesses and niche players, yet cross-synergies exist among each type of business.
4. For mass-market players, strategic brand management will be key, complemented by an extensive fine-tuning of their offerings based on a detailed understanding of their audiences and advertisers.
5. Subscription-based players should optimize the customer lifetime funnel in its integrity, while carefully watching the social media.
6. Churn management will become increasingly important in a maturing media industry and can be managed through the careful optimization of all customer touch-points.
7. CLM capabilities will become increasingly important for subscription-based companies, especially with the added complexity of online and digital; however, rather than taking a 'big bang' approach, companies should introduce them gradually, using a pilot-based approach followed by a scalable, flexible and lean roll-out.
8. Niche businesses require very different approaches and cost structures than mass businesses, but the advent of cost-effective delivering and user-generated content create new promising niche models.
9. Media companies must ensure the necessary organizational conditions for creating niche offerings and leveraging key assets from their mass businesses, such as brand extension.
10. In general, digitization entails the need to develop further capabilities, such as social media management, micro-segmentation tactics, etc.

Canal+: Keeping Consumer Loyalty in the Face of Platform Competition[1]

Canal+ is an organization long associated with quality TV content. It has weathered significant changes in recent years, and after a major restructuring effort in the early part of this century and its subsequent return to profitability, things seem to be going well.

Yet the TV industry is changing. It's going digital, and it's going online. Traditional telecoms operators (telcos) are entering the TV market through Internet Protocol TV (IPTV). Content producers are also altering the industry dynamics. Content is king, and they know this. In the United Kingdom, the BBC, ITV and Channel 4 are investing in their own online content delivery platforms. They plan to keep their content exclusive and unavailable through alternative platforms. If this trend is any indication of what could happen in the rest of Europe, content aggregators such as CanalSat will be affected.

How well positioned is Canal+ to take on competition from new entrants from the telecoms sector and to battle it out with content producers to secure rights to premium-quality content packages?

Company History

Canal+ started out in 1984 as the first pay-TV channel in France, and today is part of the Canal+ Group, which is owned by the international media company Vivendi. The Canal+ Group consists of Canal+, a high-quality premium content pay-TV channel, and Canal+ Le Bouquet, special-interest pay-TV channels, in addition to CanalSat, a satellite pay-TV division offering a bundle of over 200 TV channels mainly over satellite but also over digital cable and IPTV networks, and CanalStudio, a division responsible for financing, acquiring and distributing films in France and other European countries. Consumers have to subscribe separately to the services of Canal+ (or Canal+ Le Bouquet) and CanalSat, thus they are treated as two separate businesses within the company. The group additionally has services for video on demand and mobile phone access to its content packages.

Canal+ is involved in rights procurement, production and programming for its TV channels, with a historical focus on movies and sports. It also creates bundles of channels for various platforms, including analogue terrestrial with set-top box, cable, satellite, DSL and digital terrestrial. For many years it was very profitable because of its focus on high-quality and cutting-edge films, premier sports coverage and its large and loyal subscriber base, which in 2008 amounted to more than 10.5 million subscribers. However, it experienced some tumultuous times during the 1990s and into this century.

---

[1]This case is developed solely as the basis for class discussion. Cases are not intended to serve as endorsements, sources of primary data or illustrations of effective or ineffective management.

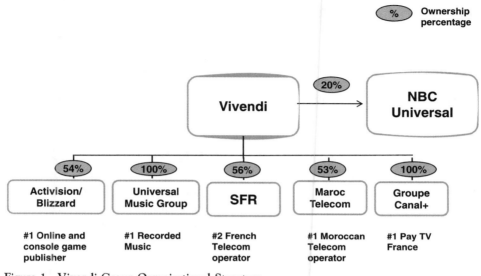

Figure 1   Vivendi Group Organizational Structure

Source: Mckinsey analysis based on data from Vivendi

Investments in satellite technology

One of the Canal+ Group's most important endeavours was the creation of CanalSatellite, in 1991. In 1996 it upgraded its network to become Europe's first commercial digital satellite television platform. With its newly upgraded network it launched an extensive digital content offering of 24 channels in addition to interactive services. CanalSat does not engage in any programming, but sources content from outside providers such as Disney, Warner and even Canal. CanalSat's business includes marketing and selling pay-TV content packages to satellite TV subscribers. Canal's original channel subscriptions via satellite are handled exclusively by CanalSat. The division broke even in 2000 when it reached 1.2 million subscribers, and continued to maintain market share against its only competitor, TPS, which it subsequently merged with in early 2007.

Vivendi

In 1999 Canal+ teamed with Vivendi to create VivendiNet, to enable Canal+'s content bundles to be accessible on mobile phones, PCs and TV. And in 2000 Vivendi bought the remaining 51% of Canal+ it did not already own for US$12 billion. Vivendi also acquired the Canadian company Seagram (whose holdings included Universal Studio and Poly-Gram) that year and combined all three firms into Vivendi Universal. Vivendi, and subsequently Canal+, went through a period of massive expansion in the late 1990s and early 2000s but financial troubles soon followed for the company.

International expansion

Throughout the 1990s Canal+ expanded internationally across Europe to the Benelux countries, Spain and Italy, and by 2002 had close to 17 million subscribers worldwide. And yet, it had expanded too quickly. It tried to become the premier pan-European pay-TV operator, but synergies across countries were much smaller than expected. As a result, the company suffered significant losses between 2000 and 2002. In 2002 Canal+'s operating losses amounted to $306 million.

Tough times: content costs and bidding wars

Things looked bleak for Canal+ in 2002/03. It was losing money and subscribers. It looked like a large, unfocused business. Its far-reaching, pan-European divisions weren't faring well. Rights to movies and sports, the core of Canal+'s content offering, are negotiated country by country, and in Western Europe 83% of premium programming (other than blockbuster films) is nationally produced. Content offerings are Canal+'s most important cost-driver and thus it was difficult for it to achieve economies of scale from its international operations.

In addition to difficulties in achieving economies of scale from its European operations, in France the brand prestige of Canal+ was under threat. Although it did continue to show some innovative programming, some felt it was losing the 'edginess' it was once known for. Furthermore, French government regulation was contributing to its profitability squeeze. Government regulation dictated that Canal+ invest 20% of its earnings in the production of French films, despite US blockbusters being more popular, and potentially bringing in more subscribers.

Another factor contributing to the tough times experienced by Canal+ was its rival in the satellite business, TPS. These two had long been rivals over the subscriber base and rights to broadcast football matches. Having the rights to broadcast League 1 matches was extremely important for Canal+ in its endeavours to maintain a large subscriber base. Yet the cost to obtain these rights was escalating owing to fierce competition from TPS. Although strapped for cash, in 2002 Canal+ bid €480 million per year for the rights to broadcast League 1 matches in the 2004–2007 seasons. At the time, it was estimated that 25% of its then 4.5 million subscribers had joined Canal+ because of its soccer coverage.

TPS was also a threat to Canal+'s subscriber base. Although CanalSat's business had grown in 2002, through adding 220 000 subscribers, Canal+ lost a net 70 000 subscribers that year to the competition, TPS. Worse still, in 2003 Warner Brothers and Disney sold pay-TV rights for their movies to TPS rather than to Canal+. With subscriber churn increasing (from 9% in 1999 to 12.9% in 2003) and escalated content costs, the organization was in need of a turnaround.

New management was brought in and the new CEO, Bertrand Meheut, and his then chief of strategy, Rodolphe Belmer, initiated a major turnaround programme to bring profitability back to the organization. The changes focused on brining Canal+ back to its French roots and restoring its brand prestige. It abandoned plans to further expand its pay-TV model abroad and disposed of several international assets. Telepiù, its Italian business, was sold to Rupert Murdoch's News Corporation in 2002. Although it still holds 100% of Canal+ in Poland, it sold off Canal+ Nordic in 2003, and Canal+ Benelux and Canal+ Netherlands in 2004.

The turnaround

In addition to scaling back its international divisions, and cutting about 15% of its workforce, several other changes were involved in the restructuring of Canal+. In an effort to strengthen its brand, its programming focus expanded from cinema and sports to news, documentaries and entertainment. The strategy was to invest in free-to-air programming, which was broadcasted at the Canal+ channel at certain fixed times during the day, to attract new customers and develop greater subscriber loyalty with recurrent programming. Additionally, a strong marketing and sales focus was adopted. The results were very positive. Sales growth was achieved through growing the number of subscribers and the average revenue per user (ARPU) without having to drastically increase the subscription price.

The following years

At the beginning of 2003 there was constant speculation that Vivendi would sell the Canal+ Group, and even speculation that it would be bought by rival TPS. After all, the group did have a €5 billion debt and was burdened with the hefty €480 million annual football rights. Yet, Vivendi did not sell Canal+. Instead, in 2006 it made a bold move and bought the exclusive soccer rights for the premier league for €600 million per year for the coming three years. In the years before it had shared the soccer rights with TPS. This move greatly affected TPS and finally convinced the company to merge with Canal+. The move put an end to the costly price wars that existed between TPS and Canal+ over programming and sports rights. Vivendi also stated that the merger would help it strengthen its market position against increasing competition from telecoms operators and Internet service providers (ISPs). This competition from non-traditional TV industry players proved to be significant.

Current Situation

Industry dynamics

Worldwide trends in TV in 2007

The market for TV services worldwide was estimated at €268 billion for 2007, with the United States, Europe and Japan accounting for 78% of this revenue. Subscriptions, public funding through licensing fees and advertising sales account for most of this revenue. Although subscription television revenues had the highest growth rates in 2007, advertising is still the main source of revenue for the TV sector worldwide. Advertising revenues were greatly affected by the economic downturn in the United States and some European countries that started in 2007.

Terrestrial television is the dominant form of television reception worldwide. Its viewers represent an estimated 47% of TV households, whereas cable represents 34%, satellite 17% and ADSL/DSL is around 1%. Yet, the growth rate of terrestrial has been steadily dropping, and there has been a recent rise in the number of subscribers to satellite services. This rise can be attributed to initiatives in many countries to phase out analogue transmission with digital TV. Satellite networks have proven to be faster at the change to digital than other types of

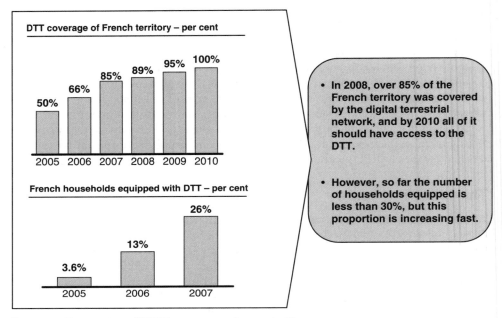

DTT coverage of French territory – per cent

- In 2008, over 85% of the French territory was covered by the digital terrestrial network, and by 2010 all of it should have access to the DTT.

- However, so far the number of households equipped is less than 30%, but this proportion is increasing fast.

French households equipped with DTT – per cent

Figure 2   Progression of DTT coverage and usage in France

Source: McKinsey analysis based on data from Mediametrie; Mediamat

transmission networks. This trend is particularly evident in emerging markets such as India and China, where cable networks have been slow to change to digital.

Trends in TV in Europe

The switchover to digital television is the dominating concern of the TV industry in Europe, with an estimated 30% of European households currently receiving digital television. Analogue terrestrial TV will be switched off in most European countries around 2012 and there is a battle raging over who will serve these households. It is expected that digital terrestrial TV (DTT) will experience major growth in the European market as one of the main substitutes of analogue terrestrial (as has already been seen in the United Kingdom, and through the launch of several DTT services in France, Spain and Italy). However, as the offering of DTT is limited to around 30 channels (or fewer when high-definition TV is broadcast) with limited interactivity, the changeover moment is seen as a big opportunity for other digital platform providers, such as cable and satellite, to offer their superior services (significantly more channels and, in the case of cable, full interactivity) to gain market share.

Another key trend emerging in Europe is the entry of telecoms and broadband operators into the TV market with IPTV platforms. Although the market share is currently small, the uptake is increasing, and the number of IPTV subscribers in Europe is anticipated to be 16.7 million by 2010.

Trends in TV in France

Although one of the last European countries to launch a DTT service, France's DTT provider, TNT, has experienced significant growth since its inception in 2005. As of 2007, an estimated 26% of French homes are equipped with DTT service, up from 13% in 2006. This growth can be attributed to a French law enacted in 2000 to ensure between 85% and 95% of the population have access to DTT by 2011. This law has shaped the TV industry within France.

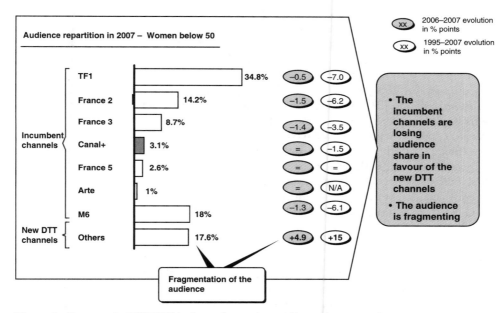

Figure 3   Increase in DTT FTA channels causing audience fragmentation

Source: McKinsey analysis based on data from Mediametrie; Mediamat

Accompanying the launch of the DTT service in 2005, 14 free-to-air (FTA) channels and two pay-TV packages were also launched. Previously, there had only been five FTA channels in France. In 2008 the number of FTA channels has grown to 21. Once enjoying an oligopoly, the seven incumbent channels (TF1, Canal+, France2, France3, France5, Arte, M6) now have increased competition for viewers.

The incumbents are losing market share to the new FTA DTT channels, and as a result the audience is more fragmented. To respond to the fragmentation of the audience, most incumbents have adopted strategies involving editing and broadcasting new theme channels and/or new mini-generalist channels in order to recapture some of the market share their flagship channels are losing. The successful launch of Canal+ LeBouquet (renamed " Les chaînes Canal+ in 2008), consisting of 4 digital channels, (Sport, Family, movies and "Décalé" (repeats)) and the main channel Canal+ sped up this fragmentation greatly. By the end of 2008 less than 1 million analogue subscribers were left, all others had moved to the digital package. Additionally, to remain competitive against the new FTA DTT channels, many of the incumbents have launched high-definition (HD) channels

(TF1 HD, M6 HD, France 2 HD, Arte HD) for free-to-air HD broadcasts. Canal+ launched the first HD channel in France on August 8, 2008 (start of Olympic Summer games).

Cable still plays a minor role in France, with the market share of Numericable, the sole provider, diminishing because of increased competition. France, however, is leading in Europe in the roll-out of IPTV platforms; the three major IPTV providers already serve 16% of the market in 2008. The large success is due to favourable regulations, which allowed new entrants easy access to the 'last mile to the home' from the telecoms networks and the very aggressive and successful market entry of a new player, Free, which offers 'triple play' (Internet, telephone, TV) services at a highly competitive price. Free entered the market in 1999 and by 2008 owned 24% of the broadband market and has over 1.4 million TV subscribers (19.4% of households).

Currently, in 2008, three players, Free, SFR/Neuf (Vivendi) and Orange (France Telecom) provide IPTV through DSL networks. Although they currently hold a small portion of the market, they are aggressively competing for subscribers with their triple play offers. Yet, DSL TV providers are having limited success monetizing their subscriber base. One major obstacle for them is that Canal+ controls the premium film and sports programming. Free, with its aggressive plan to cover 66% of the French TV market by 2008 still must buy Canal+ packages and services. Neuf, another DSL provider, was recently acquired by Canal+'s parent company, Vivendi, and merged with SFR. This may seem like the perfect opportunity for Canal+ and SFR/Neuf to engage in exclusive content distribution deals, yet this has been blocked through French anti-trust legislation.

Orange TV, France Telecom's TV brand, also offers DSL pay-TV services, similar to those of Free and SFR/Neuf. These services include specialized content packages, subscription video on demand (SVoD) and pay-per-view VoD. In 2008, Orange launched its TV services through satellite in order to expand its reach to customers who can't have access to an ADSL connection. This move, coupled with France Telecom's successful bid for the TV broadcast rights to some of France's League 1 soccer matches, further changes the TV industry in France. Through Orange TV, France Telecom will be in direct competition with CanalSat, which has had a monopoly on satellite services since merging with TPS in 2006, in addition to being in direct competition with Canal+ for sports rights.

Canal+

After its tough times in the late 1990s and massive restructuring during the early part of this century, the Canal+ brand has regained its status within French society. Not only known for cinema and soccer, it is again associated with cutting-edge material, alternative views, honest commentary and its willingness to cover controversial subjects. Today, the Canal+ group focuses on three main areas: content bundling, content distribution and film production.

Canal+'s programming is available through 20 specialized thematic channels, in addition to the Canal+ Le Bouquet, which is composed of six premium channels. Despite the Canal+ group having a subscriber base of over 10.5 million, one-third of French households still cannot receive the Canal+ Le Bouquet, as it is not available on the

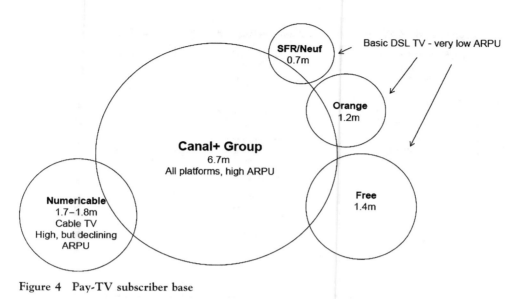

Figure 4   Pay-TV subscriber base

Source: McKinsey analyses based on data from Enders Analysis

analogue terrestrial network. This barrier will be eliminated with the switch to digital in 2011, when 100% of French households will be able to receive Canal+ Le Bouquet.

The importance of soccer broadcast rights

In early 2008 the rights to broadcast French soccer matches were up again for negotiation. The previous three-year deal was negotiated prior to the Canal+/TPS merger and cost Canal+ €600 million a year. Canal+'s management, was not prepared to pay €600 million a year again, and thus France Telecom was able to claim some of the premier broadcast rights. Together, Canal+ and France Telecom's Orange will pay €668 million a season for the rights to broadcast French soccer matches. France Telecom paid €203 million to get three of the 12 lots put up for tender by the French Professional Football League, and Canal+ claimed the remainder for €465 million. This gives Canal+ the right to broadcast all the games available on TV, however not all can be broadcasted live: out of the 10 premier league games, 1 is broadcast live on Canal+ (Sunday prime time), 8 are broadcasted live as pay per view (PPV) and 1, which is broadcasted live on Saturday prime time by Orange, is available on Canal+ PPV with a time delay.

Return to profitability

After the tough times of 2000–2002, revenues and operating income for the Canal+ Group are growing again, and its financial situation for 2007 looks solid. Revenues rose to €4 363 million, up 20.2% from 2006, and the Group's EBITA was €490 million, up 94%

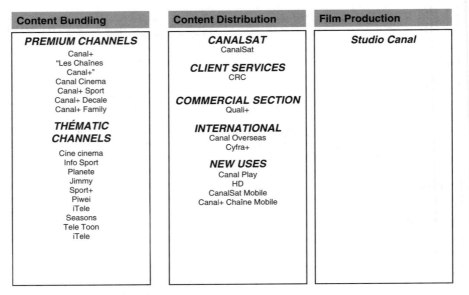

Figure 5 Main areas of Canal+

Source: Figure adapted from data from Canalplusgroup.com. Reproduced by permission

compared to 2006. Revenues benefited from the TPS acquisition, and growth in subscriptions and advertising revenues.

However, there is concern that the Canal+ Group won't meet the 2010 targets that Vivendi has set for the Group. Although Canal+ was able to attract 300 000 new subscribers (net) in 2007, there is speculation that this growth rate is too weak to

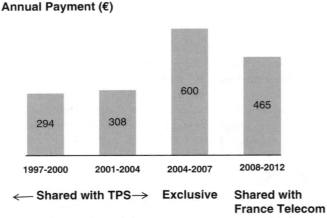

Figure 6 Canal+ payments for football rights

Source: McKinsey analyses based on press clippings

Winning bidder	Rights package
Canal+	Sunday primetime game, including the top 10 of the year
FT	Saturday primetime game
Canal+	All other games in live PPV
Canal+	Highlights magazines (Saturday, Sunday & Monday)
Canal+	Live Highlights for top four competition days
FT	On-demand highlights from Monday
FT	Mobile TV (all live games, except for the Sunday primetime game held by Canal+)

Figure 7   League 1 broadcasting rights 2008–2012

Source: Enders Analysis

meet the targets of having revenues above €5 billion (15% above 2007 results), and EBITA above €1 billion (more than double the 2007 result) by 2010.

Strategic Challenges

Although currently performing well, Canal+ must address several challenges in order to reach the 2010 targets set by Vivendi and remain profitable in the future.

Competitive threats: from TPS to Orange TV

Just as Canal+ incorporated its chief rival in the satellite business, France Telecom's Orange TV looks to be moving into the void left by the Canal+/TPS merger. In addition to launching a satellite service in France, Orange TV entered partnership agreements with satellite operators to provide television services in Spain and Poland. France Telecom also recently competed with Canal+ to acquire French Football League broadcasting rights, and won Saturday night games and VoD rights until 2012. It remains to be seen how serious a competitor France Telecom will become.

New platforms, new entrants, new technologies

Canal+ content bundles are available through satellite, DTT, IPTV, mobile-TV and VoD. But the industry value chain is changing such that some platform owners are negotiating content deals directly with content owners, as opposed to working with a content bundler such as Canal+. While Canal+ signed an agreement with several French movie

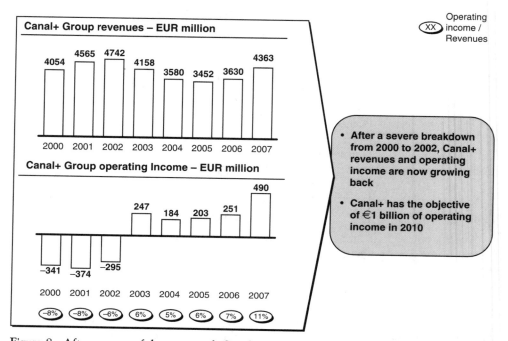

Figure 8   After a successful turnaround, Canal+ generates €490m of operating profit

Source: McKinsey analyses based on data from Canal+

organizations to enable them to show French and European movies via their VoD service, Free, an IPTV provider, has also struck a VoD deal. Free signed an agreement with Warner for the rights to distribute its catalogue via VoD. As telecoms companies encroach on Canal+'s core business of negotiating content and advertising deals, one wonders how well positioned it is to offer packages of superior quality to the Canal+ Le Bouquet.

Increasing the subscriber base

A growing subscriber base is crucial to Canal+'s bottom line. In order to negotiate attractive licensing agreements with content owners, it needs a critical mass of subscribers. Sports rights are an important factor in retaining subscribers, and it is estimated that one-third to one-half of subscribers would leave Canal+ if it were to stop broadcasting football.

Although Canal+ focuses on offering quality content to retain customers, its subscriber base is vulnerable to ISPs offering triple play bundles, FTA channels and other pay-TV channels. Over-the-top Internet TV platforms, such as YouTube or Joost, may also adversely affect their numbers in the future.

Diversifying

To remain competitive, Canal+ may have to further diversify. In an attempt to do so, it formed a new subsidiary, Canal+ Events. This division will be a sports marketing organization involved in both planning sports events and acquiring sports rights, broadcasting rights and club marketing rights.

The Group is also looking for new platforms for its content, and has recently signed an agreement with Sony Entertainment to enable its CanalPlay VoD service to be available through Sony's PlayStation games console.

Additionally, the Canal+ Group is considering investing more in its film production arm, StudioCanal. It recently announced its intention to acquire Kinowelt, a leading German group in film production. With Kinowelt, StudioCanal would be able to offer an all-media distribution network (theatres, video, audiovisual and VoD) for the United Kingdom, France and Germany.

$$* \quad * \quad *$$

Canal+ has so far been able to withstand the threats of the market entry of the digital platform operators as it had the 'early mover' advantage to create scale and thus offer more viewers to the content providers as well as build a strong brand. Will this suffice in the medium term, given that several of the new entrants have strong financial backing and can offer additional services such as telephony and broadband access? Should Canal+ itself become a (virtual) platform operator (provided the regulators approve it)? How far should it go in its diversification efforts in order not to fall into the same over-extension trap again as it did in early 2000? What can it do to strengthen one of its key assets, its loyal customer base?

EMI: Developing New Marketing Models for the Digital Age[1]

The year 2007 was a memorable one for the EMI Group. The music industry as a whole suffered yet another market decline. Although digital sales were strong in 2007, they have not yet compensated for the huge decrease in CD sales. Furthermore, in the midst of this industry-wide decline in sales, Guy Hand's private equity firm Terra Firma acquired the EMI Group.

EMI went through radical organizational changes since the acquisition, from layoffs throughout the company to the hiring of new management talent not only from inside but also from outside the music industry. But there were also some positive signs. In June 2008 Coldplay, one of EMI's signed artists, posted the highest weekly sales of any album in 2008. Much of this success is attributed to EMI's innovative marketing strategy with the Coldplay release. Caty Parry had huge success, also with her online community. In the last 3 months of 2008, 20 new artists were signed, both known and unknown. In light of these positive initial results, Morvan Boury, VP Strategy and Development at EMI France, has got his work cut out for him. Digital technology has the potential to drive new opportunities in artist and repertoire (A&R) and marketing, but how to capitalize on these digital investments is far from clear.

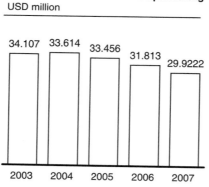

Music revenues recorded and publishing
USD million

34.107   33.614   33.456   31.813   29.9222

2003   2004   2005   2006   2007

Figure 1 Decreasing global music market

Source: McKinsey analyses based on data from IFPI

History of the EMI Group

The EMI Group was founded in 1897 as the Gramophone Company in the United Kingdom and Pathé Studios in France. It is now the third-biggest music group worldwide and it operates numerous labels and imprints across the world.

---

[1]This case is developed solely as the basis for class discussion. Cases are not intended to serve as endorsements, sources of primary data or illustrations of effective or ineffective management.

Company	Owner	Revenues EUR million**	EBITA margin Per cent	Labels
Universal Music	Vivendi	4.87	12.8	A&M, DefJam, Geffen, Interscope
Sony Music Entertainment	Sony	ca.3***	N/A	Columbia, Epic, Sony Classical, J.Records, RCA, Arista, Zomba
Warner Music	Bronfman consortium	3.39	13.9*	Atlantic, Electra, Rhino, Sire
EMI	Terra Fima	2.45**	86	Capitol, Virgin, Chrysalis

Figure 2   Major record labels, 2007

*before restructuring cost
**underlying group revenue
***before exceptional items
Source: McKinsey analyses based on data from Warner Music, EMI, eflux media, EMI, Vivendi

Early beginnings: innovative technology and international breadth

In 1887 Emile Berliner invented the gramophone method of recording and reproducing sounds using discs. Ten years later he established the Gramophone Company in London, and focused on bringing together the sound technology of the gramophone with contemporary musicians. He recognized early on that for his technology to gain popularity it was important that the music of contemporary artists be available in recorded format. The technology caught on, and by 1914 the Gramophone Company was selling nearly four million records a year.

The company obtained an international presence early on, and within a year of being formed operations were set up across Europe, and later were expanded to Russia and the Middle East as well as Australia, India, China and parts of Africa. By 1906, less than 10 years after starting up, over 60% of the company's revenues came from outside of the United Kingdom.

After the Great Depression of the 1930s, sales of records dropped by over 80%. In response to this massive decline the Gramophone Company and the Columbia Graphophone Company merged and became Electric and Musical Industries, or EMI.

Over the long history of this organization, it has focused on producing recordings from musicians worldwide, such as the Berlin Philharmonic and Vienna Philharmonic orchestras, classical artists like violinist Yehudi Menuhin and tenor Beniamino Gigli to rock and roll artists from America and the United Kingdom, such as Frank Sinatra, Nat

King Cole, Peggy Lee, Dean Martin, the Beatles, the Beach Boys, Pink Floyd, Queen and Norah Jones.

Keeping pace with new technologies

From the invention of the gramophone to establishing the world's first purpose-built recording studio complex in north London at 3 Abbey Road, to its role in developing magnetic tape used to record live performances, EMI has long been involved in fostering innovative technology within the recording industry.

A major technological development occurred in 1948 when vinyl 33 rpm LPs were released in the United States. Together with the new 45 rpm singles, these formats were cheaper, lighter, more durable and could hold much more music on each side than the older 78 records. The next major technology to change recorded music was the CD format, which came in 1983. By the 1990s CDs accounted for the majority of the albums sold by EMI. With each technological change, changes in strategy and business models have had to occur. By the late 1990s Internet and digital technologies were gaining momentum, and thus EMI had to look into ways of adapting its business to these changes.

Adapting to the Internet

The music industry was widely affected by Internet technology as early on as 1998. That year, the EMI Group utilized the Internet's powerful distribution capabilities to stream tracks from Massive Attack's album Mezzanine over the Internet. During the following year, which saw the rise of Napster and an explosion of online music file sharing, EMI launched David Bowie's *Hours* as the industry's first downloadable album.

During the first decade of this century, EMI has continued to keep pace with evolving digital, Internet and mobile technology. In response to the growing importance of digital music, and the importance of enabling consumers to copy and transfer digital music to CDs and portable devices, EMI Music released online 140 000 tracks from over 3 000 EMI artists, and by 2007 released its downloads in a digital rights management (DRM) free format. In response to the threat of digital piracy and the immense popularity of peer-to-peer (P2P) file sharing, EMI Music launched several initiatives in 2006. Although perhaps a bit late in its response, EMI was the first major music company to make its catalogue available to a legitimate P2P service. EMI Music signed agreements with ad-supported P2P service Qtrax, and with SNOCAP, a new venture by the creator of Napster. EMI also recognized the importance of Internet video and released Lenny Kravitz's video single *Dig In* in 2002, and responded to the popularity of user-generated video through signing an agreement with Google and YouTube to give fans access to EMI's music videos and recordings. With mobile technology, EMI entered into a ringtone deal with Nokia as early on as 2001, and by 2006 was trialling ad-supported mobile video with mobile carriers in the United States and the United Kingdom.

EMI has a long history in the music industry of recognizing quality talent and responding to changes in recording and distribution technology, but despite its investments in Internet and digital technologies, 2003–2007 has been a challenging time for EMI, and for the recorded music industry as a whole.

Situation in 2007

Industry dynamics

Since 2003, the digitization of music has significantly disrupted business models within the music industry and has vastly changed customers' music preferences. Digital sales account for around 15% of the total music market in 2007, compared with only 2% in 2004. Digital sales are split at roughly 50/50 between online sales and mobile sales. Furthermore, record company revenues from digital sales are estimated at US$2.9 billion in 2007, up 40% from $2.1 billion in 2004. Vast changes occurred in the digital music industry between 2003 and 2007.

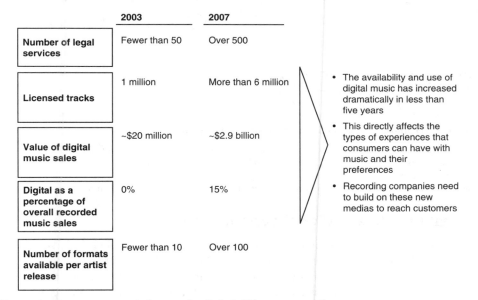

	2003	2007	
Number of legal services	Fewer than 50	Over 500	
Licensed tracks	1 million	More than 6 million	• The availability and use of digital music has increased dramatically in less than five years
Value of digital music sales	~$20 million	~$2.9 billion	• This directly affects the types of experiences that consumers can have with music and their preferences
Digital as a percentage of overall recorded music sales	0%	15%	• Recording companies need to build on these new medias to reach customers
Number of formats available per artist release	Fewer than 10	Over 100	

Figure 3   Reinventing an industry: the digital difference over 5 years

Source: McKinsey analysis based on data from IFPI Digital music report 2008

The music industry in 2007 showed both signs of progress and the presence of significant challenges in commercializing digital music. Although record companies' digital sales have experienced strong growth, they still have not offset the decline in CD sales. However, there were some exceptions, particularly in Asia and India. In Japan, the world's second-largest music market after the United States, digital sales have in fact offset the decline in CDs. Digital sales in India, China, Indonesia and South Korea have also outpaced the decline in CD sales.

Although the numbers indicate an industry in decline, there are differing opinions about the health of the industry. It is generally agreed that record companies are ailing, but music publishing, licensing, merchandising, live shows and digital-only music labels are performing well.

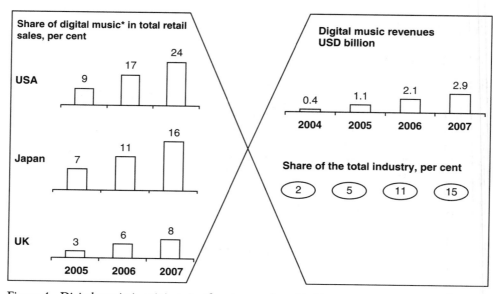

Figure 4   Digital music is gaining significant ground worldwide

*Digital music includes single-track downloads, album downloads, music video online downloads, streams, master recording ringtones, full-track audio download to mobile, ringback tunes, music video downloads to mobile and subscription income

Source: McKinsey analysis based on FPI recording industry sales report; IFPI Digital Music Report 2008

Digital threats and digital opportunities

There are those within the industry who view digital piracy and illegal file sharing as significant threats to their bottom line. The 'darknet'[2], a black market network where individuals can obtain and share illegal copies of digital content, will be difficult to destroy even through digital rights management (DRM) technology, lawsuits or greater Internet service provider (ISP) accountability. Curbing the negative effects of digital piracy may only occur when record labels learn to compete with the black market and offer free versions of their own digital content.

Yet the industry is starting to see the digital opportunities amongst the threats, and is realizing that digital can no longer be a separate branch of a record company, rather it must be an integral part of all products and services offered. There is momentum within the industry to turn the record business into a 'music entertainment business',[3] where a vast range of different and complementary products can be designed around an artist's release. Additionally, the industry is acknowledging the significant role that mobile technologies could play in the future of the music business. IFPI reports that in 2007 there was a

[2]See Biddle, P., England, P., Peinado, M. and Willman, B. (2002) The Darknet and the Future of Content Distribution. *Proceedings of ACM Workshop on Digital Rights Management*, http://crypto. stanford.edu/DRM2002/darknet5.doc. The authors, Microsoft Corp. employees, conclude that businesses selling and distributing digital content must compete with the 'darknet' on its terms.
[3]Thomas Hesse, President, Global Digital Business, SonyBMG Music Entertainment.

noticeable increase in sales of full rack downloads to mobile. The sales accounted for 12% of all digital sales in the first half of 2007, compared with 6% for the same period in 2006. There is also a move within the industry away from focusing on revenues from recorded music to developing alternative revenue streams such as live performances and merchandising. The BPI (the British Phonographic Industry), the body that represents British recorded music, disclosed in July 2008 that 11.4% of UK revenues for labels came from other revenue streams such as copyright licensing and merchandise.

EMI's performance in 2007

The EMI Group consists of EMI Music and EMI Music Publishing. EMI Music holds a catalogue of recordings of over three million individual tracks, and various record labels such as Blue Note, Capital, EMI, EMI Classics and Virgin supporting a wide range of artists. EMI Music Publishing acquires, protects and administers rights for music compositions, in addition to licensing them for films, commercials or other media.

The EMI Group's revenue for 2007 was £1 751.5 million, down from £2 079.9 million in 2006. EMI Music generated £1 350.2 million in revenue and an earnings before interest, taxes and amortization (EBITA) of £44.9 million. EMI Music Publishing performed better than EMI Music, with its revenues declining by less than 1% at constant currency to £401.3 million, and an EBITA of £105.6 million. However, the Group's digital revenues increased from £112.1 million to £162.2 million, representing 9.4% of total underlying revenue in the year.

During this difficult year for the EMI Group, it was acquired in August 2007 by Terra Firma, a private equity firm headed by Guy Hands. Since then, there have been some major changes at EMI.

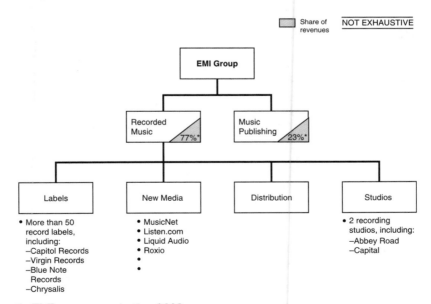

Figure 5   EMI group organization 2008

*2007 numbers
Source: McKinsey analysis based on data from EMI

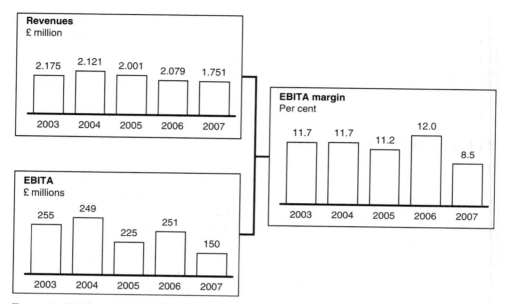

Figure 6   EMI group financials

Source: McKinsey analysis based on data from Bear Stearns; EMI

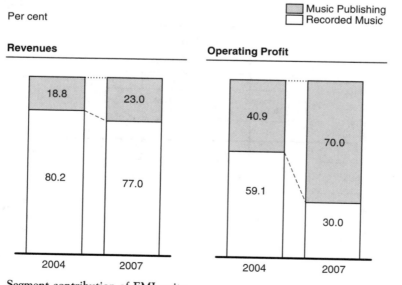

Figure 7   Segment contribution of EMI units

Source: McKinsey analysis based on data from EMI; UBS Warburg

Restructuring the EMI Group

Guy Hands introduced several controversial restructuring changes within the EMI Group. From the beginning, he faced many sceptics – artists and record executives alike – who had concerns that a private equity group could not understand how to run a creative business. At the same time there was also a group of strong supporters, both in- and outside the company who strongly believed radical change was needed.

Part of his restructuring plan for EMI was to cut as many as 2 000 jobs. Gone was the era at EMI of multi-million-dollar signing bonuses, and gone was the independence of the labels. Job cuts would, above all, take place in the administrative and support functions through centralization and increased effectiveness of functions such as marketing, production, distribution and back-office support. A&R was not to be affected, and in some cases was even strengthened. Hands also introduced dramatic changes at the senior management and board level. Managerial talent was acquired from outside the music industry, and involved several key players from the technology sector.

David Merrill was hired as President of Digital Business for EMI Music. He will be responsible for the company's digital strategy, innovation, business development, supply chain and global technology activities. Merrill, previously Google's chief information officer, was involved in several strategic efforts while there, including the company's 2004 IPO. Cory Ondrejka, a co-founder of Linden Labs, the company responsible for Second Life, was also hired by EMI. He will take the post of Senior Vice-President and will be responsible for digital strategy at EMI. Like Merrill, Ondrejka has never worked in the music industry.

Another industry outsider to enter into the management ranks at EMI is Elio Leoni-Sceti. He will join as CEO of EMI Music. Leoni-Sceti comes from Reckitt Benckiser, a consumer brand company, where he was Executive Vice-President, Europe, and was involved in successfully turning around businesses and building brands. Additionally, several board appointments were made to individuals from outside the music industry, such as Mike Clasper, who was appointed to the investor board. Clasper was formally the CEO of BAA, a leading airports group, and prior to that the President of Global Homecare at Procter & Gamble.

Also some key players from the industry were convinced to join the company, such as Nick Gatfield, who joined from Universal to become the head of Artist & Repetoire (A&R) North America and UK, and Billy Mann, who came from the independent music producers, to become the head of A&R international and global artist management.

In addition to senior management and the board, EMI Group was also restructured as a global functional matrix organization. The thought behind this matrix was to create agile A&R units which would be supported by centralized marketing, sales and production functions. These functions in their turn would not become more productive because of scale effects, but would be run more professionally. For example, the marketing function could be created around consumer segments rather than music genres, ensuring that each segment gets its preferred mix of genres. The appointment of functional managers with best practice knowledge from outside the industry was one important element to achieve these goals. The new organization was structured around the following divisions:

• Artists and Repertoires
• Marketing and Promotion
• Sales, Licensing and Synchronization

- Digital Development
- Catalogue and Archives
- Regions: North America, United Kingdom and Ireland, EMEA, Asia/Latin America/ Australia and NZ
- Global Support: Finance, Procurement and Logistics, HR

In addition to the reorganization a number of future revenue-generating sources were prioritized, which should become the focus points of the organization. Music labels were to be repositioned and partly pruned, so that their profile would become more clear and relevant to the consumer. A major effort was made to generate more digital revenues and increase revenues from unconventional sources, such as corporate sponsoring. The monetization of the huge archives of EMI, using the long tail effect from the Internet, was initiated and artist contracts were, wherever possible, revisited and redrawn so that EMI would not only share in the sales revenues of the tracks but also from the other revenue streams of the artists, such as concerts, merchandising and advertising, with the argument that the music company was instrumental in building the artists' brands.

Strategic Challenges

Amidst the restructuring of EMI and changes in senior management, the challenges facing Morvan Boury, VP Strategy and Development at EMI France, focus around understanding customers that buy digital music. Not only has digitization shifted the market for recorded music from CDs to mp3s, but also gone are the days when customers could be segmented by musical genre. Consumers of digital music have become more critical in what music they would like to listen to as they can pick individual tracks rather than being forced to have a whole album. They have also different expectations around pricing and how and when they want to have access to the music. In particular, their expectations about what music-related products should be free and which ones should be paid for are different from traditional customers of recorded music.

A major challenge is to increase the number of tracks sold. On a track-by-track basis, digital downloads are more profitable than CD tracks, in spite of the lower price, because of a much more favourable cost structure.

As consumers are not forced any more to buy whole albums, the numbers of tracks sold has dropped dramatically, leading to an absolute drop in margins. Successful stores such as iTunes are much better able than their competitors to cross-sell tracks and thus increase the number of tracks sold per person. EMI is looking at ways of providing its customers with better choice, availability and flexibility in enjoying digital music as well as incentives to increase the number of tracks sold.

Developing marketing as a core competence

Traditionally, marketing had a strong business-to-business (B2B) element in the music industry. There was one product, the CD, and marketing efforts were, above all, directed at the radio stations, as there was a clear correlation between the number of times a (reasonably good) song was played, its recognition and its sales. The other main parties

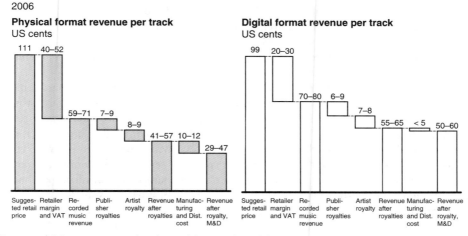

2006

Physical format revenue per track
US cents

Digital format revenue per track
US cents

Figure 8   **Margins per track, physical versus digital format**

Source: McKinsey analysis based on data from industry interviews; CSFB; Enders 2006

were the major retailers such as Wal-Mart in the states or FNAC and Virgin Music in Europe. There was relatively little interest in the actual consumer, their preferences and their habits, as the majors had no direct interaction with them and little opportunity to gather data. However, in the digital world the rules of the game changed fundamentally the moment the consumer suddenly had significant choice and influence.

One release, many products

Digital music has opened up the possibility of using one release from an artist in dozens of different products. Consumers can buy a download, a CD, wallpaper for their mobile phone, a mastertone, an e-ticket, a music video, become an artist's friend on a social network or sign up to a subscription service. Additionally, new agreements can be made such that greater revenues are shared with performers through the sales of merchandise, publishing, brand sponsorship and concerts. Consumers may, in fact, buy multiple products around a single release, as opposed to in the past where they might have just bought a single product, namely the CD.

Other initiatives being investigated are 'direct to consumer' schemes, where consumers have access to a range of artists' products directly via their websites. Artists' sites create a community environment where fans can connect with the artist and other fans, and purchase content.

Understanding the digital customer

Consumers have developed a very different perspective of the value they get and the prices they are willing to pay for music. They are increasingly unwilling to be patronized by the industry and want to determine their own music selection and way of consuming it. At the same time only 15% of consumers are really willing to go through the effort and undertake extensive searches to find their preferred music. There is also the expectation of receiving something for free. Schemes such as EMI's free download release of Coldplay's new single for a limited period and ad-supported services that allow customers to stream or download music for free are becoming the norm.

EMI is using both consumer market research and customer relationship management (CRM) techniques and technologies to enhance its understanding of different customer segments, and to build and manage profiles of its target customers. Several demand-based consumer segments are defined and their music tastes and buying habits analysed. Based on these profiles, and feedback from analytical tools, EMI is able to design marketing campaign techniques to reach highly targeted customer segments. Reaching customers may involve online voting campaigns, where fans are encouraged to download/purchase a track or album and can then identify which tracks should be released as singles or for radio play. It also may involve integrating feedback from direct-mail channels and using these to tailor campaigns through mobile channels such as SMS, WAP, Push and MMS.

Businesses as new digital customers

Engaging in relationships with businesses such as ISPs, mobile phone manufacturers and mobile phone operators as customers is also being explored by EMI. Unlimited access to EMI's digital catalogue is provided with Internet access through the French ISP Alice (Telecom Italia Group), the Sony Ericsson Walkman mobile phone comes loaded with a new album by Matt Pokora and Orange has launched a programme in France with EMI's music, such that it will provide an unlimited music download service for PCs and mobiles. In addition EMI is using its consumer knowledge and segmentation to start a dialogue with advertisers and generate advertising revenues based on a deep understanding of the music tastes of the target segments of the advertisers.

* * *

Morvan is faced with the challenge of transforming his company into a highly sophisticated marketing machine, which faces challenges that are much more complicated than those of even the most sophisticated consumer goods company. Given that marketing used to be a simple support function in the music industry and all attention was directed towards A&R, this means a fundamental change. Focus will be very important, as he cannot adapt everything at the same time. From all the strategic marketing opportunities, which should have the highest priority? Should he focus on short-term margin generation or building long-term relationships with his consumers/customers or can he do both at the same time? Where should he put the priorities in building up the marketing skills of his organization?

Telenet: Leveraging Digital Segmentation[1]

Duco Sickinghe, the CEO of Telenet, the leading Flemish cable company, was reflecting on the recent investor presentation and how analysts were likely to react to the continued strong results of the company by mid-year 2008.

Thanks to its heavy investments in 'multiplay' offerings (combinations of TV, telephone, broadband Internet as well as, recently, mobile), it could report a revenue growth of, on average, 25% per year over the last five years and an average EBITDA growth of 40%. Consequently, EBITDA margin had grown from 22% in 2002 to an expected 48% margin by 2008. This is significantly higher than the margins of its major competitor, the national telecoms incumbent Belgacom, as well as the industry average of European telecoms operators of 33%.

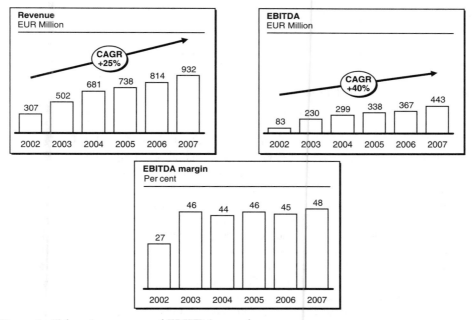

Figure 1   Telenet's revenue and EBITDA growth

Source: McKinsey analyses based on Telenet data

The growth was fuelled by the fast adoption of digital products. In December 2004, 293 000 of Telenet's 1.6 million cable TV subscribers had also subscribed to telephony (24% of all households covered by the Telenet network, or footprint), 506 000 for broadband Internet (40% of its footprint) but only a few digital TV subscribers. Three years later, in 2007, Telenet had 548 000 subscribers for telephony and 883 000 for broadband Internet, and digital

---

[1]This case is developed solely as the basis for class discussion. Cases are not intended to serve as endorsements, sources of primary data or illustrations of effective or ineffective management.

television subscribers were close to the 400 000 mark. Further, Telenet had launched a mobile product in 2006 that is used by about 70 000 customers.

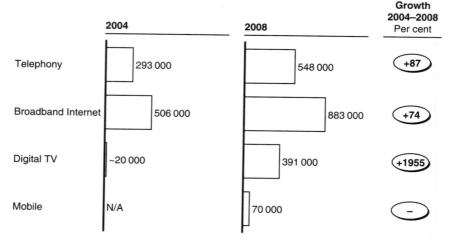

Figure 2   Telenet fast product adoption

Source: McKinsey analysis based on data from Telenet

Notably, Telenet kept and even increased its leadership position, ahead of Belgacom, with about a 67% share in its footprint for its flagship digital product, broadband. Furthermore, the shift to digital television gained momentum, with paying video-on-demand transactions nearly doubling in one year with 50% of digital video-on-demand users generating up to seven to eight transactions a month.

The fast growth of the broadband also meant that key natural consumer segments of Telenet (families with children, and young people) were reaching saturation. Tapping into other segments like the older generation would be more difficult as the old generation has more affinity with the telecoms incumbent. Furthermore, Belgacom had started to push its own IPTV offering, challenging Telenet on its core product with a very aggressive pricing scheme (€1 per month for the basic package).

Duco Sickinghe was, however, not ready to give in and offer large discounts. After all, his digital products offered good quality, a good set of fast broadband products (mid-tier 10 Mbps downstream, up to 20 Mbps for Turbo Net), while telephony products were already priced below the incumbent telecoms operator.

Looking at the marketing four *p*'s (price, product, placement and promotion), Duco decided that his company must leverage the last two *p*'s more aggressively and work out much more sophisticated segmentation strategies. Duco was obviously eager to leverage its large online customer base as a great distribution channel and interactive communication tool for Telenet. He was also encouraged by a few interesting insights gathered in his company. First, online sales were building up nicely, while micro-marketing campaigns by e-mail were returning conversion rates of close to 10% of the target population, a significant success indeed.

Per cent

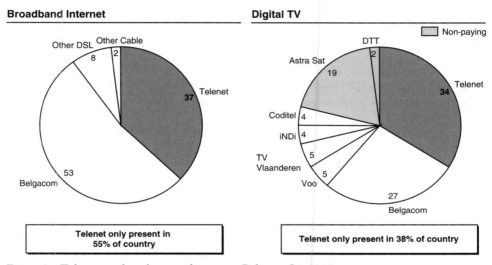

Figure 3   Telenet market share performance, Belgium Q4 2007

Source: McKinsey analyses based on data from ISPA; Telenet

Company History

Telenet is the leading provider of cable television and broadband Internet and the number-two provider of fixed-line telephony services in Flanders, the Dutch-speaking part of Belgium. It also offers mobile telephony, but its market share is still low, as it entered the market as late as mid-2006. The company was founded in 1996 with the purpose of delivering telephony and, later, Internet services to residential subscribers in Flanders through a proprietary fibre backbone network.

Its original shareholders were a mix of public and private institutions:

1. the 'mixed intercommunales' (MICs): utility companies that are owned by both municipalities and Electrabel, the former operator of the MICs' cable systems
2. six 'pure intercommunales' (PICs): utility companies wholly owned by municipalities, that hold their interest in Telenet through a jointly owned company, Interkabel Vlaanderen CVBA
3. GIMV NV: a publicly listed company that is majority-owned by the Flemish Government
4. the Financial Consortium: a consortium of regional financial institutions
5. US West International Holdings, Inc. (later re-named MediaOne International Holdings Inc.): a division of US telephone operator US WEST Inc.

In 1997 the construction of the fibre backbone was completed and Telenet was granted access to the 'local loop' coaxial networks of the MICs and PICs to have direct access to homes. In January 1998 Telenet began providing Internet and telephony services to the public. By the end of 2001 the company already generated €178 million through telephone and Internet access. The agreements with the MICs and PICs also provided for an upgrade of the local loops to a hybrid fibre coaxial (HFC) standard with bidirectional digital transmission capabilities. The upgrade started in 1996 and was completed in June 2002. The network capacity was increased to 450 MHz, which provided Telenet with 48 usable downstream channels. The infrastructure investment was financed by the MICs and PICs; however, Telenet has to repay them through a variety of different financial arrangements in the years after.

In 2001 Callahan Associates International LLC (later Cable Partners Europe LLC), a company founded in 1996 by Richard J. Callahan, a previous president of the US West International and Business Development Group, led a consortium of investors (the 'Cable Partners Consortium') which acquired a controlling interest in the Telenet group, through a subsidiary.

In the first half of 2002, Telenet entered stormy waters following the collapse of the stock market. Direct and indirect sources of capital were quickly exhausted. Through an aggressive programme of cost-cutting, operational improvements, price increases and financial restructuring, the company managed to stay afloat.

In August 2002 the Telenet group made its next major strategic move. It acquired the cable television business of the MICs. In return, the MICs' financial interest in the group increased significantly, taking 33.5% of the shares, while the Cable Partners Consortium owned 21.8%, the GIMV 15.2%, the Financial Consortium 15.2%, Interkabel 9.3% and Electrabel 4.9%. Telenet went public and got listed on Euronext. This led to a significant change in ownership. The largest cable company outside of the US, Liberty Global, bought the shares of Cable Partners, which had gotten into financial trouble, and continues to buy the shares of the other shareholders. Currently, the mix of shareholders has significantly changed, with Liberty Global owning 52%, while slightly more than 40% of the shares are publicly traded. Recently, Telenet acquired the cable business of the PICs in order to be able to deliver a cohesive full play also in the PICs region, including television.

In recent years, the company has shown a very positive financial development, with revenues increasing from €90 million in 2000 to around €930 million by the end of 2007. EBITDA went from minus €64.4 million in 2000 to above €440 million by the end of 2007. The company went cash-flow positive in the first half of 2003, and yearly free cash grew from €25 million by 2005 to €177 million by 2007.

Current Situation and Market Position

Telenet has developed a position in both the residential and business markets. Similarly to many other cable companies, its focus is, however, on the residential market, where it holds a very strong position in all three product segments where it is active and which make up more than 90% of its profit. It also introduced mobile telephony in recent years, and it's currently testing other mobile extension.

Cable television

Satellite and terrestrial broadcasting plays almost no role in the Belgian TV landscape. Almost 90% of households in Flanders are using a cable network – the largest penetration in Europe, compared to 80% in Holland, and less than 20% in both the United Kingdom and France.

Today, Telenet is concentrating on shifting its television customers towards digital and interactive television. The major difference between analogue and digital offering is the number of channels offered in the 'basic package', as well as the availability of on-demand services. Currently, the cable network analogue basic package broadcasts 27 analogue channels (as well as 14 radio channels) to all subscribers; 15 television channels of these are so-called 'must carry' channels, which Telenet is required to carry at no charge. Telenet's digital basic package offers 51 digital TV channels, as well as 33 radio channels. The price of the digital package is €1 per month less than for the analogue package as an incentive to migrate users to digital. Telenet used to have a contract with Canal+, a pay-TV provider that provided it with the exclusive use of nine 8 MHz television channels. Telenet acquired Canal+ in late 2003, integrated it and repackaged the premium TV offering under the PRIME brand name. For video on demand, Telenet has contracts with five of the top seven Hollywood majors, plus local producers such as Studio 100, a leading independent television series producer in Flanders. Digital TV users also have access to programmes they missed for one week after the broadcasting of top channels (among others, VRT's Net with Ooit Gemist, VMMA's Iwatch, SBS C-more and MTV's re:play). Finally, its interactive television platform hosts 23 innovative services. Telenet is an especially large innovator in hybrid TV/PC offerings (movies on PC, PC-TV offering, HD video sharing on its user-generated content website, Garage TV, and photo-sharing applications on the TV screen).

Compared to the IPTV offering from Belgacom, Telenet's basic package is €3 per month more expensive; however, there is no requirement to bundle the service with a fixed telephony line – furthermore, on-demand recording is free only on Telenet. The thematic pack on Belgacom TV is significantly more costly than Telenet (€14.95 versus between €5.95 to €9.95 per month on Telenet). Both Belgacom and Telenet have started offering HD channels.

Residential broadband Internet

Telenet offers high-speed broadband Internet services throughout Flanders. Currently, the company leads the residential broadband market in Flanders with a strong brand reputation. In independent market research, the standard products of Telenet (Standard Pack and Express Net) are both mentioned as a best in test and the best buy. Monthly data volumes are, however, posing challenges as average monthly downstream volume increased by 75% between 2006 and 2007, mostly owing to changing habits in consumers' Internet use (from text, to graphics, to now video).

On top of broadband Internet access, Telenet has been successfully launching a set of online media services. The Telenet portal, dubbed Zita, is the number-two portal in Flanders with 3.3 million unique visitors a month. Garage TV is the first Belgian video-sharing site, with over 70 million videos viewed since its launch. 9lives is a leading game community in Flanders.

	Telenet Digital TV	BelgacomTV
• Price basic channels (EUR, incl. 12% VAT)	12.7	9.95
• Access line (telephony) required?	No	Yes
• Set-top box rental (EUR per month)	4–8	6
• Flexview (easy recording)	Free	1.95
• Basic channels (Number)	51	60
• Sports pack (EUR per pack)*	14.95	19.95
• Film pack (EUR per pack)*	19.95	N/A
• Thematic pack (EUR per pack)	5.95–9.95	14.95
• HD channels (Number)	4	7

Figure 4 Digital TV product comparison in Belgium*

*Telenet offers combined film and sports pack for €26.95

Source: McKinsey analysis based on data from Telenet; Belgacom

zita.	• Number-2 portal in Flanders • 3.5 million unique visitors per month • Widget concept enables surfers to put any content they want
GARAGE TV	• First Belgian video sharing site • 1 million unique visitors per month • Over 70 million videos viewed since launch
9lives	• Lead games community • 0.4 million unique visitors per month • Online gaming TV launched in 2008

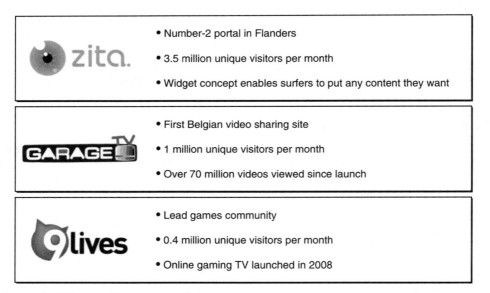

Figure 5 Telenet online service offering

Source: McKinsey analysis based on data from Telenet. Reproduced with permission

Residential telephony

Early in 2004 Telenet had already achieved a market share of 13%; by mid-2008 this had nearly doubled. Recently, residential telephony subscribers of Telenet have also been able to order additional services, such as voicemail or caller ID. The main costs Telenet incurs in its telephony business are interconnection fees (fees it has to pay to other telephony companies when the call ends in their networks). These costs are still relatively high, given that Telenet has less than one-third of the market and has thus to pay the interconnection fee for two-thirds of the calls. Another challenge Telenet faces is that the amount of payable minutes per telephony subscriber is declining.

Telenet recently launched a voice mobile offering, where customers only pay for usage if they subscribe to other Telenet telecoms products (outside analogue television). The service started in the fourth quarter of 2006. In the first quarter of 2008 it has 67 000 mobile paying users, or about 8% of its telecoms base. In parallel, Telenet invested in Wi-Fi technology and is today the leader in terms of rolled-out Wi-Fi hotspots in the country: while usage on those hotspots did take time to develop, the tipping point of usage was 2007, and numbers of session and total hours of usage have nearly doubled in one year.

Multiplay

From a consumer perspective, 33% of customers were enjoying multiple services by the first quarter of 2006 to reach 43% two years later; moreover, 12% were taking the holy grail of 'triple play' (broadband Internet, television and fixed telephony) by 2006. This proportion has increased to be above 21% by the first quarter of 2008.

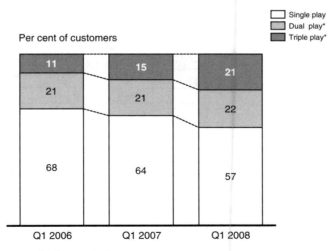

Figure 6   Telenet multiplay evolution

*Triple play is defined as TV, Internet and telephony. Dual play is defined as any two of the three products
Source: McKinsey analysis based on data from Telenet

Telenet cost of customer acquisition declined over time, as it shifted towards the most cost-efficient and controllable channels, such as online acquisition channels (standing for 12% of sales). Recently, Telenet pushed its online services, with online customer care being successfully personalized with the 'My Telenet' application (take-up was roughly 55% of total contracts) and online basic support being offered to customers (30% take-up). Telenet also launched a customer advisory portal, as well as kiosk booths in some major retailers in Flanders.

Strategic Challenges

Telenet is confident about its future. Cash flow is improving continually, as are most operational indicators. With the new acquisitions, the company has a robust product and service portfolio, enabling it to compete with its main competitor, Belgacom.

The real question for Duco Sickinghe is how the company can continue to grow its customer base in the advent of two major phenomena. First, the trend of customers deciding very quickly which product to buy once they decide to move to quadruple products (65% decide in less than one month; for online users the proportion is going up to 75%). Second, there is an increasing complexity in customers touch-points. In particular, online retailers are not substituting offline retailers but rather complementing them (of those who search for products online, 60% will still buy those products offline in stores).

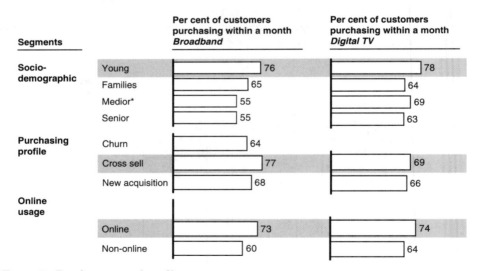

Figure 7 **Purchasing speed profiles**

*Medior are people above 50 who are still working but where the children have left home.
Source: McKinsey analyses based on data from Telenet broadband users consumer survey

In thinking through his options, Duco realizes how strong his broadband base is. Also more and more customers decide with help from online services which subscription services to choose. He bases himself on a set of analyses and market research received from his staff:

1. Close to 40% of its customers have used online one way or the other (search, Telenet website, third-party comparison sites, etc.) to buy products.

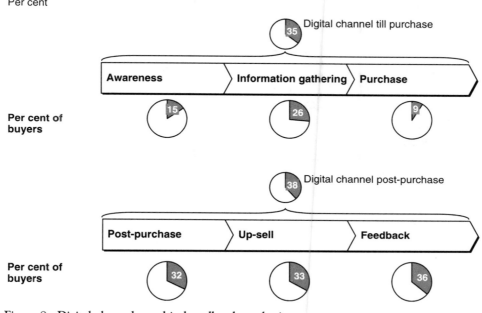

Figure 8 Digital channels used in broadband purchasing

Source: McKinsey analysis

2. Only 10% of customers have *bought* online.
3. Telenet has limited affiliated marketing and search-engine optimization programs.
4. The cost of running micro-campaigns online is three to eight times lower than offline; this is especially true with outbound calls.
5. Telenet is still spending more than 50% of its marketing budget on broadcast (TV and radio), while brand awareness is already well established for its product, especially broadband Internet.
6. Customers use as many as seven touch-points *before* they buy a product.
7. Online usage information collected from its own services (games, Garage TV, ISP surfing, etc.) provides a rich database.
8. Word of mouth is critical – affecting 17% of Telenet sales. Telenet has the benefit of being able to interact with its customer base online, and has drawn up a list of 10% of its current customers as major social brand influencers within their social networks.

Overall, Duco wants to reinforce the company's 'go to market' power, leveraging online to further refine segmentation against its major competitor, Belgacom.

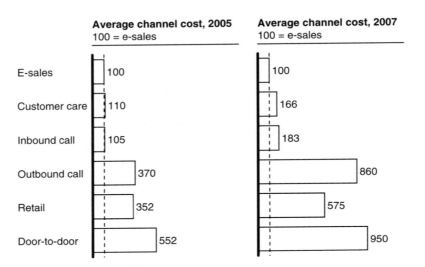

Figure 9   Sales cost per channel

Source: McKinsey analyses based on data from Telenet

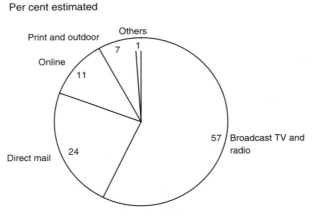

Figure 10   Telenet communication spend mix, 2007

Note: Spend includes media costs, production costs, other costs and taxes, Surcom and fees
Source: McKinsey analyses based on data from Telenet

Per cent usage

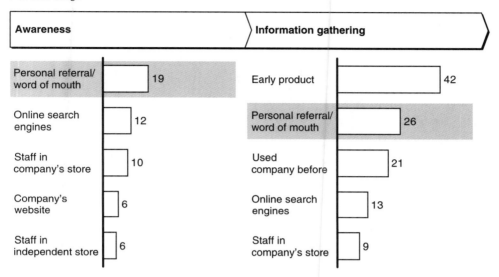

Figure 11   Top 5 touch-points influencing sales*

*Origin of touch-points for a sale, average for eight industries including media and telecoms
Source: McKinsey analyses based on data from Digital Marketing Survey, Belgium

END-TO-END SUPPLY CHAIN MANAGEMENT

Effective supply chain management has become increasingly important in media, not only to save costs but also as a way to manage new complexity arising from digitization and the increasing number of format productions and distribution channels. While media companies have started addressing their operational effectiveness issues, they typically lag behind other industries, and are in general late adopters of technology despite the rapid evolution of electronic media and the need to transition to digital workflows and platforms. This chapter discusses how media companies can best achieve operational excellence in supply chain management. Questions specifically discussed are:

1. *What is supply chain management in media? How important is it?*
2. *How can operational effectiveness in supply chain management be improved:*
   - *in standardized processes?*
   - *in project-based processes?*
3. *When should media companies in- or outsource their supply chain activities?*
4. *How can media companies effectively manage the transition to digital platforms?*

Achieving Operational Excellence in Supply Chain Management

Supply chain management is the end-to-end optimization of production, editing and distribution processes, including the selection and integration of suppliers, manufacturers, warehouses, distributors and retail channels. An efficient and effective supply chain ensures the production and distribution of the right quantities at minimal cost and optimized service levels. Superior skills at managing the chain can be a true competitive advantage for media companies.

One major benefit is cost reduction. The media industry is still characterized by a high degree of vertical integration – an array of production and printing facilities, together

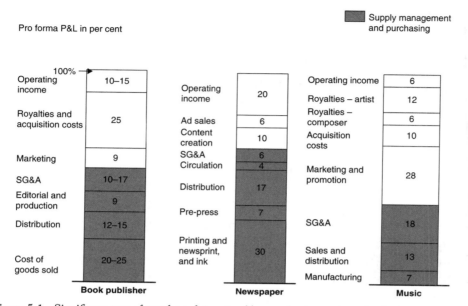

Figure 5.1 Significant part of cost base determined by purchasing and supply chain management decisions

Source: McKinsey analysis

with distribution networks, are still owned by major media companies. As a result a high proportion of the cost structure is directly related to the supply chain. Media sectors, such as book publishing, music or newspapers, can have up to 65% of their total costs linked to the supply chain (Figure 5.1). The proportion can be as high for television companies integrating into own production and technical facilities (like most of public television in Europe), but is usually lower for free-to-air television, which tends to purchase a lot of its programming. In this case, one major cost lever is the optimizing of the purchasing process.

Effective supply chain management can also make a major difference on the service quality as well as on the revenue side. With digitization, media consumers are shifting their habit to 'always on, everywhere' delivery, and are expecting, for example, constant updates in time-critical media items, such as news, etc. Facilitating a multiformat as well as continuous (versus batch-mode) supply of news will guarantee superior quality of services from the newsroom.

Today, media sectors have yet to move to a mode of continuous performance improvement, as already prevalent in other industries, such as steel, automotive and chip industries, which have been under an ongoing pressure to reduce costs over the past decades. As a result there are often still 'cost reserves' in media companies. Experience has shown that media companies which aggressively optimize their supply chain often achieve lasting cost reductions in the order of 10% of the total cost base. 'Turbo-charging' the redesign of the supply chain through digitization often can double the savings if the company is prepared to abandon its traditional practices, as such product-oriented silos in the organization, limitations on distribution channels and release windows and few IT facilitated processes.

Many leading companies in other industries have successfully adopted systematic approaches, such as lean production and six sigma, to codify and reinforce execution excellence. The key question is whether methods applied in these industries can be applied to the media industry.

The first step should be to increase the efficiency and effectiveness of *standardized* processes. This can include streamlining internal production processes, optimizing distribution, implementing shared services and outsourcing certain parts of the business. The *non-standardized* processes are much more difficult to optimize, as the output metrics are not clearly defined but their strategic relevance is often very high. However, as claimed below, these creative processes, such as TV production and editorial work, hold major potential for continual improvements if handled in the right way.

Enhancing the Effectiveness of Standardized Media Supply Chain Processes

The powerful levers that can be used to enhance standardized processes within a media company can be divided into five areas: improving production process efficiency, improving distribution efficiency, optimizing purchasing, implementing shared services and enhancing efficiency through outsourcing or offshoring. Each of them is discussed below.

Production process efficiency

Repetitive standardized operational processes – such as CD manufacturing, printing or internal product flows – are usually the first areas to review when attempting to enhance the efficiency of a company (Figure 5.2). These processes can easily be benchmarked and improved without major investment requirements, and will deliver immediate results. The governing ideas behind achieving excellence in executing both standardized and non-standardized processes are to avoid waste (e.g. waiting times for talent on the set, minimizing book returns from the stores as well as stock-outs), to minimize inflexibility (e.g. inability to offer the most up-to-date news items) and to reduce variability (e.g. unpredictable peak demand for production capacity) (Figure 5.3).

The process to continually generate these measures can be systematized, for example with lean production or six-sigma principles. Many ideas from the classic lean manufacturing concept can be transferred to the media industry (Figure 5.4). This may include just-in-time production, awareness-building, quality assurance or load smoothing.

In general, improving production efficiency is a 'no regret' move for media companies as savings can be significant. For instance, reducing downtime and increasing throughput speed has improved overall productivity for one company's printing process by 115%. Another company has managed to reduce the waste in its printing process by almost 15% (Figure 5.5).

Although the benefits seem obvious, the key hurdle media companies have to struggle with is the company culture. Not only is operational excellence often not high on the

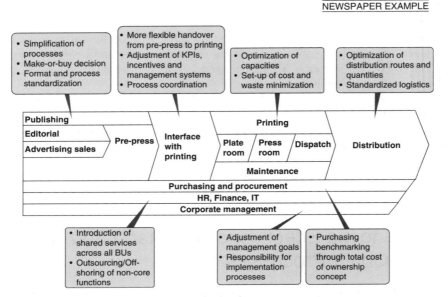

- Simplification of processes
- Make-or-buy decision
- Format and process standardization

- More flexible handover from pre-press to printing
- Adjustment of KPIs, incentives and management systems
- Process coordination

- Optimization of capacities
- Set-up of cost and waste minimization

- Optimization of distribution routes and quantities
- Standardized logistics

Publishing			Printing				
Editorial	Pre-press	Interface with printing	Plate room	Press room	Dispatch	Distribution	
Advertising sales							

Maintenance

Purchasing and procurement

HR, Finance, IT

Corporate management

- Introduction of shared services across all BUs
- Outsourcing/Off-shoring of non-core functions

- Adjustment of management goals
- Responsibility for implementation processes

- Purchasing benchmarking through total cost of ownership concept

Figure 5.2   Sample levers to optimize standardized processes

Source: McKinsey analyses

- Overproduction – e.g. too many stories written
- Waiting – e.g. press room waiting for plates
- Transporting – e.g. double handling of insertions
- Overprocessing – e.g. rework of stories
- Inventory – e.g. paper, stories 'in reserve'
- Motions – e.g. walking around editorial floors
- Defects – e.g. scrap copies
- Unused skills – e.g. experienced supervisor working as operator

Waste

Variability   Inflexibility

- Inability to react to change in customer demand – e.g. late-breaking news, sports results
- Non-flexible working practice – e.g. attitudes of journalists, established norms in press halls, union agreements

- Input variability – e.g. newsprint quality
- Process variability – e.g. breakdowns, manual work in page setting that could be automated
- Demand variability – e.g. demands from editor

Figure 5.3   Factors inhibiting operational performance

Source: McKinsey analyses

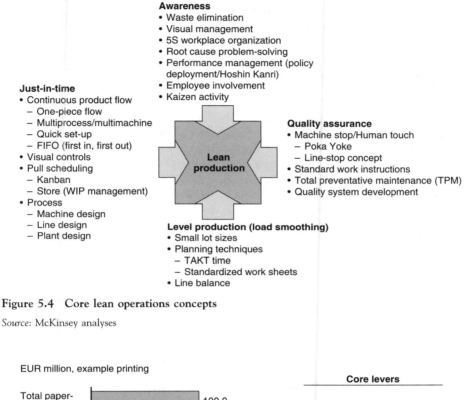

Awareness
- Waste elimination
- Visual management
- 5S workplace organization
- Root cause problem-solving
- Performance management (policy deployment/Hoshin Kanri)
- Employee involvement
- Kaizen activity

Just-in-time
- Continuous product flow
  - One-piece flow
  - Multiprocess/multimachine
  - Quick set-up
  - FIFO (first in, first out)
- Visual controls
- Pull scheduling
  - Kanban
  - Store (WIP management)
- Process
  - Machine design
  - Line design
  - Plant design

Lean production

Quality assurance
- Machine stop/Human touch
  - Poka Yoke
  - Line-stop concept
- Standard work instructions
- Total preventative maintenance (TPM)
- Quality system development

Level production (load smoothing)
- Small lot sizes
- Planning techniques
  - TAKT time
  - Standardized work sheets
- Line balance

Figure 5.4   Core lean operations concepts

Source: McKinsey analyses

EUR million, example printing

Core levers

Total paper-related costs	100.0
Administration, storage	1.6
Total paper costs	98.4
Excess orders	0.8 — Reduction by 50%
Overproduction	1.6 — Reduction by 25%
Waste	6.5 — Reduction by 10–15%
Profits from recycled paper	0.8 — Increase by 100%
Change of paper type	1.6 — 60% of profit margin
New paper-related costs	87.0

- Application of internal best practice
- Determination of number of overproduced newspapers
- Upgrade of counters on printing press
- Joint team of printing and newspaper personnel
- Adjustment of incentives
- Application of best practice between printing units (e.g. soft start-up of machinery)
- Renegotiation of contracts
- Bypassing of dealers by directly approaching customers
- Change of all volumes to paper type 42
- Printing of four additional pages*
- Others

Figure 5.5   Waste can be reduced significantly

*To compensate for thinner-looking newspaper
Source: McKinsey analyses

management agenda, but also in most media sectors, especially print, management has to cope with very strong and often inflexible unions. Changing this deadlock, for example by bringing in expertise from outside the industry, will be the major challenge.

Distribution efficiency

Addressing operational improvements should not be solely focused on opportunities to reduce costs, but also on streamlining the supply chain to enlarge and improve sources of revenues. The volatility in demand often results in stock-outs of newspapers, CDs or other goods. In the media industry especially, stock-outs represent a high opportunity cost, as most of the costs are upfront investments in content creation. Assuming a contribution margin of around 70%, an average stock-out rate of 20% would result in lost contribution of close to 15%. Therefore, it is worthwhile for all media companies to spend the time and money on optimizing the match of supply and demand for products across all areas of coverage. This can be done by reducing uncertainty through the development of tools to better predict demand (Figure 5.6). For example, sales of the soundtrack from a popular film are likely to increase each time the film is shown on TV. In book publishing, editor forecasts can be systematically synthesized and demand curves that are based on historical sales patterns can be leveraged to calculate optimal order quantities.

BOOK INDUSTRY EXAMPLE

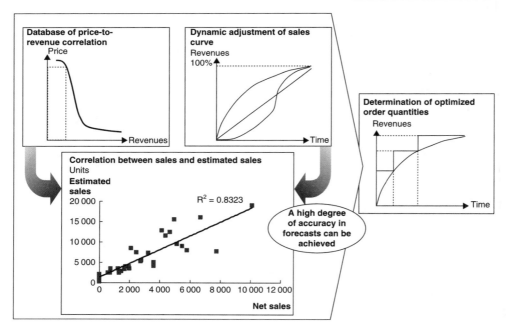

Figure 5.6 Order quantities can be optimized with help from systematic forecast tools

Source: McKinsey analyses

Optimizing the supply chain for revenues can be very effective. For example, one European magazine publisher was able to enhance sales by around 1.5% by reducing kiosk stock-outs. Of course, cost efficiency can also be enhanced in distribution. One newspaper company was able to reduce distribution costs by 12% simply by optimizing the delivery route.

The major hurdle against implementing best practices in distribution is not so much cultural but most often skills-based. Optimizing distribution requires a deep understanding of logistical algorithms and statistical forecasting techniques. Although some media companies are already very sophisticated in this field, most are still relying on experience-based rule-of-thumb approaches. Bringing in and developing high-level logistic skills will become increasingly important, as the number of products, product formats and distribution channels continues to increase.

Purchasing effectiveness

Experience shows that the total cost of purchased goods (both direct, e.g. magazine paper, as well as indirect, e.g. travel) can be decreased by as much as 10% to 15% by applying best practices from other industries. The most effective measures in purchasing create a win–win situation for the supplier and the purchasing company, for example fine-tuning and standardizing *specifications* (e.g. choosing the optimal trim, weight and grade for coated and newsprint paper) helped publishing companies save an average of 10% of annual paper costs.

As with distribution, the major hurdle media companies face in this area seems again to be skills-based. The ability to develop sophisticated pricing formulas for commodity products, such as paper, with variable input costs, such as for pulp, will become increasingly important.

Also, institutionalizing better purchasing practices across the organization requires strong IT support, using enterprise resource planning (ERP) or procurement packages.

In general, current purchasing processes in media do not match standard practices in other industries. A classic example is the broadcasting industry, where a loose purchasing process can inflate costs, and lead to poor performing programmes. Many Wild West stories can be told on how 'output' deals (deals where a TV broadcaster buys the output of a studio for the coming years) have been negotiated late at night in a hotel room without clear consideration of the schedule and TV grid economics. In practice, we still find pain points such as limited respect of purchasing rules, non-transparent selection of ideas and formats, etc. When evaluating the ideas, ROI (return on investment) evaluation metrics are still not a pervasive practice, especially those ROI metrics that take into account the full 360° potential of formats (Figures 5.7 and 5.8).

Shared services

Media companies are usually hesitant about centralizing internal services, even for administrative functions such as IT or human resources (HR), as they don't want to interfere with their profit centres. Going even beyond administrative functions, it is also possible for media companies to centralize operational functions that will benefit from

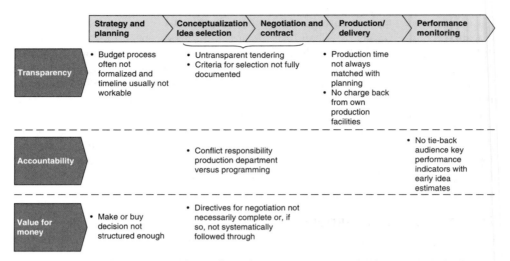

Figure 5.7 Typical pain points observed in television programme purchasing example

Source: McKinsey analyses

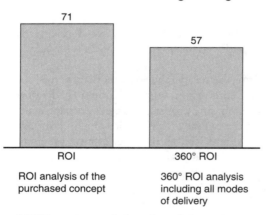

Figure 5.8 Sophisticated ROI metrics are being adopted, but not yet pervasive

Source: McKinsey analyses

economies of scale and substantially increased utilization. Bertelsmann, among others, has developed a shared printing service via Arvato for all of its relevant affiliated companies. The same concept can also be applied to studio production, warehousing, distribution and call centres. Media companies have usually achieved up to a 20% saving by establishing shared operational services; however, they usually encountered stiff organizational resistance along the way.

The key challenge in shared services – especially non-standardized operational functions – is to develop in parallel efficient interaction rules (e.g. transfer price systems and priority rules) to ensure that cooperation is devoted to improving performance.

In many cases, establishing a shared services centre can have ancillary benefits. A company can approach the open market with a well-provided service, generating additional revenues. The Burda Group, for example, has built up a very attractive direct-marketing business in just a few years, starting with its subscriber service, and is also very active in offering other so-called 'back-office activities' as commercial services to third parties.

While, traditionally, shared services have been infrastructure-based, the market for supporting business functions of the media industry (e.g. studio production, editing, printing and distribution) can develop. For example, NOB – the formerly Dutch-owned TV production studio – has spun off from the Dutch public broadcaster, NOS, to offer its studio services to the private sector.

Again, as with production optimization, the major challenges media companies face with centralizing their services are cultural. Media subsidiaries tend to be fiercely independent and are likely to fight hard to keep their own services. Finding the right balance will take a sure instinct and depend on the prevailing company culture; however, experience has shown that a more centralized approach can yield significant benefits, once properly implemented.

Outsourcing and offshoring

Besides branching out to become a business on its own, shared services can also be part of the outsourcing of entire or parts of administrative and business functions.

To date, media companies have been hesitant about outsourcing significant parts of their businesses. In the German market, for example, commercial broadcasters such as ProSiebenSat1 own significant TV production facilities. The same holds true in publishing, where printing facilities are consolidated in-house, as in the example of Bertelsmann with Arvato. Media companies have many good reasons for not outsourcing their entire business activities. First of all, in a market with high volatility, there are advantages to having production in close proximity to the media facilities to have access to capacity in case of a sudden uptake. Also owning all assets enables a media company to react very quickly to challenges from competitors. Burda, for example, launched a new magazine within two days to counteract the launch of a competitor's magazine in its core business. This was possible only because Burda had direct access to its own printing facilities and was thus able to shift priorities accordingly.

Furthermore, media companies are concerned that outsourced activities end up with direct competitors.

If properly structured, however, outsourcing can substantially reduce the capital employed and at the same time deliver comparable or better services at a lower cost. In any case, management should always consider outsourcing as a credible fallback option to ensure that internal production and administrative functions are benchmarked and operate efficiently.

Furthermore, in general, efficient outsourcing can be recommended when a liquid market of independent suppliers for the service prevails, especially in the case of over-capacity. Owing to the large and liquid market for IT services that has been established in recent years, many industries have found the outsourcing of IT operations to be a good option. For example, Deutsche Bank and J. P. Morgan have major long-term IT outsourcing deals. However, most media companies (e.g. Bertelsmann and Liberty Global) are consolidating their IT operations into their own shared services unit rather than outsourcing it. A key reason for this is the growing strategic importance of IT in the media industry. Although IT is basically seen as a support function in many industries, IT competencies and innovation in media are becoming more a part of the core competencies. Outsourcing can mean a loss in strategic flexibility.

In areas where very specific know-how is required, such as in broadcasting, it is difficult for an outsourcing company to acquire and replicate this know-how, thus making outsourcing deals prone to failure. Also, companies may experience a degradation of perceived quality when they outsource. Managing through service level agreements is usually more difficult than managing a company's own resources, as traditional escalation mechanisms may not work. Finally, many media and entertainment companies are large enough to capture much of the scale savings themselves, thus reducing the value of outsourcing.

Offshoring for Additional Benefits

Offshoring, as an extension of outsourcing services, has become increasingly common for call centres, as well as application development and maintenance. The benefits for companies have been measurably significant. For instance, GE Capital has had an offshore centre since 1996 supporting ten of its business units with new application software development for financial services and industrial systems and, in addition, providing legacy system maintenance and a help desk. A major German broadcaster has a joint-venture offshore facility in Russia, where much of the application development is done.

Offshoring applications can deliver substantial cost improvements of up to 50% versus doing it in-house. Other benefits of offshoring include:

- shorter learning curves because of expertise and familiarity of offshore partners, especially for legacy and enterprise systems
- 24/7 production and development allows for synchronized work between Europe and offshore teams with large time differences
- the ability to quickly ramp up capacity because of large pools of consultants and additional talent
- mature lifecycle processes.

Obviously, there are risks linked to offshoring; that is, companies have limited control, and offshoring concentrates risks in a few countries and on a few companies, which can go bankrupt. This must be closely monitored by companies for the duration of the offshoring contract.

Improvement Levers for Non-standardized Processes in the Media Industry

A major challenge for media companies has been to optimize project-based or semi-standardized processes. These processes are the backbone of media companies in the areas of content creation (e.g. studio production and editorial writing).

As there is no repetitive process behind the tasks that can be trimmed for efficiency, more effort must be put into motivating employees to ensure efficiency and effectiveness. Typically, this is done by creating *transparency* through allocation of costs to those who can influence them and creating clear benchmarks against which they can measure their performance and making employees directly *accountable* for their actions.

These simple rules have proved to be very resilient and successful. For example, a benchmark analysis of the throughput of TV production companies reveals that, even for the same production format, the efficiencies vary greatly. A variety show format was produced with 18 full-time equivalents (FTEs) per 60-minute show at one channel, whereas a comparable product required close to 48 employees at another channel (Figure 5.9).

Companies must thus ensure transparency and clear accountability for all cost positions from the start to be able to reduce costs in production. The blurred separation of tasks between 'creative' functions and 'service' functions results in continual budget overruns and a laissez-faire attitude. In addition, a system for tracking costs that quickly identifies sources of budget overruns is rarely in place. However, only a clear delineation of responsibilities

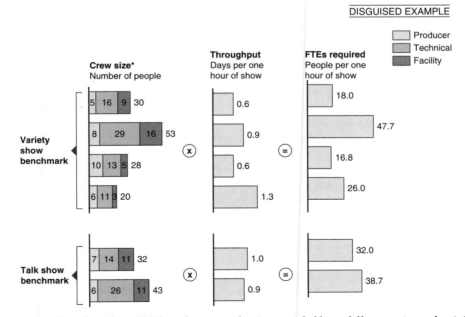

Figure 5.9 Benchmarking TV show format production revealed large differences in productivity

*Excluding talent
Source: McKinsey analyses

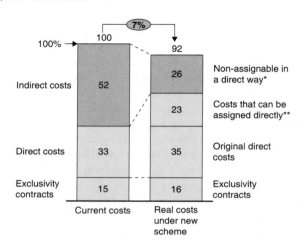

SOAP OPERA EXAMPLE

Index, 100 = current costs

Figure 5.10 Tracking costs in a more direct way by reducing indirect costs increases transparency and accountability

*Administration, corporate services, etc.
**Includes technical and non-technical services
Source: McKinsey analyses

combined with a true understanding of the underlying costs can enable management to diagnose and optimize the underlying cost base. To create *transparency*, successful production companies have created so-called 'service catalogues', based on a careful breakdown of costs, with help from comprehensive cost trees that systematically distinguish between unit costs and number of units required. This catalogue, closely linked to a sophisticated reporting system, made it possible to describe and standardize studio services and assign clear unit transfer prices to each of the services. With this modification, one studio was able to allocate otherwise non-assignable costs in the order of magnitude of 25% of its total costs, and calculate the profitability of a production more accurately (Figure 5.10).

Once transparency has been achieved, companies need to make individuals clearly *accountable* for each cost item, separating creative activities (which mostly determine the number of units used) from service activities (which mostly influence the cost per unit) (Figure 5.11).

For example, closely monitoring the utilization of talent, writers and producers has proved to be a key lever to enhance efficiency. They are often the most important cost items in TV production; however, frequently only utilized 40% to 70%. As a consequence, low utilization should be penalized or reflected in the compensation of the producer who is responsible for scheduling (Figure 5.12).

Similar examples can be found in other media sectors. At one newspaper, most stories were handed in just shortly before the deadline, resulting in costly last-minute work. Furthermore, there was a substantial amount of overproduction in the number of pages.

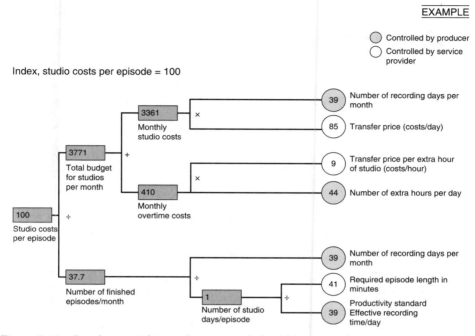

Figure 5.11 Cost levers within producer control should be assigned to owners

Source: McKinsey analyses

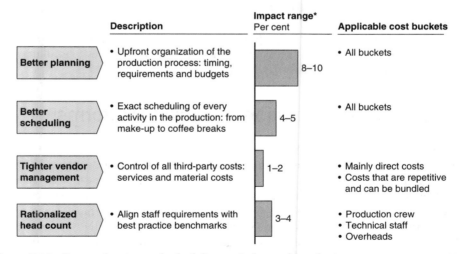

Figure 5.12 Better planning and scheduling main levers for reducing costs

*Percentage of total production costs, average results from 10+ cost-reduction projects in a variety of TV productions
Source*; McKinsey analyses

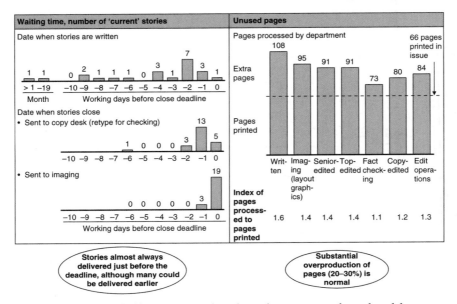

Figure 5.13 Significant hidden waste in the editorial process can be reduced by systematic planning

Source: McKinsey analyses

Substantial savings were achieved by making managers and editors directly responsible for the costs incurred (Figure 5.13).

Therefore, optimizing project-based processes is primarily a challenge of proper people management and corporate culture accomplished through transparency, accountability and the motivation of individuals.

Managing the Transition to Digital Platforms

The entertainment supply chain was in the past structured to distribute and sell media content through a simple, dedicated distribution network at fixed time windows. With the rise of digital platforms like the Web, as well as multiple digital access devices like the mobile phone, the iPod, the Kindle and the resulting change in consumer behaviour (shifting to on-demand multitasking, and always on consumption of media), the media and entertainment industry must upgrade its operations fundamentally.

In the 2000s a multitude of companies began launching the so-called digital transformation; these includes companies involved in movie production, for example Paramount Pictures, which launched its digital business in June 2006, and music production, for example Universal Music, which launched a digital platform in response to the booming demand for music content to be consumed on mobile and other Web platforms. There is great potential to be realized, as some companies have already discovered; yet the road is risky and there must be adequate planning.

High potential from digitization of the supply chain

Some media companies are already very successful in realizing profit from digitizing their supply chains.

For example, newspaper company Belo Interactive manages and feeds its news across its 17 television and online properties, using a central digital publishing system that simplifies news development and content-sharing. Tribune Interactive operates a digital content management system connecting its five major newspapers and 23 TV stations, offering greater asset utilization and improved coordination. The German sports broadcaster DSF, which has recently automated the standard workflows for sport production and diffusion, anticipates a cost savings of 25% annually. Textbook publishers McGraw-Hill and Prentice Hall use electronic textbook files to assist teachers and students to develop and propose feedback and changes, with significant returns because there are more accessible training modules, less travel support, etc.

Music companies such as Universal manage hundreds of artist websites across the globe and claim to save more than 50% of the cost of managing content by sharing it (using a content management system entered once by the repertoire owner and then used by all), instead of each affiliate working to find the appropriate clips and photos (Figures 5.14, 5.15 and 5.16).

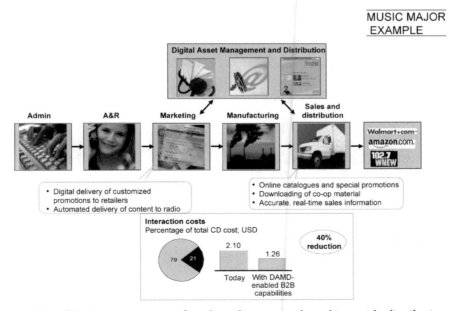

Figure 5.14 Digitization may significantly reduce cost of working with distribution and promotion partners

Source: McKinsey analyses based on data from Vogel's Entertainment Industry Economics

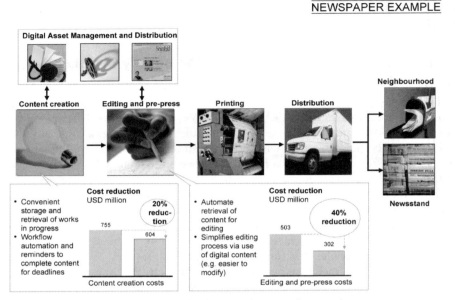

Figure 5.15   Digitization can increase speed and efficiency of internal processes

Source: McKinsey analyses based on data from Merrill Lynch (May 2001); Kagan (July 2001)

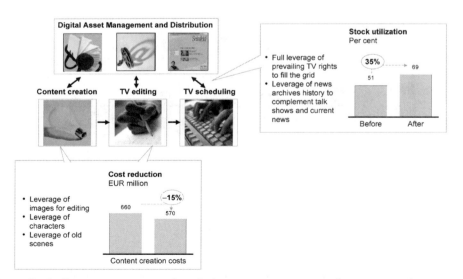

Figure 5.16   Digitization can significantly leverage assets usage and improve working capital management

Source: McKinsey analyses based on data from Merrill Lynch (May 2001); Kagan (July 2001)

Digitization: McGraw-Hill Redefining College Textbook Retailing

US-based publisher McGraw-Hill has developed a new value proposition for college textbooks. Based on content orders submitted by instructors, its Primis electronic publishing system assembles electronic textbook files that are retrieved and printed on site by university campus bookstores on request by students.

This proposition is an 'offer to assortment planning' that radically alters the traditional information and product flows along the textbook supply–demand chain. The conventional supply–demand chain has drawbacks for all parties involved. For the retailer's customers – students – books are expensive, especially when only certain parts of a book are required reading. If the bookstore underestimates demand, students must wait for the book while the publisher makes an extra shipment. If the bookstore overestimates demand, it incurs inventory and obsolescence costs. When instructors make poor choices or assumptions, the consequences may not be immediately economic, but they do face the frustration of both students and bookstore managers.

The textbook that the student buys using Primis can be customized for the instructor's course – this is the primary value offering of the publisher to the instructor; secondarily, the textbook is available in a much shorter timeframe than with the conventional book supply chain. For students, the main benefit is price, which is usually lower than a standard mass-produced book because only the required text is included. The use of on-campus printers makes the unit cost independent of batch size, thus removing obsolescence costs for the publisher (unsold returned books commonly account for up to 30% of sales) and opportunity cost for the retailer (wasted display space). With this new system, everyone wins.

Digitization RTL-TVI, End-to End Newsroom

RTL-TVI is the leading Belgian, French-speaking broadcaster, part of the RTL group owned by Bertelsmann. The RTL-TVI news programmes have been an important contributor to the success of the broadcaster. Among others, the live television 19:00 bulletin attracts the station's prime-time audience, an audience that remains with the station for the rest of the evening, every day of the week.

The management has created end-to-end news production, with the goals of remaining cost-effective while at the same time being flexible enough to accommodate 'just-in-time' editing, offering greater access to archive material, promoting wider sharing and cooperation among journalists and of increasing the news throughput for not only the channel but also other media outlets, such as the Internet. The system chosen was through EVS, another Belgian company, mostly renowned for its sports digital end-to-end system, which had software features such as, among others, replay. The most important lessons learned from this implementation were:

1. Seamless component integration: for news, this includes data from the 'new news' feeds, but also from the archives. Those data must be integrated into the complete system file, connected with the MAM (media asset management) system and enhanced by functionalities such as search and retrieval. In practice, this is difficult because the value chain elements tend to be serviced by different companies, or the

> IT system is not fully developed, using rather a gearbox approach than the flexibility of a file-based meta-data-based environment.
> 2. Value comes not only from cost-efficiency (efficiency increases due to automation of tasks such as tapeless editing, journalist cooperation, automatic back-ups and restore, etc.), but from the speed and versatility at which breaking news can be enriched and put on air or on other platforms, such as the Internet. In practice, journalists' work is enhanced, with more choice to edit and develop news quickly.
> 3. The business cases were costs and benefits of newsroom automation are calculated shows a strong return on investment (ROI) yet typically, a period of training and experimentation must be planned for. ROI increases significantly if the IT platform and application investments are scalable and interoperable. Fundamentally, the ROI is boosted by the potential to offer many more minutes of news in multiformats and multichannel environments, such as online.

Manage the 'road' cautiously

While some early-mover media companies have been quite aggressive and successful in using digital production and content management technologies, it is fair to say that, for many others, this has not always produced the desired results.

One reason is historical: one of the unwritten tenets of the inner workings of many media and entertainment companies was that technology planning and creative endeavours did not mix. The creative side was allowed and, in many organizations, encouraged to function without a comprehensive strategy for technology and how it could be leveraged across the business. If a producer wanted a piece of equipment, they procured it, if the budget was approved by the business side. If a news director did not like a particular technology or process, it was ignored in favour of one with which the news team was more adept.

Some companies have been burned by false starts with the centralization of assets. They embarked on well-meaning technology-driven projects, including extensive efforts to identify every photo, video, piece of artwork and audio clip/track to create an all-singing, all-dancing digital asset database. Inevitably, these efforts developed into mainly an infrastructure project, with very little payoff for the various users, which resulted in enormous costs. Gaps in early technology infrastructure (e.g. network bandwidth, storage) had proved to be a further bottleneck to implementing new digital solutions, but now this is finally being sorted out.

Another, and possibly much more crucial, reason for failure was that companies did not revise their production processes. Rather than adjusting their processes to optimally leverage the advantages of digitization, companies have been reluctant to adapt their workflows. Instead, many silo solutions were created in each function, hindering the capture of the additional value created by integrated solutions.

Time to jump!

Technology has advanced to the point where it is now a true enabler rather than a barrier. For one, production automation technologies have become cheaper and easier to use as far as they have shifted to IT software solutions.

Second, vendors of digital asset management (DAM) products offer more comprehensive solutions, making it easier to capture digital assets and enabling the storage and sharing of a growing inventory of valuable content. Finally, there is an exponentially declining cost of storage and distribution, making it possible to store and exchange large media assets electronically.

Owing to these trends, media companies must jump and master two key success factors to capture the full business value in the supply chain.

- *Creating a cross-functional business programme:* This means that all key stakeholders – from producers to broadcast operations – must be on board, working together. New business demands and improved technology are beginning to blur the line between traditional production, ad sales and distribution. Building the digital infrastructure and effectively introducing new production tools require a holistic perspective, and inevitably a change in organization to avoid the classic silo approach so popular in media.
- *Overcoming the challenge of changing production and other creative processes:* The key is to create and implement a standard set of process enablers (e.g. production workflow management, scheduling, budgeting) that cut across the production lifecycle. These components represent the link between the core digital infrastructure and the applications that will support the customized needs of end users.

Key Takeaways

1. Effective supply chain management has not been a key feature of the media industry, but there is a large cost potential to be realized by managing media processes carefully.
2. Furthermore, effective supply chain management through the digitization of workflow processes is becoming a key competitive advantage in the shifting world of linear media towards 'always on', everywhere multimedia.
3. Standard processes in production, distribution and purchasing can be optimized systematically with help from proven approaches, such as lean production; major hurdles are currently cultural resistance and missing analytical skills.
4. Creation of shared services, outsourcing and/or offshoring can yield significant savings; however, this should be carefully balanced against the need of the individual business unit to be flexible and reactive.
5. 'Back end' services can be developed into attractive stand-alone businesses when managed with full commitment.
6. The transition to digital production platforms can yield significant cost and revenue benefits when managed correctly; there is a significant competitive advantage for early movers.
7. Media companies should not be afraid to hire new experts from industries that are known for their need for operational excellence, e.g. several European media companies are now hiring managers from other industries such as the automotive industry to install a lean manufacturing culture in media.

RTL Group: Creating a Digital Value Chain[1]

RTL Group, like many other TV and radio broadcasters in Europe, is faced with updating its business models as digitization and the Internet change the industry. As part of its digital strategy, RTL Group wants its content to reach customers via multiple platforms, ranging from traditional TV channels and mobile phones to online social networking websites such as MySpace and digital retailers such as iTunes. The wildly popular television show *Idols*, produced by RTL Group-owned FremantleMedia and first launched in 2001 as Pop Idol in the UK on ITV, proved to be the perfect vehicle to test the early phases of this digital strategy. For example, Germany, in addition to Grundy Light Entertainment (part of FremantleMedia) producing the show for RTL Television, the format was also featured on the catch-up service RTLnow.de and on its video community Clipfish.de. The sister channel Super RTL aired an additional "behind the scenes format" and there are merchandising, brand extension activities as well as revenues from voting. M6 in France is pursuing a similar strategy with "La Nouvelle Star". RTL Group is looking for ways to repeat this success on a continuous basis.

Elmar Heggen, CFO and head of RTL Group's Corporate Centre, wonders what this entails, and how whatever it is will be leveraged through RTL Group's multiplatform digital strategy. Furthermore, as head of the Corporate Centre, he is tasked with facilitating sharing amongst RTL's many profit centres, Elmar wonders how to best profit from the accumulated experience as they all attempt to launch content online, through video on demand (VoD), mobile platforms or innovative new platforms.

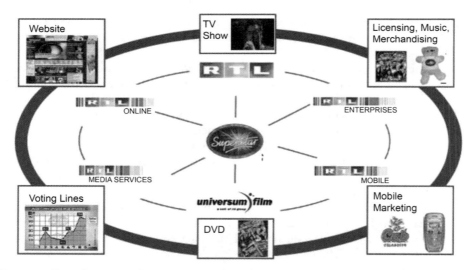

Figure 1 Digital strategy: Superstar example RTL Germany

Source: RTL presentation to INSEAD, 2008. Reproduced with permission

---

[1]This case is developed solely as the basis for class discussion. Cases are not intended to serve as endorsements, sources of primary data or illustrations of effective or ineffective management.

Company History

The RTL Group, one of Bertelsmann AG's major divisions, is one of the global leaders in free TV and radio broadcasting and production. The TV channels it owns and/or holds significant stakes in include RTL Television, Vox, RTL II and Super RTL in Germany, M6 in France, RTL-TVI in Belgium, Five in the United Kingdom and RTL 4 from the Netherlands. Additionally, there are channels in Spain, Eastern Europe and Russia. RTL Groups' radio stations broadcast from Paris, Berlin, Brussels and Hilversum (the Netherlands), amongst several other European cities. And in content production and rights management, RTL Group has holdings in the United Kingdom, the United States, Germany, Australia and Luxembourg through its worldwide production arm Fremantle Media (Talkback Thames, UFA Film & TV Produktion, Grundy Television and CLT-UFA International).

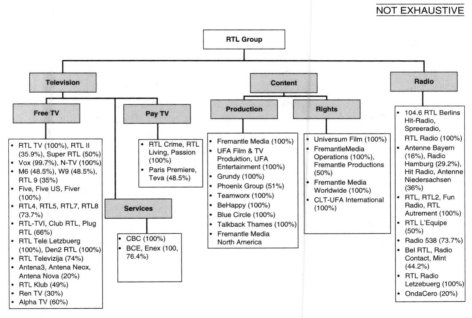

Figure 2   RTL group: key divisions 2007

Source: McKinsey analyses based on data from RTL Group

RTL Group's beginnings date back to 1931 when the Compagnie Luxembourgeoise de Radiodiffusion (CLR) was incorporated in Luxembourg as the country's national radio agency. One of the early strengths of CLR was its international and multilingual programming. Owing to the more relaxed radio and TV regulations in Luxembourg, commercial radio was allowed there before the rest of Europe. This regulatory environment permitted CLR to transmit its programming in a variety of languages and to locations outside of Luxembourg. In 1933, owing to advanced radio transmission capabilities, its broadcasts in French, German and English were able to reach listeners in Germany, Great Britain, France and Belgium for the first time. CLR's French-language radio station broadcasting, now known as RTL, was one of the most popular stations, and has continued to perform well for decades. Building on its success in radio, CLR diversified into free-to-air (FTA) television as it gained popularity in the 1950s. And in 1954 CLR became CLT (Compagnie Luxembourgeoise de Télédiffusion).

The regulatory environment in Europe changed in the 1980s, and with it came new competitors from commercial radio and TV stations in the rest of Europe. CLT remained focused on building a strong position in both radio and TV throughout Europe. Using the RTL brand, CLT entered the German, French, Belgian and Dutch markets. Over the course of the last century and into this one, the group has further expanded into radio and TV. In 2008, it holds stakes or owns 45 TV channels in 11 countries, and 33 radio stations in seven countries.

In addition to FTA holdings, the group expanded into content production, and eventually became one of the largest independent content distribution companies outside of the United States. In early 1997, Audiofina, the holding company of CLT, decided to merge with the Hamburg-based UFA Film und Fernsehen GmbH, a subsidiary of the German media giant Bertelsmann, to create CLT-UFA. CLT-UFA emerged as a strong player in broadcasting and programming production and rights management. In 2000, Bertelsmann, Groupe Bruxelles Lambert (GBL)/Electrafina (the original owners of Audiofina) and Pearson Television decided to merge their interests. Pearson had a strong offering in content production, as it had acquired several production companies since 1993. The joint company was renamed RTL Group. It includes all the assets and activities of CLT-UFA and Pearson Television. As a part of the merger, Pearson Group's stakes in Antena 3, a Spanish TV channel, and in Channel 5 (renamed Five) were brought into the RTL Group. The production activities of Pearson Television and the German UFA Group were combined to form the worldwide production arm of RTL Group, which adopted the new company name Fremantle Media in 2001. With Pearson's activities as a global production house in the United Kingdom, United States, Australia and Europe, and with CLT-UFA's broadcasting network, the newly formed company became Europe's leading private production house and broadcaster.

Bertelsmann

In a move to gain a majority shareholding in the RTL Group, Bertelsmann engaged in a share swap with Groupe Bruxelles Lambert (GBL). In 2001 Bertelsmann took over a 30% stake in the RTL Group owned by the investor GBL. In return, GBL received 25.1% of capital shares and 25.0% of voting rights in Bertelsmann AG. Bertelsmann continued to increase its shareholding of RTL Group with the takeover of another 22% in January 2002, this time from Pearson. As the media industry was fragmenting and moving online, gaining control over a major producer of video content was seen as vital for Bertelsmann. Today, the RTL Group is Bertelsmann's largest corporate division, and its share in RTL Group now amounts to a 90.3% stake. The remaining 9.7% are publicly traded on the Brussels and Luxembourg stock exchanges.

Bertelsmann is a family-owned business that wants to remain as such. In an effort to have all of Bertelsmann's shares controlled by Bertelsmann Stiftung and the Mohn family, they negotiated a share buyback from GBL. In July 2006 Bertelsmann AG bought back the 25.1% block of capital shares previously held by GBL for €4.5 billion. The share buyback was financed with a €4.5 billion bridging loan. Yet the €1.63 billion in proceeds from the sale of BMG Music Publishing to Vivendi in 2006 considerably reduced the size of this loan. Currently Bertelsmann is a privately held stock corporation, the ownership of Bertelsmann AG has been split between Bertelsmann Stiftung holding 76% of the capital shares and the Mohn family holding the remaining 23.1% held via intermediate companies. The Bertelsmann Verwaltungsgesellschaft (BVG) controls 100 percent of the voting rights.

Recent Years

In recent years, the RTL Group has strengthened its FTA offerings, expanded into digital TV and radio, enhanced its online presence and focused on diversifying its operations outside of TV and radio.

Traditional TV and radio

RTL Group has continued to focus on its traditional markets of the United Kingdom and Western Europe, where it has had a strong presence for decades. Since the early 2000s RTL Group has acquired various TV and radio assets in this region, such as the 2002 acquisition of n-tv. This German news channel helped to improve RTL Group's offering in the news segment in Germany. Additionally, in 2004, RTL Group launched Plug TV in Belgium (renamed plug RTL in 2008) and acquired Paris Première through its French TV channel M6. Another important move for the RTL Group came in 2005 when it purchased the remaining shares in UK TV channel Five, and gained a 100% control over the channel. In 2007 several key activities focused on the Netherlands market with the launch of the family's fourth free-TV channel, RTL8, which was the successor to Talpa, later renamed Ten, a free-TV channel launched by John de Mol only a few years before and who sold certain key TV rights following an asset deal to RTL Group after a disappointing market entry. RTL also closed a deal with John de Mol's Talpa Media Holding to bring the radio station 538 into RTL.

Parallel to the acquisitions, came the sale of some assets to bring more focus into the portfolio. The RTL Group retreated from the UK radio market with the 2001 sale of Atlantic 252. Additionally, the RTL Group divested from the French satellite market through the 2007 sale of TPS, in which TF1 and M6 contributed 100 percent of TPS to Canal+ France for a shareholding in the new group of 9.9 percent and 5.1 percent respectively.

The RTL Group has also expanded further south into Spain and Portugal. Starting in 2004 the RTL Group acquired in several steps a 32.9 percent stake in Grupo Media Capital, a leading Portuguese media company with holdings in FTA TV and radio stations. However, this stake was eventually sold off in 2007 after the Spanish media company Grupo Prisa acquired the majority stake. In Spain, RTL Group has a minority shareholding (~29%) in

Grupo Antena 3 comprising the TV Channels Antena3, Antena.Nova and Antena.Neox, and in the radio stations Spain Onda Cero and Europa FM.

Although the RTL Group expanded further east into Poland as early as 1996, its holdings continue to be mainly minority investments in the Eastern European region. RTL currently has stakes in TV and radio stations in Hungary, Croatia, Russia and Greece. It sold off its investment (RTL 7) in the Polish TV market in 2001. In Russia the RTL Group has a significant investment (30% shareholding) in the Russian TV network Ren TV.

In addition to its many investments in free-TV and radio stations, the RTL Group does have some pay-TV interests. The rise in digital and Internet TV, along with the European Union ruling to make European TV fully digital by 2012, influenced RTL Group's expansion into digital pay-TV channels.

Digital TV and the Internet

In 2006 RTL Group launched several digital channels both through Five and through RTL Television in Germany. Five launched Five Life (renamed Fiver in 2008) and Five US, while RTL Television started RTL Crime, RTL Living and Passion. M6 launched in France the channels W9. RTL also started to offer video-on-demand (VoD) services in 2006, when Five launched Five Download (relaunched as Demand Five in 2008). It continues to build this VoD offering through online platforms such as M6Replay.fr in France and RTLnow.de in Germany or RTLgemist.nl in the Netherlands. RTL Group also provides online services such as the video communities Clipfish.de and Video.fr. Additionally, RTL is expanding its mobile TV activities through its 2008 agreement with T-Mobile Germany and the launch of the mobile channel RTL 24 in the Netherlands. Although digital radio has not experienced the same growth as digital TV, in 2007 RTL Radio France launched the digital radio stations RTL Autrement and RTL L'Equipe.

Diversification

In addition to expanding into Southern and Eastern Europe, building a presence on the Internet and entering into the digital TV market, the RTL Group has diversified its offerings, albeit with mixed success.

In 2001 RTL Group launched the RTL Shop in Germany, a cable and satellite TV home-shopping network. However, this venture did not prove successful and the disinvestment of the RTL Shop is executed in 2008. Additionally, in 2001 the RTL Group, the Canal+ Group and the Groupe Jean-Claude Darmon signed an agreement to merge their sports rights activities to create SPORTFIVE, the leading sports rights company. RTL sold its interest in SPORTFIVE in 2004 and relaunched instead UFA Sports in 2008.

Diversifying into content production has been a great success for RTL. Fremantle-Media has played a key role in this success as it has produced many international hits. Furthermore, owning content has allowed RTL Group to explore new distribution channels for this content, such as online, mobile and on-demand. Yet, monetizing these new distribution formats and platforms continues to be a critical issue for RTL Group and others within the TV industry.

2007 Situation

Industry dynamics

Television in the new millennium

The switchover to digital television dominates the TV industry in Europe, with an estimated 35% of European households receiving digital television in 2008. It is expected that digital terrestrial TV (DTT) will experience major growth in the European market, as has already been seen in the United Kingdom, and through the launch of several DTT services in France and Spain. In Germany, DTT penetration is also progressing quickly, even gaining market share from the dominant cable distribution platforms. However, digital satellite is the current digital market leader in Germany with 60% of all digital homes receiving satellite coverage.

In addition to modifying the TV distribution platform, digital TV has other effects. It significantly increases the number of channels available to subscribers. This increase in channels is causing greater fragmentation in the market, as traditional leaders lose market share to increased competition from specialized digital FTA and pay-TV channels. In the United Kingdom, for example, one of the most advanced countries with regard to digital TV, the peak-time viewing market share of the FTA broadcasters declined from 92% in 1997 to 72% in 2007. The FTA broadcasters have, in part, compensated for this by the launch of additional niche channels; however, although it helps to defend the market share of the company, it also increases costs.

Not only does digital TV increase the number of possible channels, it also enables new ways to view TV content. Time-shifted viewing, the ability to watch shows outside the traditional scheduled time, is becoming increasingly popular. Additionally, personalized TV viewing, made possible through Video on Demand (VoD), personal video recorders (PVRs) and the Internet, is experiencing significant uptake. In Europe, estimates suggest that the number of individuals using a personal TV system will exceed 170 million by 2012.

Digital world	Number of channels possible ANALOGUE	Number of channels possible DIGITAL
Terrestrial	5–6	30–40
Cable	30–40	200+
Satellite	200+	500+
DSL / IP-TV		unlimited
Mobile TV (DVB-H, DMB)		15–30

Figure 3 TV distribution in the digital world

Source: RTL presentation to INSEAD, 2008. Reproduced with permission

The effects of time-shifted and personalized viewing on broadcasters are mixed. On the one hand, studies suggest that it increases the number of minutes viewed and market shares are shifting back to programmes from the main TV channels. On the other hand, viewers can skip advertisements. In addition to the slowdown in TV advertising revenues, as advertising dollars shift to online alternatives, skipping adverts will put further pressure on the bottom line. However, with the personalization of TV comes the ability to personalize advertising. Although a new trend, the ability to insert contextualized ads based on users' consumption patterns may prove to greatly increase the advertising effectiveness and with that its revenue potential.

Radio in the new millennium

Radio, like other players in the music industry, has been negatively affected by online piracy of music. Additionally, through Internet sites such as last.fm and pandora.com, traditional music stations are now competing directly with online music websites. However, traditional talk radio programmes have remained popular.

The uptake of digital radio has not been nearly as successful as the uptake of digital TV. Lack of standards, the relatively small amount of spectrum freed for switching to digital and the already large number of good-quality FM transmission stations has made the benefits of digital radio less obvious to consumers. However, a move by the French government to approve a technological standard for digital radio may improve its uptake. France anticipates digital radio will officially be launched in late 2008. Although Germany pioneered digital audio broadcasting (DAB), a standard used to broadcast digital radio, it has abandoned its original target of phasing out analogue terrestrial radio by 2010.

Content production

As the entire TV industry shifts to accommodate the Internet and digital TV, the value chain is also changing. Disintermediation is threatening traditional TV broadcasters, whose focus has typically been on creating innovative content bundles for viewers. Some content production houses are looking into distributing their on-demand content through online platforms directly and bypassing broadcasters. Another trend seen in content production is the move to create content with international appeal and interactivity from viewers. Given the success of *Big Brother* and *Pop Idol*, content that scales well to different geographical locations and content that is suited for different platforms such as digital TV, websites and mobile phones is increasing in popularity.

The RTL Group

RTL Group's position as a leader in several TV and radio markets is in part due to its organizational structure. RTL Group is heavily decentralized, with each country's TV and radio stations run as independent profit centres. Additionally, FremantleMedia, the content production arm, is run as an independent profit centre. Each centre has its own CEO and is managed with an arm's-length approach by RTL Group and its owner,

Bertelsmann allowing for maximum entrepreneurship and adoption to local taste. Yet recently there has been a greater focus on cross-centre collaboration, in particular related to technological expertise. This has become an important task for the Corporate Centre, which focuses on creating a milieu for sharing ideas and experience across profit centres. This was supported by the creation of the Operations Management Committee (OMC) where all the CEOs of the profit centres are members and three synergy committees (Sycos), which report to the OMC on Programming, Radio and New Business Models, each with several sub-meetings.

RTL Group's strategy is based on three components. One component involves building and strengthening families of channels ranging from generalist to niche, in order to counter fragmentation resulting from digital TV. An additional component involves diversifying revenue streams to become less dependent on advertising. This is extremely pertinent given the worldwide shift in advertising dollars to online. Additionally, RTL Group is looking to expand geographically in order to benefit from growth in emerging markets. In addition to its overall strategy, RTL Group's digital strategy focuses on ensuring its TV and radio channels are platform-neutral, and thus available to consumers through a wide range of choices including digital TV channels, on demand/catch up TV and through intensifying online publishing activities through "vertical" websites as Kochbar.de (cookingbar) and Frauenzimmer.de in Germany and Turbo.fr and Deco.fr in France and by becoming more active in social networking websites e.g. the acquisition of the social network Wer-kennt-wen.de in Germany.

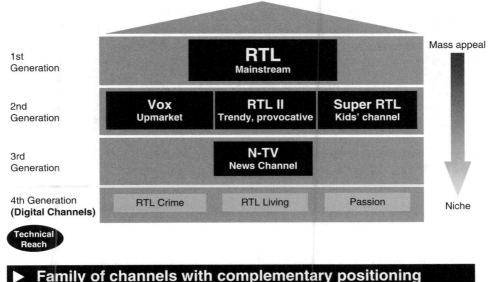

Figure 4   Family of channels: the RTL family in Germany

Source: RTL presentation to INSEAD, 2008. Reproduced with permission

Diversification

Although TV advertising revenues still account for 60% of RTL's total revenue, it has made gains to reduce its dependence on this type of advertising. RTL has developed non-advertising revenue streams, such as T-commerce, merchandising and premium-rate services.

Some subsidiaries within RTL Group, such as the Groupe M6, have been very successful in systematically diversifying away from TV advertising revenues. In 2007 49% of Groupe M6's revenue came from non-advertising sources. This group has a broad offering of revenue streams consisting of distance-selling services such as a home-shopping service and an e-commerce site. It is also involved in magazine and music publishing and events through M6 Interactions, content rights trading, and interactive, mobile and Web-based services. M6 Mobile by Orange allows Orange customers to have access to M6 content on their mobiles. Additionally, M6 has diversified through acquisitions and strategic partnerships such as its 9% stake in the US movie production company Summit Entertainment, and its joint venture with PagesJaunes, an online classifieds site. On top of this, this group has an extensive Web division consisting of 50 websites, a catch-up TV service (M6replay.fr), a social networking site and a video sharing site.

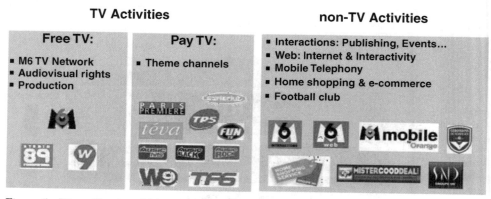

Figure 5 Diversification: M6 example

Source: RTL presentation to INSEAD, 2007. Reproduced with permission

International presence

Although RTL Group has content production operations in North America and Australia, most of its expansion activities are focused on Europe. RTL Group is concentrating on obtaining a greater market share in the UK TV market, in addition to expanding further into Eastern and Southern Europe. Furthermore, RTL Group is moving away from its dependence on Germany for generating the majority of its profit. In 2002 Germany contributed 51% to RTL Group's EBITA, while today it contributes 37%, with other countries continually increasing their contributions.

Digital presence

Technology, and in particular Internet technology, evolves at a rapid pace. Rather than banking on a particular technology, RTL Group has adopted an all-encompassing approach to selecting platforms for its content. Each profit centre is involved in exploring all emerging technologies and determining how content can be best applied to the platform, be it VoD, mobile TV, interactive digital TV, online networks and communities, gaming or new distribution devices such as iPods and game consoles.

Furthermore, RTL Group has developed a 'cat strategy' for digital content, such that it has 'nine lives and a long tail'. New content, in addition to long tail content such as repeats, brand extensions, pre-views and archives, are leverage and reused on as many platforms as possible. For example, in 2008 FremantleMedia Australia provided MySpace with licensed video content from its traditional TV broadcasts of *Project Runway Australia* and *Neighbours* FremantleMedia and YouTube closed a contract agreement in 2008 in which a multitude of new online formats will be created and YouTube's webplatform will be used as an exclusive distribution platform for current and future TV shows, all based on an advertising revenue sharing agreement. Also in 2008 FremantleMedia Archive signed a deal with Deutsche Telekom to use old footage of Paul Potts, the winner of the talent show "Britain's Got Talent", in an highly successful advertising campaign.

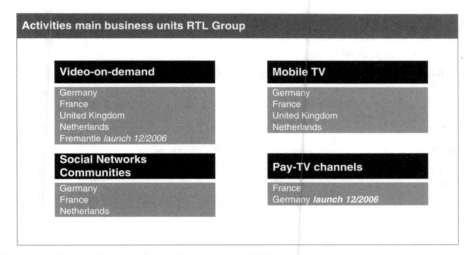

Figure 6 **New platforms to reach the customer: RTL examples**

Source: RTL presentation to INSEAD, 2008. Reproduced with permission

Financial performance

RTL Group's net profits in 2007 were €563 million, down from a record of €890 million in 2006. This decrease in profits was due in part to a €96 million fine imposed against one of RTL Group's advertising sales houses. Despite fairly strong financial performance in both 2006 and 2007, RTL Group is limited in its ability to use these funds for new investments, as Bertelsmann is actively reducing its debt of approximately €3 billion, which was incurred when it bought back shares in its own company from GBL in 2006.

2003–2007

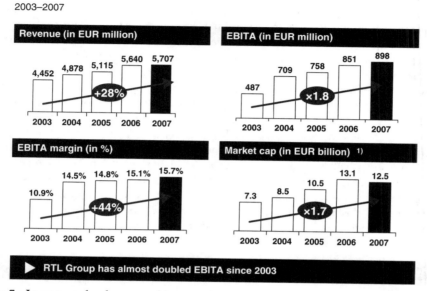

Figure 7   Long-term development of key metrics

Source: RTL presentation to INSEAD, 2008. Reproduced with permission

EUR million, 2007

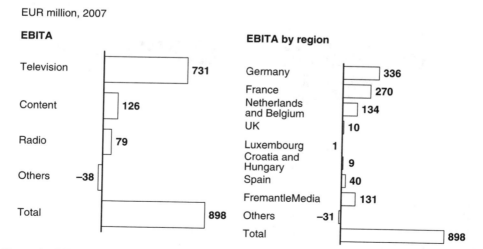

Figure 8   RTL's profitability by sector and profit centre

Source: McKinsey analyses based on data from RTL Group

Strategic Challenges

In addition to being limited in the size of investments it can make, RTL Group has the challenge of maintaining profitability, and of leveraging its organizational structure as it transitions its business to the digital world.

Profitable growth in the digital world

Digital content

Online or offline, what brings in viewers is killer content and innovative formats. Without a winning TV series, either produced in-house through FremantleMedia or acquired through rights negotiations, financial growth will be difficult.

Yet, even if RTL does have winning content, determining what form it should take on which platform is not obvious. There's a clear first-mover advantage in format innovation. In Germany, RTL Television's *Who Wants to be a Millionaire?* (first aired in 1999 in Germany) captured more than the combined audience share of the four most successful copycat formats. Going forward, RTL Group will need to provide the right content in the right format to retain and grow its audience share. RTL Group has employed techniques such as versioning, which enables the same content to be used across a variety of platforms ranging from digital niche channels available on VoD to Web clips available on mobile phones. Yet it remains to be seen how sustainable the approach of exploring and exploiting all new platforms is, in particular when new Internet players, such as Joost and Bubblegum, are entering the market and are launching innovative IPTV platforms. RTL has yet to explore this platform.

Fads versus money-making trends

Making money through online ventures can be elusive. In 2008 Google, who acquired the widely popular YouTube, is still working on how to monetize this form of user-generated content (UGC). Although RTL Group is planning to explore all new platforms for content, some platforms may not be conducive to revenue generation. For example, although social networking communities are popular, how traditional broadcasters can make money from these ventures isn't immediately clear.

Synergies across profit centres

In the physical world, each of RTL Group's profit centres functions as an independent business, based on a geographical region, or in the case of FremantleMedia on content production. This model has proved successful, and has helped RTL Group gain market leadership in several markets. Yet as digitization changes the TV industry, collaboration, particularly collaboration related to technological expertise, is increasingly relevant. To facilitate collaboration across profit centres, RTL Group has tasked its to Corporate Centre, with promoting cross-centre cooperation. As some profit centres, such as Groupe M6 in France, have more advanced digital offerings than other centres, collaboration may facilitate the roll-out of services in less advanced centres. Yet, given that content rights are negotiated by country, and mobile operators are often tied to a specific geographical region, will cross-centre collaboration through OMC and Syco's be fruitful enough? Furthermore, given the lack of geographical boundaries in the digital world, will RTL's profit centres be able to compete against the online giants?

*   *   *

Looking at the speed and purposefulness with which single-minded Internet giants such as Google, Yahoo!, eBay and Amazon, and increasingly social networks, are conquering the digital world on a global scale, will RTL Group's current approach deliver enough traction? Should funds be concentrated on a few digital opportunities rather than a broad approach being taken? If yes, where should RTL Group place its bets? Will content really be king or are there other opportunities? Can a decentralized, entrepreneurial approach survive in a world of global Internet giants which are strongly steered from the centre?

WAYS OUT OF THE ADVERTISING COMMODITY TRAP

Advertising is, to date, the major revenue source of the media industry, but advertising revenues, as well as the advertising value chain, will change significantly. The question is to what extent the recent evolution towards more accountable advertising formats, as well as the deployment of online and other digital platforms, will create structural shifts in advertising spend and delivery, which will require traditional media companies to adapt. In this context, this chapter addresses the following main questions:

1. *What structural changes are to be expected in advertising practices? Will there be a fundamental shift in the industry, and by when?*
2. *What roles will Google and other new kids on the block play in this advertising evolution, and how will they animate the advertising ecosystem?*
3. *What strategies can media companies follow to cope with these changes?*
4. *How should media companies upgrade their capabilities (advertising product offering, impact measurement, pricing, sales force deployments, back-end services) to effectuate this structural shift?*

Traditional Advertising under Increasing Pressure

Advertising is one of the key pillars upon which the media industry has been built. Some 60% of media revenues come from advertising, although with significant variance between media sectors (Figure 6.1). Radio, newspapers and the portion of free-to-air TV are especially dependent on advertising revenue.

Advertising spend has historically always been strongly correlated to gross domestic product (GDP) growth,[1] making up 0.8% to 1.4% of GDP in Western countries.[2]

---

[1] The time-series correlation is usually very high (in the range of 90% to 98%), depending on the country analysed. With the recent fluctuations of ad spend (see later in the text), the correlation has started to decline, e.g. it went from 96% to 92% if one contrasts the early period 1988–2000 with 1995–2007.

[2] Ad spend in Europe is significantly below that of the United States. This is explained by different boundary conditions such as regulations with regard to maximum amount of TV advertising and the

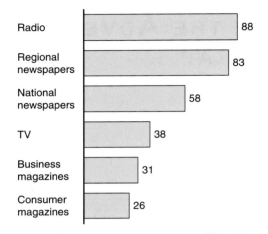

Figure 6.1   Advertising share of gross revenues in per cent UK, 2004

Source: McKinsey analysis

Deviations from this equilibrium have obviously occurred. With the birth of the Internet and the ensuing boost of a large number of companies launching and building their brand presence online in the late Nineties, advertising grew on average 1% per annum faster than GDP in Europe. But since the collapse of this boom in 2001, advertising spend has been readjusted to go back to the typical ratio of ad spend to GDP.

Going forward, we see several trends which may affect this ratio. The first is the Internet. With the rise of the Internet, and especially search advertising, advertising has become affordable and attractive to a large number of medium-sized companies. In old days, these companies would at the most post small ads in yellow pages and local newspapers. This emergence of 'the long tail' of advertisers is a significant source of growth for companies like Google and, to a lesser extent, the advertising market as a whole. Another effect of the Internet is that large advertisers have become increasingly critical regarding return on investment (ROI) of their marketing spend. On the Web, the effectiveness of ad spend can be measured more precisely, leading to more scientific scrutiny of marketing plans.

A second trend is that regulatory changes may remove some of the restrictions on advertising that were imposed on European media companies. In France, for example, the ban on advertising by retailers has been lifted and TV advertising regulations with regard to time and placement of advertising blocks and rules around product placement have been relaxed.

How the combined effects of these trends will work out is difficult to predict; for the time being we expect the equilibrium of total ad spend to GDP to roughly hold. There will likely be, however, significant changes in the allocation of advertising money and the type of products advertised, which will affect media companies' performance.

---

much stronger role of public service broadcasters, etc. Within Europe, the southern European countries are lagging behind the northern European ones. Advertising is likely to remain a local business for the time being, in 2008, only 5% was pan-European.

The First Wave of Advertising Spending Shift: Direct Marketing and Below the Line

Historically, major advertisers have spent a large share of their marketing budget in the mass media on building brand awareness. This was key for sectors such as fast mover consumer goods (FMCG) or for industries launching new products (like automotive companies).

But the cost of mass-market campaigns is high: only 10–15% of all companies advertise on prime-time television, and not surprisingly these are the largest companies. The long tail of small and medium enterprises cannot afford the risk of large mass-market advertising campaigns. As many of the smaller companies sell services rather than products, they prefer to spend their marketing money on inducing sales rather than creating awareness. They prefer a 'push' marketing approach, such as direct marketing or 'below the line' store promotions.

As the overall economy shifted more and more to services and small and medium enterprises, this resulted in a slow but persistent shift of marketing money to 'below the line' and direct marketing such that they made up the bulk of total marketing spend as early as the year 2000 (Figure 6.2).

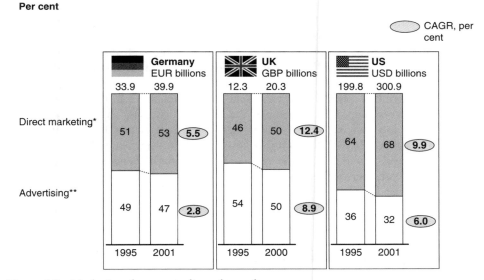

Figure 6.2 **Marketing share expenditure by medium**

*Includes direct mail, telemarketing, database marketing, press and magazine displays, door-to-door, inserts and new media
**Includes TV, radio, press
Source: McKinsey analysis based on data from Advertising Association; Direct Marketing Association 2000/01 Census; 2001 Survey on Direct and Interactive Marketing Activities in Europe; FEDMA; ZAW; Zenith Media; Direkt Marketing Monitor; Deutsche Post

Digital Technology at the Core of the Second Wave

The digitization of media is causing a number of fundamental changes in the advertising world. First of all, the fragmentation caused by digital offering caused market shares of most mass media to decline by 20% to 30%. Consider television: digital thematic TV services have grown significantly at about 15% a year, representing in some markets, like France, 20% of audience share; in Poland or Romania, 30%; and more than 40% in the United Kingdom, the United States and Canada. This viewing shift towards thematic channels is obviously divided among a larger number of channels; but those channels can still significantly affect the allocation of ad revenue. In fact, 20% of the worldwide television ad market is now within the hands of thematic, instead of generalist, channels. Generalist media companies have usually tried to compensate for this extra competition with price increases. The mass media that have the highest relative market share succeed in combating the threat posed by the rise of thematic channels, as, relatively speaking, they are increasingly the ones best placed to guarantee a mass-market audience. Generalist media companies that are third or fourth in the market have a significantly harder time to keep/raise prices. (It is indeed a case of 'winner takes all'.)

Another effect of digitization is that as the distribution constraint on content has been retrieved (once content is digital it can be distributed around the world at almost no cost), more and more content is available for free. This is not only the case for content on the Web, but also increasingly on TV, such as video on demand: a large share of video downloads are advertising financed rather than paid-for content. Even 'non-digital' media are moving towards the free-content model in order to stay competitive with digital content. Free newspapers such as *Metro* and *20 Minutes* are cases in point: they are by now market leaders in several countries. The complication of this is that the media revenue mix is shifting from paid to advertising-financed content. This can create major imbalances in the demand/supply balance of advertisements. If, for example, the current advertising share of total media revenues would shift from 60% to 70%, as implied by the early success of free content, this would require a growth in the advertising market of over 16%, something which is not likely to happen in the short term, given the correlation between GDP and advertising spend.

Last but not least, there is the move of the advertising spend mix away from traditional media to digital media. This reallocation of advertising money to the Web is driven by the fast growth of the Internet. A large online advertising market has developed in recent years around search engines, with Google as the major player.

Industry dynamics: demand side

Advertising markets are two-sided markets. On the one hand, there is the audience; on the other, the advertisers. Both are fundamentally changing their behaviour as the result of the rapid growth of digital media.

Audience impact

The evolution of traditional advertising formats expanding towards digital, while being offered to an increasing number of providers, means a very large explosion in terms of

United States, hours/day

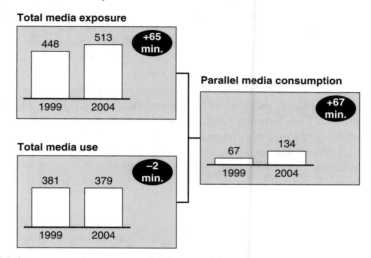

Figure 6.3   Media consumption patterns 8–18 years old

Source: McKinsey analysis based on data from the Kayser Foundation

messages trying to get through to consumers. As a case in point, the number of traditional commercial messages that a UK consumer is exposed to each day increased eight-fold in the period from 1975 (173 messages) to 2001 (1 300 messages). In addition, there is a clear trend towards more parallel media usage, especially with younger children, who often use three to four media in parallel; this parallel media consumption has doubled in the years 1999–2004 from 67 to 134 minutes a day in the United States and there are many indications that this trend is continuing.

The implication of this is that the likelihood that consumers will switch to another media the moment an advertisement is shown is high. Although measurements tell us the time spent watching television is not declining, the amount of time TV gets primary attention is declining and it runs the risk of becoming 'wallpaper' for part of the time it is on (Figures 6.3).

The battle for attention thus started a long time ago, and is inevitably increasing with the shift of usage towards online. In the beginning of this century, this was not necessarily a major issue: the Web was still limited, and ad banner click-through rates were very low, less than 0.5%. This is obviously changing dramatically. *First*, the market penetration of the broadband online platform has grown at an unprecedented rate and in the major OECD (Organization for Economic Cooperation and Development) countries more than half of all households are online. In fact, according to research,[3] 57% of

---

[3]See among others the various research studies made by the European association of interactive advertisers. Research extracts are available at http://www.eiaa.net.

Europeans now regularly access the Internet each week in 2007, and young people (aged 16–24) are now spending more time on the Internet than they are watching TV. *Second*, with the venue of broadband, and the rise of more highly engaging applications on the Web, such as multi-person games and social networks, time spent online is also increasing. European Internet users are spending an average of 12 hours online each week in 2007, or close to two hours a day. Twenty-five per cent of German, Italian, French and Spanish Internet users spend even more than three hours a day, surpassing TV viewing time. *Third*, the Web is becoming much more influential with regard to buying decisions. The Internet plays an increasingly important role throughout the whole purchasing process, with regard to information-gathering, product comparisons and social recommendations (e.g. Amazon ratings, and others) and also purchasing. Online purchasing itself is growing at 20% per year.

Impact on advertisers

After a significant delay, advertisers are following their consumers online. Currently, the share of online advertising spend as a percentage of total media spend still significantly lags behind the share of time spent online as a percentage of total time spent on media (Figure 6.4).

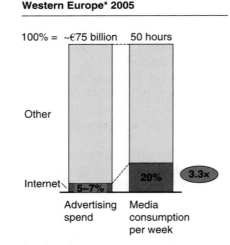

Figure 6.4 Advertising spend and media consumption time

*Germany, United Kingdom, Sweden, Denmark, Norway, the Netherlands, Belgium, France, Italy, Spain
Source: McKinsey analysis based on data from Jupiter; EIAA; IAB

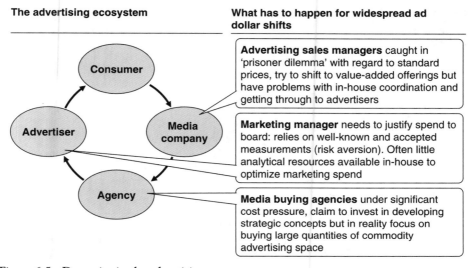

The advertising ecosystem

What has to happen for widespread ad dollar shifts

Advertising sales managers caught in 'prisoner dilemma' with regard to standard prices, try to shift to value-added offerings but have problems with in-house coordination and getting through to advertisers

Marketing manager needs to justify spend to board: relies on well-known and accepted measurements (risk aversion). Often little analytical resources available in-house to optimize marketing spend

Media buying agencies under significant cost pressure, claim to invest in developing strategic concepts but in reality focus on buying large quantities of commodity advertising space

Figure 6.5   Dynamics in the advertising ecosystem

Source: Author analyses

The main reason for this is the inertia in the advertising ecosystem (Figure 6.5): marketers are under significant pressure to justify the ROI of their marketing spend and find it easier to rely on well-known ratios and proven advertising effectiveness measurement models that have been developed for traditional media, especially TV, than to justify highly complex cross-media or online campaigns with new, different and often inconsistent measurements. Also, the effort of developing such a campaign is often very high and most marketing departments have only very limited resources. Media-buying agencies would in principle like to take on the role of strategic media advisers; however, they are only being paid for their media-buying services and the buying of traditional media space is still simpler and more profitable for the agency than digital media space. Finally, although media companies are starting to sell their online offerings more aggressively, they are still hesitant to cannibalize their traditional media offerings. Very often, the sales of off- and online media are done by different sales forces, so it is difficult to come up with an integrated offering where on- and offline are bundled. Even when the media companies offer bundles, this very often results in a discussion on additional discounts rather than strategic effectiveness.

For the advertising ecosystem to adapt to the digital world, it must make changes to its systems of payment and for measuring advertising effectiveness, as well as to its skills and organizational structures (integration of off- and online advertising activities). For this to happen, there has to be significant market pressure, as is shown by the historic example of US cable TV. Initially, the cable channels had major problems getting

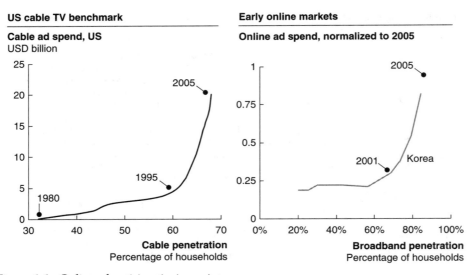

Figure 6.6 Online advertising tipping points

Source: McKinsey analyses based on data from US Bureau of Census; Veronis Suhler; Universal McCann; Media Dynamics; Television Bureau of Advertising; ZenithOptimedia; Jupiter Media

advertising revenues in spite of the fact that they had significant viewer share. Again, this was mostly due to the ecosystem, as advertisers were not adapted to measuring the cable audience and allocating their advertising over a multitude of local channels rather than a few national networks; however, as the channels reached a 60% penetration and time spent watching cable TV surpassed time spent watching the major TV networks, the pressure got too great and the ecosystem changed. US cable advertising has subsequently skyrocketed at the expense of broadcast television networks (Figure 6.6).

Online advertising is now also nearing this tipping point with broadband penetration above 60% in many countries. In the United Kingdom and France online advertising already represents more than 10% of the total advertising spend, bypassing spend for radio and magazines. In the United Kingdom online spend is expected to surpass TV advertising spend in 2008 (19% market share for online versus 18% for TV).

Although there is still significant uncertainty as to how big the online ad market will be, most optimistic forecasts estimate that online will be the second-largest medium for ad spend by 2011, larger than newspapers, and just below the combined advertising spend of radio and television broadcasting.[4] As a consequence of this, it is expected that online advertisement worldwide will increase from US$36 billion in 2006 to US$81 billion by 2010 (Figure 6.7).

---

[4]Veronis Suhler Stevenson estimates, as reported in Les Echos, Tendances, August 10, 2007. This was confirmed by a McKinsey survey of more than 300 companies worldwide, where online spend will be 24% of total spend, above newspapers and television.

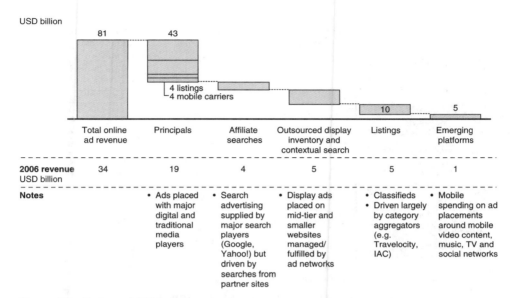

USD billion	Total online ad revenue	Principals	Affiliate searches	Outsourced display inventory and contextual search	Listings	Emerging platforms
	81	43			10	5

4 listings
4 mobile carriers

2006 revenue USD billion	34	19	4	5	5	1
Notes		• Ads placed with major digital and traditional media players	• Search advertising supplied by major search players (Google, Yahoo!) but driven by searches from partner sites	• Display ads placed on mid-tier and smaller websites managed/ fulfilled by ad networks	• Classifieds • Driven largely by category aggregators (e.g. Travelocity, IAC)	• Mobile spending on ad placements around mobile video content, music, TV and social networks

Figure 6.7   Estimated 2010 ad revenue

Source: McKinsey analyses based on data from eMarketer January 2007

To know more about how exactly online marketing will evolve, a survey was conducted by one of the authors, with McKinsey colleagues, amongst a large set of marketing executives from public and private companies around the world in July 2007 and June 2008.[5] Three key insights emerged regarding shift in advertising demand.

Fact 1: The importance of all areas of digital marketing. Two-thirds of companies are using digital marketing tools in the five major marketing areas (advertising, sales, customer care, product development and, to a lesser extent, pricing). At least two-thirds of companies using digital tools view them as very important for their marketing (Figure 6.8).

Fact 2: The rise of new advertising formats. Spending on digital advertising is set to increase significantly across the board. In the 2008 survey, 90% of companies were already spending some budget online, versus 72% one year before. A third of companies that advertise online were already spending more than 10% of their

[5]Bughin, J., Shenkan, A. and Erbenich, C., 'How companies market online: a McKinsey survey', July 2007 and Bughin, J., Shenkan, A. and Singer, M., 'How companies are advertising online: a McKinsey survey', July 2008.

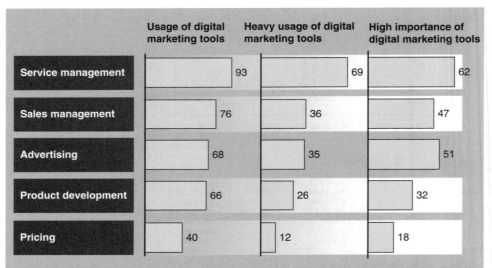

Figure 6.8   Penetration of digital marketing tools

Source: Jacques Bughin, Aly Shenkan and Christoph Erbenich, 'How companies market online: a McKinsey survey', July 2007

advertising budget by 2007. It is estimated that by 2011 twice as many will be spending at least that much online, and 11% will be spending the majority of their budget online.

Finally, spend on different online advertising formats is quite broad, including new formats such as rich media videos ads and Web 2.0 elements. E-mail marketing is still

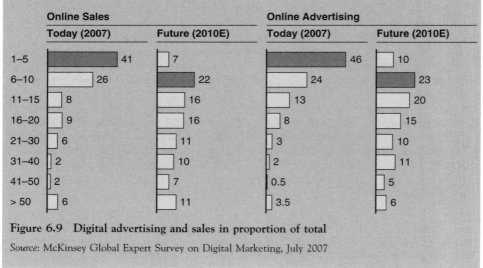

Figure 6.9   Digital advertising and sales in proportion of total

Source: McKinsey Global Expert Survey on Digital Marketing, July 2007

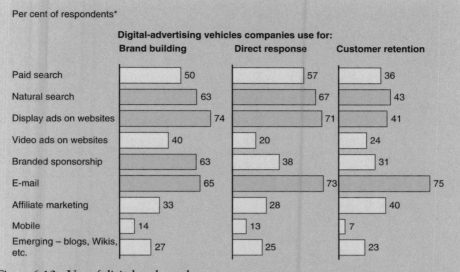

Per cent of respondents*

Digital-advertising vehicles companies use for:

	Brand building	Direct response	Customer retention
Paid search	50	57	36
Natural search	63	67	43
Display ads on websites	74	71	41
Video ads on websites	40	20	24
Branded sponsorship	63	38	31
E-mail	65	73	75
Affiliate marketing	33	28	40
Mobile	14	13	7
Emerging – blogs, Wikis, etc.	27	25	23

Figure 6.10   Use of digital tools used

*Respondents who answered 'other' or 'don't know' excluded
Source: McKinsey Digital Marketing Survey, July 2008

dominant, however, and the majority of online advertisers also use ad banners and search advertisements (both classified and natural search). By 2008, 40% of companies used online video advertising for brand building, and 27% used emerging vehicles such as blogs, social networks and Wikis, as well as widgets and virtual worlds like Second Life. Mobile advertising had only just taken off in 2008, and in that year was used by 14% of companies (Figures 6.9 and 6.10).

Fact 3: New types of online marketing spend. Companies spend increasingly on direct involvement with online users, rather than online advertisements. This includes sponsoring, typically for communities online. Such is the case for companies like Apple or Victoria Secrets, both of which have sponsored their own communities on major online social networks (for both this is Facebook). Also, companies are using collaborative tools such as blogs, Wikis and social networks for product development and customer service. For example, at the most basic level, 22% of companies host a user forum for customers to help each other. Some two-thirds of the companies surveyed use online tools for product development; about a quarter do so frequently. The focus is on testing concepts and screening ideas or on involving customers in the use of collaborative design. This process of close cooperation with users is not new, but is gaining momentum as the size of the online population grows (Figure 6.11).[6]

---

[6]This involvement of customers translates into media and user-generated content and peer production (see chapter 3 in this book).

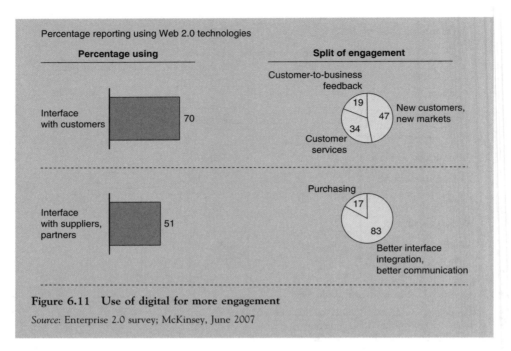

Figure 6.11 Use of digital for more engagement

Source: Enterprise 2.0 survey; McKinsey, June 2007

Also within the traditional media there will be significant changes as the ability to skip advertisements with help from digital video recorders or video-on-demand offerings increases, advertisers will turn more and more to sponsoring and product placement; they even want to develop direct-branded content. Although the bulk of the ad market is still ad-spot based (for instance 90% of all TV advertisements), the alternative revenue from advertising is growing at double the rate of the ad display market and is likely to represent 14% of the total ad spend by 2012. This is even larger than what advertisers are likely to spend on online videos ads (Figure 6.12).

These alternative vehicles will be promoted by advertisers looking to create the fastest, if not immediate, brand association with their product, and will be facilitated by the rise of digitization, which enables advertisers to enjoy closer and more direct contact with their audience and so engage more deeply with it. As a result, a lot of new media branded content production companies have seen the light in recent years, from UK-based Cake to US-based Deep Focus and many others.

Industry dynamics: supply side

The advertising value chain is traditionally composed of ad inventory providers (mostly media companies such as a television network offering 30 second ad spots or a newspaper offering classifieds and display page inserts). These companies capture roughly 80% of the revenue. Other parts include media planning and buying services as well as agencies which perform the creation and production of the advertisements (both the media planning and

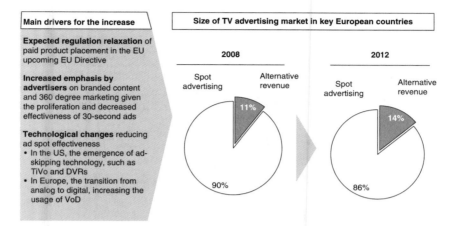

Figure 6.12   The rise of new alternative ad business.

buying as well as the creative agencies are mostly owned by large advertising conglomerates such as WPP, Publicis and others) (Figure 6.13).

The digital evolution significantly affects the complete industry structure and conduct.

Dynamics of advertising services

The service part of the value chain has witnessed a dramatic concentration of media buying groups, with the top five groups making 80% of the revenue. While this concentration meant more strength for these groups, this development did not extend

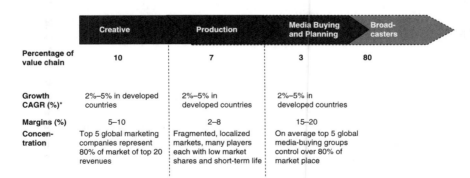

Figure 6.13   TV advertising value chain dynamics

Source: McKinsey analysis

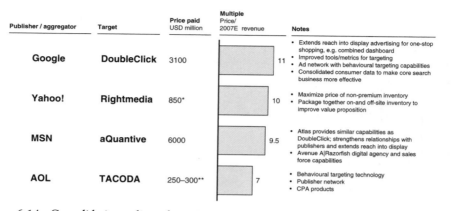

Figure 6.14 Consolidating online ad services

*Yahoo! paid $680 million for 80% of equity it didn't already own
**Companies did not publicly disclose deal value; *Wall Street Journal* pegs the acquisition between $250m and $300m
Source: McKinsey analysis

to the online world. In 2007 alone, more than US$12 billion were invested to concentrate the ad services online, including Microsoft's acquisition of aQuantive for about $6 billion, and Google's acquisition of Double Click for more than $3 billion. Traditional agencies have also entered this arena, for example Publicis' acquisition of Digitas for more than $1 billion and WPP's acquisition of 24/7 media (Figure 6.14).

In general, the jury is still out about how the market will consolidate, but one factor seems important for the development of the online advertising service market in the near future: our research shows that advertisers moving online are still, on the whole, using the services of the traditional media agencies for online, but in exchange they expect much more online analytical competencies. As this could not always be provided, some advertisers (about 30%) have shifted to specific online agencies.[7] Most online players have aggressively developed those analytic competencies, either in-house as well as through acquisitions, for example Yahoo!'s acquisition of BlueLithium and AOL's acquisition of Tacoda (behavioural targeting technology services).

Finally, on the advertising creative side, things are changing too, as new forms of relationship between advertisers and a new breed of creative agency is being created, moving more towards the concept of 'branded content' with direct ownership of the content by the advertisers. One such example is the show *The Gamekillers*, produced by a US-based digital creative company called Radical Media and sponsored by Unilever's Axe Deodorant. The producers marketed the show virally on the Internet, launched a MySpace page that enabled people to become 'friends' with the contestants on *The*

---

[7]Bughin, J., Shenkan, A. and Singer, M., 'How companies advertise online: a McKinsey survey', June 2008. The survey includes about 300 companies worldwide.

Gamekillers and supplemented the show with a print campaign. The concept produced strong impact. The show drew 10 million viewers over 10 days, and most importantly for the brand, sales of Axe Dry deodorant increased by a staggering 60%, even though the show never mentioned the brand.

The impact of this trend on the industry's structure is still to be seen, but it is likely to create new competition if early successes prove scalable.

Dynamics in ad inventory provision

Media companies typically play a major role in this part of the advertising value chain. The dynamics in this segment are likely to change fundamentally in the coming years. Competition will increase on three fronts. As discussed earlier, smaller niche players in traditional media will increase their activity and market share as they move to digital. Second, pure online players such as Google, Yahoo! and many others will aggressively fight for advertising revenue (Figure 6.15). Third, platform operators such as cable companies and telecoms operators, or original equipment manufacturers (OEM) such as handset are increasingly intending to use their reach and direct customer relationships to take a slice of the advertising pie.

On the Web, the major players, such as the search engine Google, the major portals or the major content sites like C/Net are offering the bulk of the new ad inventory. Google, specifically on the market for paid search, is dominant in almost every country (with the exception of a few markets like Russia or South Korea, where the domestic search portal dominates, given language and indexing barriers). But niche content sites are

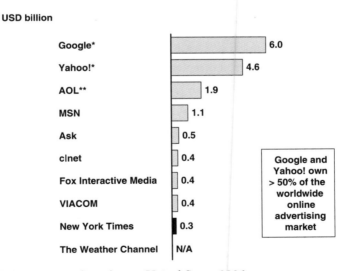

Figure 6.15   Revenue top online players, United States 2006

*Yahoo! and Google estimates are gross revenue before traffic acquisition costs
**AOL data are inclusive of Advertising.com revenue, which is gross (before traffic acquisition)
Source: McKinsey analysis based on data from Interactive Advertising Bureau (IAB); company filings; Piper Jaffray Investment Research

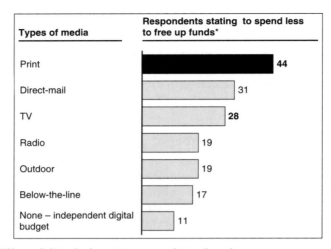

Figure 6.16   Effect of digital advertising on traditional media

*Base is total of respondents that use digital tools for advertising (n = 280)
Source: McKinsey Global Expert Survey on Digital Marketing

also increasingly trying to get their share of the market, directly competing with traditional media. In the United States, Next New Networks (or NNN) has set up 101 personalized 'micro-television' networks focused on cars, fashion, politics and other topics. San Francisco-based 80/20 Publishing has launched highly successful crowd-sourced community magazines, such as *JPG* (photography-based community) and *Everywhere* (travel-based community).

Online advertisement inventory is not always a substitute for traditional offline inventory, but can serve as a good complement. This is because a mere 10% of Internet consumers are taking decisions *exclusively* online. Since most customers will remain multi-touch-point and multichannel in their buying decision process, it remains critical to deploy a cohesive media-mix approach to support sales. In our survey of advertisers, we found that 50% of the advertisers who spend money on online marketing are actually considering the online budget as being complementary to offline and thus not affecting the offline spend. For those which don't, they substitute money from offline to online, and more frequently, at the expense of print (Figure 6.16).

Reaching New Capabilities in Advertising

Given the above trends, media companies risk an oversupply and commoditization of traditional ad space, while media agencies face a risk of being partially made superfluous by "direct booking" online players such as Google.

To avoid those pitfalls, companies must quickly build new capabilities, as well as refocus on customer needs and find better ways to fulfil them. This, however, requires a fundamental rethink.

This includes three core elements: (a) a much more B2B-like marketing approach to advertising sales, (b) a different approach to advertising product offering, impact measurement and pricing and (c) a better trimming of the ad sales force. Those 'hygiene' factors must be mastered no matter what, and extended with digital capabilities online.

Systematic use of B2B marketing approaches

Other industries, which have already faced fierce competition, have fine-tuned B2B marketing approaches, and many of these can be applied to the media industry. The predominant thought behind these approaches is to avoid the 'commodity trap', that is sell the same product as everyone else, and the resulting price-based competition, and instead focus on creating (unique) value for the customer. Applied with the right approach, this even works for industrial commodity businesses, for example one steel producer managed to increase its return on sales (ROS) by 5% by systematically applying all B2B marketing levers (Figure 6.17).

Effective B2B marketing strategies require four steps:

1. Define segment needs of the customer with regard to the type of products/services offered.
2. Develop tailored value propositions that encompass the entire value delivery process rather than just the product.
3. Create differentiated offerings to deliver on the value proposition.
4. Set prices that reflect the true total customer value rather than competitive spot prices.

Given the historical, relatively simple structure of the media advertising offering (30-second TV spots, classified columns and magazine pages), it is not immediately obvious

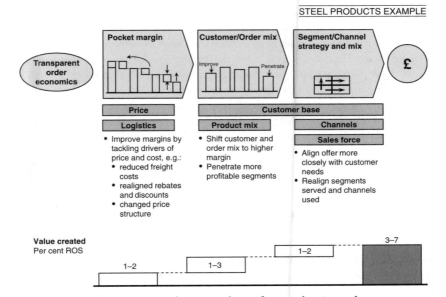

Figure 6.17 **B2B marketing approaches created significant value in steel sector**

Source: McKinsey Business-to-Business Marketing Practice

how to apply these principles. However, in the digital world there are new options and, at the same time, the necessity to create more B2B customer-oriented offerings.

Define segment needs directly related to product/ service offering

The key competitive advantage of large-scale media such as TV, radio and newspapers is that they are unique in offering immediate, large-scale access to end consumers. Therefore, the key customers of these media are those companies that want to invest in (fast) brand building for a mass audience. The defined target groups are broadly defined, based on demographics (adults 16–49), and prices are based on the gross rating points (GRPs; percentage of target audience reached) and CPM (cost per thousand contacts). The reach of a medium is based on real-time panel research (TV) and/or circulation tracking (print) combined with an intermittent market research to translate circulation into typical readership profiles. For TV advertising, the more advanced advertisers use an econometric 'black box' to assess an advertisement's impact on sales and to improve the micro-placement of ads. These models are mostly developed and owned by the media-buying agencies or special service providers.

These practices have been in place for many years, with slight variations on a country-by-country basis. With the advent of digital media, the model shows three major drawbacks:

1. **Consumer segmentation:** advertisement placement in traditional media is mostly based on demographic segments. More and more advertisers, however, do not segment any more based on demographics but on 'usage and attitude' (U&A) based criteria. A bank, for example, would look not only at the wealth of its customers but also at whether they want personal service or prefer the Internet; a mobile operator is above all interested in whether its customers use the phone just for voice or also for additional services; a car manufacturer wants to lure drivers of French cars away to German cars. When setting up a traditional marketing campaign, these segments have to be translated into approximate demographic segments in order to select the right media. Research has shown that there can be, however, major differences in media usage between groups with a similar demographic profile but different U&A profiles not only with regard to the type of media they use but also with regard to how they use the media, for example advertising filtering behaviour (Figure 6.18). Basing reach calculations solely on demographic profiles can thus lead to significant misplacement of advertisement (Figure 6.19). Digital media can often offer much more detailed information on consumers as their media usage can be followed on a real-time basis (what sites do they click on, what digital TV programmes do they watch, etc.) and usage data can often be linked to the subscription data of the digital platform (cable, telecom, ISP) which the consumer uses to access the media offerings.
2. **Single-media approach:** traditionally there is a strict separation between media with regard to sales of advertising inventory, measurement of reach and payment practices. For example, an advertiser very often does not know when an advertisement in a newspaper in the morning reaches 30% of its target group and an advertisement on TV

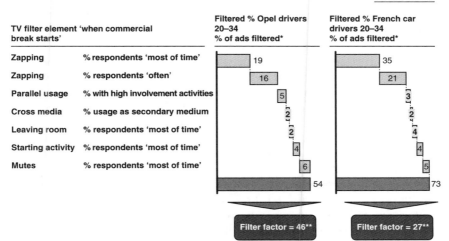

Figure 6.18   Advertising filtering behaviour of drivers of French vs. German car drivers (aged 20–34) in the Netherlands

*Exact weighting of filter elements to be statistically determined
**(100% filtered percentage) * 100
Source: McKinsey MediaMatics

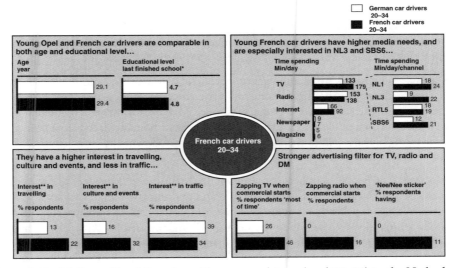

Figure 6.19   Media profile of French vs. German car drivers (aged 20–34) in the Netherlands

*On a scale from 1 to 7, with 7 representing highest
**Stated as (very) important topic
Source: McKinsey MediaMatics project

in the evening reaches 30% of its target group, whether he reached 30% of its target group twice or 60% once that day, as he does not know the overlap between the media. Often advertisers confine a major extent of their advertising budget to one medium, where they can optimize the reach/frequency trade-off (i.e. what percentage of the target group is reached, and how often, in a certain period). With the fragmentation of media and the reallocation of time to the Internet, it will become more and more important to reach consumers at different points in the day with different media in order to get a critical mass of touch-points and profit from the mutual relation between media. It is especially important to understand the relationship between traditional media usage and the Internet, as marketing efforts in these forms of media often complement each other (for example searches on the internet for a product tend to go up significantly after a TV-ad).

3. **Marketing needs:** depending on the lifecycle of a product, an advertiser is likely to have different marketing goals for the same product and target segments over time, for example creating brand awareness, creating interest in the product, inducing trial and ensuring repeat. Some media are more appropriate for ensuring certain marketing goals than others, for example TV is often used for brand building, magazines for advertisements which appeal more to emotions and newspapers for functional advertisements, such as store promotions. The role of the Internet is still evolving. Initially, Web advertising was, above all, used to generate leads; however, with the rise of rich internet media and social networks, the Internet has become an increasingly important tool for creating brand awareness and loyalty. Although there are many rules of thumb on which medium to use for which marketing goal, and several ad hoc researches on the effectiveness of certain media, there is little systematic, comprehensive academic research on the topic, and advertisers must often rely on empiric models from media-buying agencies, which are based on historic correlations rather than forward looking insights. In the digital era it will become much more important to understand what the joint effect of using various media will be in order to fine-tune the media mix.

Increasingly, advertisers are becoming aware of these drawbacks and the demand for a new value proposition from the media companies increased.

Rather than just selling advertising inventory in bulk ('tonnage') to media-buying agencies, media companies will thus also need to do their homework to gain a proper B2B understanding of the needs of their key customers. The following five-step checklist offers the basic components of this homework:

1. *Importance of brand:* Research by the MCM Institute in Munster, Germany, and McKinsey & Company shows that the role and importance of brand varies by product category (Figure 6.20). Not paying attention to this has caused, for example, consumer goods companies to overinvest in building brand awareness rather than actually pushing the products in the market. By segmenting their customers according to brand importance, media companies can tailor their mass-marketing image campaign propositions to product categories with high brand value, or offer direct-selling campaigns for product categories where brand is less important.
2. *Bottleneck in purchase funnel:* Companies lose many potential customers along the purchase funnel (Figure 6.21). A detailed analysis of where these customers get lost

Scored 0–5
Product markets

Image benefit	(0–5)	Information efficiency	(0–5)	Risk reduction	(0–5)
Designer sunglasses	4.86	Cigarettes	4.12	Headache pain relievers	3.41
Compact cars	3.81	Detergents	3.72	Designer sunglasses	3.40
Mid-class cars	3.77	Beer	3.67	Cigarettes	3.27
Telephony (fixed wire)	2.41			Small cars	3.20
		TV listings magazines	3.28	Washing machines	2.99
Detergents	2.36			TV listings magazines	2.87
		Bonus	2.63	Coffee percolators	2.32
TV listings magazines	2.13	Coffee percolators	1.86		
Energy	1.72	Electricity		Paper handkerchiefs	1.83
Paper tissues	1.43		1.51	Electricity	1.78

Figure 6.20   Importance of the three brand functions from the MCM/McKinsey brand relevance survey

Source: McKinsey, analyses based on data from MCM; GfK GfK

can help the company focus on which part of the funnel to allocate its spending. Consequently, companies must decide what marketing tools are most effective. Purchase funnel analyses can be conducted by media companies for their customers, to help develop proactive marketing strategies (Figure 6.22).

3. *Target end-consumer segments:* Advertisers vary greatly in the specificity with which they approach consumers, ranging from very broad segmentation (all viewers between

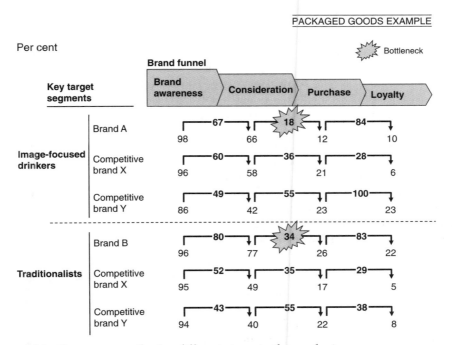

Figure 6.21   Consumers get 'lost' at different stages in the purchasing process

Source: McKinsey analyses

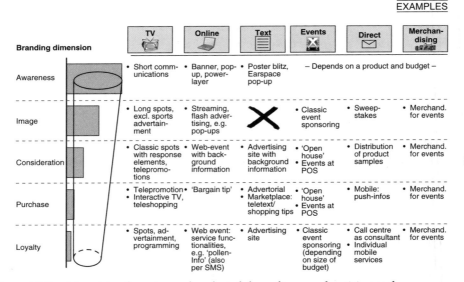

Figure 6.22   Advertising formats can be adapted depending on advertising goal

Source: McKinsey, SevenOne Media

14 and 49 years) to a bundle of highly specific, mostly non-demographic segments. By specifically mapping the target audiences for media offerings to the advertisers' needs, high-fit versus low-fit segments can be defined.

4. *Segment according to value orientation:* A large European magazine group segmented its advertising customers into three groups – concept buyers, value buyers and efficiency buyers – based on their respective focus on value-creation versus cost-sensitivity. Each group had a clearly different attitude towards the type of products in which they were interested and the price they were willing to pay. Understanding these differences can result in different strategies per segment as best-practice examples show (Figure 6.23).

5. *Differentiated service needs:* In addition to the advertising space and price, other factors in the booking process can play an important role for advertisers, for example order lead times, flexibility, ease of incorporating the ad into the programme or text, customer service and payment terms. Although these factors are not all-determining in the ad-purchasing process, they can play an important role in swinging the balance.

As developing this knowledge requires significant investment by a media company, it should be very clear beforehand which of its key customers it wants to focus on or, in the case of smaller customers, what are the key branches it wants to develop these insights for. In selecting its target customers/branches several best practices should be taken into account. First, media companies should strive for a large market share in selected segments rather than a small market share in the market as a whole. Second, they should focus on those one or two key purchase factors that really matter to the customer segment rather than try to be a 'jack of all trades' and, third, they should have

Segment	Advertiser behaviour	How to extract more money

Concept buyers	• Willing to buy premium products and seek to be associated with premium brand	• Create premium offers, e.g.:
		  – Special editorial sections
		  – One-of-a-kind placements
		  – Special inserts
		  – Targeted magazine segments
		  – Gatefold advertisements

Value buyers	• Seek privileged access to influence purchasing behaviour through integrated packages that add value by leveraging synergies across properties and media	• Provide integrated marketing solutions to surround audience across media platforms
		• Demonstrate distinctive ways in which your media can influence purchasing decisions, e.g.:
		  – Ziff Davis and Survey.com alliance, providing custom market research through on line panels to technology- and consumer-oriented companies
		  – Fusion techniques, currently used by market research firms Nielsen and Kantar, combine information from respondents to more precisely target specific audiences

Efficiency buyers	• Maximize reach and frequency into a target demographic at the lowest possible cost	• Lock-in multiyear commitment in exchange for fixed-price increases • Create lower price products (e.g. half-page supplements) to tap 'pocket price' advertisers • Demonstrate value and share of 'attention' vs. alternative buy • Optimize pricing according to publication

Figure 6.23 Advertising buyers can be segmented according to their focus on value vs. price

Source: McKinsey analyses

a deep understanding of the profit potential and ability to win business per segment in order to keep efforts focused.

Develop unique value proposition

Once there is a good understanding of the need of the advertisers, media companies need to develop an offering which caters specifically to these needs. Media companies (e.g. Time Warner, Viacom) have taken the first steps along this road by offering cross-media, all-inclusive packages to their major accounts. However, results so far have been mixed, as very often the organizational effort to create these media packages is high, the willingness of the customer to pay premium prices is low (or the customer even expects additional discounts) and measuring the effectiveness of the campaign is complex.

In order to create true value and lasting customer relationships media companies need not only to strategically design their advertising products but also to go beyond just delivering advertising inventory and add value along the whole advertising value chain.

Strategically designed advertising products

Media companies have been struggling with the 'commodity' character of their advertising products, which allows for little differentiation except in audience reach. Cross-media offerings are often just a combination of the available standard products offered at a discount. Creative companies go successfully beyond this approach:

- *Use innovative forms of advertising:* Especially in TV and online, advertising offerings greatly increased during the first decade of this century. Not only new formats but also new approaches such as sponsoring and branded content (see the beginning of this chapter) are developing fast. Media companies should be very aware of these trends, especially through the Internet, and incorporate them early on.
- *Integrated advertising concepts:* Although first hailed as an industry innovation and then spurned as a tool used by advertisers to negotiate volume discounts, integrated advertising concepts (i.e. combining multiple media) can create a value-added offering when applied correctly and segment-specifically. The key is that integrated offerings must be concept- rather than advertising inventory supply-driven, that is they should be built around a certain theme relevant to the target customers. A prime example of this is the Dove campaign, where a strategic message which is core to the brand (women with normal bodies are beautiful) is used as a basis for storytelling and interaction on several fronts. As this campaign is not a one-off but the basis for a multi-year thrust, the effort to create the campaign is worthwhile and, as it uses many community aspects, part of the content and involvement is created by consumers (Figure 6.24). Synergetic cross-media campaigns need products with a strong, well-known brand personality.

Figure 6.24 Dove multimedia campaign: real women have real curves

Source: Unilever. Reproduced with permission

Redesign the value chain

Just offering innovative, value-added advertising products will not be enough. Advertisers (and media agencies) tend to be conservative and risk-averse and very often do not have the resources to redesign and experiment with their marketing approach. For things to change, media companies will have to push for change in the whole advertising value chain:

- *Advertising content creation:* Media companies, especially those which cater to more niche audiences, very often have an in-depth understanding of their audience – the way they feel and think, their preferences and concerns and the way they consume media – which can be matched by few. At the same time advertisers are looking more and more to create stories for their consumers (à la Dove) rather than simple, single messages, in order to capture attention and involvement in a market which is flooded by advertising messages. By using their storytelling competence and in-depth knowledge of their consumers, media companies can create unique value for the advertisers. The audience can even be used for testing concepts and direct feedback.
- *Measuring reach and impact:* A key bottleneck in transitioning advertising space from commodity to strategic products is the lack of ability to easily and objectively measure the effect of these new approaches. Traditional advertising effectiveness research such as TV panels and print sales statistics are not geared to cope with the increased complexity. Innovation of the measurement of media consumption and advertising impact is 'make or break' for the innovation of advertising strategies – and digital technologies can offer those means, but, alas, the bulk of companies are still far from mastering those technologies:

> Our survey on digital marketing demonstrates that the unique capabilities to deliver measurable and targeted results through digital technologies are used inefficiently.[8]
>
> When asked to rank the top three barriers preventing their companies from spending more on digital advertising, the primary reason, cited by almost 20% of the respondents, was insufficient metrics to measure impact (Figure 6.25). Those companies that rank Web analytics as the digital marketing tool or technology that would drive the most value to their companies mostly use separate outside agencies for their digital advertising.
>
> A lack of specialized Web skills may also explain why almost two-thirds of respondents say they use qualitative, rather than refined quantitative, analyses when deciding how to allocate their ad budgets. Barely more than half look at the click-through rate or click-based conversions for direct response ads and two-thirds have yet to measure the combined impact of online on offline in their measure of online effectiveness spend (Figure 6.26).

---

[8]Bughin, J., Shenkan, A. and Singer, M., 'How companies advertise online: a McKinsey survey', June 2008. The survey includes about 300 companies worldwide.

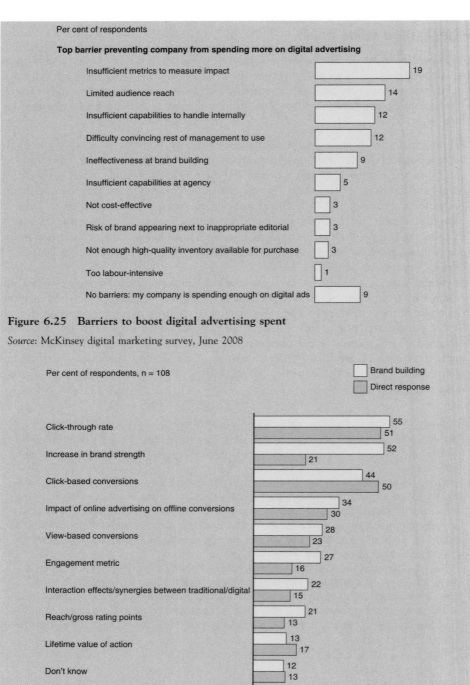

Per cent of respondents

Top barrier preventing company from spending more on digital advertising

Insufficient metrics to measure impact	19
Limited audience reach	14
Insufficient capabilities to handle internally	12
Difficulty convincing rest of management to use	12
Ineffectiveness at brand building	9
Insufficient capabilities at agency	5
Not cost-effective	3
Risk of brand appearing next to inappropriate editorial	3
Not enough high-quality inventory available for purchase	3
Too labour-intensive	1
No barriers: my company is spending enough on digital ads	9

Figure 6.25   Barriers to boost digital advertising spent

Source: McKinsey digital marketing survey, June 2008

Per cent of respondents, n = 108

Brand building
Direct response

	Brand building	Direct response
Click-through rate	55	51
Increase in brand strength	52	21
Click-based conversions	44	50
Impact of online advertising on offline conversions	34	30
View-based conversions	28	23
Engagement metric	27	16
Interaction effects/synergies between traditional/digital	22	15
Reach/gross rating points	21	13
Lifetime value of action	13	17
Don't know	12	13

Figure 6.26   Tools for measuring digital advertising effectiveness

Source: McKinsey digital marketing survey, June 2008

Digital technologies also open up completely new opportunities to measure media consumption in real time, across media, for example measuring digital TV and Internet usage with help from smart set-top boxes. Many parties are experimenting with new ways of measurement, for example TiVo in the United States, P&G and Nielsen with the now discontinued Apollo project also in the United States, the Touchstone project in the United Kingdom and the Mediamatics initiative in the Netherlands. All these experiments show that major benefits can be gained from improved cross-media measurement, for example the Mediamatics pilot in the Netherlands showed that advertisers can increase their reach by between 10% and 40% for the same advertising spend by having better information on advertiser segment-specific media usage.

- *Create an integrated approach:* Media companies have the unique chance to interact with advertisers in the concept phase, based on their understanding of target groups and storytelling abilities; in the media selection phase, based on their knowledge of media-usage patterns; and finally in the measurement phase, by providing consumer-usage data. Tying these all together into a coherent approach will make the media company a strategic partner for advertisers rather than suppliers of ad inventory. It will also be an important way for traditional media companies to compete with industry innovators like Google, who are trying to leapfrog the industry by creating innovative and highly efficient automated platforms which optimize media space booking with help from algorithms and auctioning procedures and deliver impact measurement with tools like Google Analytics. By delivering much more in-depth and qualitative concepts, media companies can differentiate themselves from these types of offerings. To truly deliver on this several media companies are already deciding to integrate vertically.

Online companies are leading the vertical integration of the advertising value chain. Google has evolved from a provider of basic information retrieval to a powerful online information marketplace, and now continues to expand, building up its own analytic and display advertising service competencies through its AdSense network and its acquisition of Double Click. Other major online players such as AOL and Yahoo! are also expanding their presence along all the elements of the advertising value chain (Figure 6.27).

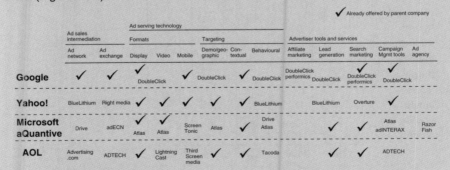

| | Ad sales intermediation | | Ad serving technology | | | | | | Advertiser tools and services | | | | |
| | | | Formats | | | Targeting | | | | | | | |
	Ad network	Ad exchange	Display	Video	Mobile	Demo/geo-graphic	Con-textual	Behavioural	Affiliate marketing	Lead generation	Search marketing	Campaign Mgmt tools	Ad agency
Google	✓	✓	✓ DoubleClick			✓ DoubleClick		✓ DoubleClick	DoubleClick performics	DoubleClick	✓ DoubleClick performics	DoubleClick	
Yahoo!	BlueLithium	Right media	✓	✓	✓	✓		✓ BlueLithium		BlueLithium	Overture	✓	
Microsoft aQuantive	Drive	adECN	✓ Atlas	✓ Atlas		Screen Tonic	Atlas	✓ Drive Atlas		✓	✓	Atlas adINTERAX	Razor Fish
AOL	Advertising.com	ADTECH	✓	Lightning Cast	Third Screen media	✓	✓	Tacoda		✓	✓	ADTECH	

✓ Already offered by parent company

Figure 6.27   The vertical integration play in online ad value chain

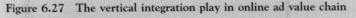

Source: McKinsey analyses

Traditional media can react by also integrating vertically (through acquisitions such as Lagardere did by buying Jumpstart, or through organic growth, for example the Belgian newspapers building their own cooperative online ad network). In all cases, however, vertical ownership requires new analytic and service capabilities that traditional media must master in order to compete with the online players.

Performance-based pricing

With the advent of the Internet, advertisers are getting more and more used to performance-based pricing. The first major shift was from CPM (reach-based prices) to CPC (cost per click), and companies like Google and MSN are increasingly experimenting with prices which are based on actions (e.g. the online booking of a test ride at a car dealership) or even sales resulting from the click. Advertisers really like these types of payment models, as they greatly reduce their risk and increase transparency (Figure 6.28).

For offline media it is, of course, much more difficult to link prices directly to performance; however, through intimate knowledge of the audience and of the real-time demand for and supply of advertising space, even offline yields can be increased significantly.

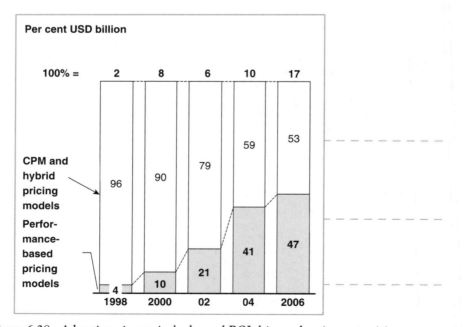

Figure 6.28 Advertisers increasingly demand ROI-driven advertisement pricing

Source: McKinsey analysis based on data from PWC Global Outlook/IAB, interviews; SFN Research, 2006

For media companies, this implies that they should try to shift the price focus of offline advertising space away from GRP (gross rating points; a price based on the number of viewers within a predefined target group) and sales volume to include other factors such as price elasticity, capacity restraints, time of booking, booking flexibility and quality of media surroundings as well as disciplining the sales force on when and how discounts should be used.

Sellers of ad space/time need to adapt their inventory allocation and pricing schemes continually, taking into account what exactly their key advertising clients seek in terms of audience share, frequency, segmentation and timeline. While the logic of this is well known, the level of sophistication still varies significantly across the European media landscape. Although actual allocation and placement trade-offs are essentially driven by advertisers' concrete briefing constraints, media planners in general note 'rigorous execution', 'audience stability' and 'placement flexibility' as the top three properties they seek in ad-sales departments.

Programming for Money: Free-to-Air TV Revenue Optimization

Especially for free-to-air TV channels, business is fundamentally about maximizing advertising revenue per time unit/viewer, as advertising is usually their main revenue source and advertising time is limited by regulators (typically to a maximum of 12 minutes per hour in most European countries). Revenue maximization can be achieved by selling targeted contacts for specific audiences rather than net airtime. The TV channels should be free to deliver the contracted number of contacts through inserts at different timeslots (e.g. one prime-time insert typically equals four lunchtime inserts). Sub-optimal matching of target viewers and advertisers in each specific timeslot still prevents many media players from capturing the fair value of their available ad minutes. In a 2002 survey, 22 out of 25 TV channels in 14 countries said that they designed their programming to maximize audience share rather than revenue or profit potential.

The most obvious move is to adjust the programming grid to maximize revenue potential rather than audience share, taking into account that each ad minute will be sold to a particular commercial target. Many viewers who happen to be watching the surrounding programmes may be outside the targeted contacts sold and hence wasted from a revenue perspective, allowing for improvements through a better fit of programming and ad minutes. A sample advertiser may have bought 60% reach with housewives between 25 and 49 years of age through three or more contacts over a period of two weeks. The programming challenge is to find a combination of ad slots that delivers that specific buy, and minimizes accidental viewers outside the profile (e.g. upscale males or children) who could generate revenues through other advertising clients (see Figure 6.29).

When it comes to pricing, TV channels can learn from the yield management that airlines apply when filling a plane. Currently, two-thirds of commercial TV channels have pricing schemes based on ratings (number of viewers) and/or time slots, rather than precise value to advertisers. Only 12% engage in actual yield management of their advertising inventory, while most others allocate it on a first-in, first-served basis.

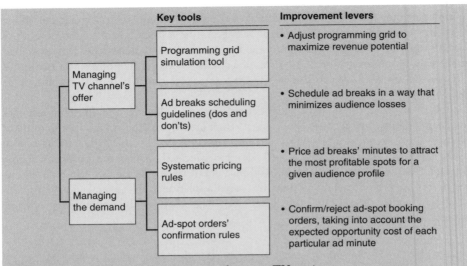

Figure 6.29 Overview of monetization levers at TV stations

Source: McKinsey analysis

As a first step, companies such as Mediaset in Italy and TVI in Portugal have introduced a more differentiated approach to the GRP system. Traditionally, advertising rates were determined by the number of viewers within a predefined generic target group (e.g. in Germany, the number of viewers between 14 and 49 years old). Rather than applying this 'one size fits all' approach, these companies discuss a more precise target group with the advertisers (e.g. males between 16 and 25) and agree on rate per viewer only for this target group; this rate is, of course, above the 'average rate' for the generic target group. By making multiple deals along these lines, the TV channel can start to arbitrage, for example allocate advertisements to programmes, where the share of the specific target group desired by the advertiser is the highest, and thus optimize overall revenue. The key challenge here is timing: should an advertisement booking request, which does not really fit with the audience of a programme, be accepted or should the channel wait for another potential request where the target group fits better?

Designing pricing schemes based on potential demand – taking into account effective demand when pricing any particular ad break and favouring shorter, more profitable spots over longer spots ̃ can help to extract five times the value generated without any such yield management. Revenue potential can be further enhanced by establishing rigid, value-based guidelines for the acceptance or rejection of ad-spot booking orders, depending on expected demand, price sensitivity of programme and target value. Best-in-class players take into account the opportunity cost of any particular ad minute before pricing and accepting or rejecting a booking order. For example, an advertising client booking a large number of short spots to a top audience during prime time and requested two weeks before air time will be, in terms of both discounts and acceptance probability, favoured over a client booking fewer, longer spots to a lower-value audience during lunchtime and requested at the last minute (Figures 6.30 and 6.31).

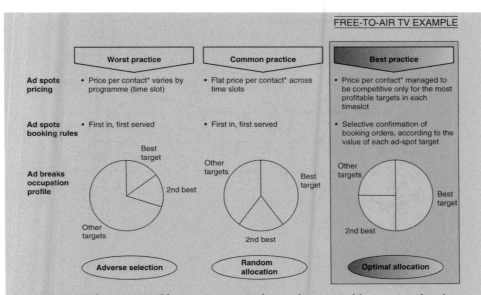

Figure 6.30   Advertising yield management can be much improved by mass-media players

*Usually measured through gross rating points (GRP)
Source: McKinsey analyses

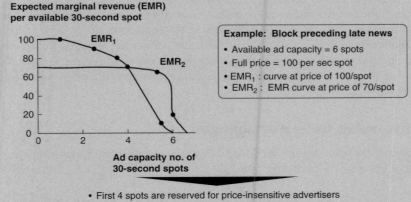

- First 4 spots are reserved for price-insensitive advertisers to be sold at 100 per spot
- Last 2 spots may be sold at 70 per spot to price-sensitive advertisers
- Booking limit full price = 6; booking limit discount price = 2

Figure 6.31   Ad-block allocation should be based on expected marginal revenue potential

Source: McKinsey analysis

Total discount on corporate accounts
Latest 12 months

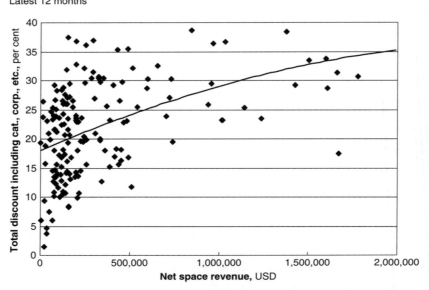

Figure 6.32   Wide variations in discounts per advertiser often exist, revealing pricing inefficiency

Source: McKinsey analyses

Another important element with pricing is the trade discount. Although most media companies have relatively clear, mostly volume-based guidelines for their list prices, actual prices often vary greatly (Figure 6.32). This is usually the case for a variety of reasons, which can be addressed when systematically analysed. Excellent B2B marketers base their prices on a careful analysis of value delivered to the customer over the lifetime of the product/service compared to the competition – rather than on spot market prices – taking into account both tangible and intangible value elements (Figure 6.33).

Effective sales force management

Even the best thought-through B2B marketing strategies fail when the people involved in the execution are not properly managed.

Trimming the field sales force for effectiveness

With increasing complexity owing to differentiated value propositions by segment and a more diverse product offering, it will become even more important to ensure an optimal deployment of the sales forces' time and skills. Key levers are:

- *Ensuring correct customer focus:* Very often salespeople allocate their time relative to the size of actual revenue per customer, rather than potential revenue. This is usually

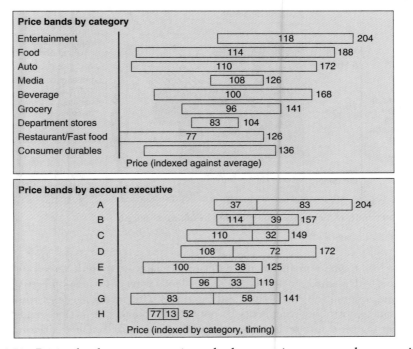

CABLE EXAMPLE

Figure 6.33 **Pricing bands across categories and sales executives can reveal opportunities to improve discounting policies**

Source: McKinsey analyses

the result of too narrow a definition of the potential market. Expanding the market definition – for example by including ad spend on other media – companies can identify potential opportunities to increase sales. A shift in focus from maximizing revenue to maximizing contribution margin can also result in a shift in customer focus. It is important here to look not only at revenue and discounts but also at other factors which indirectly affect the profit margin, such as the type of inventory (ad space) the advertiser uses (e.g. peak vs. off-peak) and their booking behaviour (when booked, how many changes occur). One major European TV channel, for example, calculated that its top 21 to 100 customers were significantly more profitable than its top 20 customers, thus resulting in a shift in resource allocation (Figure 6.34). A ratio which is increasingly used by TV channels to measure the attractiveness of advertisers is the so-called revenue inventory ratio, that is the share of total revenues from an advertiser versus the share of inventory it used. Although this ratio, of course, does not take into account many underlying aspects, it gives a good first indication of the attractiveness of an advertiser.

- *Pragmatic sales force structure:* Although organizing the sales force according to the defined customer segments seems, at first sight, the most logical approach, in practice

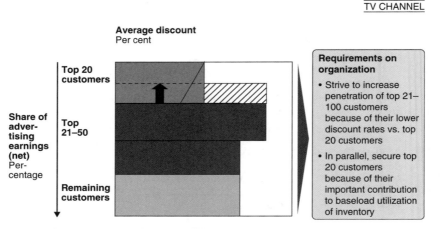

Figure 6.34 Shift in customer focus needed to improve margin

Source: McKinsey analyses

this can lead to major inefficiencies, resulting in a large geographic spread and multiple interfaces with media agencies. There is a need for a pragmatic trade-off between, on the one hand, minimizing travel time and interfaces with media agencies while, on the other hand, controlling complexity by limiting the number of products and clustering customer segments into groups that require similar sales skills. Differentiating the sales

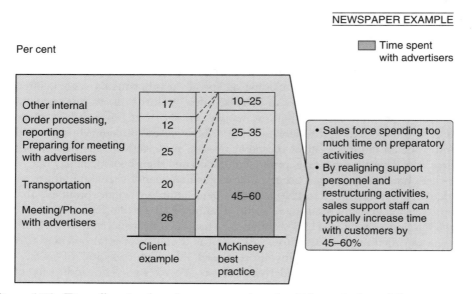

Figure 6.35 Time allocation for sales representatives should be tracked carefully

Source: McKinsey analyses

ILLUSTRATIVE

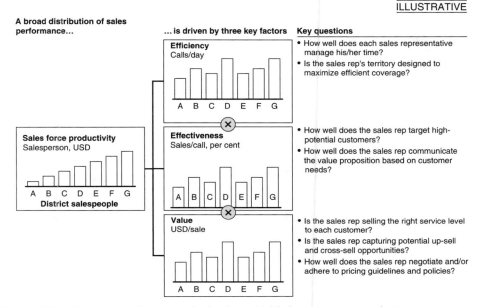

Figure 6.36 Relative productivity of sales force highlights opportunities for improvement

Source: McKinsey analyses

force between hunters (acquiring new customers) or farmers (penetrating existing customers) has also proven very effective given the different skill set and personality type required for each task.

- *Maximizing effective use of time:* The time of frontline salespeople is often cluttered with administrative and travel activities, such that relatively little time is left for actual sales visits. By delegating more administrative tasks to back-end support services and minimizing travel time (see above), customer interface time can be increased significantly (Figure 6.35).

- *Strengthening incentives:* In the past, the advertising market, especially in TV, was often more demand- than supply-driven, and the quality of the individual salesperson had limited impact on the sales figures. In the current market, however, large differences can often be seen in the individual productivity of media salespeople. This can be caused partly by differences in quality and skills, and partly by an inadequate incentive system. This implies the need for a much more consistent personnel management and for the laying-off of underperforming salespeople as well as a fundamental revision of incentive systems (Figures 6.36 and 6.37).

- *Integrating sales forces:* In many media companies the sales forces for offline and online media are still separated. Special skills are needed to sell online products, which have quite different pricing and measurement schemes from offline products, and the volume of online products is often still significantly lower than that of offline products, and they would not get enough attention when sold jointly. Also, on the advertiser side, they are often different parties buying online and offline products. With the growth of online

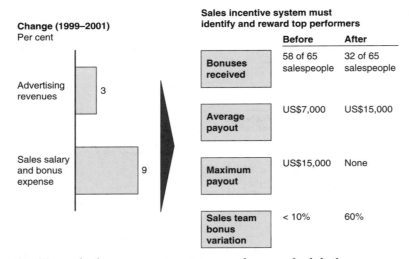

Figure 6.37 Many ad sales compensation structures deserve a fresh look

Source: McKinsey analyses

media and the increased need for integrated offerings, this approach will have to be revisited. Several companies, such as the Axel Springer group in Germany, already have fully integrated sales forces offering full-services marketing concepts.

Win–win cooperation with media agencies

The large media agencies are also trying to expand their role from ad space buyer/reseller to full marketing services agency, developing increasingly sophisticated tools for analysing media use and impact. Advertisers stimulate this by increasingly outsourcing their media-planning activities to agencies in order to save costs. As such, media agencies see themselves more and more as the owners/originators of the media strategies and tend to object if media companies attempt to take too much of a consultative role with the advertisers. This leads to conflicts of interest as media companies are trying to become strategic partners of the advertisers.

Given the pending demand–supply unbalance and the strong market position of the leading media agencies, an attempt to bypass the agencies is not likely to work, at least not in the short term. For these reasons many media companies are integrating vertically with media agencies. When this is not possible, the challenge will be to develop win–win cooperation models where both the media company and the media agency are aligned to offer maximum value to the advertiser segments. As media agencies work with competing media companies simultaneously, implementing this strategy is not trivial. The main incentive for the agencies to cooperate is to make a credible argument that, by jointly improving the value proposition to the advertisers, the total market will grow, rather than having market shares shift. However, as good ideas filter through to the competition, the onus will be on high-performing media companies to continually innovate and refine offerings for their clients.

* * *

Media companies will have to manage the transition from price-based to value-based competition in advertising sales. This will entail a fundamental shift in mindset and innovative approaches in creating value for customers. Managing the complexity of more differentiated offerings, ensuring an effective use of resources and securing a constructive cooperation with the media agencies will be the main challenges in implementing this strategy.

Key Takeaways

1. The advertising market will change structurally in the coming years; key drivers will be a shift towards more tailored/direct-marketing approaches by advertisers and an increasing role for innovative online advertising forms, especially search, together with emerging new rich media and participatory ad services.
2. The shift towards digital is reaching the tipping point for the exponential growth of online advertising, creating a significant multi-billion-dollar market in the future.
3. In parallel to online shift, there will also be increasing competition within traditional advertising (TV, print), trying to defend their market share, with a significant risk of downward price pressure and 'commoditization' of standard ads.
4. To cope with these changes, media companies should follow the example of other, more mature industries and shift from a sales approach to a true B2B marketing approach.
5. For this, they will have to develop a much deeper understanding of their customers' needs, such as the way they define their target segments, how these segments use media and what the marketing goals are for these segments.
6. A value-added value proposition has to be developed, based not only on strategically designed (cross-media) advertising products but also on a service offering along the whole advertising value chain. Developing innovative measurement systems for media reach and advertising impact will be key.
7. More performance-based pricing models are becoming increasingly important, especially online. Offline differentiated prices for different segments, as well as 'yield management' approaches, can significantly increase revenues.
8. The new sales strategy will require a different approach from sales force management. Key issues are: ensuring the right customer focus by understanding the true profitability and potential of each customer, a structure which is a pragmatic trade-off between segment orientation and efficient sales force deployment, an increasing focus on time spent with the customer and ensuring adequate and aggressive personal evaluation and incentive systems.
9. Media companies and media agencies will in parallel significantly upgrade their services in digital; this will not only mean buying or building companies making those services but also include a real step change in the capabilities to measure and fine-tune digital marketing strategies.

Schibsted: Diversifying the Advertising Source[1]

Kjell Aamot, the CEO of Schibsted ASA, is reviewing the first-quarter results of 2008. He is considering the major transformation the company has been able to undergo. Especially, he is looking at his company's shift to new media, with a strong presence in online classifieds, both nationally and internationally, and attractive online revenues from editorials. Today, excluding associated companies, close to two-thirds of first-quarter results arise from this online transformation.

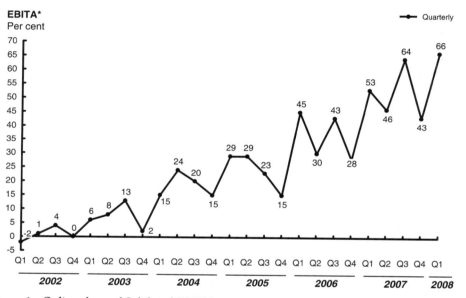

Figure 1   Online share of Schibsted EBITA

*Reported EBITA excluding associated companies
Source: McKinsey analyses based on data from Schibsted

With the recent approved merger with Media Norge, the company would possibly use the synergies to further boost the online transformation in its core market, Norway.

Company History

Schibsted has transformed itself significantly over the years.

[1]This case is developed solely as the basis for class discussion. Cases are not intended to serve as endorsements, sources of primary data or illustrations of effective or ineffective management.

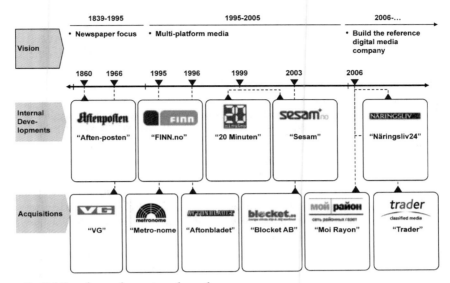

Figure 2   Schibsted transformation along the years

Source: McKinsey analyses based on data from Schibsted.com

Schibsted's founder, Christian Schibsted, started a small printing business in Oslo in 1839, Christian Schibsted's Forlag. In 1860, he launched a newspaper to leverage spare printing capacity. The paper was eventually named *Aftenposten* and became Norway's leading morning paper.

In 1966, Schibsted acquired the tabloid *Verdens Gang* and turned it into Norway's single-copy market leader by aggressive growth in the largely unexploited tabloid market. In the early 1980s, Schibsted launched its diversification strategy and expanded into the film industry through investments in film production, starting initially with a film laboratory.

After 150 years as a family-owned and family-managed company, Schibsted became a joint stock company in 1989 and went public in 1992.

Following the course set by the 1980s' expansion into film, Schibsted achieved further diversification through a series of strategic investments, acquisitions and launches in broadcasting and online and print publishing in the 1990s.

In 1991, Schibsted successfully applied for a television licence and launched the country's first national commercial TV channel, TV2. In 1995, it acquired the Internet service provider Oslonett AS, which was eventually divested some years later.

In 1996, Schibsted acquired the Swedish broadsheet *Aftonbladet*, thereby taking control of Scandinavia's leading broadsheet. In 1998, this was followed by the acquisition of *Svenska Dagbladet*, Stockholm's number-two morning paper. The paper was loss-making when it was acquired, but a successful turnaround programme brought it back to profitability by 2003. Sweden continued to be a core second market, with the development of new, mostly online, ventures, with Blocket, a consumer-to-consumer (C2C) commerce site, and Hitta, an online directory service.

Starting in 1999, Schibsted launched a series of free commuter newspapers, based solely on advertising revenues. The paper *20 Minutes* was published in Switzerland, Spain and France. Schibsted had tried out other markets, such as Germany, but competitive/regulatory difficulties gave it a difficult start, and its German activities were discontinued in 2001.

In recent years, the company has diversified online, starting with the launch of FINN in 2000, by now the leading online classified platform in Norway. It launched Sesam, a local search portal, in 2005 and acquired Internettkatalogen, an online directory business, the same year. In 2006, it launched the online classified sites Willhaben in Austria and Leboncoin in France. The company took an active role in the consolidation of the European classified market as it acquired part of Trader, a classified company present in many major countries in Europe. Schibsted took over the Western European business with strong footprint in, among others, France, Spain and Italy. Schibsted also restructured its traditional media portfolio; the company divested its shares from TV2 and TV4, the two lead free-to-air broadcasters in Norway and Sweden, and got the approval of the Norwegian Media Authorities to form Media Norge, the leading newspaper group in the Norwegian region.

Schibsted is one of the Nordic region's leading media companies today, generating NKr13.6 billion revenues by 2007 (roughly €1.7 billion), and an operating profit of 1.8 billion, or 13% margin.

NKr millions, per cent

	2007	Margin
Operating revenues	13610	—
Operating expenses	(11996)	—
Income from associated companies	149	—
Operating profit (EBITDA)	1763	13.0
Depreciation	(586)	—
Operating profit (EBITA)	1177	—
Write-down goodwill	(8)	—
Other revenues and expenses	77	—
Operating profit (EBIT)	1246	9.0
Net financial items	(218)	—
Profit before taxes	1028	7.5

Figure 3   Schibsted Group's 2007 profit breakdown

Source: McKinsey analyses based on data from Schibsted

Even if most of the profit comes from the Nordic countries, Schibsted's revenue base is well diversified internationally, with Norway generating less than 50% of total revenue and Sweden generating approximately 30%. Other territories stand for 20% as of the first quarter of 2008.

NKr million, Q1, 2008

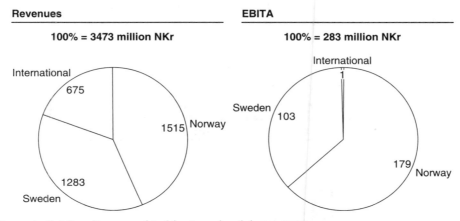

Revenues

100% = 3473 million NKr

International — 675

Norway 1515

Sweden 1283

EBITA

100% = 283 million NKr

International — 1

Sweden 103

Norway 179

Figure 4 Schibsted's geographical business breakdown, 2008

Source: McKinsey analyses based on data from Schibsted

1. *Online diversification:* The trends in print are dismal, with fewer people reading newspapers and advertisers starting to shift print media advertising towards other media, especially online. In fact, many studies suggest that newspapers must have more than 25% of their revenue online by 2012 to compensate for the drastic decline in the print marketplace.

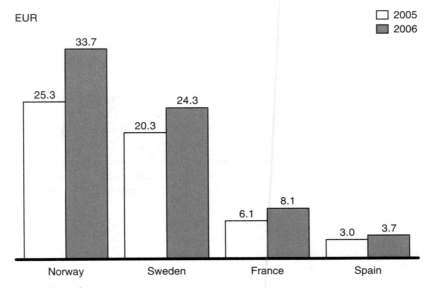

EUR

☐ 2005
■ 2006

	Norway	Sweden	France	Spain
2005	25.3	20.3	6.1	3.0
2006	33.7	24.3	8.1	3.7

Figure 5 Online advertising per capita

Source: McKinsey analyses based on data from Jupiter Research; Zenith Media; IRM

Schibsted was one of the first print companies to move towards digital, perhaps driven by the fact that advertising migrated online much faster in Scandinavia than in other Continental European countries.

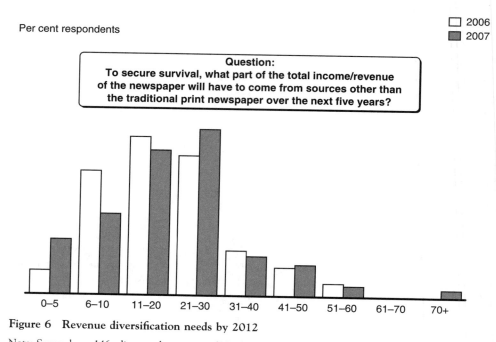

Per cent respondents

☐ 2006
■ 2007

Question:
To secure survival, what part of the total income/revenue of the newspaper will have to come from sources other than the traditional print newspaper over the next five years?

0–5   6–10   11–20   21–30   31–40   41–50   51–60   61–70   70+

Figure 6   Revenue diversification needs by 2012

Note: Survey base: 146 editors and managers of Nordic newspapers
Source: Wilberg Management as 'The Nordic Future and Change Study for Newspapers 2007', August 2007. Reproduced with permission

By 2008 the company was close to the 25% mark. From 8% in 2005, online stands close to 23% of revenue in the first quarter of 2008. Moreover, the importance of online contributions to the group's EBITDA (which excludes operating losses for new business development) has surpassed the 60% mark in the first quarter of 2008; in 2003 the online EBITDA margin was negative. The difference in profitability and revenue contribution is linked to the strong margin the group has been able to secure online, for example while the EBITDA margins of the newspapers are just about 10%, margins online are more in the region of 40%.

2. Print paid newspapers: The newspaper publishing division generated more than NKr9 billion in revenue by 2007. While newspapers still stood for 83% contribution to the company's total net income (2003), it was just below 50% by the first quarter of 2008. Schibsted is the market leader of both the Norwegian and the Swedish single-copy markets with *Verdens Gang* (VG; about 290 000 circulation copies) and *Afton-bladet* (370 000 copies per week day), respectively. It also publishes the leading morning

Per cent, Q1, 2008

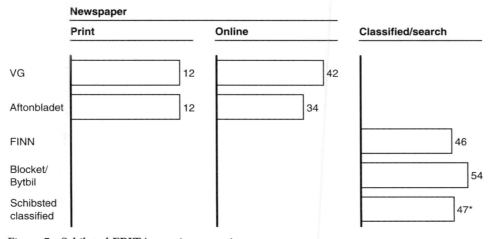

Figure 7 Schibsted EBITA margin comparison

*2007
Source: McKinsey analyses based on data from Schibsted

papers in both countries (*Aftenposten* and *Svenska Dagbladet*), with *Aftenposten* enjoying morning and evening circulations of 255 000 and 221 000 copies on a daily basis. *Svenska Dagbladet*'s circulation is just above 200 000 copies on a week day. The advertising volume is significantly driven by *Aftenposten*. The title alone makes 50% of the total print advertising revenue of the newspapers, while it is also the major source of revenue, that is two-thirds of the total revenue of the title.

3. *Free newspapers:* The free newspaper *20 Minutes* was launched in the late 1990s to cater to commuters and to the younger generation, who normally would not read a newspaper. In 2008, it is present in France and Spain; in both cases *20 Minutes* is the most read newspaper in the country. While growing in France, it had a weaker performance in Spain, but both papers have reached EBITDA break-even.

4. *Print classified:* With the acquisition of *Trader*, Schibste owns classified print businesses in Spain, France and Italy. Given fast migration online, the business is quickly shrinking, with a 41% revenue decline last year. Part of this decline comes from the closing of marginal titles; up to 40 of the 110 in the Spanish portfolio were closed. Large titles like *Secondamano* retain a good standing in major cities in Spain and Italy. The EBITDA margin is, however, close to zero.

5. *Broadcasting and film production:* Schibsted used to have a large TV and film production business generating €57 million in revenue in 2003. This has been reorganized significantly with large divestitures of the ownership stakes in the leading commercial TV channels in Norway (TV2) and Sweden (TV4). The new unit, called Live Pictures, stands now for NKr1.35 billion (2007), but is still only at break-even.

□ Revenue
■ EBITA

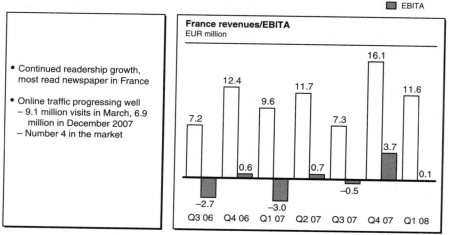

* Continued readership growth, most read newspaper in France

* Online traffic progressing well
  – 9.1 million visits in March, 6.9 million in December 2007
  – Number 4 in the market

France revenues/EBITA
EUR million

Figure 8 Profile of *20 Minutes*, France

Source: McKinsey analyses based on data from EPIQ; AIMC EGM; OJD, March 2007; Schibsted

Strategic challenges

In most European countries, newspaper readership has been declining over the past 20 years. Not only do younger people read less than the older generation; also the number of readers within one generation declines over time.

The real challenge is, however, the migration to digital. In a recent study by Wilberg Management, surveying 146 editors and managers of Nordic newspapers in August 2007,[2] more than 70% quoted the Internet in general as the most formidable competitor for the next five years.

There are many channels through which online will affect the traditional business of newspapers.

First, newspapers' business advertising revenues are facing online substitution not only for classified ads but also for display advertising. The overall shift of advertisers towards online is increasingly visible. Around 45% of online display advertising growth is directly substituting offline advertising. The effect on print is greater than on television, as television still has some minimal protection thanks to its mass-reach potential. Like other newspaper publishers, Schibsted saw its classified advertising business – recruiting, property and cars in particular – come under pressure from online players already during the late 1990s as online classifieds can offer better prices/efficiency, more depth and greater convenience than their offline counterparts.

---

[2]Wilberg Management, 'The Nordic Future and Change Study for newspapers', August 2007, quoted by WAN world digital media trends report, 2008.

Searches in online databases are usually cheaper for both advertisers and readers than offline databases, for example recruiting through newspaper ads is five times as expensive per new hire as through online databases.

Online classified databases also offer a much broader choice than newspaper classified sections, for example already in 2001 the leading German online recruitment player carried eight times the number of new listings than those in the leading national newspaper's classified section.

Finally, online players offer more comfort and functionality than newspapers; features of leading online classified databases include comprehensive search facilities, permanent/ real-time availability, personalization, e-mail alerts and enhanced information on advertisers – none of which are available to newspaper readers.

As a consequence, online competition is capturing a substantial share of classified revenue today, for example 30% of total recruiting revenue in the United States was generated online in 2006. In most countries newspapers have been very late in entering the online classified market and leading positions have already been taken by new entrants.

In the long run, online players have the potential to dominate the classified market, thereby adversely affecting newspaper circulation and non-classified revenues. Most newspapers' current revenue mixes and overall economic models will be jeopardized and may eventually turn out to be unsustainable.

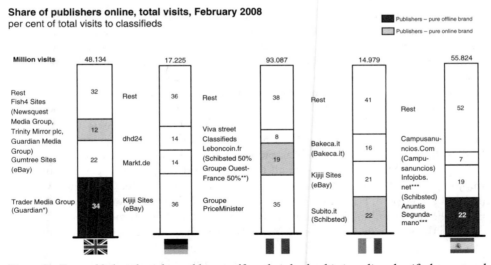

Share of publishers online, total visits, February 2008
per cent of total visits to classifieds

Figure 9   **Few publishers have been able to reaffirm their leadership in online classifieds, a natural sweet spot for publishers offline**

*Jointly owned by Guardian and Apax
**Schibsted acquired Leboncoin.fr through acquisition of parts of Trader International in 2006
***Segundamano (of which infojobs is also a part) was acquired in 2006 through the acquisition of parts of Trader International
Source: McKinsey analyses based on data from Advertising Association and Enders Analysis; comScore

Schibsted, however, has managed to counter online competition in classifieds through different actions.

First, it created a competitive advantage by venturing as early as 2000 into online classifieds. The company foresaw cannibalization of offline classifieds and decided to control it rather than let it happen. Through a subsidiary, *Aftenposten*, Schibsted created the FINN brand for online and offline classified advertising. FINN was featured both on the front page and in the classified sections of *Aftenposten* and the major regional newspapers. By creating a unified brand and leveraging the newspapers' audience and trust across channels, Schibsted created a substantial competitive advantage over the new online-only entrants.

Second, to offset lower placement prices online, the company included value-added services early on, both for consumers, such as search customization, and for advertisers, such as targeted placement of supporting services, for example special car maintenance offers placed alongside car sales ads. In particular, FINN online offers extensive customization functionality (a personalized search engine, offer tracking, an integrated CV solution, service plug-ins), as well as third-party editorial content on topics pertaining to the classified segments, such as interior decoration, insurance and car repairs. FINN was developed as a separate organization to ensure it received sufficient management attention, but offline ad sales, especially for *Aftenposten*, were consistently aligned and coordinated with online advertising. Special online deals – for example based on number of items offered rather than space – were created for high-value advertising clients. As a case in point, in car classifieds, FINN equalled *Aftenposten*'s revenue by 2003, to stand for 90% of total car classified revenue of the group by now.

FINN is currently Schibsted's most profitable business. As the price level of online classifieds in most categories is significantly below the level of newspaper classifieds, FINN's revenues had to make up for the loss of revenue experienced by the traditional newspapers. FINN continues to grow at a fast pace, more than 30% per annum, and has continued to expand, for example in verticals such as travel.

FINN will be part of Media Norge as the merger takes place. In addition Schibsted developed Schibsted Classified Media SA(SCM), for its international classified businesses, by now one of the biggest online classified players in Europe, with a leading position in markets such as Sweden, Spain, France and Italy.

In Spain, SCM is number one in all traditional verticals, such as recruitment (with Infojobs, 2.2 million monthly unique visitors), cars (with Coche, 0.8 million visitors) and real estate (with FotoCasa, 1.2 million visitors). It holds Caradisiac/La Centrale in cars in France (combined, about 3.9 million visitors) and Bytbil in Sweden. SCM also operates the C2C commerce sites like Blocket, which is still growing significantly and can be easily replicated in SCM's other markets. Hitta, SCM's online directory search business, is also growing and is going head-to head-with Eniro, the incumbent yellow-page player in Sweden. SCM mostly includes the assets of *Trader*; given the large shrinkage of *Trader*'s offline businesses, SCM share of online revenues were 61% by the first quarter of 2008. In EBITDA contribution, the picture is even more dramatic. Owing to the substitution of offline to online classifieds, however, SCM's revenue and EBITDA have shrunk. Expectations are that the next few years will show a bottom- and top-line growth recovery for SCM as a whole.

Figure 10   Schibsted classified international leadership*

*Also present in Austria (Willhaben), Lithuania (Autoplius), Malaysia (mudah), Slovenia (Bolha) and Latin America
Source: Schibsted. Reproduced by permission

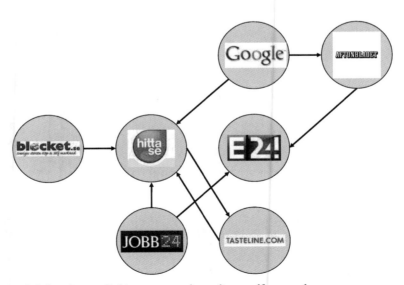

Figure 11   Schibsted cross-linking strategy for online traffic growth

Source: Schibsted. Reproduced by permission

Online extensions of newspapers have been quite successful too, for example with the launch of a Web venture for online readership, including Web video services, and an investment at 60% in Netby. VG multimedia continues to grow at double the pace of the online market. Its EBITA margin is already 40%. VG.no attracts three million unique visitors and is the number-one site in Norway. *Aftonbladet*'s online revenue is similar to VG's, with margins of 34% and four million monthly unique visitors. It is the second-most-visited site in Sweden after MSN. Another strong online presence is *20 Minutes*; it is the number-three site in Spain with 4.8 million monthly users, and has 2.7 million visitors in France.

Schibsted interlinks all its properties to create a network. Schibsted claims this aggressive traffic 'machine approach' has resulted in a major boost of its traffic, for instance in Sweden, in recent years.

With this successful picture, the company managed the best transformation known in the industry to online and digital. Most newspapers barely derive 5–10% of their revenue from online services; Schibsted is already at 20%.

The current focus of the company is MediaNorge, which will include FINN. The real concern in this respect for the CEO is selling this compelling success story to the stock market: will this be seen as a traditional print disarray stock, a much diluted online company or the unique case of a transformational company?

CORPORATE STRATEGY IN MEDIA

In the wake of constant changes and digitization, media companies need to constantly rethink their business units, their overall corporate strategies and the way they manage their portfolios. Specific questions addressed in this chapter are:

1. *What is the historical logic behind the activity scope and structure of media corporations?*
2. *What rationale exists for different portfolio logics?*
3. *What are the implications of new market forces for current corporate management and ownership models?*

Current Media Landscape

In the United States the 'big four' media companies (Viacom, Disney, Time Warner, News Corporation) are active in almost all media sectors and are vertically integrated as they produce content in their own studios, package content and often also own cable platforms to distribute content.

The current continental European media landscape is somewhat different. It has been strongly influenced by the Second World War. Many of today's European media companies were founded following the end of the war as newspaper or magazine publishers. The industry was characterized by a multitude of owner/entrepreneurs, each publishing a limited number of print products, very often with a strong regional bias. Many of these companies prospered in the post-war boom and a few – for example Bertelsmann, Lagardère, Elsevier and Pearson – expanded more aggressively by acquiring other media players. Most European media companies are still strongly influenced by founder-family ownership.

Another outflow of the Second World War was that most European countries became heavily regulated, with the original intent of guaranteeing media independence, avoiding opinion monopolies and restricting foreign ownership.

Not surprisingly, the geographic scope of the largest European companies is much more international than their US counterparts', as their home markets are significantly smaller.

EUR million, *media* revenue only

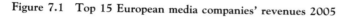

		Revenue split by sector Per cent rounded				
		Broadcasting (TV, radio, production)	Professional publishing/ business information	Consumer publishing (newspapers, magazines, books)	Music	Other media
Bertelsmann*	14022	~40	—	~40	~20	—
Vivendi*	8355	~65	—	—	~35	—
Lagardère Media**	7905	~10	—	45	—	45
Reed Elsevier	7542	—	100	—	—	—
BSkyB	6066	100	—	—	—	—
Pearson	6030	—	60	40	—	—
BBC	5857	100	—	—	—	—
Fininvest***	5496	50	—	45	—	5
ITV	3184	100	—	—	—	—
DMGT	3126	6	27	67	—	—
RAI	3062	100	—	—	—	5
EMI Group	3042	—	—	—	100	—
TF1	2874	86	—	14	—	—
Axel Springer Verlag	2392	—	—	87	—	13
Sanoma Group	2216	18	—	68	—	14

Figure 7.1 Top 15 European media companies' revenues 2005

*Vivendi outside telecoms; Bertelsmann outside Arvato services
**Lagardère includes Lagardère services
***Includes Mediaset, Mondadori and Medusa
Source: McKinsey analysis based on data from E-media institute

They tend to remain more focused on a limited number of sectors, with the exception of some of the largest European media companies, Bertelsmann AG and Lagardère (Figure 7.1).

Most European media companies do not own electronic distribution platforms; however, a few companies, such as Lagardère and Sanoma Group, do have significant stakes in print distribution, with Lagardère's services division accounting for close to 45% of Lagardère's total revenue.

The main historical reason European companies did not invest in distribution platforms such as cable is that such infrastructures, other than in the United States, were often owned by the state, the municipalities and/or the incumbent telecoms operator and were not available for sale. Companies rather invested in platform services like pay-TV over satellite, like Murdoch with BSkyB, TF1 and RTL with TPS in France, etc. In general, however, the capital intensity of the business and its related risks were such that private equity firms and US companies investing in Europe, such as UGC (owned by the Schneider family) in the late Eighties, and later John Malone, with Liberty Global, gained great influence over most cable companies when they were privatized.

In most European countries, there are one or two dominating national players that are active in multiple segments, such as Sanoma Group in Finland, Schibsted in Norway,

Bonnier and Kinnevik in Sweden, Fininvest in Italy, Bertelsmann and Axel Springer in Germany, Media Capital in Portugal, etc.

The growth pattern of media companies has typically been based on related diversification, either geographically or in adjacent media. Often European media companies invested in emerging media offerings (e.g. commercial TV in the Nineties) to compensate for the slowing growth in more mature sectors, such as print. Also, their presence in multiple media has allowed the media companies to build a significant external voice. The degree of internationalization in Europe is larger than in the United States given the small market size, especially for the largest groups. But in general, for smaller groups, it was either into neighbouring countries (e.g. Schibsted moving from Norway to Sweden) or into emerging countries, mostly in Eastern Europe (Burda, MTG, Sanoma and others).

Market concentration

The degree of consolidation varies by media. Magazines have strong local leaders, pursuing international diversification (e.g. Lagardère). Newspaper publishing is still dominated by strong regional players and, given the strict regulations still governing the industry, consolidation remains difficult.

The book publishing industry, traditionally one of the most fragmented, with local market leaders owning 10–15% revenue share, is seeing an increase in consolidation, with Random House, a division from Bertelsmann AG and Hachette/Lagardère emerging as clear winners.

The television market largely consists of national oligopolies, where leaders can get locally more than 25–30% audience share (e.g. TF1 in France). Only the RTL Group and ProSiebenSat1/SBS play a full European-wide role (with MTG being present in many countries in Scandinavia and Eastern Europe too).

Truly international players can be found only in the music industry, the professional information sector and in the emerging Internet market. This group includes leading global players such as the four music majors (EMI, Warner Music, Universal and Sony), Reed Elsevier, VNU. Online leaders such as Google, Yahoo!, Microsoft, MSN, eBay and Amazon are present too in Europe, but national Internet 'darlings' have also developed a successful international strategy, like auFeminin.com just bought out by Axel Springer, or Netlog, a Belgian-based social network focusing on many small markets with less Englsih language affinity. Cable companies are still local, except for Liberty Global, which is present in many European markets (excluding the big five: the United Kingdom, France, Germany, Italy and Spain). Some groups, like Vivendi, embarked on major internationalization through their affiliates like Canal+, but the restructuring of pay-TV made Vivendi re-centre (so far) its pay-TV activity in France.[1]

As opposed to US companies, the degree of consolidation at the European level remains low, with the top five leaders in most of the sectors owning less than 50% of the total European market (Figure 7.2). This means that in several sectors it is difficult for European

[1]See Canal+; case study in Chapter 4.

Top player example	UK	Germany	France	Italy	Spain
FTA broadcaster (RTL)	✓	✓	✓	—	—
Pay-TV broadcaster (BSkyB)	✓	(✓)	—	✓	—
Magazines (Lagardère)	✓	—	✓	✓	✓
Newspaper* (FT-Pearson)	(✓)	(✓)	(✓)	(✓)	(✓)
Radio (RTL)	—	✓	✓	—	—
Classified (Schibsted)	—	—	✓	✓	✓
Broadband (France Telecom, Orange)	✓	—	✓	—	✓

Figure 7.2 Diversification of top five markets

*Niche paper *Financial Times*
Source: McKinsey analyses based on data from E-media institute; Analyst reports

media companies to systematically leverage core competencies in managing the business across geographies and, to a lesser extent, leverage economies of scale.

Diversification to Internet

With the rise of digital media, and especially the Internet, most media companies started to acquire stakes in emerging digital companies. The strategy was similar to what happened in other industries, with an overheating of investment in order not to miss the call option, then a recalibration after the bubble bursts, and now back again, a reinvestment, but often too late, when the play is no longer 'call' but real business migration. In Europe specifically, only a few companies, such as Schibsted (with the early launch of its online classified portal Finn) or Bertelsmann (with its acquisition of a 5% stake in AOL) dared to be true early movers in the Internet in the Nineties. Once early enthusiasm turned into hype, and so into a major overvaluation of the Internet, in the late Nineties, many European media companies, not wishing to miss out, embarked on a set of major investment and acquisition strategies. This was partly driven by over-optimistic capital market expectations. But also, media companies believed that through diversification across media sectors significant cross-sector synergies could be gained, that is by cross-selling to end consumers, by sharing content or by bundling advertising sales. Expectations were not met, except by a few.

After the collapse of the bubble in early 2000 most leading media companies, such as News Corporation, Lagardère and Bertelsmann, downsized or discontinued their Internet investments and did not invest further. A few smaller, mostly print-based, companies – such as Hubert Burda Media (a German-based magazine publisher), Sanoma Group with ilse media in the Netherland and Schibsted in Norway – kept on investing in Internet-based businesses, which turned out to be a very successful strategy in the medium term. Around 2005 media companies realized that they had to have a significant digital presence to stay in the driver's seat and started to reinvest in the Internet again, this time mostly in the then emerging Web 2.0 businesses. ProSiebenSat1 in Germany took a first stake in MyVideo, an online video-sharing site; News Corporation invested in MySpace; Axel Springer bought auFeminin, one of Europe's leading women websites, etc. Like in the first wave, most of the Web 2.0 websites still have to prove a clear revenue model, at least on a par with the traffic they generate. Expectations are that, owing to the large reach, the potential deep knowledge of their consumer preferences and the possible way to trigger the core node of social networks to create powerful viral marketing, these sites will be able to come up with attractive monetization models in the near future.

Corporate governance: mostly family-owned

Most European media companies, even the larger ones, remain majority-owned or controlled by the original founding families or family foundations (Figure 7.3). This can have both advantages and disadvantages: on the one hand, it allows for more risk-taking and a longer-term view, as News Corporation with its strategic investments in BSkyB and Star TV has shown. On the other hand, the owner can be too risk-taking, as shown by the example of the Kirch Group in Germany, which went bankrupt in 2002. Also, owners often have other than just purely economic goals. Unlike most consumer products and services, media products often fulfil an 'idealistic mission' in society, and the owner families tend to uphold this grail.

This idealistic mission often results, from a purely economic point of view, in the family's preferences for certain businesses or products, sometimes preventing divestments or close-downs that would have been advantageous in terms of economic value. Further, as with most family-owned businesses, defining the management role of the second-generation owner is not always clear. These risks are especially apparent in companies that are not publicly listed (or are only nominally listed), as there is no 'outside' market correction.

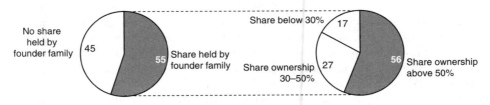

Figure 7.3   Family ownership influences of European media companies, 2006

Source: WUV; Google; McKinsey analysis

However, many of the original media founders/entrepreneurs have retired recently, and their companies are transitioning from an entrepreneurial, or even patriarchal, culture to a professional management structure. The challenge now is to move fast in an era of rapid change and digitization.

Emerging role of private equity investors

Over the last year, private equity investors acquired a significant stake in cable companies. But following the recent S-curve of broadband adoption, many of these investments have been withdrawn. They are now taking large stakes in media companies such as PagesJaunes (yellow page classified business), Pro7Sat1SBS (free-to-air television), EMI (music), Endemol (television production) and the Mecon group (a newly established newspaper group which buys up regional newspapers across Europe). At first sight, this seems surprising as private equity firms generally prefer classes of assets which generate stable and predictable cash flows and the current transition of digital may limit this potential. However, private equity investors also believe that in the short to medium term significant value can be created by a much tighter management of these companies and by the consolidation of the industry. There is a strong feeling that many media companies have been poorly run, as they have been in a growing industry for many years and family ownership has partly protected them from the pressures of the capital market. Looking at the figures, there is some evidence to support the private equity investors' beliefs: the margins in yellow-pages business in Europe can vary from 30% to 48%; magazine groups' margins oscillate between 8% and 18%, and even more in the television business. How this type of ownership will work out for media companies in the long run is still unclear. On the one hand, they can profit from an inflow of new management with fresh perspectives (as in most industries, the media industry tends to hire mostly from within its own ranks) and an objective, performance-based orientation. On the downside, there is the risk of too much focus on short-term cost reduction and too little on the long-term investments needed to make the digital transition, especially as that transition is aggravated by a heavy debt burden.

Organizational structure moving to customer-centric model

Traditionally, the majority of European media companies were organized in a highly decentralized manner with very strong product-oriented divisions. As an example, Lagardère has four divisions: Publishing, Sports, Services and Active. This structure worked well in the era of growth and for the building of market share in sequentially emerging new markets, as it fostered strong entrepreneurship and allowed for quick decision-making. In the current environment, however, digital platforms cut across the different media. Blockbusters must be leveraged quickly and in all directions to be profitable. Multichannel customer relationship management will become increasingly important in keeping the customer's attention. Lagardère Active is, for instance, pushing for a complete cross-media deployment, and has recently developed a cross-media model for news.

Many media companies initially reacted to this trend by building up centralized structures to make divisions work together more effectively. Most of these structures have, however, not succeeded in breaking through divisional barriers. As a result, several media companies have decided to revert, in part at least, to the old structures, such as, for example, Bertelsmann. Other companies, however, have pushed for more global integration. As an example, Telenet, the leading Belgian cable company, has achieved a reorientation of the company from a product-based marketing organization to a consumer-segment-based organization, which offers several products based on consumers' needs. Also for this reason, Schibsted went from an international product-based organization to a country-based organization, where consumer segments play an important role. Other companies, such as EMI, the music major, are experimenting with matrix-like structures, where product development (A&R, artist and repertoire) is still decentralized but other functions such as marketing are being centralized and organized around consumer segments. Many newspaper companies are actively integrating their Internet and print divisions, both on the editorial and advertising sales side. What model will work is still unclear and depends on the industry and company specifics. However, overall, it is becoming increasingly clear that the traditional 'mono product' divisional structures will have to make way for more end-consumer-oriented organizations. It will not be sufficient to attempt to coordinate this via corporate functions, because they lack critical mass. More fundamental reorganization will be needed.

Strong role of regulators in most countries

Despite emerging harmonization of regulations at the European level, most countries have far-reaching media regulations in place, which are aimed at preventing any one media company dominating a given market. The regulations are especially strict within media sectors. But the regulations also cut across media sectors, for example, limitations on cross-media ownership (e.g. the rejection by the competition authorities to approve Axel Springer's attempted takeover of ProSiebenSat1) (Table 7.1). Additionally, several countries still have guidelines regarding foreign investments in media, although these rules are being increasingly relaxed as a result of the European market.

The public sector not only regulates mergers and acquisitions, it also plays a gatekeeper role for the allocation of scarce analogue broadcasting infrastructure. The allocation of cable placements and broadcasting frequencies, the limitations of advertising volumes and content, and television and radio licences – including content limitations and, in certain sectors, even prices (e.g. cable subscription fees, fixed book pricing) – are mostly determined by public authorities. These directives are a major determinant of the profitability boundaries of media companies and, in most cases, can only be influenced through effective stakeholder and policy management.

Another specific phenomenon resulting from regulators' and governments' strong influence on the media industry is the domain of the public service broadcaster (PSB). On the one hand, PSBs have the positive effect of relieving the private sector of certain obligations with regard to domestic programme content and the broadcasting of quotas on certain types of programmes, like education, parliament and children. Furthermore, most PSBs are subject to restrictions on advertising and programming mix. This has resulted in available ad inventory accruing mostly to commercial TV and radio channels – this means that more commercial shows (with hence a larger reach) appear on commercial channels, which means that the ad inventory can be advantageously sold in favour of commercial broadcasters. However, the role and therefore the offering of the PSBs have expanded continually over time, and the overlap with the offering of private players is increasing, making the role of the PSBs a subject of heated debate. For instance, the BBC has invested significantly in Freeview, the free-to-air digital terrestrial platform in the United Kingdom, which managed to take more market share in this multichannel environment than other broadcasters; the BBC also launched various Internet ventures, like the iPlayer, and intends to launch its broadcast-centric partnership of on-demand videos, called Project Kangaroo. The PSBs justify this as part of their public mission 'to educate and inform the public'. The debate is obviously not closed, but can be country-specific, such as recently France's decision to re-allocate the funding mix of the public broadcaster France Television towards public endowment, and by limiting the advertising minutes in prime time in the first years.

Future challenges and opportunities

A few elements may accelerate the change towards further market consolidation: corporate governance changes, portfolio reshaping and new growth models in media. First, the slowing or declining growth in traditional sectors such as newspapers, magazines, music and free TV calls for industry consolidation, not only within countries but also across countries. In addition media conglomerates will start actively looking for growing markets to complement their portfolios, such as games or Internet. Finally, the increasing need to leverage rights across media and the need to secure attractive content could be strategic impulses to diversify the portfolio to adjacent media sectors, merchandising or life events or to integrate backwards into content generation.

At the same time the conditions to fundamentally reshape portfolios and corporate governance structures seem to be increasingly favourable. Many media companies are, as part of the post-Internet restructuring wave, finally willing to sell non-core assets to get their balance sheets back in shape. Many long-held properties are for sale or have already been sold. Financial markets are increasingly rewarding companies that follow a strategy of 'moderate diversification', meaning that those media conglomerates that streamline their portfolios will be rewarded with improved valuations. Simultaneously, regulators are demonstrating more willingness to loosen industry guidelines, with the EU challenging national protectionism and many national governments creating more liberal policies with regard to media regulation.

Future Portfolio Logic

Successful media companies have built their portfolios based on a consistent value-creation logic.

The portfolio is structured around specific core competencies, such as exploiting unique content in multiple ways, or is based on achieving economies of scale and/or cross-sector synergies. Achieving market power through vertical integration is another important driver. Some companies do not look for synergistic effects between their media investments but take a pure portfolio optimization approach, trying to balance growth businesses with the cash flow from more mature businesses.

All these approaches are discussed in detail later in this chapter. Corporate governance models will have to consistently support the value-creating logic behind the portfolio, and this is not always the case.

Building the portfolio around core competencies

Many success stories from the media industry are based on the consistent development of certain unique capabilities, which are then rolled out and adapted to local situations.

Content production as core competency

These competencies can display a variety of dimensions. Disney, for example, based its expansion on its content capability. Its entire business philosophy was created around the unique Disney characters and the company's ability to market these characters in as many forms as possible. *The Lion King* is an excellent example of how Disney, at the height of its success, managed to systematically extract value from the product's content (Figure 7.4).

Disney's performance slumped in the early 2000s as it could not keep up the production of interesting new content, mostly because it was too late in the transition from two-dimensional drawings to three-dimensional computer-animated films. The acquisition of Pixar – the highly successful computer-animated film company (formed by Steve Jobs from the ex-computer division of Lucasfilm in 1986) that had produced great hits like *Toy Story* (1995), *Finding Nemo* (2003) and *The Incredibles* (2004) – was necessary to maintain the flow of blockbuster content production, confirming Disney's strong focus on content competency as portfolio logic.

Although the Disney story is very compelling and often quoted, there are very few other examples of companies who have managed to build their portfolio around content competency, other than on a minor scale. In fact, independent production companies in television, the largest media to leverage content competency, is still very fragmented, even at a local level, and only Endemol, with its global distribution network and its library of over a thousand formats, could claim to echo Disney's success.

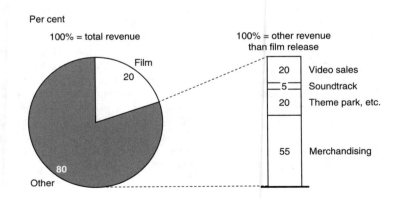

Per cent

Figure 7.4 *Lion King's* revenue split until 2008

Source: McKinsey analysis

The most likely reason for this is that Disney occupies a unique blockbuster content niche that allows blockbusters to be manufactured almost industrially (although the atmosphere of the studio has to remain a creative one). Also, Disney's positioning as 'family entertainer' has greatly helped its ability to sell its content through so many different channels and create evergreens.

Superior management as core competency

Another approach, which is used frequently as portfolio logic, could be described as 'superior media sector management skills'. Companies that have developed superior skills in managing the key processes of a certain media sector are often very successful in buying underperforming businesses and rejuvenating them through the transfer of these existing skills. Very often this approach is combined with an international expansion strategy, where companies invest in emerging markets and bring over the best practices from the more mature markets.

Hubert Burda Media, one of Germany's leading magazine publishers, is an example of a portfolio based on successful skill replication. The company managed to increase its share of foreign magazine sales to 32% in 2006 through entering Eastern Europe and investing in Turkey and France. The recipe used was simple: a team of specialists would enter the new country and acquire one or two attractive magazine properties. The local management would be assessed and replaced by other locals when needed. These people would then be coached and trained extensively, both by the international team and through visits to Germany in how to most effectively produce magazines. At the same time they would keep significant freedom in creating local content. Once the local management and editorial team were sufficiently up to speed, the international expansion team would withdraw to a more extensive coaching role and focus its attention on another country.

The correct recipe seems to be to find the right balance between introducing sophisticated management practices while respecting the need for local content. Axel Springer illustrates this balance even better:

Axel Springer decided to replicate the enormous success it had with the German tabloid *Bild* and launch a similar paper in Spain. The country had no real tabloid offering at that time. The *Bild* concept was copied and launched. The newspaper, however, did not appeal to the Spanish as the format was too much based on the German approach. The newspaper was withdrawn from the market. A few years later the company decided to give it another try in Poland, where there were also no good tabloid offerings. This time the company took a very different approach and made sure that with the help of local editorial staff both the content and the layout of the newspaper were closely aligned with local taste. The newspaper *Fakt* was launched in 2003 and became a resounding success. It is now the leading newspaper in Poland. The launch of *Fakt* was followed by the launch and acquisition of other newspapers and by 2008 Axel Springer has 43.5 percent of the Polish national daily newspaper market, with over 500,000 copies.

Transferring management and creative skills often plays a greater role in this strategy than economies of scale. The successful exploitation of sector skills can be seen in a number of medium-size sector-focused media companies such as Westdeutsche Allgemeine Zeitung (WAZ) in newspapers, Random House in books and the RTL Group in television.

Customer access/service as a core competency

Another emerging core competency around which to build new businesses is customer access and service. This is an approach mostly followed by platform operators such as cable companies or ISPs. Some companies, like Telenet in Belgium, are in the process of successfully developing a customer-centric approach, with cohesive integrated multiple touch-points and micro-segments so as to offer the best communication and service to its customers. Companies such as Free in France have adopted a simpler approach by being the first to offer a lean 'triple play' offering, with limited customer care: the value lies in the price point of their service and in the simplicity and innovativeness of their access offer. In general, however, mass-market ambition requires more than a 'one size fits all' approach, à la Free (with a stable market share in France of 20% of broadband), and requires more complex competencies of customer touch-point services.

Analytics as a core competency

Advertising services and subscription services increasingly require strong competencies in analytics, respectively through ensuring best yields from all forms of advertising and through sophisticated customer lifetime management techniques. In fact, analytics are becoming more and more important for digital marketing services (Figure 7.5), and many companies, from Google with Double Click and AOL with Tacoda to MSN with aQuantive, are quickly acquiring those analytical capabilities to serve the market.

	Offering	Key players
Web analytics	• Measures site visits by referring URL • Tracks traffic from natural search • Analyses visitor pathways	• Omniture • Web Trends
Ad serving	• Serves online advertising • Tracks ad interaction (views and clicks) and connects to site-side behaviours/conversions • Allows for behavioural and IP targeting	• Atlas • DART
Rich media	• Serves rich-media advertising • Tracks ad interaction (time spent, panels viewed, clicks, etc.)	• Atlas, DART • Pointroll, Eyeblaster, Unicast
Bid management	• Manages paid search campaigns via bid- and conversion-based rules • Provides one interface for all engines	• Atlas, DART • Omniture, e-Frontier
Multivariate testing and site optimization	• Allows for dynamic offer testing within landing pages • Measures intra-page interactivity for optimization	• X+1, Optimost, Omniture • AA/RF • Google

Figure 7.5 The wave of technology analytics for digital media

Source: McKinsey analysis

Building the portfolio around scale

Economies of scale only tend to play a significant role in national markets. A company's sales force and distribution power can create attractive competitive advantages – Germany's Axel Springer Verlag has proved this, with its dominant position in the distribution of newspapers. Leading television groups in most European countries have managed to extract a price premium in their advertising sales versus the rest of the market. For companies in which purchased goods and services play an important role, such as the newspaper industry with paper (15%–25% of costs) or the television industry with programme licences (also 15%–25% of costs), scale advantages can be achieved by bundling purchasing power. In consolidating mature markets, such as newspapers, book publishing and magazines, in Western European and US markets, more and more media companies are taking radical steps and doing away with the independent profit-centre structures of newspapers, magazine clusters and book labels and radically centralizing not only back-office functions but also production, marketing and sales. British regional newspaper companies were early movers in this respect and concentrated their back offices as early as the 1990s, as did Hubert Burda Media, which installed a profit-centre structure in the mid-Nineties in which support services, including important functions such as advertising sales, offered their services on an arm's-length basis.

It is significantly more difficult for media companies to realize international scale effects, the main reasons being that content is to a major extent national and the rights for content with an international appeal are mostly sold on a country-by-country basis. There are obvious exceptions, like in the music industry, where artists mostly sign global contracts, or in some genres in television, where international channels can stand local competition, like sports (e.g. Eurosport) and documentaries (e.g. Discovery). But in this latter case, the scale benefit comes as much from the power of the brand of the channel as from pervasive distribution (scale): in fact, premium-brand channels are able to negotiate rates two to five times larger than 'tonnage channels'.

Selective opportunities to build the portfolio around international scale effects apply mainly to companies in which the technical platform plays an important role; in traditional media this applies, for example, to professional information providers. Reed Elsevier is a good example, with its scientific and legal databases, which are leveraged globally. In the Internet world international scale through superior platform development and Internet marketing skills is a very important driver behind companies like Google, eBay and Amazon.

Building the portfolio around cross-sector synergies

Cross-sector synergies have been the driving force behind many acquisitions in the 2000s. Major players, including Time Warner, Bertelsmann and others, have invested heavily in building their company portfolios around these anticipated synergies. They and many other media companies optimistically assumed that cross-selling and/ or -promoting the products from one division by another division would result in significant additional revenues. The anticipated synergies between media sectors have, so far, barely materialized for two main reasons. First, there was significant organizational resistance with most of the powerful product-oriented divisions unwilling to surrender their entrepreneurial freedoms. Second, the companies focused on creating synergies between the properties that happened to be in their portfolios (broad push), which often had limited overlap in target consumer groups and tastes. Offerings built around the specific needs of clearly defined consumer groups are significantly more successful but are mostly created within one division rather than across divisions. There are a few examples of successful cross-promotion (e.g. *Deutschland sucht den Superstar*, the quest for new stars created by RTL) which have shown that cross-synergies are possible, but only as an outflow of systematically developed offerings, for example format creation or customer-segment focus, rather than trying to cross-market an eclectic portfolio. The fact that there has been little follow-up of these examples shows that they are few and difficult to find for companies which have historically grown business portfolios.

Vertical integration

Historically, vertical integration was above all driven by the lack of infrastructure: publishers needed to have their own presses and distribution systems as there was no alternative infrastructure available. As the print industry matured, some of the players decided to divest and outsource capital-intensive activities, such as printing, or develop industry-wide solutions, for example for newspaper and/or magazine distribution. Others, such as Bertelsmann with its subsidiary Arvato, actively expanded their service activities to become global players.

With the advent of digitization, we see increasing activity in backwards integration. Operators, such as Telenet in Belgium (cable, investing in premium pay-TV) and Comcast in the United States (cable, with its recent failed bid for Disney), (are trying to) integrate backwards into content businesses, mostly to secure their access services or to expand their product ranges to sell to subscribers.

Large commercial TV groups are also increasingly integrating backwards, to be less vulnerable to the fragmentation of the TV market and the decline in advertising revenues. The acquisition of Fremantle by RTL, of Endemol in part by Mediaset and of a number of smaller TV producers of the already vertically integrated ITV group are driven by the need not only for a constant flow of high-quality content, but also to ensure that rights can be leveraged through all channels and also for video-on-demand offerings. Most European media companies try to run their production houses at arm's length and thus have the benefits of portfolio diversification with some form of privileged access while not smothering the content production companies. An exception are those content companies such as the NBP 'soap factories' owned by Media Capital in Portugal, where a very close link is needed between the TV channel and the production company to continually fine-tune the story in order to maintain ratings.

Vertical integration is a self-reinforcing process: once a few important players start to integrate, others feel forced to do the same, in order to ensure future access to content (for platform operators) or to distribution (for media companies). The US TV market is a good example of these dynamics, where major studios own their own networks (ABC, Disney, etc.) and TV production is almost exclusively done by home-owned major studios.

Performance-based portfolio optimization

'Pure' portfolio optimization – that is, building the portfolio systematically based on the growth and cash flow potential of individual businesses, without paying much attention to possible synergies between these businesses – is not usual in the media industry. During the industry growth phase, most media conglomerates bought a broad array of businesses. They were striving to expand their portfolios by adding high-growth, high-margin businesses. However, few companies consistently divested businesses that were under-performing or had strict portfolio criteria, such as those that GE developed for managing its portfolio. In a maturing environment, it is an increasing challenge for media companies to create high-performing portfolios, as the numbers of growth businesses and margins are declining. However, the recent downturn in the industry has led to radical portfolio pruning by some players, which is a first sign of a possible fundamental reshaping of industry practices.

Defining new 'plays' based on consistent portfolio logic

Once a media company has decided on the key value-creating logic behind its portfolio, it must choose its portfolio-reshaping play accordingly. At this point, several interesting new play options have emerged:

- *Multi-local-sector dominance:* A few media companies consistently maintain their sector dominance on a multi-local basis. VNU, Reed Elsevier and Pearson have reshaped their portfolios, investing in core sectors and divesting properties that were not critical to these sectors, even if they were highly profitable (Figure 7.6). The RTL Group has duplicated its model of broadcasting quite successfully in many markets. On the Web, Google aims to dominate the digital advertising services industry, through search and other display ad services, offering its services through its own destination sites (search and others, like YouTube) and affiliates, and extending them to the mobile.
- *National multi-sector dominance:* Many media companies are attempting to build a dominant national position across sectors. The national players mentioned at the beginning of this chapter are good examples of this strategy. Mostly, these companies were newspaper companies which, in their prosperous years, began to diversify their portfolios by investing in local/regional radio stations, TV production, etc. These strategies were very worthwhile from a political influence point of view; however, at the same time regulatory constraints prevented media companies from truly optimizing their positions. The portfolios have usually been too diverse and the company culture too decentralized to leverage common competency-based synergies between media sectors. However, with digitization, reaching customers over multiple channels and leveraging rights over multiple media will become more important and media companies will have to start looking for ways to do this effectively. A major hurdle for this strategy is still national regulations, preventing media companies from investing significantly across sectors, as Axel Springer experienced when it was blocked in its planned acquisition of the leading German TV group ProSiebenSat1.

EUR million, per cent

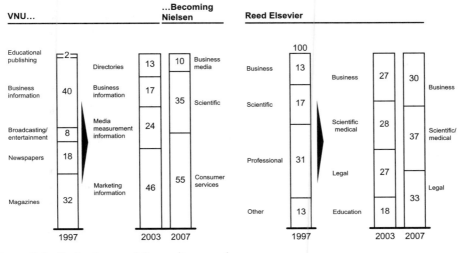

Figure 7.6 Reshaping portfolio media examples

Source: McKinsey analysis

- *Customer-segment dominance:* Here, several successful businesses have emerged, for example MTV addressing young audiences or Eurosport. However, there have been no success stories to date of media companies who built their business portfolio consistently around a customer segment, except for more B2B-oriented companies such as Reed Elsevier, which clearly focuses on a few B2B customer segments. This is partially attributable to the fact that a large amount of B2C media company revenue is derived from consumer reach, which makes it difficult to focus on specific segments. The only exception is maybe Disney, with its focus on the (very broad) family segment. The digitization and growing fragmentation of traditional mass media such as TV, however, signal that a customer-segment strategy could become an attractive add-on to a more mass-oriented sector or regional strategy.

- *Radical transformation:* It has been very rare to see media companies taking the risk to fully transform themselves. VNU was a clear exception. It anticipated the maturity of business-to consumer (B2C) magazines and shifted its strategy to become a B2B information provider, radically disinvesting from its early days of being a B2C print company, and continued to invest in its core capacity as a provider of media solutions. It acquired Nielsen, and took on that company's name. In general, digitization could increase the occurrence of such corporate strategy paths. Schibsted in Scandinavia developed an aggressive approach to digitizing its business by systematically launching or acquiring online technology platforms for classified services (e.g. FINN and Blocket) and local search. Other companies seem to be considering other forms of transformation, rather than investing heavily in digital media. For example, Bertelsmann is focusing its portfolio more and more on B2B services, as it is divesting its music business and actively growing its Arvato service division.

Merger and acquisitions

In general, research on the 'granularity' of growth by McKinsey demonstrates that long-term growth is usually driven more by M&A and adjacent markets' diversification than by fighting for market share. There are some additional rationales in media to use M&A as a way of operating the growth strategy. For instance, organic growth takes time, and usually content businesses are quite risky, with, for some media, a large sum of sunk costs (one-time costs which are spent irretrievably at the beginning of a project, e.g. television). With M&A, media companies can bypass the long phase of growing and break-even development, while possibly buying less risky assets. Sanoma, by buying the consumer magazines of VNU, managed to acquire in the deal also strong digital assets like ilse media; Schibsted managed to diversify south of Scandinavia through the acquisition of Trader, etc. The corollary is that the price of assets in the market can be bid too high, as mispricing on the potential of acquisitions. Vivendi is an example of this risk, which arose after the flurry of acquisitions made during the first Internet bubble early 2000. M&A can be a strong vehicle for revenue growth, as more than 50% of top-line growth for high-growth media companies is inorganic and that lower-growth companies are mainly hampered by inadequate M&A. (Figure 7.7)

(Re)shaping the corporate governance model

Once companies are clear about the value-creating logic behind their portfolio, they must ensure that their corporate governance model, including the role of the corporate centre,

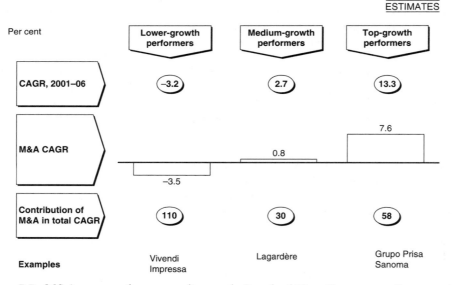

Figure 7.7   M&A as a contributor to media growth: Sample of 10 top European media companies among top 20*, 2001–2006

*Corrected for any exchange rate effect
Source: McKinsey 'granularity of growth'

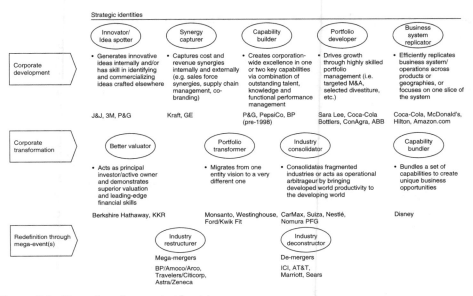

Figure 7.8 Examples of strategic identities

Source: Three modes and some strategic identities, identity definitions and examples from John Cook, 'Corporate Strategy', presentation to McKinsey Oxford Learning Symposium, September 1998

is (re)shaped in such a way that it is clear the corporate centre will add value accordingly. The corporate centre must have a clear strategic identity, which, in turn, depends on the company's strategic mode (i.e. development, transformation or redefinition of the company).

Clearly, the corporate centre will possess nuances of several strategic identities, but experience has shown that it can credibly fulfil its role only when it maintains one primary identity and a maximum of two secondary identities (Figure 7.8). Which identity to choose depends upon the company's corporate strategy. An international sector strategy will, for example, require the corporate centre in the role of 'business system replicator' (assuming no major business transformation is needed). A regional, cross-sector approach requires a 'capturer of synergies'. In either case, the corporate centre must play a more active role than in the historical hands-off profit-centre approach. The key to successfully reshaping the role of the corporate centre involves defining a clear role and ensuring that business unit management is actively involved in the process of shaping this role.

The corporate governance and ownership structure must be aligned with the value-creating logic behind the corporate strategy. Actively reshaping the portfolio will, in many cases, imply that financial investors – be they private equity firms, banks or financial markets – will take on partial ownership. Ideally, this means that 'neutral' economic interests will counterbalance the family values. This will be especially important in cases where due to, for example, a generational handover there is no longer a consistent entrepreneurial vision.

Concentrating efforts to enable regulatory alignments

Whatever the portfolio strategy chosen, media companies must focus their efforts on working with regulators on those areas that create the greatest barriers to their strategy, rather than trying to challenge all regulations at the same time. If an international-sector strategy is chosen, the focus should be on regulations preventing foreign acquisitions and on historical rights in frequency allocation. Further, a concerted effort across media sectors and geographic boundaries will be necessary to achieve critical impact. This means a much higher degree of cooperation between all industry associations, with a common understanding of areas of regulatory focus. Such fruitful cooperation is happening around digitization. For instance, cooperative models of analogue switch-off of TV signals are proposed by OFCOM, the regulatory entity of the United Kingdom, while Telenet, the major cable operator of Belgium, has worked hand in hand with the government to develop a digital platform for Flanders. There is still much to be done – but the trend is moving in the right direction.

Key Takeaways

1. Since the end of the Second World War, the portfolios of most European media companies have been influenced by national growth opportunities in the different media sectors. On a European level the industry is still very fragmented.
2. Family (majority) ownership is common in European media companies, resulting in different priorities from those of the capital markets. Meanwhile, private equity players are increasingly investing in media companies, which puts pressure on (short-term) performance.
3. Many media companies are still organized along strong, independent divisional structures. Attempts to change this structure have so far enjoyed mixed success.
4. There are still strong regulations with regard to foreign and/or cross-media ownership, creating clear boundaries within which media companies can optimize their portfolio.
5. There will be the need for media companies to rethink their portfolio structures as traditional media sectors are maturing, new growth sectors emerge and the need to leverage rights across several media increases.
6. Media companies should be clear about the portfolio logic they want to follow when reshaping their portfolio: core competency-based, scale-based, cross-sector synergies, vertical integration, portfolio diversification. M&A plays an important role in all these strategies as organic growth in media tends to be slow and risky.
7. There are successful examples for each logic, but one should expect more corporate transformation as a major way of redesigning strategy for digitization.
8. The role of the corporate centre should be clarified and focused on the portfolio logic.

Liberty Global: Multichannel Portfolio Play[1]

Shane O'Neill, the Chief Strategic Officer at Liberty Global, Inc. (LGI), and President of Chellomedia, the content arm of LGI, was looking at the latest results. Overall, the results of the company were very satisfying. The portfolio was developing well. On one hand, LGI's European cable distribution division UPC has been developing well, especially within their central and Eastern European region, where more and more consumers were buying multiplay services (a combination of TV and/or telephony and/or broadband). LGI had developed into the largest cable operator outside of the United States, serving 16 million customer homes with video, broadband and telephone services, with over 30 million homes passed. LGI's content division, Chellomedia had also significantly developed its business, with a turnover of around €260 million annually.

On the other hand, although this overall development was a source of satisfaction, Shane was particularly proud of his reorganization of Chellomedia, which had transformed it into a true content business of LGI. The company had turned around in only a few years through the acquisition of, among others, Zonevision and Sport1 and Sport2 in Hungary, and combining these new assets with existing channels, such as Extreme Sports.

Yet Shane had one concern. He made the choice to organize Chellomedia to allow for maximum entrepreneurship (most acquisitions were integrated 'as is' into Chellomedia, keeping their momentum intact, except for a consistent rebranding as Chello). However, he was still worried about the future of his niche thematic content business. Would fostering entrepreneurship be enough, or would a more integrated structure be necessary? Would it, for instance, be better to concentrate on a few, dominating genres rather than to invest broadly and opportunistically in a variety of channels? Would thematic channels continue to expand with the shift to digital TV, or would they be crowded out by 'non-linear' content, such as video on demand? Would the rise of the personal video recorder lead to consumers to record more well-known programmes and watch them at a later time rather than browse through live programmes available on thematic channels? How severe would the competition from Web video content networks such as YouTube, Dailymotion and others be?

Company History

LGI has a complex history. Its core cable distribution arm is centred on UPC. UPC was founded in 1995 as a 50/50 joint venture between UnitedGlobalCom (UGC), headed by Gene Schneider, one of the founding fathers of the US cable industry, and the Dutch Philips NV. Mark Schneider, Gene Schneider's son, came to Europe to transfer the successful US cable business model and create a pan-European cable group.

UPC started out by acquiring cable systems across Europe, eventually establishing a presence at one point in more than a dozen countries. The acquisitions were mostly debt-financed. The strategy was to create distribution scale quickly and roll out digital 'triple play' services (Internet, digital television and telephony). In 1999, the company went

---

[1] This case is developed solely as the basis for class discussion. Cases are not intended to serve as endorsements, sources of primary data or illustrations of effective or ineffective management.

public with 50% of its shares on the Amsterdam Stock Exchange and NASDAQ in order to raise further funds to continue its expansion.

In March 1999, UPC launched its broadband ISP in five European countries (the Netherlands, Norway, Belgium and Austria) under the Chello brand, leveraging its existing cable infrastructure. One month later, UPC TV launched its first proprietary television channels, which then combined with Chello to create the UPC Chellomedia Division.

As the dot.com bubble burst, the share price tumbled. The company realized it needed to restructure fundamentally in order to meet the financing costs it had incurred during its acquisition spree of 1997–2000 and its triple play investments. A fundamental strategic realignment was undertaken as well as a significant reduction of costs. Having successfully restructured the business and turned around its operating performance, the company was able to negotiate financial restructuring under Chapter 11.

After the financial restructuring, the US company Liberty Media emerged as the controlling shareholder in UGC, and after a number of further restructurings LGI emerged as the new company combining all the former assets of UGC and several Liberty Media assets (the main one being a controlling stake in J.com, the leading cable company in Japan). In 2007 LGI took control of Telenet, the leading Flemish cable operator in Belgium to become the largest cable operator outside of the United States. Mike Fries became the new CEO.

Under the new structure two main divisions were created in Europe. UPC Broadband is the distribution arm which bundles triple play cable services for residential customers and also offers digital satellite services. The other division is Chellomedia, which was redefined to include digital media centres and post-production services and, more importantly, thematic TV channels. In addition, Chellomedia manages the on-demand services and owns Liberty Ventures, the non-consolidated investment assets of Liberty Global.

Chellomedia's operations are run through five operating companies. The first is focused on on-demand products and services. The other four relate mostly to thematic channels.

Three of these four operating units, Chello Benelux, Chello Multicanal and Chello Central Europe are dedicated to exploiting regional opportunities.

Chello Benelux is the leading supplier of premium channels to the Dutch TV market distributing its premium pay TV channels Film1 and Sport1, as well as Weerkanaal (weather channel) to cable networks and satellite operators. It also runs the Digital Media Centre (DMC) in Amsterdam, which provides a full range of broadcast services for channel production, origination and distribution, as well as play out and propagation for third party TV channels.

Chello Multicanal is the leading independent provider of thematic television channels in the Iberian market, operating eight channels, which reach 14 million subscribers. Its TV brands include Canal Panda, Canal Hollywood, Canal Cocina, Sol Musica, Odisea and Decasa. It also operates joint venture channels with AETN (Canal de Historia and The Biography Channel).

Chello Central Europe's portfolio of channels includes: Sport1 and Sport2, the leading providers of sports entertainment in Hungary, the Czech Republic, Slovakia and Romania; and Minimax, the leading children's channel in the region; as well as a joint venture with MGM and three channels acquired in 2007; TV Paprika, TV Deko and Filmmuzeum. Combined, these channels reach 18 million subscribers. Chello Central Europe also

100% owned channels as of end 2007

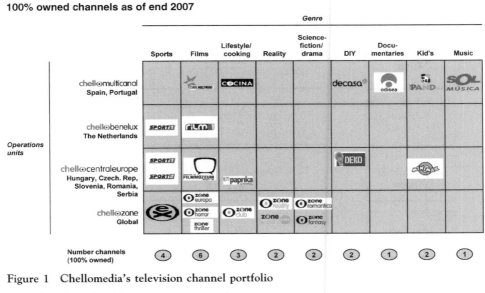

Figure 1   Chellomedia's television channel portfolio

Source: LGI. Reproduced by permission

Example Chello Multicanal

Genre	Spain	Portugal
Films		• Hollywood is the leading basic movie service; only outperformed by series-based channel (e.g. Fox)
Lifestyle cooking	• Largest lifestyle channel	
Documentaries	• At par with Discovery channel	
Kids		• Lead kids' channel • Three times greater ratings than the Disney channel

Figure 2   Chellomedia's channel strength

Source: McKinsey analyses

operates AT Media, Poland's leading thematic channel advertising sales agency, and Mojo Productions, a full service production house catering to local as well as international channels in the region.

Most of these channels have shown their worth, Minimax, for example, has become the leading children's channel for Hungary as has Panda in Portugal. Meanwhile, in Spain,

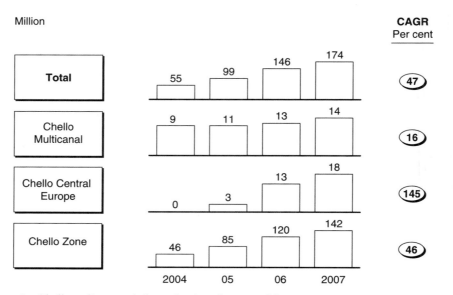

Figure 3   **Chellomedia-owned channel subscriber growth***

*Outside Benelux
Source: Liberty International. Reproduced by permission

Odiessa is challenging Discovery's dominance. The fourth business unit, Chello Zone, is a leading international broadcast and distributor of thematic television channels and operates nine thematic channels: Zone Reality, Zone Europa, Zone Romantica, Zone Club, Zone Horror, Zone Thriller, Zone Fantasy, Extreme Sports Channel and pre-school TV channel, Jim Jam, an international venture with Hit Entertainment. The channels are broadcast in over 120 countries in 23 languages. Total subscribers for Chello Zone has reached 142 million by the end of 2007, up from fewer than 50 million in 2006.

Altogether Chello Media's subscriber base has grown by 50% annually to reach close to 200 million in 2008.

Revenue has grown by between 15% and 25% annually and was estimated to be about €300 million by 2008, with a sizeable EBITDA margin.

Sport1 and Film1 in Belgium are costly premium channels, which are used to drive digital TV penetration. Meanwhile the other 25 channels have more modest annual budgets of €3–5 million each.

The bulk of Chellomedia revenue is derived from carriage fees paid by operators to distribute the company's thematic channels (68%) and advertising (22%). Only in the UK do channels not receive subscription revenue, living solely on advertising. The remaining 10% of revenue comes from third-party representation, programme sales and ad services fees.

Geographically, Chellomedia is present in 120 territories, but Benelux (21%), Iberia (19%), Poland (11%) and Hungary (11%) make up more than two-thirds of the revenue. The mix of genres is well balanced. Based on agency revenues, the three main genres are: films (22%), sports (21%) and reality (6%).

Strategic challenges

The challenges of Chellomedia, as Shane sees them, are threefold.

Continued growth

The market for multichannel TV is set to continue to grow significantly in the near future, possibly at 10% a year for the number of subscribers and up to 15% for ad revenue, according to various industry sources.

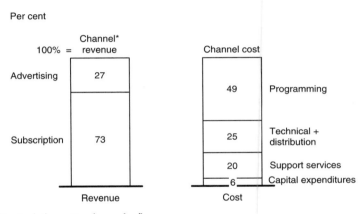

Figure 4 Typical thematic channel p/l

*Outside channel representation, programme sales or production
Source: McKinsey analyses

Will Chellomedia's revenue match or even exceed this pace? Should Chellomedia continue to enlarge its offering of genres and channels? Should it buy further channels in order to consolidate the market or expand into new markets?

Channel design

In recent years, the channels managed to generate and monetize sufficient reach to be profitable in spite of their nimble programming budgets; but what if platforms started paying ever smaller carriage fees to channels? Channels would have no choice but to live off advertising revenue alone, which as witnessed in the UK, is currently not sufficient to break even, due to the low ratings achieved by low budget programming. What kind of products would channels need to be profitable in such a world?

On-demand

The rise of on-demand TV raises another issue. Viewers will not only be able to decide when they watch television, but will also have more opportunity to watch their favorite

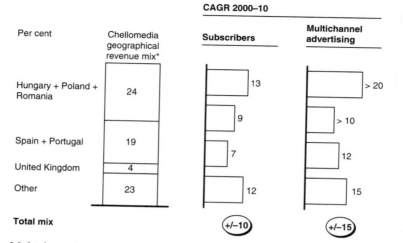

CAGR 2000–10

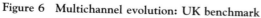

Figure 5 Multichannel revenue growth driver

*Estimated
Source: McKinsey analyses based on data from PricewaterhouseCoopers Global entertainment outlook; *Screen Digest*; Zenith Optimedia; Chello data

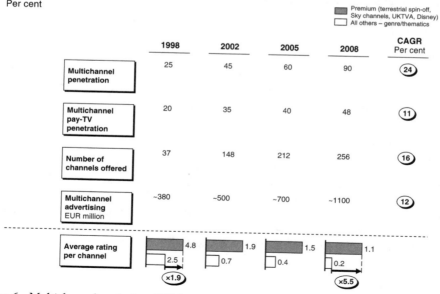

Figure 6 Multichannel evolution: UK benchmark

Source: McKinsey analyses based on data from Zenith Optimedia; Ofcom; Barb; Chello Zone

programmes. They will therefore be more likely to focus their viewing to fewer programmes. Again, the United Kingdom, as the most advanced digital TV market in the world, demonstrates that households which own a personal video recorder (PVR) graze and surf significantly less across thematic niche channels and thus reduce their ratings. What threat does this pose to Chellomedia? Is this a short-term or long-term phenomenon?

Lagardère Active: Restoring Growth Through Operations[1]

The Lagardère Media Group is one of the largest media companies in Europe, present in book publishing, print magazines, radio and thematic TV, as well as sports marketing. It generated more than €8.5 billion in sales in 2007, reaching a size similar to the other major French media company, Vivendi.

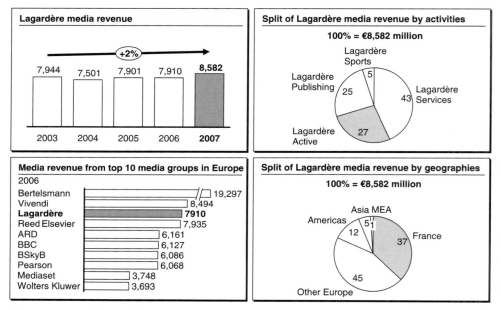

Figure 1 Lagardère media revenue

Source: McKinsey analysis based on annual report; company website

In recent months, the Group has added to its portfolio of activities Lagardère Sports, through the acquisition of Sportsfive from the RTL Group. Although the publishing division stands for the largest profit contributor to date, Lagardère Active together with the sports division are the businesses with the largest short-term expected profit growth (6%).

Didier Quillot, the CEO of Lagardère Active, knows how difficult it is to operate in the magazine environment, where circulation is on the decline, or in the area of generalist radio, such as Europe 1, which must face the fragmentation of the radio market. While the CEO knows the importance of digitization to transform the Active division, he is also aware that there will be a transition phase between the offline and digital space that

---

[1]This case is developed solely as the basis for class discussion. Cases are not intended to serve as endorsements, sources of primary data or illustrations of effective or ineffective management.

2007, EUR million

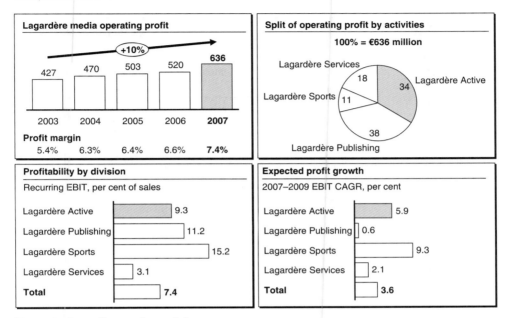

Figure 2   Lagardère media profit*

*Excluding EADS
Source: McKinsey analysis based on data from annual report; company website; ING forecasts

requires him to achieve a strong profitability boost on his current portfolio if he wishes to achieve his short-term profitability goals.

Company History

Lagardère started as a one-man publishing and bookstand business nearly 200 years ago and grew into a highly diversified player operating across many segments and countries.

Louis Hachette laid Lagardère's foundation in the early 1800s. A schoolteacher by profession, Hachette bought a small bookstore and publishing business in 1826. He soon began acquiring the rights to primary-school texts, and received an order for 500 000 alphabet primers from the French Ministry of Education when free primary schooling was introduced in 1833.

Inspired by the example of WHSmith in London, Hachette was convinced that rail travellers would be an ideal target group for pocket-sized books for passing the time during trips. Beginning in 1852, he signed contracts with French railways, securing prime bookstand locations, and launched the Bibliothèque des Chemins de Fer (Railway Library) one year later – a series of light reading and travel guides targeted specifically at railway passengers.

2007 performance EUR million				Valuation multiplier
	06–07 revenue growth	NOPLAT** EUR million	Capital employed* EUR million	Broker range***
Publishing	9%	199	993	8.6x–9.8x
Audiovisual	–13%	54	206	14.5x–17.1x
Press	2%	101	1675	8.0x–8.6x
Services	3%	81	18	9.9x–10.0x
Sport	N/a	45	865	16.4x–20.0x
	3.2%	480	3,757	

Figure 3 Lagardère value creation potential

*Excluding investments in associates
**Net operating profit less adjusted tax
***Morgan Stanley – 9/04/2008, ABN Amro – 31/03/2008
Source: McKinsey analysis

The Bibliothèque was a huge success, and, to enhance his newsstand offering, Hachette launched his first magazine, Le Journal pour Tous (Everyone's Magazine) in 1855.

The company grew by acquiring the leading French newspapers' distribution, printing and binding companies in the early 1900s, and launched its blockbuster magazine Elle in 1945, which has a strong circulation in 32 countries today. Shortly after the launch of Elle, Hachette began to diversify in both publishing and distribution. This included taking over prestigious publishing houses like Grasset et Fasquelle and Fayard, launching the paperback imprint Livre de Poche (1951), starting his own book distribution centre (Centre de Distribution du Livre) and, especially, creating the newspaper and distribution agency NMPP (Nouvelles Messageries de la Presse Parisienne) in 1947. In the 1970s, the company diversified in a number of directions, making it a prime target for acquisition.

Filipacchi Médias, Hachette's rival in magazine publishing, grew throughout the postwar era through a series of launches (Lui, Photo, Union), and became one of the largest French magazine publishers in 1976, when it acquired Paris Match. In 1981, the company acquired Hachette together with Jean-Luc Lagardère, then director general of Matra Automobiles, and later CEO of Lagardère.

Per cent

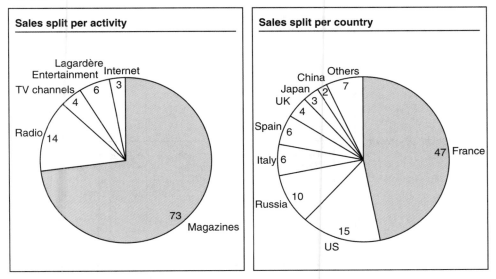

Figure 4   Lagardère active sales by activity and geography, 2007*

*Excluding regional dailies
Source: McKinsey analyses based on data from annual report; company website

In the 1980s, the newly merged company was systematically developed further. These years witnessed the partial IPO of the magazine division (Filipacchi), in 1984, and a number of international magazine spin-offs, for example the US version of *Elle* in 1985, as well as further acquisitions in neighbouring publishing areas. Aimed at diversification across not only countries but also various areas of the media industry, Lagardère acquired a 25% stake in the French TV network La Cinq in 1990, which was losing money at the time. The investment resulted in write-offs exceeding €630 million a year later and nearly caused the collapse of the company. To cover the debt, a holding company (Lagardère SCA) was formed in 1993, with Filipacchi Magazines, Hachette Publishing and Matra Automobile as its subdivisions.

Matra Automobile was sold ten years later, in 2003, when Lagardère SCA took a minority share in aviation and space company EADS. After the takeover of Vivendi Universal Publishing in 2002, Lagardère Média has become the largest publishing company in France. It also acquired a sport marketing company, Sportsfive.

Lagardère is still family-managed. In 2008 the company was managed by the son of, the now deceased, Jean-Luc Lagardère, Arnaud Lagardère. The media company has four divisions, Lagardère Active, managed by Didier Quillot, Lagardère Publishing, managed by Arnaud Noury, Lagardère Services, under the leadership of Jean-Louis Nachury, and Lagardère Sports (the branding of Sportsfive), under the leadership of Oliver Guiguet.

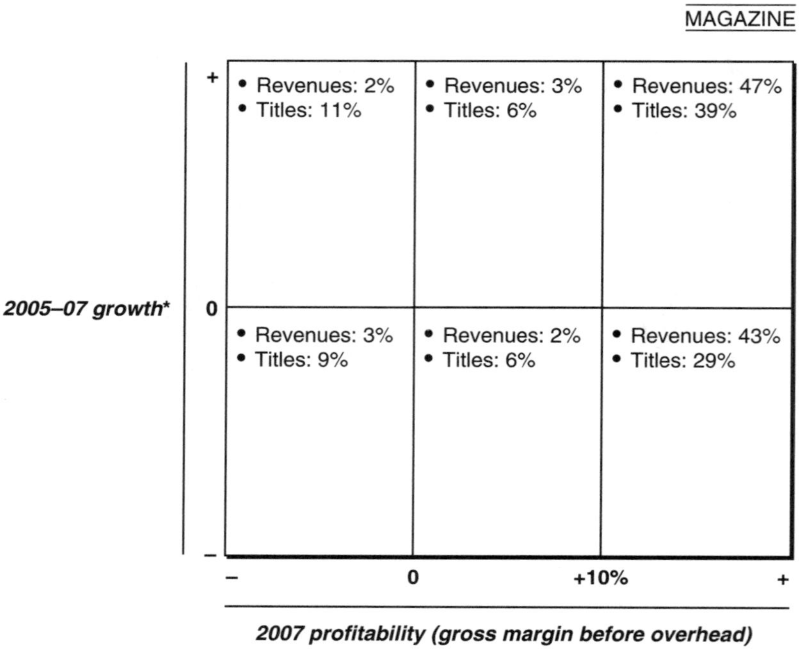

MAGAZINE

• Revenues: 2% • Titles: 11%	• Revenues: 3% • Titles: 6%	• Revenues: 47% • Titles: 39%
• Revenues: 3% • Titles: 9%	• Revenues: 2% • Titles: 6%	• Revenues: 43% • Titles: 29%

2005–07 growth*   0

−   0   +10%   +

2007 profitability (gross margin before overhead)

Figure 5   Lagardère Active magazine portfolio mix

*Excluding countries in JV
Source: McKinsey analyses based on data Lagardère investors' day releases

The divisions vary in revenues and profitability. Currently, 43% of revenue comes from Lagardère Services, with an operating margin of less than 4%. Lagardère Active is the second revenue contributor with a significant international footprint, as it makes more than 53% of its revenue outside of France. Close to three-quarters of the revenue accruing to Lagardère Active arises from print magazines; nevertheless, audiovisual activities have close to twice the margin of magazine activities. Lagardère publishing contributes 25% of the revenue, with an operating margin of 11%.

On a capital investment basis, outside-in analysis suggests that publishing generates strong value creation, as do services, which do not employ a great deal of capital (most of the real estate is not owned). The Sports division's current return on invested capital is likely to be below its cost, reflecting the price paid, claimed by many as high, for acquiring Sportsfive; the value creation potential will have to come from significant future growth in the business acquired.

Within Active, audiovisual has most likely a strong ROIC, reflecting the cash cow status of top radio station Europe 1 in France. The print magazine business has large capital employed in relation to the revenue generated. It is likely that the division will not

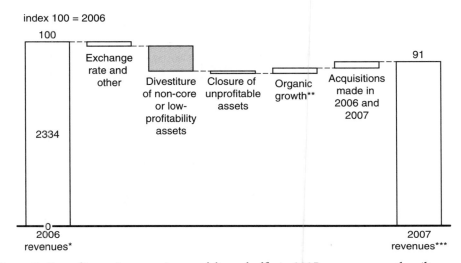

index 100 = 2006

Figure 6   Lagardère active magazine portfolio reshuffle in 2007: revenue growth spilt

*2006 proforma
**Including launch of new titles/activities
***2007 proforma, net of regional dailies divestiture
Source: McKinsey analyses based on data from investor days releases

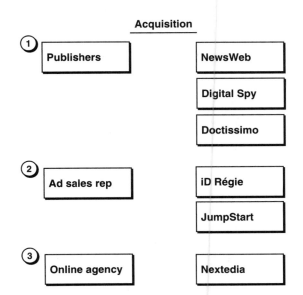

Figure 7   Lagardère active Internet acquisitions: examples

Source: McKinsey analysis

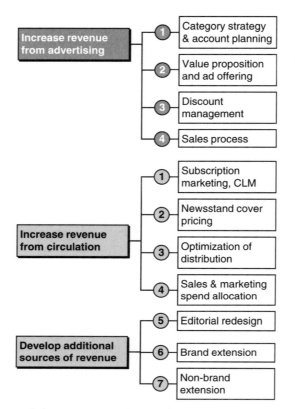

Figure 8   Organic growth levers in magazines' top line

Source: McKinsey benchmarks; Team analysis

generate large shareholder value unless Active succeeds in creating profitable growth and margins in the coming years.

Strategic Challenges

Didier Quillot knows that he must act on his digital strategy, both as a defensive move and as a growth platform. Nevertheless, the Internet is still a relatively small part of his business, and this is not likely to build the company's growth and profitability platform in the short term on its own. He has already improved the margins, through cleaning up his magazine portfolio: unprofitable titles went down from 36% of titles, or 10% of revenue, to 11% of titles, or 5% of the revenue. The extent of divestiture shrunk the top line, but will hopefully help to further grow the business. Eleven per cent of remaining titles have been

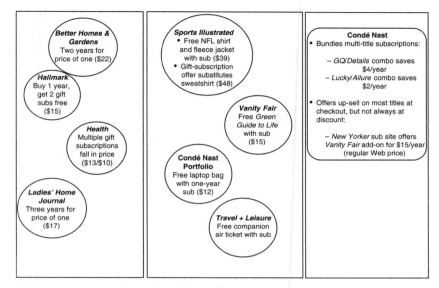

Figure 9   Innovative magazine subscription offerings

Source: McKinsey analysis

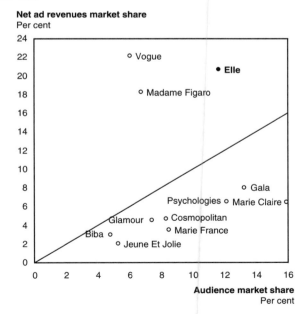

2005–2007

Net ad revenues market share
Per cent

Figure 10   Magazine ad bonus ratio, women, France

Source: McKinsey analysis based on data from TNS Media Intelligence; OJD; AEPM

restored to a positive growth trajectory now, yet the size of their revenue (2%) will not contribute significantly to the bottom and top lines.

What is really needed is to look at how to be more efficient and how to generate significant additional revenue per magazine sold – this will not only create top-line growth but also significantly boost marginal profitability. Growth levers to be considered could be increasing copy prices, to improve advertising yield or to develop brand and non-brand extension revenues.

Should lead brands like *Elle* be able to generate as much advertising revenues per circulation as *Vogue*? Should top titles be bundled as those of CondeNast, the *GQ/Details* combo, *New Yorker* with *Vanity Fair*, etc? Should advertising discounts be better aligned with ad pages revenues? How many of those levers can be pulled to boost the profitability growth of the print portfolio?

Sanoma Group: Restructuring the Portfolio for Growth[1]

Throughout Europe, market leaders in the media industry are feeling the effects of the Internet on their magazine divisions. Total magazine circulation is flat or slightly declining, and advertising dollars are shifting to online alternatives. Some companies have already sold off their magazine divisions, as was seen with the sale of Dennis Publishing's magazine *Maxim* to a private-equity business and the recent sale of emap.

However, in Finland, where Sanoma Group, one of Europe's largest media companies, still generates 50% of its sales, the Internet has had less of an impact on the media industry in spite of the world's third-largest broadband penetration (61% of households in 2008). Finnish media companies are lagging behind the rest of Europe with their online offerings. When comparing the amount of online advertising, the number of visitors on media companies' websites or the amount of money spent on online advertising in relation to the number of visitors, Finland ranks near the bottom in comparison with Western European countries.

Sanoma Group has been able to avoid the negative effects of the Internet boom while the rest of the European media majors have been suffering. This is largely due to the fact that it does not have a significant presence in the English-, German- or French-speaking media markets, which have been most affected by the Internet. Instead, it has focused on Finland, Benelux and Central Eastern European markets, such as Hungary, Czech Republic, Romania, Russia and Adriatic Region. Yet signs of the increasing importance of the Internet are emerging. This can be seen, for example, in the popularity of online financial information or the migration of tabloids online.

As Hannu Syrjänen, CEO and President of Sanoma Group, ponders the future direction of his organization, he wonders if they waited too long to build a solid online presence, or, if they are in fact in an ideal position to learn from the mistakes of others in the European media industry. Another issue concerning Hannu is how much the organization should focus on developing its online presence compared to continuing to grow its traditional (and very successful) magazine, educational publishing businesses internationally.

Company History

The Sanoma Group was formed in 1999 when the Sanoma Corporation, Helsinki Media and WSOY merged. Prior to this, each company had a strong history within the media industry in Finland. WSOY was founded in the nineteenth century by Werner Söderström, and later became one of Finland's leading book publishers. Sanoma Corporation, whose stronghold was in newspaper and magazine publishing, started when Eero Erkko founded the newspaper *Päiälehti*. In 1904 the paper was renamed *Helsingin Sanomat*, which became the core of Sanoma's newspaper and magazine business. The Helsinki Media Company was formed in 1993 from two divisions (Sanomaprint and New Media) of Sanoma. Over

---

[1]This case is developed solely as the basis for class discussion. Cases are not intended to serve as endorsements, sources of primary data or illustrations of effective or ineffective management.

the years Helsinki Media built up its magazine portfolio, in addition to entering the TV industry through an associated company, Ruutunelonen. Rautakirja, the newsagent, was already founded in 1910 by a group of companies, including Sanoma Corporation and WSOY. Rautakirja sold newspapers and books through kiosks primarily located at Finnish railway stations. Throughout the first half of the twentieth century, Sanoma, WSOY, the Helsinki Media Company and Rautakirja all grew steadily.

When Sanoma Corporation, WSOY and the Helsinki Media Company merged in 1999, they became Finland's largest media company. As both Sanoma and WSOY together owned a majority of shares in Rautakirja, when the companies merged, Rautakirja also became a subsidiary of the newly formed company. It later was fully integrated into the Sanoma Group (in 2003, when the company was still called SanomaWSOY). The newly formed company continued to invest in educational publishing, magazine and newspaper publishing and newsagent kiosks, in addition to television and online services.

Book publishing

Although Sanoma Group sold off some of the operations in its book publishing divisions (calendars, special printing), it has continued to invest in this area throughout the 2000s. In particular, it further built up its portfolio of education materials through the acquisition of Dutch publisher Malmberg Investments BV, in 2004, that of Hungary's leading educational publishing and training company, Láng Kiado & Holding, in 2006 and the acqustion of Nowa Era in Poland in 2008.

Magazines and newspapers

Throughout the 2000s, Sanoma Group greatly expanded its magazine business within Europe. In 2001 it acquired the Dutch magazine publishing business from VNU and became Europe's fifth-largest magazine publisher. Additionally, in 2002, it set up a company in Croatia, and in 2003 moved into Bulgaria. The year 2003 marked the launch of the Hungarian, Croatian and Romanian editions of *National Geographic* and the Croatian editions of *Elle* and *TV Story*. In 2005 Sanoma Group acquired a leading consumer magazine publisher in Russia, which held a portfolio of 28 consumer magazines and three newspapers in both Russia and the Ukraine. Additionally, in 2005 Sanoma Group cooperated with German Gruner + Jahr and Austrian Styria to expand their magazine publishing activities in the Adriatic region (Croatia, Serbia and Montenegro, Slovenia). Onwards from 2005, Sanoma Group continued to invest in Eastern Europe and launched dozens of magazines in this region.

Digital and Internet technology

At the height of the Internet boom Sanoma Group decided to form a subsidiary group called SWelcom (nowadays Sanoma Entertainment) to focus on electronic media. Through SWelcom, Sanoma Group launched digital television channels, increased its holding in Channel Four (Nelonen) to 90.55% and formed a joint venture with two other digital-TV multiplex managers to provide technology platforms for Finland's digital TV service. Further expansion into digital TV, Internet TV and video on demand (VoD) occurred through Sanoma Group's holdings in Welho, Finland's largest cable TV operator. As part of its acquisition of VNU's Consumer Information Group it had also become the owner of a few leading Dutch websites such as Startpagina.nl, a very popular search site, and nu.nl, the leading Dutch news site.

Additionally, Sanoma Group launched and acquired various online offerings such as an online market places for consumers online portals. The years 2005 and 2006 brought about the launch and acquisition of several online portals, such as the Hungarian car portal site Vezess.hu, the Dutch price and product comparison site Kieskeurig.nl, the Romanian bridal community site Miresici.ro and the Russian women's portal Ameno.ru.

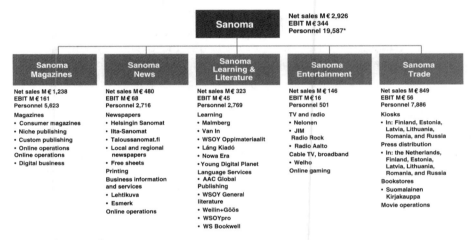

Figure 1   Sanoma Group

*Personnel under employment contract, average at the end of 2007.
Source: Sanoma presentation to INSEAD, 2006. Reproduced by permission

Current Situation

Industry dynamics

Educational publishing in Europe

Although the major publishing companies Sanoma, Pearson, Reed Elsevier and Kluwer all have educational publishing divisions, there are no dominant players in the European market, and as a result it is fairly unconsolidated. According to preliminary information from the Finnish Book Publishers' Association, the educational material market in Europe is estimated to have grown by between 1% and 2% in 2007, and is expected to have huge growth potential in the coming years, particularly in Eastern Europe. Estimates suggest that Central and Eastern Europe will have a compound annual growth rate (CAGR) of 5.1% through 2012, compared with the expected 2.3% CAGR for the much larger Western European market.

Often government policies strongly influence education and academic publishing, and can have a major impact on the publishing strategies and operations that exist in different countries. Sales of educational materials and academic books are often very dependent on national or local government expenditures. Currently, many governments in Eastern Europe are investing heavily in educational materials, thus motivating some of the expected growth in this market.

Developing electronic educational materials is another key trend gaining traction. Several companies, such as Pearson, are planning to gradually develop more textbook-free materials for schools. Lower production costs, which can be half what it costs to produce a book-based programme, are driving this trend. Sanoma Group has also developed digital educational (e-learning) materials, in addition to publishing traditional educational materials.

While educational material publishing is a niche market in Europe, magazine and newspaper publishing is a large-scale industry. Yet the trend of Western European companies moving into Eastern Europe can be seen in this market as well.

Magazine publishing in Europe

With a market size of around €40 billion in 2007, the magazine industry in Europe is experiencing several key trends. Despite the fact that the number of new titles is growing faster than overall circulation, and the cost of attracting and keeping subscribers has risen, the big publishing houses are still buying or launching more new titles both in their home markets and in Eastern Europe. Additionally, the market is thematically also becoming more fragmented. There has been a strong trend towards specialized offers, especially in women's, leisure and hobby magazines. Also, there is increasing pressure from online alternatives both for magazine content and advertising dollars.

Although advertising revenues are increasingly being affected by revenue shifting to online alternatives, not all European regional markets have experienced slowed growth. According to ZenithOptimedia 2007 estimates, in both the Netherlands and Belgium magazines experienced a declining market share of advertising revenue. However, expenditures on print media advertising in Russia increased by 24%.

The Internet has also had a mixed effect on the magazine industry. In France, America and Italy, men have quickly switched from magazines to online services. For example, automotive Internet sites are more popular with men than print editions. However, there is a trend for Internet sites to act as complements to, rather than substitutes of, the hard copies of magazines. The majority of consumers still prefer to read hard copies of magazines, although 60% expressed interest in accessing content via the Internet in addition to having the physical magazine. This is due, in part, to the inability of online sites to match the pleasing characteristics of magazines: their portability and glossiness, which appeal to many. That notwithstanding, there is a consensus within the industry that an online presence is critical for a magazine company.

While it is clear that a Web presence is good at attracting and retaining subscribers, how to make money from the Internet is not clear to the majority of magazine companies. In general, companies are earning a fraction of what they earn from print subscriptions and advertising. Additionally, consumers often expect to pay much less for digital content than for printed materials.

Currently, Sanoma Group, one of Europe's largest media companies, is continuing its expansion in Eastern Europe in both educational publishing and magazine publishing, in addition to investing more heavily in its online presence.

Sanoma Group

Today, Sanoma consists of five divisions: Sanoma Magazines, which publishes over 300 magazines internationally; Sanoma News, which focuses on newspaper publishing and printing in Finland; Sanoma Learning & Literature, which is responsible for educational and book publishing; Sanoma Entertainment, with its electronic media focus; and Sanoma Trade, which oversees press distribution, kiosks, bookstores and movie theatres. Across the five divisions it has pan-European activities in Finland, the Netherlands, Belgium and in the Central Eastern European markets of the Czech Republic, Slovakia, Poland, Hungary, Romania, Bulgaria, Estonia, Latvia, Lithuania, Russia, Ukraine and the Adriatic Region.

With its focus on Finland and small- and medium-size European markets, Sanoma Group has been able to occupy a top-five position in consumer magazine publishing in addition to being the sixth-largest educational publisher in Europe. At the moment, it holds market leadership positions in Finland, the Netherlands, Belgium, Hungary, the Czech Republic, Slovakia, Bulgaria and Russia.

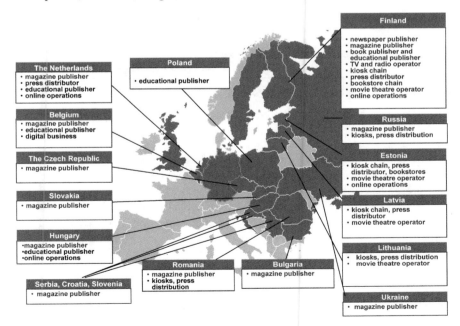

Figure 2 Sanoma's expansion East

Source: Sanoma presentation to INSEAD, June 2006, 2007 Annual Report, 2007. Reproduced by permission

Sanoma Group's current strategy focuses on expanding internationally in magazine publishing, educational publishing, press distribution, kiosks and digital media. In line with this strategy, magazine publishing operations exist in 13 countries in Europe and in 2007 accounted for 41% of Sanoma Group's net sales, educational publishing operations existed in five countries and occupied 7% of net sales and press distribution and kiosks accounted for approximately 28% of sales and operated in seven countries. Digital operations, which were grouped with publishing activities, in 2007 accounted for 10% of net sales. Sanoma Group has begun to focus more extensively on building up its online operations. Through Startpagina.nl in the Netherlands and Startlap.hu in Hungary, Sanoma Group now occupies leading market positions in each of these countries.

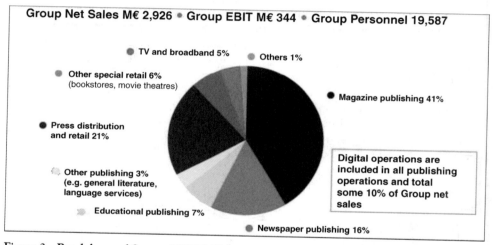

Figure 3   Breakdown of SanomaWSOY Net Sales (EUR)

Source: Sanoma Group, Roadshow Presentation, Investment Highlights, May 2008. Reproduced by permission

To build up its digital and online offerings in Finland, Sanoma Group formed Sanoma Digital, at the beginning of 2007, and has recently entered into an agreement with Google for keyword advertising in addition to working with Microsoft on a search advertising solution for the *Helsingin Sanomat* publication. Sanoma Group has also further developed its Internet presence in Eastern Europe. In 2008 it acquired 68% of the shares in Net Info. BG AD, Bulgaria's leading Internet company.

Financial performance

Sanoma Group has a long history of strong financial performance, and 2007 was no exception. In 2007 Sanoma Group's operating profit increased by 17.5%, totalling €343.8 million, compared with €292.5 million in 2006 and €301.3 million in 2005. Additionally, its net sales increased by 6.7%, totalling €2 926.3 million compared with €2 742.1 million in 2006, and €2 622.3 million in 2005. Forty-nine per cent of net sales came from Finland, 46% from other EU countries and 5% from non-EU countries, 21% came from Central and Eastern European countries, Russia and the Ukraine (partly included both in other EU countries as well as in non EU countries). Additionally, all divisions increased their net sales, with the greatest growth coming from operations in Russia, Belgium and Hungary, as well as online sales in the Netherlands. By 2008, 22% of net sales will come from countries such as Russia and Ukraine.

Geographic net sales breakdown 2007*

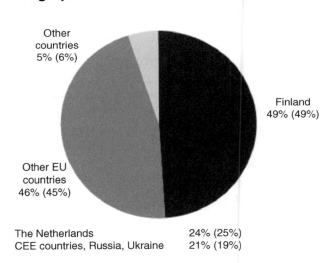

Other countries 5% (6%)

Finland 49% (49%)

Other EU countries 46% (45%)

The Netherlands 24% (25%)
CEE countries, Russia, Ukraine 21% (19%)

Figure 4 Breakdown of SanomaWSOY net sales by geography

*( )=2006

Source: Sanoma Group, Roadshow Presentation, Investment Highlights, May 2008. Reproduced by permission

Diversification in terms of business operations and geography helped lessen the impact of the weakening Western European advertising market on Sanoma Group. While many Western European magazine and newspaper companies were affected by a slowdown in advertising revenue, advertising sales remained stable for Sanoma Group. Advertising sales accounted for 24% of the group's total net sales, with online sales showing strong growth over 2007. They accounted for 11% of the group's total advertising sales.

To keep up its strong performance in 2008, Sanoma Group will need to execute its strategy well to expand its educational publishing into Central and Eastern Europe, and online, in order to sustain its financial success.

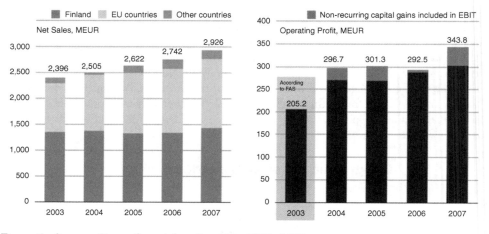

Figure 5   Sanoma Group financial performance 2003–2007

Note: The number of EU countries has increased. Figures for 2003 according to FAS. Since 2004 according to IFRS. Net sales of 2003 not comparable with earlier years due to change in accounting practices.
Source: Sanoma Group, Roadshow Presentation, Investment Highlights, May 2008. Reproduced by permission

Strategic Challenges

Although to date the Internet has had the strongest influence on the media industry in the Anglo-Saxon world, and print media is still growing in Eastern Europe, Russia and parts of the Far East, this is expected to change rapidly in the coming years. In continuing with its international expansion plans, Sanoma Group will need to understand the stages and directions of technological development within the different markets in which it operates.

Digital world

Currently, Sanoma Group online operations in the Netherlands and Hungary are very successful. In these countries it operates search portals Startpagina.nl and Startlap.hu. In addition to search portals, Sanoma Group also has news and entertainment portals (nu.nl), classified ad sites (huuto.net), virtual communities (Nlcafe.hu) and e-commerce sites (suomalainen.com). Other digital offers include digital content and broadband solutions available through Welho broadband, and digital TV, IPTV and VoD solutions offered through Sanoma Entertainment.

In expanding its digital presence it's not clear how best Sanoma can use its current assets. Its portal offering is extensive, and its operations for the Netherlands and Hungary have been successful. But will mirroring these portal services into new regions be fruitful?

Besides this, the portfolio does not seem to be very coherent: on the one hand Sanoma Group has a selection of portal sites and on the other hand it has investments in telecoms and digital television infrastructure. It is not entirely clear how both of these offerings can be combined or leveraged to strengthen Sanoma's digital offering.

Furthermore, Sanoma Group is building up its electronic-based educational tools. In Finland, Sanoma Group provides the Internet-based electronic learning environment Opit for schools. In Poland, Young Digital Planet is a world-leading educational software publisher and e-learning technology and content developer. Given the success of these offerings, launching these services in new markets such as Eastern Europe seems attractive.

Yet how quickly will Internet technologies be adopted in these emerging markets?

International Expansion

It is clear to Sanoma Group that expanding into Central and Eastern Europe is lucrative. Having said that, what approach it should take is less obvious. In the past it has focused mainly on small countries with small audiences for local language media (with the exception of Russia); however, these markets are getting saturated, as many other magazine players have entered too. Should they continue to focus on small, emerging markets and move even further east?

It is also not clear what operations Sanoma Group should roll out in these emerging markets. Should it focus solely on online and digital expansion projects in Central and Eastern Europe or invest broadly in magazine publishing, educational materials, online portals and print distribution outlets? Given that Central and Eastern European countries are investing heavily in education, e-learning, and Internet-based services, focusing on online and digital learning tools may be an ideal strategy. However, magazine publishing currently accounts for most of Sanoma Group international revenue. Additionally, its print distribution and kiosk operations are very strong, with around a 70% to 90% market share in Baltic countries, 35% in Romania and very strong growth expected in Russia.

* * *

Although Sanoma Group's strategy has yielded very good results so far, the company is faced with several dilemmas. Through its strategy of entering smaller markets, it was protected from the fierce competition taking place in markets like Germany. On the one hand, most markets have quite different characteristics with regard to media consumption and online penetration. This requires a strong focus on local management, which on the other hand makes it more difficult to coherently develop new business fields, such as digital media. Can it keep on growing in many different markets and at the same time create enough critical mass to transition to digital media? Where should it put its emphasis?

THE FUTURE ROLE OF ONLINE MEDIA

8

The previous chapters have made clear that the media industry is being transformed by digitization, affecting both market competition and the way traditional media are to be managed. This chapter takes a more in-depth look at online media and the impact they have on the industry, and addresses the following questions:

1. *What can be learned from the first wave of online digitization, and what are the implications of the new '2.0' digitization wave for media companies?*
2. *Which online media models are currently functioning well or could function well?*
3. *What should traditional media companies do to become part of the online world?*

Online Start 1995–2001: 'Overestimate in the Short Term'

Digitization as technology has been around for several decades, but was first, and above all, adopted for B2B (business-to-business) transactions. Even in 2008, 90% of all digitized transactions were B2B, and only 10% B2C (business-to-consumer). The Web was expected to revolutionize the possible use of digital technologies for both B2B and B2C. It was expected that the Web would enable an effective and openly inter-connected set of IT platforms between individuals and companies, leading to new models of distribution, exchanges, infomediation, etc. A lot of this did not happen as planned.

On the B2B side, IT and software platforms for distribution, supply chain, customer relationship had already been adopted quite extensively by many industries in the early Nineties, and led to, among other things, a major boost of B2B electronic data exchange (EDI) between firms. This was not very relevant for media companies, as most had a limited volume of intermediary goods, in contrast to, for example, manufacturing companies.

The development of the Internet was supposed to render B2B transactions even more efficient. Marketplaces arose such as Covisint or Commerce One and many others. In retrospect, most of those platforms failed for two reasons. First, the EDI exchanges of the recent past were effectively functioning models; moving to the Web for the extra gain of efficiency and with the risk of poor functioning was a no-go for many companies, and so most of those Internet marketplaces were limited to non-strategic elements like basic current goods. Second, those marketplaces got to trade only the small volumes ('the long tail') as large companies preferred to use their own Web interface for most purchasing, even that of current goods. Covisint, while created by automotive industry giants, remained in competition with its own founders, as GM and Ford continued to do online purchase via their own sites.

On the B2C side, the story was not much better. Various new Web-based business models were developed, such as transaction commerce (e-commerce) and advertising-based content services. Transaction commerce has worked somewhat, but for only a few categories of products, such as travel, high-tech products and some media commerce (like books and CDs).

For the media ecosystem, the Web was also generating great hopes. On one hand, *distribution and access platforms* such as cable operators were all foreseeing a major growth in consumer Internet connections augmented by the digitization of telephony and television services. Cable and telecoms quickly decided to compete for this new market by offering 'triple play' services (Internet, TV and telephony via the IP protocol). On the other hand, media *services* companies saw that those connections were offering the possibility of a new major interactive platform to engage consumers.[1] The figures were compelling: Internet usage grew in less than eight years to 600 million access users in 2002. Media services companies reasoned that this new reach could be monetized like any traditional media platform. They could place targeted ad banners online, offering the holy grail of a combined high-reach and selective media. Further, once digitally created, content could be sought for, replicated and distributed at hardly any additional cost: the prospect of new consumption windows was really appealing.

Here as well, the reality caught hard on the promises. Internet connection adoption was fast, but the cost of the necessary network upgrade was heavy and the transition to triple play was not as rapid as expected. Most cable companies in Europe, which fully rolled out upgrades of their network, fell into a cash trap and were obliged to enter bankruptcy. In the worst time, their accumulated debt traded at less than US20 cents per USD. For media services and content companies also, the picture was far from rosy. Digital piracy increased significantly, while advertising online did not really take off as fast as expected. Further, the early Web was mostly creating 'hyper-competition', leading to high competitive pressure and limited returns for media companies.

This was caused by the fact that at that point market entry into the Internet did cost about one-tenth of what is required to enter the offline media market. In addition, the major upfront investments to establish a brand, attract customers and achieve critical mass were funded by the billions of dollars of venture capital available on the market at that time (e.g. in 2000 US$92.9bn was invested by venture capitalists in the United States; in

---

[1]Media services companies are defined as media companies that deliver media content and services to find and evaluate the content, such as search, for the consumer.

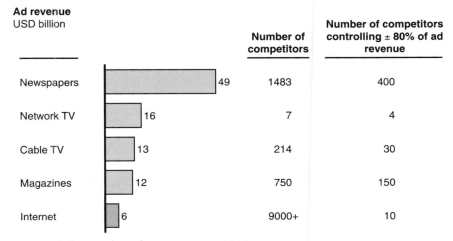

Ad revenue USD billion		Number of competitors	Number of competitors controlling ± 80% of ad revenue
Newspapers	49	1483	400
Network TV	16	7	4
Cable TV	13	214	30
Magazines	12	750	150
Internet	6	9000+	10

Figure 8.1 Online media industry structure 2001

Source: McKinsey analyses based on eMarketer; McCann-Erickson; NaH Cable TV Associate; Editor and Publisher; ABC Trends

2002 this amount had plummeted to US$6.9bn). This resulted in an avalanche of media service start-ups entering the market, ultimately creating an unsustainable economic structure, while at the same time advertising revenues gravitated more and more to a few large players (Figure 8.1). A situation of excess supply developed – a typical feature of the birth phase of a new industry.

In addition the optimistic advertising revenue forecasts in 2000, which formed the bulk of revenue potential for many Internet business models, did not materialize. In many cases, the actual revenues started to be far off the projected growth rates, essentially for two main reasons. First, banner advertising was not receiving the expected attention as click-through rates (i.e. the proportion of site visitors who click on an ad to reach an advertiser's website) fell to less than 1% in 2003. Second, there continued to be a clear time lag between changes in media usage by consumers and media mix changes by advertisers, driven by the conservative attitude of the advertising industry and their preference for established, high-reach, offline media platforms such as TV and print. Advertiser preferences remained in favour of traditional media, and this was also reflected in the spending behaviour of major corporations, with only 2% of the total Internet-marketing budget spent by the Fortune 500 companies by 2003 (Figure 8.2).

With advertising accounting for around 80% of the revenues of a content site, the slow uptake of Internet advertising made most digital media businesses struggle. The market suffered some key drawbacks, like the exit of Disney's portal Go.com. If about 20% of the surviving transaction-based B2C retail business models, such as Amazon, did turn profitable, only 5% of the portal players, such as Yahoo!, and a mere 3% of content players, such as CNet in the United States, eventually turned cash-flow positive.

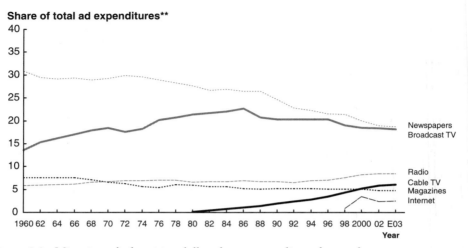

Share of total ad expenditures**

Figure 8.2 **Migration of advertising dollars from one media to the next***

* 'Migration' refers to the transfer of the proportion of total ad spend from traditional forms of media such as newspapers to cable TV and, more recently, the Internet
** Total ad expenditures include the following categories not graphed here: direct mail (19.7% of total ad expenditures in 2003), yellow pages (5.9%), outdoor (2.2%), other (13.7%)
Source: McKinsey analysis based on data from Salomon Smith Barney (2003)

Period of Consolidation 2002 to 2008: Building the Digital Platform

After the promises and the burst, the various industry segments for online services consolidated, some disappeared altogether (e.g. hosting services and many e-commerce offerings, etc.) and e-commerce as well as digital media models were revised. In this new era, Internet migrated to broadband lines. B2C companies such as Amazon and eBay started to make a big business out of selling niche products which were not available in normal stores. Others focused on building and monetizing search, comparison and social recommendation sites. Google made its famous appearance, and the 'social web' (so-called Web 2.0) allowed the rise of new darlings such as YouTube and many others.

Mass-market broadband

Until the bubble burst, in the early 2000s, the Web was primarily seen as a medium for searching for information and for simple exchanges. The development of broadband access technologies, primary cable, DSL (and later fibre to the home) for the residential home offered a new compelling value for consumers, who were willing to pay a significant price premium for always-on and speed. With broadband, new products like downloads, streaming, telephony over IP and IP-TV emerged and, with them, the opportunity for

Internet Service Providers (ISPs) to expand their offering from a pure Internet access provider to a 'multiservice' ISP.

An early example was Yahoo! broadband in Japan, which was one of the first to supply an IP telephony line at major discount via its access connection. By using the IP infrastructure, IP telephony providers could avoid the 'origination fees' telephone operators had to pay when using the traditional copper lines. As Yahoo! passed these cost savings on to its users, Yahoo! could convince 45% of its broadband subscribers to take a secondary telephony line, in barely 18 months.

In Europe, France led the way. Very early on, France offered favourable fees for local loop unbundling, that is the access fee companies pay to the telecoms operator to use their local lines which can connect a core network ('backbone') to individual homes. As a result, aggressive and innovative players like Free built their own backbone and launched a service that could offer television and telephony on top of Internet, at virtually no extra cost. Following this strategy, Free managed to attract close to 20% of the broadband access market in France in less than two years.

Multiservice ISP offerings are usually very disruptive for the telephony industry as telephony is used to cross-subsidize broadband access. For instance, in mid-year 2004 Free offered access to telephony and free local calls, as well as 2 MB/second Internet access, for less than €30 a month under local loop unbundling. The same Internet access product is offered for exactly the same price by Wanadoo, the ISP from France Telecom in France, yet without counting the telephony line.

Cable companies, which did build their own digital infrastructure all the way to the home, used triple play offerings to secure product penetration on their networks, while securing a greater loyalty from their customers. The strategy has been paying off: the churn of customers who have triple and double play offerings is one-third and two-thirds of the churn of a single product customer respectively, while more than half of cable customers are multiplay (Figure 8.3). By 2007, cable companies in Europe enjoyed better EBITDA margins than telecoms companies.

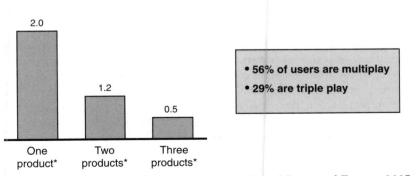

Figure 8.3 Monthly cable churn: 10 cable companies, United States and Europe, 2007

* Average of broadband, telephony and digital television
Source: McKinsey analyses

In 2008, the typical broadband penetration in Western Europe was about 30% of the population, or about 60% of *households* (assuming one paid connection per household). Put another way, this means that broadband has become a true mass-market platform, which will drive new behaviours and services in the near future. Perhaps the best way to anticipate what the future may hold is to look at a pioneering digital market like South Korea. By 2008, South Korea has achieved a household broadband penetration level of about 94%. Average downstream bandwidth speed was about 50 MB/second, compared to about 6–8 MB/second in Western Europe. Furthermore, 95% of South Korean mobile handsets offer Internet capabilities, with 3G-HSDPA technology, providing bandwidth higher than that of a typical DSL line in rural areas in the United States.

Three elements are worth noticing from such a pervasive 'broader-band' environment. First, 'broader-band' drives usage intensity. Almost 50% of South Koreans use the wireless Internet on a daily basis, while daily time spent online is 50% greater per user in Korea than in Europe, or more than one hour a day, which is much more than time spent on print media, or on the lead generalist television broadcaster. Second, the market has experienced a massive explosion in video-on-demand usage: South Koreans have been able to get their favourite television shows on the Internet for five years. Third, peer-to-peer usage has also expanded dramatically. In fact, by 2008, 45% of Koreans were using Cyworld, an online social network, via both their mobile handsets and online. This penetration rate is much higher than the penetration of other, more famous social networks, such as Facebook and Bebo in the United States and Western Europe. The main reasons for this are that bandwidth availability has led communities on Cyworld to start developing 3D environments, while social sharing has become much more personalized, to the point that by 2008 45% of South Koreans had their own online avatars (a user's digital depiction) as a form of online identity.

From access to services

In the early days of the Internet, at least in Europe, the most dominant, as well as profitable, players in the Internet market were the companies holding the key to Internet access services. Also in the broadband world, access is priced at a good margin, a margin that, in absolute terms, is significantly higher than what any Web ad revenue-generating model can hope to receive per user. Yet, even if advertising income was small, incumbent telecoms companies, which often owned the leading national ISP, combined their access with a portal gateway to the Web early on. As the leading websites receive a disproportionate share of ad revenue, their strategy was to become the leading portal. These telecoms ISPs were not only the first in the market, which helped their portals to achieve high reach, but also were typically in a strong position to leverage their portal as a preset starting point for the new user. On average, 75% of online users did not change their pre-settings, which were, in 50% of the cases, the ISP's Web page.

This dominance evaporated over the years, because people started to change their behaviour from browsing to searching, and would rather go to much more engaging destination sites for entertainment activities (like games and online video), for socialization (like social networks) and for many other activities on the Web, like e-commerce and exchanges. Second, the broadband reach had created enough of a mass-market platform to see advertising finally adapting to the new world, which led advertisers to target their investments at compelling destination sites and to limit their spend on portal gateways.

This phenomenon is not new: it took between five and seven years for radio to displace print advertising, and US cable TV only got to receive a significant share of the television network ad money when it had attained mass-market reach. Interestingly, the tipping point where ad money started to move disproportionately to cable networks was 1995, when cable had a penetration of 60% of US homes (see Figure 6.7).

This tipping point of 60% broadband penetration of all households has been achieved in many countries in Western Europe and online ad spending shifted from a few per cent of total ad spend to be more than 10% of total spend in many countries by 2007. For companies already using the Web for advertising, online is already 10–15% of their ad spend, and this percentage could double by 2010, making the online advertising category the largest category above any offline medium, like broadcast TV or news-papers and magazines (see Figure 6.10). This is a significant change from 2002, when the top companies' online ad spend was often no more than 3% of their total advertising budgets.

A large part of this online ad money has not come from conventional display formats. One of the first surprises of Internet usage was the extent to which search was such an extremely powerful way of attracting advertising online. Search engines, epitomized by Google, have demonstrated that they are a 'killer' application used by almost all Internet users (Figure 8.4).

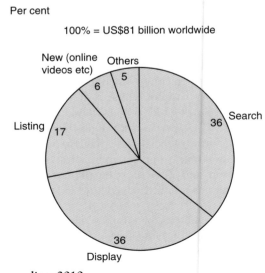

Per cent

100% = US$81 billion worldwide

Figure 8.4 **Ad dollars online, 2010**

Source: McKinsey analyses

The future of search is positive for many reasons. Search frequency increases with broadband. Together with the growth in Internet penetration, this will make search an even more powerful direct-marketing engine. Also, with broadband most search categories will become more effective and more fun to search for – this includes dating services (picture downloads and instant messaging), travel (video streaming of best hotels, etc.) and shopping experiences (music download). The more attractive offerings will increase the volume of the search market and boost the profitability of the leading search engines as many more advertisers get interested in bidding for ad keywords.

The Web as a social platform: Web 2.0

The Web continued to evolve and was significantly boosted by the emergence of a set of new technologies, called Web 2.0. In the past, Web users faced significant barriers to interaction: they had to build their own Web page, host it at great cost and get other people to do the same, in order to have a possible meaningful 'conversation' and 'community exchange'. The essence of Web 2.0 technologies is that they solved these bottlenecks.

The Web 2.0 technologies have made it very simple for people to post, share and forward any form of digital content. Not surprisingly, they have been accompanied by the rise of a new breed of online property, which taps into the social and participatory nature of the Web. Social networks, from Orkut and LinkedIn to MySpace or Facebook, are now attracting millions of visitors online; YouTube was launched by late 2005 as the first user-generated video content site, not only facilitating the posting of short videos but making it easy for people to forward videos virally, even outside the YouTube universe. This resulted in YouTube becoming one of the most recognized brands on the Web to date in less than three years.

The power of social media is visible through many elements. The growth of engagement (as measured by pages viewed) on the top 100 brands on the Web has been about 40% a year; Web 2.0 companies have grown at close to 200% a year, or five time faster. In 2005, social Web 2.0 sites accounted for less than 3% of time spent on the top 100 brand properties; 18 months later, this percentage stood at 31% (Figure 8.5).

It is estimated that the size of content which is digitized and stored on the Web is growing at more than 55% a year, of which 70% is consumer related, and half is linked to activities close to social Web 2.0 properties, such as posting videos, writing comments on Wikipedia or designing the features of social games like *The Sims Online*. Further, the effect of the social Web is not only visible on pure content sites: it drives social recommendations for extra sales on Amazon, new social shopping sites are launched and companies are leveraging users to design their own online advertising campaigns, such as Doritos for its Super Bowl advertisement.

By 2008, the advertising revenue attached to these social networks and other Web 2.0 sites still lagged behind the volume of traffic these new sites attracted. One of the reasons was the very large number of posts with few visitors; another reason was the context of those sites (people on Facebook are not interested in seeing ads), or the profile of users (teens on MySpace), but things can change quickly on the Web too, as the past has

Per cent

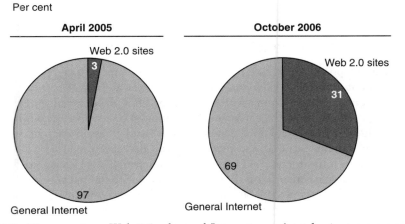

Figure 8.5 Time spent on Web 2.0, share of Internet users' total minutes consumed, top 100 sites

* Web 2.0 does not include e-mail time
Source: McKinsey analyses based on data from Piper

demonstrated. Sites such as LinkedIn, a Web 2.0 directed at professionals, started to make some members pay for some special services. Facebook and MySpace are starting to monetize their various brand communities, such as Apple or Victoria Secret, etc., through sponsorship and merchandising models.

Other Web innovations will continue to flow. Social sites are already moving to immersive 3D (three-dimensional) virtual worlds. Second Life, the largest of these 3D virtual worlds, in 2008 exhibited the same kind of growth as other social-based destination sites (Second Life users logged 3.3 million user-hours in May 2006; less than one year later, that number had increased to more than 20 million hours). Second Life users also tend to immerse themselves deeply in these worlds: an average resident of Second Life spends 15 to 20 hours a week flying through the virtual landscape, meeting friends and 'partying', or even developing his or her own business online.

Many sceptics believe online metaverses like Second Life are likely to remain a niche phenomenon except where they are connected to popular videogames; a Second Life platform may, indeed, appear complex for newcomers and empty at first sight. Balancing this scepticism is the recognition that social virtual worlds address certain fundamental human needs, and that technologies are evolving very rapidly to support complex virtual realities. Virtual worlds provide life-like experiences to users that go beyond the physical constraints of real life. In principle, this opens a wide array of applications in the areas not only of entertainment but also of education (simulation, learning, testing) and commerce. Several 3D virtual worlds allow their users to create objects and build their own environments. This ability appeals to the human need for control, self-expression and creativity, but also opens the way for new models of the co-creation of products and services.

Online Media Business Models

'Rebalanced' broadband media value chain

The above developments demonstrate that the broadband media value chain is rebalancing with content and service providers capturing a larger and larger part of the value.

Outside of commerce, we estimate that in Europe 95% of the revenue of the Web is based on access; this is simply the consequence of a limited B2C market for online services, a nascent online ad market and price points for broadband access in the range of €25 per month per connection. By 2010, this proportion will have been reduced to 74%. Much more, in value, the infrastructure and network provision will likely be less than 50% of the total online media value chain. This shift is, first of all, due to limited bottom-line growth on the access side. The demand for broadband lines will mature and emerging competition on the multiplay has been aggressive, recently leading to close to flat broadband rates. Also, the extent of capital expenditure needed to sustain the infrastructure will likely not decrease, due to the growth of bit usage by the consumers, which is doubling every 18 months (Figure 8.6).

However, media services are developing quite quickly, and several will develop enough scale to be profitable. Lead media service aggregators, like online classified sites, portals, etc., are generating margins of 30–40%, close to double the margin rate of offline; content producers and syndicators can generate margins as strong as in offline, and in the case of content deployed for multiplatform (say TV and the Web), the margins can be significantly stronger. Further, new services, like online ad networks, can boost their margin and create a significant opportunity online.

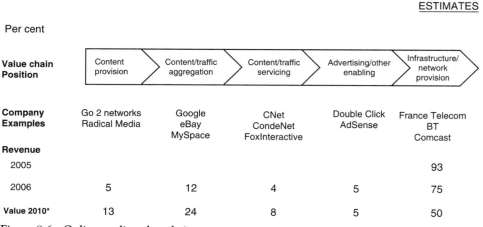

	Content provision	Content/traffic aggregation	Content/traffic servicing	Advertising/other enabling	Infrastructure/ network provision
Value chain Position					
Company Examples	Go 2 networks Radical Media	Google eBay MySpace	CNet CondeNet FoxInteractive	Double Click AdSense	France Telecom BT Comcast
Revenue					
2005					93
2006	5	12	4	5	75
Value 2010*	13	24	8	5	50

Figure 8.6 Online media value chain

* Based on margin development, top-line growth and capital spending to sustain business
Source: McKinsey analysis

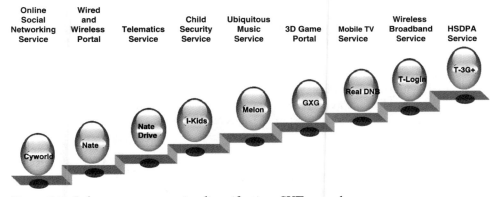

Figure 8.7   Infrastructure to service diversification: SKT example

Source: McKinsey analysis

In general, the play in the value chain will continue to evolve, and we have seen a very large number of movements in the value chain by players vying to consolidate their online position. Infrastructure providers have been trying to move into services as a way of compensating for growth pressure, but also as a way to prevent a 'free ride' of other service providers on their infrastructure. This strategy, put in place early on by some ISPs, has not been very successful so far, except in a few cases: Telenet, for instance, has been diversifying actively in games and online video, and Korean Telecom, a telecoms player, was a fast innovator of services like social networks (Cyworld), music (Melon) and games (GxG) (Figure 8.7).

Large traffic aggregators have actively diversified to online ad networks. This includes Google and its AdSense offering plus the recent acquisition of Double Click for online ad serving, Yahoo! and Overture, etc.

Online business opportunities

As discussed earlier, incumbent media companies have to develop their own strategy and positioning with regard to online, not least because a large part of the online value chain development comes in part as a substitution to offline advertising and media usage.

In the first place, companies should frame their strategy right: defending offline revenue is likely to delay the problem of maturity but will not provide a great platform for growth. Meanwhile, aggressively building online requires a clear understanding of the opportunities, together with the necessary (but not sufficient) advantage of being the first to market. Those companies that were first into the market were able to gain and maintain market share. For example, Ilsemedia's site "Startpagina" was launched in the late Nineties and offered a simple interface in the local language and ten years later was still the leading content site in the Dutch market. Similarly, those search portals which were able to resist Google were those that had been the first into their local markets, such as Naver in South Korea or Yandex in Russia, but competing against Google on paid search is likely to be difficult in Western Europe, where the Google share of search is averaging 80% and systematically ranks as a top five property for visitors online in each market.

All in all, entering the online world might remain a challenge for traditional media companies, especially for those who withdrew after the bubble burst in the early 2000s. A checklist to frame the online opportunity is offered below.

Checklist #1: Do not exclude growth. It is still generally good to be part of the media business. Even though new technologies and approaches will continue to crowd into the marketplace, traditional media will still be the major access to media in the next few years. Media companies such as News Corporation have been able to grow at more than 10% during the first years of the new century, by surfing tailwind markets like pay TV or by diversifying through acquisitions like MySpace and others.

Checklist #2: Complement with online. Against this global evolution, the combined online advertising market (including formats such as search, display and classified) of the US and European markets will keep growing fast even during the expected recession years in 2009/2010. Various surveys of advertisers demonstrate that about half of this $40 billion growth will come as substitution to traditional media, making advertising growth relatively challenged for incumbent media companies relying on advertising for their bottom line.[2] But the flipside is the most reassuring: the other half is new money, and the margins online can be drastically better too. Companies, such as Schibsted in the print media, have demonstrated that it can be done. Schibsted generates more than its fair share of revenue from online (23% of revenue for 10% online spend in its core markets in 2007) and delivers a 40% margin online.

Checklist #3: Consider media as global. Another changing industry dynamic involves the fast globalization of media. Global Internet brands attract users in proportion with Internet usage distribution. If about 20% of Internet users originate from the United States, 72% of Yahoo! users, 78% of Googlers and 77% of Wikipedians come from outside US Internet protocol addresses (Figure 8.8). Since mid-2008, more than 50% of Google revenue comes from outside of the United States. In contrast, traditional global media companies have diversified globally but with less speed and success. Media companies such as Axel Springer bought auFeminin.com, a woman-based portal of to develop a pan-European footprint. It also uses key working communities like cooking in one country to consolidate in other markets (while auFeminin had bought Marmiton in France, Axel Springer bought Chefkoch in Germany as a quick 'cut and paste' strategy).

---

[2]Bughin, J., Erbenich, C. and Shenkan, A., 'How companies are marketing online: a McKinsey survey', *McKinsey Quarterly Online*, 2007.

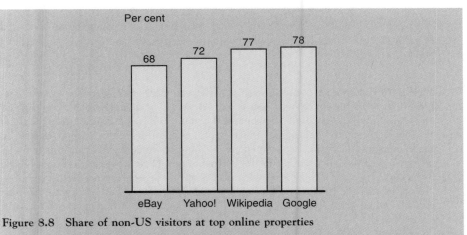

Figure 8.8   Share of non-US visitors at top online properties

Source: McKinsey analyses based on data from comScore; Morgan Stanley

Checklist #4: You can still act local. It has been shown time and again that global coexists with local, that is music brands like MTV could be coexisting with local music channels like Viva in Germany or MCM in France; *Cosmopolitan* could coexist with local young female magazines, etc. Increasing numbers of media participants are learning that paying attention to local needs may even rival the global powerhouses on the Web. Google's presence remains notably limited in Russia because, as of 2008, the company still had to create a major local index in the Russian language or to deploy significant resources in Russia to address local needs. Consider, as well, NHN's Naver in South Korea, which created a compelling search platform based on a people-created database rather than a computer-based algorithm. Naver had 77% of the search market in Korea in 2008, beating Yahoo! and Google by a wide margin. The driver of Naver's success lies in the creation of a local information knowledge database for the country that has over 490 million entries, captured solely on the basis of providing loyalty points to people who contribute local content and information in a question and answer service (Figure 8.9).

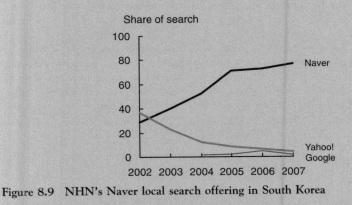

Figure 8.9   NHN's Naver local search offering in South Korea

Source: McKinsey analyses

Telenet,[3] the Flemish company, has also used the local flavour of communities and social proximity to design its online services: it now has the lead as the local YouTube (GarageTV) and as the local games platform (9lives).

Checklist #5: Espouse content with a different 'persona'. Media relevance goes hand in hand with great content quality and diversity. The digital revolution is bringing YouTube and the long tail of user-generated content (UGC), but this is only the tip of the iceberg of creative changes. In fact, digital creation increasingly finds its base in niche communities formed around common interests. Some players ride this trend by re-inventing traditional media. In the United States, Next New Networks (or NNN) has set up 101 personalized 'micro-television' networks focused on cars, fashion, politics and other topics. In-house creatives produce 50% of the content, with the rest contributed by site viewers; in 2008 NNN was the most watched bouquet on YouTube channels.

In the same way, San Francisco-based 80/20 Publishing reverse-engineers the Web by developing UGC communities of interest online and by selecting the best as offline and highly successful, and pricey, crowd-sourced community magazines.

Checklist #6: Build for 360°. The development of digital media goes hand in hand with designing, creating and producing 360° media. Not surprisingly, new agencies are quickly showing their competencies in this domain (such as GoTVNetworks, which has been working closely with Procter & Gamble to develop *Crescent Heights*, a show about a recent college graduate moving to Los Angeles, and whose new life is distributed and commented online and over mobile phones).

Sanoma Group[4] is one company that is developing an aggressive strategy of 360° media. For instance, in Hungary, it has succeeded in relaunching its flagship gossip magazine *Story* magazine on the Web (StoryOnline), cable TV (*Story TV*) and at major events (*Story* award galas), and all of these media are based on the original print magazine's focus on celebrity gossip (Figure 8.10).

Checklist #7: Do not understate the online baby boomers. Last but not least, media should not only focus on early-mover segments. The online media industry has focused, quite rightly, on the younger demographic segment, because that age group has substituted traditional media consumption online. In Europe, for example, the Web already reached up to 8% of the population by 2008, which is mostly composed of younger demographics. By focusing on this uniquely, traditional media may overlook the vital but ageing 'baby boomer' audience. This may be a mistake. After all, other demographics, like the baby boomers, have the money to spend and can therefore be very attractive

---

[3]See case study in Chapter 4.
[4]See case study in Chapter 7.

Figure 8.10   360° media

Source: Sanoma Magazines. Reproduced by permission

targets for advertisers. As the Web matures, the baby boomers will engage online too. Older audiences can be very participative in social media. For example, the bulk of edits on Wikipedia are done by the cohort of Web users aged between 41 and 59. While representing less than one-third of American Internet users, US Internet users in the 50+ age demographic spent in 2008 over 40% of the total time on the Internet (Figure 8.11).

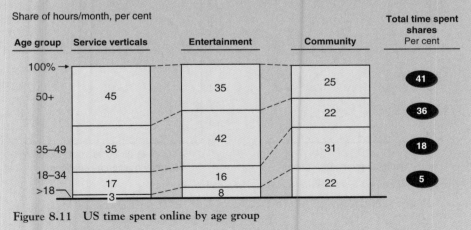

Figure 8.11   US time spent online by age group

Source: McKinsey analyses

Whatever the challenges for media companies, a few 'non-regret' moves must be tried out, even if their success will require improved capabilities derived from digital technology.

Online marketing

A first move for media compares to use the web is to use online to market *offline* entertainment. As for other industries, the Web offers tremendous opportunities. For example, RTL is heavily promoting its own films and features online, by combining TV films with online trailers, theme-related communities and fan-article shopping opportunities. Traditional channels seen on YouTube have encouraged audiences to come back to television channels, in some instances pushing up to 20% extra new younger audiences back to the old television.

Pushing social recommendations for media products has been rather successful. The probability of buying for someone receiving a recommendation on Amazon was boosted by 3% for books, but up to 10% for DVD purchases according to some research.[5] And some communities fare even better: for books, for instance, success rates of recommendations are close to 5% for medicine and professional, versus basic fiction books like romance or childrens books (less than 2%) (Figure 8.12).

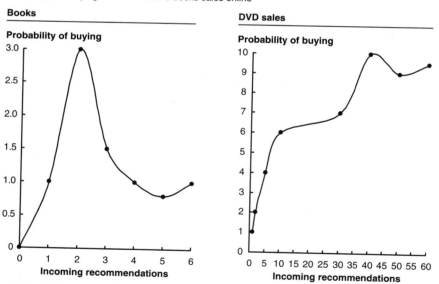

Figure 8.12   The power of online social recommendations

Source: McKinsey analysis based on data from Leskovec; Adamic and Huberman; Carnegie Mellon

---

[5]Leskovec, J., Adamic L. and Huberman, B., 'The dynamics of viral marketing', School of Computer Science, Carnegie Mellon University, PowerPoint presentation.

Despite being a non-brainer, leveraging online marketing is surprisingly not well used by media companies. Only a few companies are truly using the analytical tools (Buzzmetrics, Offermatica, Webtrends and others) to allocate their media spend.

Online co-creation

With Web 2.0, the Internet has proven to be a global platform for creation and UGC. Media companies could go the extra mile by engaging customers in the co-creation of services and products.

Co-creation has been recently recognized as a powerful innovation mechanism used by companies like Procter & Gamble and many others. In industrial co-creation activities, such as open-source software development, active participants tend to make up 20% to 30% of the community. 3D virtual world members appear to be more than willing actors in this new method of innovation: close to 60% of Second Life members, for example, have reported building their own virtual space. Within these 'creators', about 60% would be interested in co-creating with a brand they trust.

The idea of co-creation remains, however, limited in media, as most of the market is well structured in terms of talent management and market availability. There are, however, attempts to bypass this course especially if it concerns more products than pure talent creation. In order to boost its video sales, Netflix opened its video recommendation algorithm to users; Disney's Virtual Image Kingdom is extending the brand of its favoured theme parks to help co-create a compelling media universe for its audience and more than one million character images have been created in less than seven months.

Online distribution

Online distribution models for accessing or selling traditional content supported by broadband have the great potential to change the media industry's current business models and, eventually, its structure.

Using subscription-based or pay-per-download business models for physical goods, successful players will be in the powerful position of being able to bypass the entire physical supply chain. There is always the danger with virtual goods of piracy obviously – as seen in the case of music – but new distribution models (streaming) and new incentives (like extra pre releases and exclusive content online) can alleviate (part of this) risk. For instance, when launching a new music production, music tracks can be sold exclusively as premium online product for a few days in pre-sales in order to capture the willingness-to-pay of fans, while creating the marketing buzz of exclusivity. After this, the music can be sold offline exclusively as a second window to capture the full mass market and to maximize protection; then, in the third window, the music can combine both offline and online channels, while later in the cycle the music can be provided solely online (to minimize the costs of physical storage and distribution).

Video is the next distribution platform. YouTube, reinforced by its synergy with Google, its parent company, has quickly developed as a favourite platform, and some broadcasters have been trying to carve their own route with online video. In the United

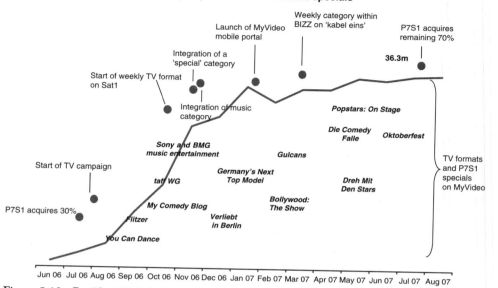

Monthly visit development (IVW) and selected content specials

Figure 8.13   Pro7Sat1SBS deployment of MyVideo

Source: McKinsey analyses based on data from Pro7Sat1

States, up to two-thirds of prime-time programming of the major US networks was already available online for the 2006/07 season. In 2008 the major TV stations launched their own destination Web site, called Hulu.com. Through affiliate marketing, 90% of US web traffic was marketed to Hulu.com by the end of 2008. In Germany, an online video site similar to YouTube, MyVideo, is owned by one of the leading broadcasters, the Pro7Sat1SBS Group (Figure 8.13). The group successfully cross-promoted shows and audience across television and Web platforms, and is now extending its Web properties to social networks.

Online communities for offline

Finally, community-based online models are emerging as profitable on the Internet. Early on, successful community models were paid-contents models such as most of the online dating services. Now those models are increasingly funded from advertising, again leveraging the key broadband community needs and the search advertising boom.

Traditional media have been slow in engaging in the community route. New models have, however, been created, showing the path to success.

Here again, the main risk is to get the right capabilities to scale the model. For instance new online community players work with much faster throughput of editing, work in a much more cooperative environment, and with much smaller teams to develop the media product than offline publishers.

Key Takeaways

1. The initial economic failure of Internet business models was mainly caused by a supply excess of new Internet businesses and a severe overestimation of the development of Internet advertising revenues.
2. The online value chain is now quickly growing even if still much in flux:
   - A number of attractive online media business models have emerged, moving from access to online ad-based platforms, such as search engines and online classified portals.
   - Now, with the reach of mass-market broadband, and the advent of the social Web, new service and content models can reach scale and be profitable.
3. In general, the rise of profitability in the service part of the value chain comes in part as a reallocation of ad mix online, putting most media companies in the situation where they must act urgently.
4. While many possibilities exist for traditional media companies, four of them are non-regret moves which should be pursued in any case (digital marketing, 360° distribution, co-creation and communities-powered media). In general, however, those moves require the mastering of new digital capabilities.

Second Life: Peer Production Through Co-creation[1]

Robin Harper, CMO of Linden Lab, the developer of the 3D virtual world Second Life, was reflecting on the press release which announced that its board of directors had named Mark Kingdon to serve as CEO, to work alongside Linden Lab founder, former CEO and current chairman Philip Rosedale.[2]

To her the press release demonstrated the team spirit of the new leadership: 'Our search for the leader of Linden Lab demanded both tremendous business skills and a deep understanding and passion for Second Life and where it is going. Mark is the perfect choice,' said Philip Rosedale.

'Joining Linden Lab with so much growth and opportunity on the horizon is incredibly exciting. I am looking forward to work with Philip. Until Second Life, we experienced the digital world passively in two dimensions. By enabling users to create a rich and immersive virtual world, Second Life is transforming the way we connect, collaborate, learn and transact online. I am thrilled to be part of this epic transformation,' said Mark Kingdon.

In her initial years at Linden Lab, Robin led the development of the Second Life brand. In the past few years, she shifted her focus to the interface between the Second Life Residents and Linden Lab. In 2008, Robin resumed the leadership of marketing but also continued to implement new programs in Second Life. Before joining Linden Labs, Robin had been a vice president of marketing at Maxis, where she, amongst others, established SimCity as one of the most recognized brand names in entertainment software.

Robin agreed fully with her new CEO on the nature of transformation happening in 3D virtual worlds. In the traditional gaming model consumers would only come in at the end of the supply chain, where the only thing he/she could do was to accept or reject to buy the engineered product or service. With the advent of Web 2.0 and of more powerful 3D virtual platforms such as Second Life, this model changed significantly.

- 1978: The first 1D (text-based) chat world, MUD (Multi-User Dungeon/Domain) is created by academics at Essex University, England.
- 1987: Habitat, the first 2D chat world, or 'graphical MUD', is launched. Habitat is the first successful attempt at a large-scale commercial 2D virtual community.
- 1994: Knowledge Adventure Worlds (renamed Worlds Inc. '95) launches the first fully navigable 3D virtual world on the Internet, and creates the world's first avatar-based chat.
- 1996: Meridian 59, the first 3D MORPG (multiplayer online role-playing game), by Archetype Interactive, is launched.
- 2003: Second Life debuts, the first 3D persistent virtual world that allows its users to retain property rights to the virtual objects they create in the online economy.

Figure 1 A history of 3D virtual spaces

Source: McKinsey analysis

---

[1] This case is developed solely as the basis for class discussion. Cases are not intended to serve as endorsements, sources of primary data or illustrations of effective or ineffective management.

[2] See: http://lindenlab.com/pressroom/releases/04_22_08.

There are today about one billion people online, many of them visiting social network sites and creating large communities that, among other things, get together to discuss and try out new brands. A unique virtual marketplace will develop, and with it a new model of distributed co-creation.

In fact, a large portion of key online business models rely on turning users into contributors – from eBay through consumer-to-consumer (C2C) auctions, Amazon.com (recommendations), Google (relevance of search links) to YouTube (video posting), Wikipedia (encyclopedia) or OhmyNews (citizen journalism[3]). Similarly, many companies are making full use of the Internet as a means of testing new ideas through forums and user participation. Lego launched Lego Digital Designer, enabling users to design their own Lego with the option to upload their design to the Lego Factory gallery for other users to view, download, edit and republish to the gallery. Since its launch, more than 77 000 models have been designed. Swarowski, a crystal jewellery designer, launched a Web-based toolkit for users to create crystal designs – and more than 20% of online visitors contributed to the new design.[4]

With Second Life, Linden Lab was convinced that they were pushing the limit even further. The 3D virtual worlds, such as Second Life, are very immersive, with people

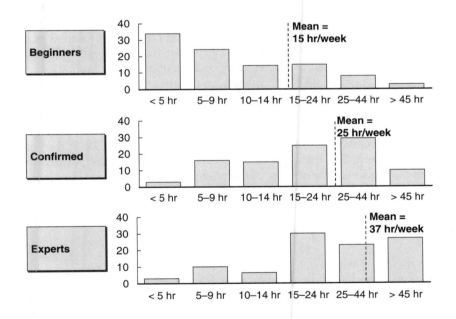

Figure 2   Time spent on Second Life

Source: McKinsey analyses based on data from Reperes market research, 2007

---

[3]See separate OhmyNews case study in Chapter 3.

[4]Fuller, J., Bartl, F., Ernst, H. and Mulbacher, H., Community based innovation: How to integrate members of virtual communities into new product development, *Electronic Commerce Research*, 6,

spending an average of 15 hours a week on the platform. This is a significant amount of time, much more than with leading websites such as Google or Yahoo!, or even YouTube.

Over time, Robin had gained experience on how to maximize profitability of the platform. *First*, from her early experience in multiple-player game platforms, she learned that virtual worlds can be easily outsourced – a game-based virtual world such as *The Sims Online* was built for 90% by a few of its community users, even though the benefits of the Sims' creations went fully to the game publisher, Maxis.[5]

Second, from other successful virtual worlds such as Habbo Hotel and Cyworld Club Penguin and There.com, she observed that members prefer to participate actively within smaller sub-communities. Often those communities could easily be built around brands or sponsors, like the Apple fans on Facebook, or the Coca-Cola drinkers on Habbo Hotel.

Third, Second Life's own experience had shown an unexpected revenue potential. The platform has the added feature that allows both individuals and businesses to participate, enabling everyone to create their own shop, build their own economy and even exchange and trade goods via their own currency (the Linden Dollars). Initially, the management of Second Life envisioned the platform as a consumer entertainment service, which would be subscription-based. The notion of an economy came later as Second Life saw that people started to sell their creations and the company began to realize the parallel between building Second Life through economic growth and the way that developing countries use their economies to drive their economic take-off. The Linden Lab revenue model got adapted and was based on business transactions rather than subscriptions. People and companies would rent virtual land where they could build their own business and attract audiences to visit. They could build virtual learning and education environments or co-create and design new goods and service for companies.

Today, the success is there, but the platform is complex to run and close to its limits in terms of accepting concurrent users. On the other side, for many renters of land, the number of people coming to their island is still relatively small, let alone those coming back after first visits. This questions the attractiveness of their rental place. Robin was convinced that technical constraints of the platform could be solved – her role was to generate more visits to renters and to sustain revenue growth.

Company History

Linden Research was originally located on Linden Street in San Francisco. The company is now doing business as Linden Lab and has nearly 300 employees worldwide. It has a multiple location office structure with the core campus in San Francisco and additional satellites in Mountain View (Seattle), Davis (California), Boston (Massachusetts) and Brighton (United Kingdom). Linden Lab is currently expanding its operations into Europe and Asia.

---

[5]As discussed in Chapter 3, contribution is skewed towards only a few participants, i.e. 5% of *The Sims* Online users were 'creators', benefiting both Electronic Arts and the rest of *The Sims'* community. Ironically, if this co-creation element helped build the game at the start, *The Sims Online* has been criticized for not harnessing it further.

Linden Lab was founded in 1999 by Philip Rosedale, the former CTO of RealNetworks, where he pioneered the development and deployment of streaming media technologies. Investors include Catamount Ventures, Benchmark Capital, Globespan Capital Partners, Omidyar Network and Bezos Expeditions.

Second Life was not conceived as a user-created metaverse. The blog rumours go that CEO Philip Rosedale wanted a simulation of the natural world; CTO Cory Ondrejka wanted a game development platform. They only realized what Second Life really stood for after they had created the underlying technology and started playing around in the world themselves. The development team refocused its efforts on creating a virtual environment instead, and the software project *LindenWorld* was born.

Second Life was released for beta testing in 2002 and went public in June 2003. At the same time Linden Lab introduced an updated version that included more realistic 3D landscapes, with an improved mapping and navigation system. Linden Lab also recognized at the State of Play Conference in November 2003 that in-world content made by residents was owned by its creator. This enabled residents to retain full intellectual property protection for the digital content they created. By 2004, a variety of new features was launched, enabling the residents to more fully develop and personalize their identities.

In December of 2005, Linden Lab celebrated 100 000 registered accounts. In October 2006, Second Life hit one million registered accounts and, by July 2007, eight million, climbing to 13 million by March 2008. At that time, as many as 65 000 concurrent users were on the platform. The user-to-user revenues from Second Life went up from $5 million in January 2007 to $8 million one year later.

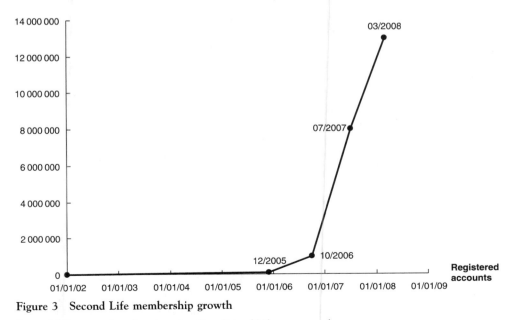

Figure 3   Second Life membership growth

Source: McKinsey analyses based on data from Second Life.org; press releases

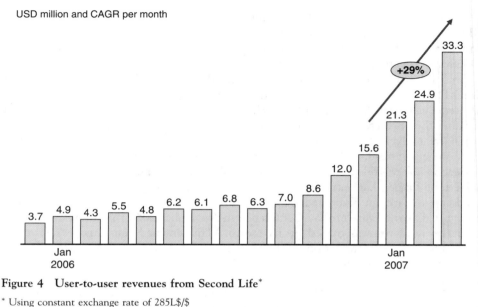

Figure 4 **User-to-user revenues from Second Life***

* Using constant exchange rate of 285L$/$
Source: McKinsey analyses based on data from Second Life.org

Today, a typical Second Life member is engaged in many activities, the three most frequent being meeting people (86%), discovering new places (85%) and shopping for avatars (68%). Fifty-seven per cent of users have engaged in building something; overall, 95% of the Second Life landscape has been built by its residents.

Internal sources estimate that Linden generated about $40 million of revenue in 2007, up from $10 million in 2006. This could double by 2008. The operating margin is estimated at 30–40%. There is no fee for registering an account or participating in Second Life. All one needs is to file payment information to be able to buy land or to use the Lindex. One needs a premium account ($9.95/month) to own land on the Second Life mainland, and support is tied to the amount of money you pay per month.

The bulk of revenue comes from virtual land sales (70–75%), which have a monthly maintenance fee, as well as user subscriptions and commissions on the issuance of Linden Dollars. About 50 000 users make a profit from their in-world businesses and about $1 million worth of Linden Dollars changes hands every day.

At the same time, about half of the active user base spends $2 or less a month in-world. Merchandising (selling real products by promoting them in a virtual world) has only interested the media industry so far. Music and video companies experiment with the virtual merchandising of their own catalogues of music, video and games, etc. Another virtual world, There.com, signed an agreement with Capitol Music Group to bring its musicians into virtual social nightclubs and concerts, enabling fans to engage directly with the artists and the music publishers to stimulate music sales. Also some early experiments exist in other industries. Dell and Reebok sell actual products through their virtual store in Second Life.

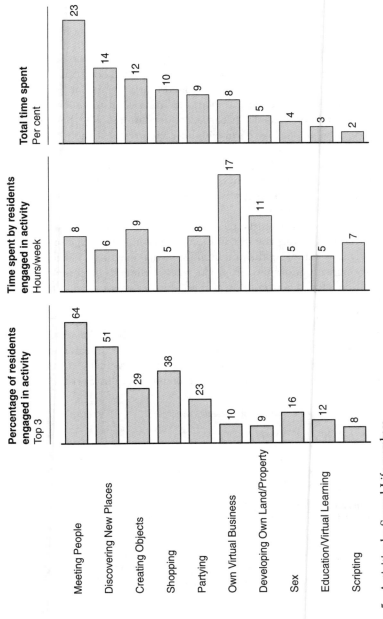

Figure 5   Activities by Second Life members

Source: McKinsey Reperes study, 2007

The technical complexity of linking virtual worlds to e-commerce systems, the lack of scale and a lack of understanding what works and what does not still create barriers.

Challenges

Second Life is facing several challenges. Although approximately 13 million accounts are registered, a large percentage of these are inactive. Realistically, about 550 000 of all accounts are active users, of which 65 000 are concurrently online at peak times. Furthermore, as noted above, the Second Life platform has several technical problems and will need a large boost to be scalable. It can accommodate roughly the amount of concurrent users it has now at peak as its maximum concurrency. Second Life's user interface is still quite confusing to many.

The 3D software is now available through GPL licence, partly backed by IBM, Cisco and others. This may lead to 3D worlds like Second Life supplanting the 2D Web interface, or more realistically, as Robin believes, a 2D interface enhanced by 3D elements in some key areas, such as commerce.

For Robin, this evolution will be essential to creating a seamless mass-market platform and an environment that will enable the distribution of learning on a large scale. Some corporations are already now exploring the potential for virtual meetings, virtual training and virtual product shows with customers. In product development, 3D computer-aided design is already a well-developed concept that will find further creative opportunities in highly realistic virtual worlds.

Furthermore, virtual worlds could become a powerful platform for engaging customers in co-creation activities. At user-generated content sites such as YouTube, about 10% of the people participate, while the large majority of users visit the site to search and watch videos. In industrial co-creation activities such as open-source software development, active participants tend to make up 20–30% of the community. In Second Life, the

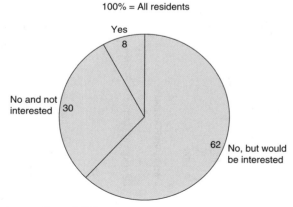

Figure 6   Co-creation on Second Life

Source: McKinsey Reperes study, 2007

Per cent

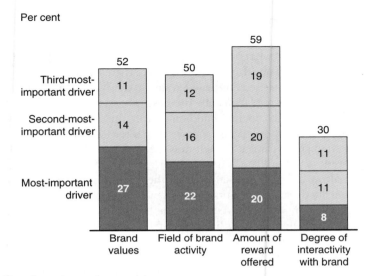

Figure 7   Brand as trigger of co-creation

Source: McKinsey Reperes study, 2007

proportion of co-creators is still less than 10%, but the key bottleneck is the absence of awareness of the possibility to co-create. In principle, up to 60% would be interested in co-creating, especially with a brand they trust.

Furthermore, time spent on creative activities is up to eight hours a week, and time spent on co-creation could top up to 15–20 hours a week, which constitutes a significant production and creation capacity.

Exploiting the will to create can also be powerful for media players. Disney's Virtual Image Kingdom is a powerful example of this, pushing the brand analogy of its favoured theme parks to help co-create a compelling media universe for its audience: more than one million character images were created in less than seven months.

Robin Harper was already familiar with this epic transformation. By mid-2007, she was sharing her own thoughts on how to harness participation on the Internet and how 3D virtual worlds will become the new platforms for creation. And she did this as an insider, as the CMO of Linden Lab's well-known 3D virtual platform Second Life.

YouTube: Building Social Media[1]

Chad Hurley can be proud of what he has achieved in recent years. With his former PayPal colleagues, he founded YouTube three years ago. Since then, the site has been acquired by Google to become the most visited online video site on the Web by far. *Time* magazine did not get it wrong when it named YouTube the best invention of 2006.

YouTube is one of many companies building their business models on the principle of social media. Those companies leverage a new set of Internet technologies, dubbed Web 2.0, that enable inexpensive ways to facilitate user participation and social sharing of media-rich content and services. These properties created the ideal conditions for 'network externalities', that is the effect that the larger the number of participants, the more the benefits these participants will get out of their participation. On one hand, visitors are more and more willing to visit the site as the freshness of content and size of the library increases, while, on the other hand, posting content is increasingly rewarding as the audience grows. This network externality functions as a self-reinforcing mechanism: the larger the site, the better it gets, and the more difficult to imitate.

Clearly, YouTube has enjoyed a very large network externality momentum. Coming out in mid-2005, it already entered the list of the hundred-most-visited sites by early 2006, and became the fifth-most-popular site on the Web by July 2007. One year later, it bypassed its mother company, Google, in the Alexa ranking (this measures site popularity as a combination of page views and reach), with close to 300 million monthly visitors in June 2008.

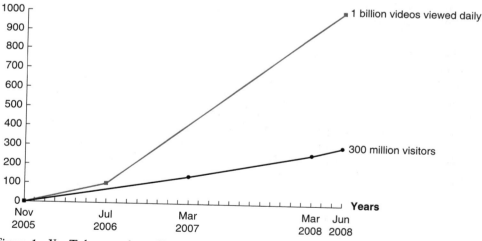

Figure 1 YouTube growth profile

Source: McKinsey analysis based on data from Morgan Stanley; comScore; Alexa; Forbes

---

[1]This case is developed solely as the basis for class discussion. Cases are not intended to serve as endorsements, sources of primary data or illustrations of effective or ineffective management.

In the video category, in the United States more than one video in three is viewed on YouTube, significantly above its major competitors Fox Interactive Media (with a 4.2% share) and Yahoo! (with a 2.9% video share).

Per cent

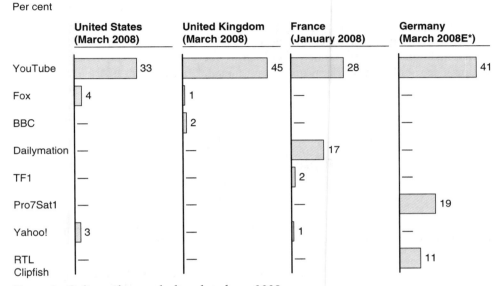

Figure 2   Online video watched market share, 2008

* Based on visitors, December 2007, and average videos viewed by end of 2007
Source: McKinsey analysis based on data from comScore; Alexa

Despite this, Chad was still eager to understand more about how to maintain the momentum. He identified three main issues:

First, Chad was quick to acknowledge the flipside of network externalities, that is a small reduction in interest by some visitors or participants can quickly initiate a negative spiral and deflate the momentum of YouTube. In an environment of hyper-competition like the Web, new darlings are continually replacing old darlings, like Google bypassing Yahoo! or Friendster being replaced by Facebook. On the other hand, the more YouTube manages to extend its popularity, the more the 'winner takes all' effect will become evident.

Second, Chad was clearly seeing the very positive development of YouTube outside the United States. According to many web sources, YouTube was replicating its US dominance in the United Kingdom, with a 45% market share of video viewed versus 1.2% for BBC sites.

However, expansion success does not apply to all countries. The rapid copycat launches of localized 'YouTubes' meant that market benefits he enjoyed in the United States and the United Kingdom (same language) were not likely to be replicated across the board. In France, YouTube was dominant, but a 'copycat attacker', DailyMotion, had appeared early in the market, and managed to get 17% of the video viewership. Further, US television networks finally started to retaliate. They first launched lawsuits against YouTube for copyright infringement and then offered free series download on their own websites, or launched their own user-generated content (UGC) sites, such as Hulu.com. They have only recently started to cooperate with YouTube.

Foreign television networks were faster to react. They started building their own UGC video sites early on: the leading French TV broadcaster TF1 with WAT; RTL, Europe's leading TV group, with ClipFish; and Pro7Sat1 with MyVideo in Germany. In Germany, network television sites were running neck-and-neck with YouTube, and could leverage their core business to cross-promote their sites or to even broadcast the most high-profile online video, which of course meant instant fame for the creator.

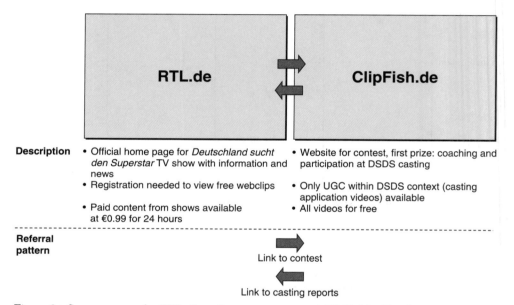

Description	• Official home page for *Deutschland sucht den Superstar* TV show with information and news	• Website for contest, first prize: coaching and participation at DSDS casting
	• Registration needed to view free webclips	• Only UGC within DSDS context (casting application videos) available
	• Paid content from shows available at €0.99 for 24 hours	• All videos for free

Referral pattern

Link to contest

Link to casting reports

Figure 3 Synergy example: RTL SuperStar programme and ClipFish's Clip-Contest

Source: McKinsey analysis

Third, the open architecture of social video sites meant that a contributor could freely choose to post on *all* sites deemed interesting to him or her. The evidence is that the majority of top contributors post at least on all top content sites.

And even if a small time lag could be observed of about 10–15 days between first preferential and a second site, the most appealing videos would remain on the top views for months, meaning that the offering of videos was not likely to be a major differentiator among sites.[2]

---

[2]Gill *et al.* report in their YouTube study that 73% of videos in the top-100 list were more than one month old, and 5% are over one year. Gill, P., Arlitt, M., Li, Z. and Mahanti, A., 'YouTube traffic characterization: a view from the edge', http://www.imconf.net/imc-2007/papers/imc78.pdf, accessed 10 November 2008.

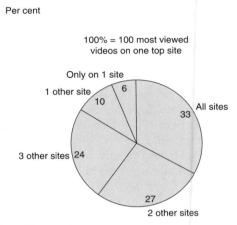

Per cent

100% = 100 most viewed
videos on one top site

Figure 4   **Pervasive online video posting**

Source: McKinsey analysis based on data from MyVideo; YouTube; Google Video; ClipFish; Sevenload websites

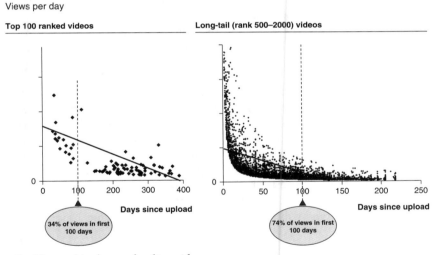

Views per day

Figure 5   **Viewership decay of online videos**

Source: McKinsey analyses of Web log file of online video sites

Chad reasoned that there was much still to do to lure more users and to deepen usage. YouTube continued its search for new innovations, like offering online video 'verticals' (video offerings concentrated around certain themes such as music, allowing people to rate videos and forward them to friends) and enabling YouTube on mobile. But he was ready to learn any new tactics to consolidate the site's competitive advantage.

Company History

Chad Hurley, together with his former PayPal colleagues Steve Chen and Jawed Karim, activated the domain YouTube.com in February 2005 and launched it in November 2005. This debut was supported by an early funding of US$3.5 million by Sequoia Capital, and an additional funding of $8 million six months later. By mid-2006, YouTube's growth accelerated, outpacing other darlings of the moment, such as MySpace. It was already delivering more than 100 million video views a day.

By October 2006, YouTube was acquired by Google for US$1.6 billion in stock. The site continued its growth momentum and rapidly became the most visited online video property on the Web. From the beginning, YouTube had to face strong negative reactions from television networks. NBC, for example, asked for the removal of *Lazy Sunday* and other channel-owned content. CBS followed suit. So YouTube decided to set a limit of ten minutes on video run time, in order to limit direct competition with the networks, and the networks started to reverse their course. They started to look at the company as a possible complementary marketing platform for their own shows. An NBC channel was established on YouTube, promoting high-profile series such as *The Office*. The same happened with music companies: Warner Music signed a deal with YouTube whereby YouTube could host Warner Music videos in exchange for a portion of the advertising income received on music video inventories.

The success of the company led to public recognition and fame: YouTube was declared the best innovation in 2006 by *Time* magazine, and *PC World* magazine put YouTube on the top-ten list of best products in the same year. Its exponential growth continued, with the site crossing the one-billion-views-per-day mark worldwide by March 2008, making it by far the biggest video network worldwide.

At the time that Google purchased YouTube (in October 2006), the site was generating $15 million a month (YouTube's revenue model is advertising based). YouTube will likely generate $200 million in 2008 and $350 million in 2009. Owing to the amateur nature of its production, the typical video posting is unlikely to deliver significant advertising income. Therefore, YouTube is pushing for more professionally produced content, such as movie trailers and television series highlights. YouTube also started to offer branded communities in the form of destination channels. Hundreds of channels are now being sold to advertisers as brand content, such as Nestlé and P&G, for a sponsoring tag of $200 000 a piece.

Features of the online video market

Though virtually nonexistent a few years ago, the online video market is already characterized by the following features:

Mainstream Internet video

Many statistical sources show that, in most countries where YouTube is present, up to two-thirds of broadband users in their teens or twenties have watched or downloaded videos

Per cent, estimates

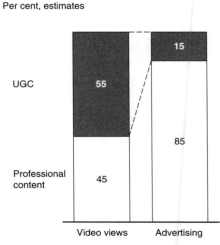

Figure 6 **Professional online video content significantly more attractive to advertisers: US market projection 2010**

Source: McKinsey analyses based on data from Handelsblatt, January 2007; *Screen Digest*

made by other people via their computer. The phenomenon is spreading to older cohorts, as half of the broadband users in the 25–44 age bracket access online videos.

Long-form Internet video

Sites like YouTube usually only post short-form videos as a policy to prevent copyright issues but also because most personal videos are short clips.

However, there is a clear appetite for longer videos, with more than 50% of those not watching long videos expressing a wish to do so. In a recent survey on a Pennsylvania campus, it was discovered that students were watching 2.6 TV series per season on TV (of which about 1.7 were from the top five networks) and 1.4 authorized websites, but that the growth on websites was more than 100% in a year versus just above 10% on traditional TV.[3]

Concentration of consumption

Media consumption exhibits a long tail distribution, with viewership being concentrated on a relatively limited number of users. UGC video is no exception. YouTube has recently revealed that its 100 heaviest users spend up to 100 minutes a day on the site versus the 100 minutes per month for the average user. The same is valid for video popularity: the

---

[3]Waldfogel, J. 'Lost on the Web: Does Web Distribution Stimulate or Depress Television Viewing?', October 2007, *NBER Working Paper*, No. W13497.

Per cent

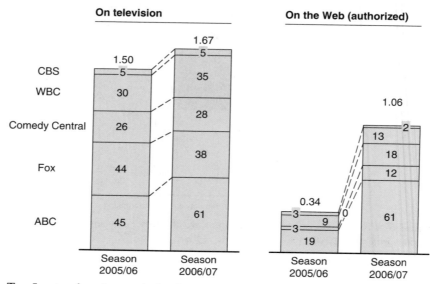

Figure 7 Top 5 network series watched online versus on TV

Note: Sample of undergraduate students at University of Pennsylvania; series viewed include both frequent views as well as ad hoc viewing
Source: McKinsey analysis based on data from Waldfogel, 2007

ten-most-viewed videos contribute to approximately 40% of YouTube's traffic in the United States (see Footnote 2).

Concentration of participation

In the United States, only 6% of people visiting Google Video in 2006 had ever posted a video on the site. In Germany, only between 3% and 6% of people visiting one of the top three video sites have posted videos. This percentage, however, increases with time, doubling every 18 months in Western Europe.

Social media relevance

Top video websites have all embedded social features on their site, including video rating, video forward or user-feedback. Those social features are important for the dynamics of the Web video market. In a recent study on the German video market,[4] 25% of videos were watched following friends' referrals; furthermore, 41% of German

---

[4]Bughin, J., 'How companies can make the most of user generated content', *McKinsey Quarterly Online*, August 2007, http://www.mckinseyquarterly.com/Information_Technology/How_companies_can_make_the_most_of_user-generated_content_2041, accessed 10 November 2008.

Per cent

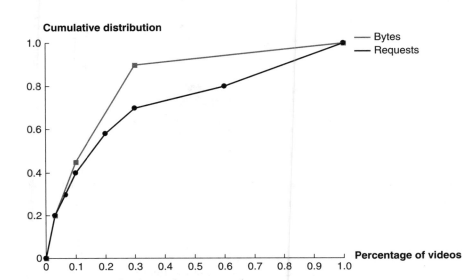

Figure 8   **Concentration of online videos requested**

Source: McKinsey analysis based on data from Gill, P., Arlitt, M., Li, Z. and Mahanti, A., 'YouTube traffic characterization: a view from the edge'

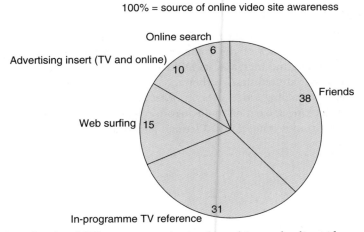

Figure 9   **Friends' referral and TV cross-promotion are large drivers of online video awareness**

Source: McKinsey analysis based on data from SevenOne Media (2007); McKinsey Survey (2007)

Percentage of uploaders

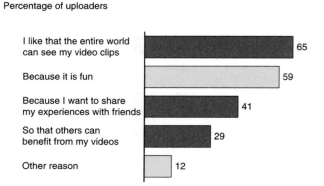

I like that the entire world can see my video clips	65
Because it is fun	59
Because I want to share my experiences with friends	41
So that others can benefit from my videos	29
Other reason	12

Figure 10 **Personal reputation and creative pride are the main drivers for uploading videos**

Source: McKinsey analysis based on data from Online survey SevenOne Interactive, 2006

video uploaders were quoting 'sharing with friends' as a main rationale for posting their videos online. Also, social media is a good brand builder for online video sites: about one-third of brand awareness in Europe comes from friends' referrals.

The fame effect

Financial incentives, as proposed by YouTube, for top contributors have an impact on the incentive to post more and more videos. Yet the desire for fame is still the strongest driver in most of the studies on contributor motivations.[5]

Strategic challenges

Looking at the data in the German markets, Chad sees that video viewership is challenged by the online video sites of the commercial broadcasters. Although YouTube is still gaining momentum and increases its relative share, everything can reverse quickly as a result of network externalities. Furthermore, broadcasters are posting their programmes only to their own online video sites, in order to restrict the appeal of YouTube.

Chad only looking at what he could do to accelerate its growth and wonders how he can win the concentration game in the German and other Continental markets with strong local competitors.

---

[5]Beenen, G., Ling, K., Wang, X. *et al.* (2004) Using social psychology to motivate contributions to online communities. In *Computer Supported Cooperative Work: Proceedings of the ACM Conference On Computer Supported Cooperative Work*. New York, ACM Press.

PEOPLE MANAGEMENT IN MEDIA COMPANIES: CREATIVE MANAGERS OR MANAGED CREATIVITY?

People are at the core of any media business; however, people management in media companies is often more an art than a skill. Given the challenges ahead and the new skills which will be needed, people management is and will stay a clear strategy differentiator in the future. This chapter discusses how media companies can improve people management skills; the main questions addressed are:

1. *What are the current people management practices at media companies?*
2. *Should different groups within the organization be managed differently?*
3. *What people management practices should apply to all employees?*
4. *What is the best way to manage and motivate the creatives?*
5. *What are the implications of the digital transition for people management in media?*

Current People Management Practices in the Media Industry

'Media is a people business.' This opinion is often voiced by senior media executives. Or, as one music industry manager expressed it, 'We don't have a product produced in just one factory; instead, we have 500 little factories.' The product has to be created anew every day, which is on the one hand a large opportunity but on the other makes the media company very dependent on the day-to-day performance of its people.

Many media companies feel, however, that their people management processes do not ensure systematic, high-quality output. Structural 'best practices' are often missing in regard to talent development and guiding day-to-day performance (Figure 9.1). Also the role of the HR department in many media companies is still more focused around administration and union negotiations than strategic people management (Figure 9.2).

Most media companies rightfully believe that systematic people management processes will become increasingly important with the digitization of media, requiring new skills, mindsets, behaviours and leadership for success.

Current practice

Percentage not agreeing*

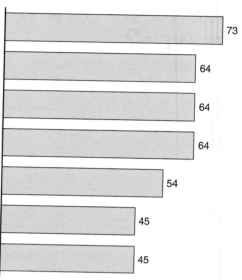

Systematic mentorship of high potentials — 73

Those creatives are promoted to managers who have also clear managerial skills — 64

Being a good people developer is highly recognized — 64

Employees have detailed job descriptions — 64

Rewards are explicitly linked to individual (and possibly group) performance and influence, compensation more than 30% — 54

Institutionalized, regular feedback conversations — 45

Systematic career development plans for high potentials — 45

Figure 9.1   Performance gaps in HR management in media

* Strongly disagree, disagree to some extent
Source: Author survey with 11 leading media companies, 2004

'The HR department in my company has a strategic human development role rather than an administrative role...'

100% = 11 HR managers of leading European media companies

Strongly agree 36

Agree to some extent 18

Strongly disagree 28

Disagree to some extent 18

Figure 9.2   HR departments predominantly administrative in media

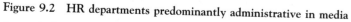

Source: Author survey with 11 leading media companies, 2004

Current Challenge: Embrace 'Creators' Yet Do Not Understate 'Transformers'

The profitability of traditional media companies is often determined by a few decisions; the bulk of revenues in the music industry, to take one example, come from only a small number of products. Indeed, 80% of new CD releases fail to generate positive earnings. Also in less volatile industries, such as magazine publishing, a large share of the earnings often comes from a few formats. In television, the rights for the following season's programme grid are only negotiated once every half year and there is limited flexibility to change the programme schedule once it is set.

This imbalance means that only a few people are involved in making what can be crucial business decisions. These people are mainly 'creators' and senior management has to trust their opinion. In fact, the companies are dependent on their investment choices, which can either translate into valuable call options (the blockbuster) or prove to be costly decisions.

Book editors, talent scouts in the music industry, TV programme managers, film producers and newspaper journalists are all creators. Creators have two quite different tasks. First, they have to generate or discover new content or artists and assess their likelihood of success. Second, creators have to develop the talent or concept into a lasting success, for example managing a singer's career or producing a new TV programme format. Both these types of activities are highly creative – meaning they need both subjective opinions and, often, individual approaches.

However, not all people in a media company are creators. In fact, the proportion of people involved in the actual generation or purchasing and packaging of content within a media company, the 'content creators', is relatively small. The largest group of people working in the industry is that made up of people who transform the content offering generated by the creators into revenues, the so-called 'content transformers' (Figures 9.3).

There are three subgroups of content transformers: people working in functional departments, support staff and 'crafts people'. The functional departments are generally responsible for the three other core processes: content delivery, ad sales and consumer interaction; they are also responsible for the last step in the content generation process: the marketing of the content (see Chapter 2). Support staff work in the traditional support functions such as HR, finance, PR and legal departments, and the 'crafts people' include set designers, stylists and camera operators.

Rather than having to make the big decisions that often confront the creators, content transformation is characterized by a large number of people making many small decisions on a daily basis. The processes are standardized and do not differ fundamentally from those in other industries. In addition, the end products of these processes (e.g. advertising space sold or levels of customer service) can be measured relatively easily.

However, although content transformers' activities do not differ from those in many other industries in terms of the skills required, media companies rarely exhibit top-notch people management processes for these people either. Even simple people development activities or systematic performance measurement systems are often not present. Furthermore, the digitization of media requires the upgrading of skills, that is the Web analytics of measurable online media campaigns are much more difficult to execute than the simple management of gross rating points (GRPs).

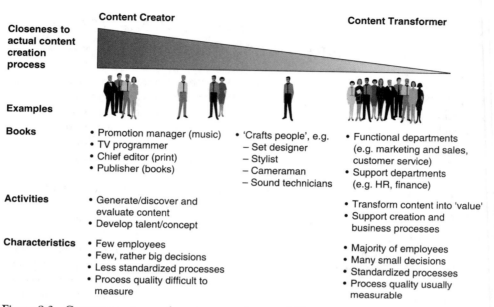

Figure 9.3   Content creators and content transformers differ in activities and characteristics

Source: McKinsey analysis

Common Principles of People Management Processes for 'Creators' and 'Transformers'

Systematic talent development

Although media companies in general put a lot of effort into finding and hiring talent, especially in the creative area, many are still quite weak in systematic talent development. High potentials are often spotted early on, but their way through the organization is not planned systematically; often the company relies too much on the 'apprenticeship' model (i.e. learning by working with/for an experienced creator or manager).

Also too little attention is paid to soft factors, such as the availability of mentors, something which is especially important in a more 'emotion-driven' environment. Companies such as Bertelsmann and Schibsted in Scandinavia have already put, or are in the process of putting, in place programmes to develop and retain their talents; however, it is a slow process (Figure 9.4).

Clear performance evaluation

Media companies are often not very clear about the tasks and responsibilities of each person and how success will be measured. Regular, institutionalized feedback conversations are not common practice and incentive systems are often not in line with the performance criteria (Figure 9.5).

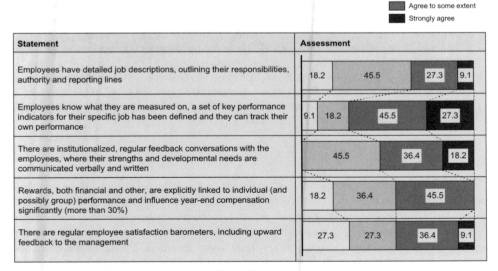

Strongly disagree
Disagree to some extent
Agree to some extent
Strongly agree

Statement	Assessment		
Identifying and recruiting top talent is a high priority on the top management's agenda and is seen as a board level activity	36.4	27.3	36.4
High potentials are identified early on and supported actively	18.2	72.7	9.1
Systematic career development plans are made for high potentials and followed through	18.2	27.3	45.5	9.1
High potentials are expected to work in different parts of the organization	18.2	36.4	18.2	27.3
Mentorship of high potentials is managed actively	27.3	45.5	9.1	18.2
The HR department has a strategic human development role rather than an administrative role	27.3	18.2	18.2	36.4

Figure 9.4   Systematic talent development in the media industry

Source: Author survey with 11 leading media companies, 2004

Strongly disagree
Disagree to some extent
Agree to some extent
Strongly agree

Statement	Assessment		
Employees have detailed job descriptions, outlining their responsibilities, authority and reporting lines	18.2	45.5	27.3	9.1
Employees know what they are measured on, a set of key performance indicators for their specific job has been defined and they can track their own performance	9.1	18.2	45.5	27.3
There are institutionalized, regular feedback conversations with the employees, where their strengths and developmental needs are communicated verbally and written	45.5	36.4	18.2
Rewards, both financial and other, are explicitly linked to individual (and possibly group) performance and influence year-end compensation significantly (more than 30%)	18.2	36.4	45.5
There are regular employee satisfaction barometers, including upward feedback to the management	27.3	27.3	36.4	9.1

Figure 9.5   Use of formal processes in the media industry

Source: Author survey with 11 leading media companies, 2004

One important improvement lever is the introduction of strict(er) formal steering mechanisms, built on a differentiated set of key performance indicators (KPIs).

Best-practice KPIs in the Media Industry

KPIs can be established along three areas: strategic, operating and financial indicators. A *strategic indicator* focuses on those performance measures which are the most critical factors for the medium-term success of the company. For advertising-driven businesses, this may be the average audience reach during peak time or the average CPM (cost per thousand, i.e. price paid by the advertiser per thousand people reached within the agreed target segment). For 'copy sales'-driven businesses, this may be the hit ratio and/or the lifetime value per artist. For subscription-based businesses, it may be the consumer satisfaction average and distribution or lifetime value per subscriber.

Operating and financial indicators are the most commonly used KPIs for content transformers. *Operating indicators* are daily measurements which tie closely to the most important value drivers per function. For example, as mentioned in Chapter 2, customer service is increasingly focusing on retaining existing customers rather than attracting new ones. An operating indicator within this newly defined function would, therefore, focus on quality rather than on productivity in terms of number of calls or call duration. A *financial indicator* focuses on the key financial parameters within the profit-and-loss and balance sheets of a company. For example, in TV production this could be cost-per-format.

The key to defining successful KPIs is that there should be no more than 10 to 15 KPIs that are understood and shared by everyone. Defining these KPIs is not a trivial task, as it requires a very deep understanding of what at that point in time are the crucial determinants for success of a company. KPIs can shift significantly over time, for example as the company is entering or going through the digital transition.

The first step to implementing these KPIs is to define clear accountability of creative and functional costs and output so that the people responsible can be identified. This requires clear targets, for example set benchmarks, that can be broken down into individual goals and linked to the incentive system. All indicators need to be measurable, easily allocated and reachable, and individuals must be able to influence them. Incentive systems should then be tied to performance.

Original KPIs that trigger the right behaviour of performance in the adequate company and market contexts are rarely seen in the media industry, although there are some exceptions. For example, a leading music group is developing a differentiated set of targets that go beyond sales numbers. In the difficult market environment, success can no longer be judged solely on the number of platinum discs awarded. Product managers are increasingly judged on their fulfilment of specific strategic goals, such as whether they managed to set a new trend by investing in a specific artist, even if the artist him- or herself was not a major hit, or whether they got attention from the right media. By focusing on both short-term sales and long-term market development goals, the company aims to motivate its people even during the recession.

Lucas Digital, a special-effects subsidiary of Lucasfilm, targeted KPIs that ensure constant learning and development to state-of-the-art technologies. It evaluates creatives based on their eagerness to take on new work and to learn new technologies and techniques. Lucas Digital's first project was *Star Wars* in 1979, and since then it has scooped 29 Oscars.

The extent to which the introduction of KPIs is possible depends on the industry, the phase it is in and the kind of project. Standardized processes, such as traditional newspaper production, are easier to measure than a one-off project, such as creating a TV series. Introducing digital media requires specific KPIs that focus on the speed of innovation and the effectiveness of the digital offerings rather than on efficiency. Even when operating and financial indicators are relatively easy to define, such as in the traditional print business, it still does not mean that they are always used. Comparing efficiency in editorial offices reveals big differences and highlights where there is room for improvement. Of course, efficiency measures will have to be handled with care, as they do not say anything about the quality of output; however, they are an important element in creating a holistic performance picture.

Management of 'Transformers'

The media industry is an attractive employer for many 'non-creatives'. In Germany, for example, graduates with a business background rank it second only to consulting. Many people involved in the transformation process in media are motivated by exciting products and the creative environment. Transformers need a great degree of flexibility to deal with last-minute changes and a tolerance of ambiguity. Media companies should, however, be aware that attempts to nurture such an open mindset can run the risk of distracting from effective process management. A music company, for example, reported that it is standard to hear loud music coming from the controlling department. In spite of this environment, transformers still require strict and professionally managed processes. As a headhunter working for the European media industry expressed it, 'Profitable media companies also have boring people who focus on getting their jobs done.'

Just as important is having a high-quality functional leadership of content transformers. For example, in the finance department deep functional expertise is crucial because cost allocation is complex, as most activities are project-driven and involve many different parties. However, many functional managers in media companies are still home-grown, and have little functional experience outside the industry.

Selectively bringing in people from the outside who have gained high-level functional experience can help generate a huge leap in performance, as a leading newspaper group experienced. It brought in an external CFO and IT manager, who introduced new best practices, learned in industries which were more sophisticated in these areas. A more extreme example is EMI, where after the acquisition by Terrafirma, a major part of the top management was replaced by managers from outside the industry coming from companies such as Reckitt Benckiser, BAA (British Airport Authorities), Procter & Gamble and Google. It is important to point out, though, that integrating these people has to be managed very carefully and it is unclear to what extent a company can absorb these changes.

There is also clear evidence that home-grown capabilities do not adapt easily to the requirements of digitization; most of the media companies which diversified successfully to online have developed the online processes and culture outside of the main company. Sanoma in Holland operates Ilsemedia as a separate entity; FINN is a separate online affiliate for Schibsted, and most of the online diversification for the BBC (e.g. the Kangaroo platform pilot) was done separate within the BBC Worldwide.

Management of 'Creatives'

Many media managers are wary of interfering in the creative process, believing it will demotivate their creators and lead to run-of-the-mill results. Also there is in many cases, for example with newspapers, the famous Chinese wall between the business people and the creators exists to prevent that content being corrupted by commercial interests. Best-practice media companies, however, realize that a systematic and professional approach to the management of creators can significantly increase both productivity *and* job satisfaction. They, therefore, manage talent systematically through the job lifecycle (attraction, development, retention and transition) while taking care that in day-to-day management they maximize the productivity of the content management process.

Set up systematic processes along the job lifecycle

In many media companies, the attraction, motivation/integration and development of, as well as the transition/phase out of, creative talent is handled informally rather than systematically. However, those companies that do shape these processes consciously – such as, for example, Bertelsmann – are generally known as highly attractive employers and are less dependent on the charisma of a few people, be it the CEO, owner or outstanding creators (Figure 9.6).

Attract

Two different approaches to building top talent have to be pursued in parallel; however, the balance between the two can vary. Two of Europe's most successful soccer clubs illustrate the distinction. Companies can, like Manchester United, develop talent internally or, like Real Madrid, they can simply buy it. Few media companies are good at retaining their talent; in most cases, talent jumps from one company to another in an attempt to get a better position. Those companies, like BBC and Bertelsmann, that have invested significantly in growing their own talent (both managers and creative staff) are, consequently, among the most popular employees for young high-flyers in their respective markets.

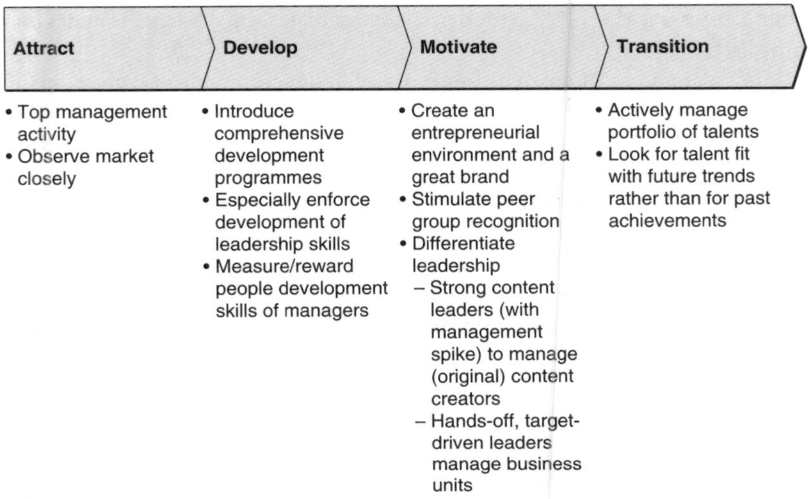

Attract	Develop	Motivate	Transition

• Top management activity
• Observe market closely
	• Introduce comprehensive development programmes
	• Especially enforce development of leadership skills
	• Measure/reward people development skills of managers
		• Create an entrepreneurial environment and a great brand
		• Stimulate peer group recognition
		• Differentiate leadership
		  – Strong content leaders (with management spike) to manage (original) content creators
		  – Hands-off, target-driven leaders manage business units
			• Actively manage portfolio of talents
			• Look for talent fit with future trends rather than for past achievements

Figure 9.6   Key success factors of managing creators

Source: McKinsey analysis

Identifying Creative Talent: Top Management Task at Hubert Burda Media

Recruiting talent externally is a task for senior management. Board members at Hubert Burda Media spend a significant portion of board meetings discussing the company's own talent base and that of its competitors. As people working within one industry are usually very well connected, it is not generally difficult to identify top talent; the real challenge is to create an environment that motivates these talented people to join the company, and then stay.

Develop talent

The systematic development of creators is rarely found in media companies. A major exception is the former UK regional newspaper group Thomson, which introduced sophisticated people-development processes 30 years ago.

Superior Development Processes at Thomson Regional Newspapers

Thomson developed an extensive training programme for all levels in the company, including both creative people and managers. The programme was given high priority and was greatly appreciated by the participants. In fact, in 2002 three CEOs of the four leading UK newspaper groups had started their careers at Thomson.

Another example is the BBC, which actively manages top creators' careers by rotating them into different areas.

Developing a creator can mean either functional development or career development. Not all creators are aiming for a management career, and they should be allowed to prosper in their creative field, for example by being given increasing degrees of freedom and budgets to work with.

For those who do want to move to a management role, a careful assessment of their management capabilities together with a strong management training programme is needed. Some companies, such as Bertelsmann with its 'corporate university', have established systematic programmes. However, the general culture of the industry seems to regard educational programmes as unnecessary and equate good performance as a creator with good management capabilities.

Introducing People Development Programmes at a German Publisher

In an attempt to overcome resistance to formal training, a German publisher implemented a programme that, along with instilling the values and goals of the publisher, laid out some leadership guidelines. These set the ground for systematic people management principles. Based on this, the programme offered access to further qualification measures necessary to attain goals.

Motivate and integrate

Creators are strongly motivated by the intrinsic value of their work, that is the content they generate, and are, therefore, often driven more by intangible incentives than by tangible ones. As Allison Polly, a vice president at marketing communications company McCann-Erickson said, 'Realize that the best creatives are, at their very soul, artists who would be creating whether or not they chose to make a living at it.' The main factors that motivate creators can be divided into environmental factors, specific rewards and type of leadership.

The main environmental factors which motivate creators are entrepreneurial opportunities provided by the company and the company brand.

Financial Times' Value Proposition for Journalists

The Financial Times offers its journalists a clear value proposition. First, they can leverage the paper's prestigious brand to earn income outside the newspaper, for example by writing a book. It also gives its journalists the freedom to write distinctive stories and, finally, it offers relatively high job security and top-end compensation.

Opportunities stem from a high degree of freedom and autonomy in multiple dimensions. Creators should have freedom not only in terms of content but also in terms of budgetary autonomy.

HBO Creates Entrepreneurial Freedom

TV company HBO is releasing one successful programme after another and is clearly attracting top talent. One Hollywood screenwriter describes its success factor as follows, 'It's an amazing place to work. Once they have hired the right people, they give you the liberty to do what you want.' (*Economist*, 18 January 2003.)

Creators are also attracted to a company's brand. A strong brand helps in both attracting and retaining talent as it enhances the individual's status within their peer group. The desire to be part of a community is a universal characteristic of the media industry as a whole and is especially strong in some sectors, such as the music and film industries. Working for a strong brand enhances social standing. Leading companies, such as Bertelsmann, build on this by treating image-building as a core people process.

Brand Yourself at Hubert Burda Media

Hubert Burda coined the slogan, 'Brand yourself'. Editors are encouraged to position themselves as experts and commentators. This ensures highly motivated employees and recognition for the whole company. A good example is Helmut Markwort, the editor-in-chief of Burda's German magazine *Focus*, who earned a national reputation.

It is also important to ensure that creators buy into the company's overall strategic direction and vision, which means that they must be aware of what this direction actually is and be involved in the strategy development process. Successful media companies such as Schibsted, Pearson and others have all spent significant time and effort to develop a shared vision translated into clear internal company values and guiding principles, which are shared by everyone and in some cases even result in charters which are signed by all employees.

Creating a Vision at Schibsted

Schibsted, one of Scandinavia's leading print and Internet companies, has revised its vision several times. In 1995 it became an early mover in the Internet age as reflected by the vision it formulated then: 'Schibsted's vision is to be a leading Scandinavian media company by being the preferred content supplier to consumers and advertisers, irrespective of their choice of media.' After successfully having pursued this mission through major acquisitions in Sweden as well as the building-up and acquisition of highly successful online classified portals, the company felt in 2005 that this vision was not stretching enough to cope with the major changes ahead, and so came to a new vision: 'Schibsted will be the most attractive media group in Europe, through people who dare, challenge and who create.' The emphasis had shifted from where to compete to how to compete, as the company believed that in these fast-changing times a powerful, flexible and innovative organization was the only guarantee for a successful transition.

This process is repeated on individual media brand levels, where the core brand values are clearly defined and translated into principles which are valid for all departments in the organization. The processes followed for defining these values are highly interactive and involve sessions with all parts of the organization, so that at the end all, including the creators, *feel ownership* of the principles. To keep these alive the values need to be revisited.

Defining Company Values at Pearson

Pearson PLC, the owner of amongst others the *Financial Times*, Pinguin Group and a wide array of educational publishers, has translated its three core values – imaginative, decent, brave – into key attributes it looks for in its key employees. A Pearson employee:

- Thinks beyond the here and now. Key attributes: smart, strategic and creative.
- Uses business acumen to make smart decisions. Key attributes: character, knowledge, drive.
- Achieves results with others. Key attributes: insight, judgement, influence.
- Connects with customers and embraces different points of view. Key attributes: responsive, curious, inclusive.

These attributes play an important role in recruitment, where the CEO herself is involved, and form the basis of extensive development and leadership programmes, high-potential events and discussion forums.

Creators should not only feel ownership for the strategic goals, but also be enabled to contribute actively to their attainment. This may be difficult, as creators are usually not used to dealing with financial or other business-related issues. It is, therefore, important to train and coach them. The BBC, for example, sends creators to a three-month management course at a US business school. Hallmark also sends its creative managers to a business leadership course, where they have to make decisions about distribution, advertising and technology.

Transition

Finally, a step which is seldom managed consistent enough in the lifecycle of a creator is the transition out of the company. In challenging times, it is essential that low-performing creators are identified and phased out. Even when things are going well, companies need to employ creators who can meet the demand for new trends and take them to the next level. Media managers have a tendency to focus on the success history, the 'stock' of a creator, rather than on the continuing success rate, the 'flow' of new ideas. Such a culture increases the risk of the company getting stuck in areas where these people have already shown their strengths and passing up new opportunities. Rotating creators, even if they have had great successes in the past, is crucial to staying open to new ideas.

To execute these processes, there needs to be a systematic performance review system that follows clear measurable criteria in multiple dimensions. Managing the transition itself is a task for senior management, as the potential risk in terms of damage to reputation or the loss of contact with artists is significant.

Overall, much remains to be done to improve the people management processes along the lifecycle and to build up motivated and well-educated employees in the long run. While that is being done, processes must be put in place that ensure the efficient day-to-day management of creators, without reducing their freedom and opportunities too much.

Ensure effective and efficient content generation processes

Michael Eisner, ex-CEO of Disney, emphasized the counterintuitive value of discipline in the creative process: 'Steven Spielberg and George Lucas, two of the most creative people, are the most organized individuals you'll ever meet.' Or in the words of Woody Allen, 'If show business wasn't a business it would be called show show.' Recent changes in senior management at several media companies show how the industry is starting to refocus on effective and efficient management. Bertelsmann, Vivendi and EMI have all migrated from having visionary 'big bet' leaders to having leaders driven by basic day-to-day management principles. These leaders are trying to revert to strongly operational and bottom-line-oriented management principles. Striking the right balance between freedom on the one hand and the effective transition to new digital processes on the other is one of the biggest challenges for creative people management in media companies.

The balance between freedom and control varies according to media segment. In those that are very hit-driven, such as music, books and TV/film production, the creators need significant freedom, as the opportunity costs of missing out on a hit are very high. Some segments are more sensitive to error than others, for example free-to-air TV financed solely by advertising is much more dependent on actual ratings than subscription-based TV. Those segments that need a high degree of freedom and at the same time strict downside risk control (e.g. free-to-air TV and film production) need a different approach from those with a low dependency on hits and low downside risks, such as Internet, newspapers and magazines (Figure 9.7).

A frequent cause for resistance against increasing control is the 'prima donna' status of some top creators, which can complicate the acceptance of any kind of rules. And yet freedom is one of the cornerstones of the creative process. In order to avoid destroying

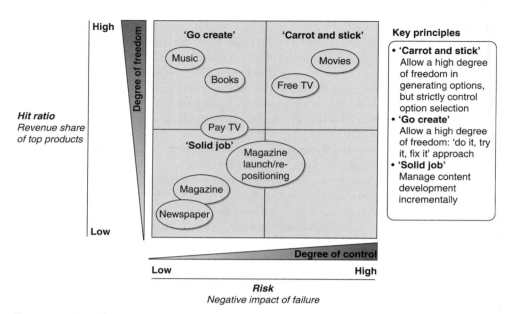

Figure 9.7   People management adapted to level of risk and hit ratio

* Existing titles
Source: McKinsey analysis

creative potential, a balance has to be struck between the demands of day-to-day management and the need for an unfettered creative environment.

There are media companies that do strike a good balance. The secret is to make creators use their creativity, not only to produce outstanding content but also to be creative in how the content is brought to the consumer and what content processes should look like. In short, the challenge is to increase the scope of creativity rather than to curb it. Successful companies, therefore, try to channel creativity, rather than bureaucratically control it. The best way to do this is to integrate creators into the overall strategic process, translate the strategy into clear goals backed by KPIs and give the creators full responsibility for achieving these goals.

Rewards

In terms of monetary rewards, media salaries are comparable with those in other industries or are sometimes lower, except for those of the top talent and certain creators. Often the better the brand, the company's status and the learning opportunities, the lower the salary expectations, especially with young high-flyers who see the company as a step on the career ladder rather than as their final destination. On the other hand, those creators who

Compensation Practices at Music Major

An international music publisher pays the majority of its creative staff below the industry average. It does not need to pay more as the brand is so attractive. However, it does pay disproportionately more to retain its best people. One reason for the high market value of these top employees is that artists are often very closely linked to their managers. Therefore, losing a manager would mean losing the artist.

have strong personal relationships with top artists or are a trademark themselves can command salaries far above those of senior management.

Besides salary, creative people are typically influenced by peer recognition, as a sign of community success and as a way to signal competencies. This element is so important that it has been one of the main drivers of the rise in user-generated content (UGC), where a major reason for contribution, like creating a video on YouTube, editing a comment on Wikipedia or posting a recommendation for a book is recognition (Figure 9.8).

The flipside of 'peer recognition' as a key part of (intangible) reward is that creatives can be more concerned about creating peer-recognized output than about being efficient for their employee organization. Giving full accountability of budget to creatives can be an effective way to better control efficiency. In fact, experience shows that once budgets are really agreed to very creative ways are found to adhere to the budgets, with no major impact on quality.

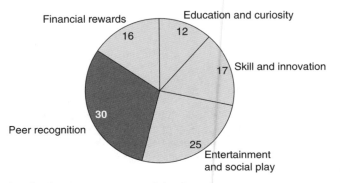

100% = contributors to six user-generated content projects*

Figure 9.8 Rationales for user-content participation

* Various surveys of Wikipedia, YouTube, MyVideo, Second Life, ClipFish and Dailymotion
Source: McKinsey analysis

Giving Full Responsibility to Creators to Achieve Goals

Ten to 15 years ago, the BBC started to assign budgetary responsibility to creators – in this case TV program producers – to control costs more efficiently. It was initially very difficult to convince creators of the importance of cost control, especially as they were used to just saying how much money they needed. To gain acceptance, creative decision-makers were included in strategic discussions and implementation programmes. Eventually, the scheme improved cost-efficiency enormously, and the corporation halved its costs. Alongside budgetary responsibility, the BBC also introduced a structured performance measurement system. It conducts peer group comparisons, annually comparing quality and efficiency. Targets were broken down, based on each division's goals.

A German publisher introduced budgetary responsibilities a few years ago, thereby strengthening its decentralized organization. Senior editors were involved in the strategic discussion and, together with the CEO, defined the travel and expense budgets for the editorial departments. Each editor-in-chief also received support in breaking the budgets down for different departments. Although it was difficult at the outset, it turned out to be a very successful way of bringing costs under control.

Leadership

Leadership in media is increasingly recognized as a crucial role in attracting and retaining creative talent. As Disney's vice-president of HR said, 'The most important element in retention is the leader.' Two successful but distinct media leadership styles emerge: the inspirational and hands-on creative style, exemplified by the likes of Endemol's previous CEO and current co-owner, John de Mol – a charismatic person, known for his continuous creation of successful innovative ideas – and the highly performance-oriented hands–off style, used by managers like Tony Ball, former CEO of BSkyB, who lead by setting clear goals that are systematically translated into individual targets.

BSkyB: Lead by Strategic Goals

Every year, BSkyB's former CEO, Tony Ball, formulated specific strategic goals that were then broken down to the next level of 10 to 20 managers. They cascaded into individual goals for the different functions, which, in turn, linked back to the overall strategy. By setting one overarching goal every year (e.g. regarding the number of new product introductions or an increase in revenue per customer), Ball managed to align the whole company and set the right framework, even for the creators. Given the changing and increasingly competitive environment, his successor, James Murdoch, pursued a more hands-on management style.

Determining which style of leadership fits best depends on a number of factors. In industries in which original content is created within the company (magazines, newspaper, TV production), the leader of a group of creators is often a creative person, with a deep knowledge of the relevant content, for example a chief editor of a magazine or a programme manager at a TV channel. This level of content knowledge is crucial for winning acceptance. <u>The challenge, of course, is to find a leader who combines a good head for business with creative competence</u>. Too often, creatively talented employees are promoted, based on their creative performance, and are not assessed rigorously for their managerial skills.

In the music industry, for example, promotion managers, who used to work mostly by themselves, can suddenly find themselves in charge of a whole group of people. As one senior music executive said, 'Unfortunately, many of our best talent promoters have definite autistic traits; they are lone fighters, penetrating specific music scenes.' Worse still, when these sorts of managers are given more responsibility, they do not receive sufficient training in such basic management skills as giving feedback, project management or budget development. Also although high-quality, hands-on creative leaders can be very inspiring for young creators, they can stifle the more senior people to such an extent that they decide to leave and take on an own-leadership position. It is the role of top management and the HR department to make sure that these senior creators get either enough freedom to develop their own ideas or are rotated to other parts of the organization, where they can take on more responsibility.

Allow more cooperation between 'creatives' and other parts of organizations

A final element to ensure better leverage of 'creators' is to ensure that they have all the means necessary for developing a closer cooperation with other parts of the organization. Doing so with finance and admin will help control investment costs; doing so with marketing will help understand the design–revenue relationship of the creation; doing this with distribution will help creatives understand how products of their creation can or cannot be consumed and truly exploited.

Improving Cooperation between Finance and Product Management at a Music Major

At an international music publisher, the controlling department and the music production departments were increasingly drifting apart, developing their own momentum. Controllers and creators worked totally independently of each other, with controllers setting budgets without knowing exactly what the goals and requirements of creators were. Creators meanwhile never received feedback from the controllers as to their results and steered their artists down commercial blind alleys.

When the company moved to new premises, it took the opportunity to co-locate administrative functions and creators. As a second step, it set up processes in which controllers and creators had to interact. Controllers were dedicated to specific product managers, with weekly meetings to set up and control the budget. In addition, creators were also included in further administrative tasks, such as negotiating legal contracts with the lawyer.

Increasing Understanding between Marketers and Content Creators at Bertelsmann

Bertelsmann conducted a 'Content meets Marketing' event. Thirty to 40 leading content creators and the same number of marketing executives spent two days together and exchanged views and ideas. The degree of understanding between the two groups grew tremendously.

People Management in the Digital Media Era

How does the transition to the digital world affect the traditional best practices in people management in media? Old beliefs and role divisions will have to be shed with major implications for organizational structures, and new skills will be required. Not only traditional media companies will have to rethink their people management practices as they enter seriously into Internet businesses or integrate vertically with content creation businesses; also, pure Internet businesses face significant challenges as they have to transition from the entrepreneurial start-up to the multi-billion-dollar conglomerate within only a few years. Finally, Web 2.0 technologies are entering the sphere of the media enterprise and can be leveraged for better cooperation and learning for 'creatives'.

New (digital) skills

New digital skills need to be developed online. This will not only require facing the general truth that media employees need to be more literate in using digital tools and technologies (see Chapter 5) but also mean that some functions are radically adapted by the transformation to digital. These include:

1. *Editorial:* The value proposition of a typical website is directly correlated with the freshness of its content. Typically, content in news must be refreshed at least every hour to have a chance to be compelling to online users. Compare this velocity of news production and update with traditional media, where newspapers are published once daily, TV news several times daily, etc. productivity has to significantly increase, and writing styles must be much more fine-tuned to headlines and short articles .

2. *Ad sales:* before the digital revolution, ad sales' value propositions were directly linked to reach and, in some cases, selectivity. With online, the same holds true, but the medium holds the promise of much more measurability and accountability, like click

and video conversion, brand-strength enhancement, etc. Advertising sellers must upgrade their skills from basic inventory management to much more comprehensive analytics to measure and market the performance of their new media.

Media companies are still struggling with this need to upgrade skills, but it is unavoidable. Companies such as ilse media within Sanoma Group already have developed the digital media HR skills, as they have in Schibsted. Yahoo!, Google and others have invested in the wholesale retraining of many of their employees to master these new skills, and ad creative agencies, like JWT, have bought digital agencies and their people to inject new skills into their traditional ad planning and creative businesses.

Pure Internet businesses: mastering the transition from start-up to corporation

People management in Internet businesses has been very different from the start. The businesses had highly entrepreneurial settings, roles were flexible and employees highly motivated to do whatever was necessary. As the content which could be provided was to a major extent dependent on the technical platform, 'creatives' and technicians had to work together intensively from the outset. Creativeness by the engineers was as important as content creativity. On top of this, the marketing function had to be intimately linked to the entire process. The divide between content and commerce was much less stringent than in traditional media and the advertising-sales function was an integral part of the core organization. Open platforms and interactive content creation have become increasingly important, increasingly putting the 'content' people into a director rather than a creator role. Initially, most Internet businesses relied on strong informal communication structures. People were incentivized by the entrepreneurial challenge and often attractive stock option schemes. However, as the Internet became a serious business the successful players, such as Yahoo!, Google and Amazon, were faced with the challenge of introducing new organizational and reward structures. For those Internet companies which were bought up by traditional media companies such as MySpace, Bebo and AOL (although initially AOL bought Time Warner), there was the additional challenge of integration in/cooperation with a very different culture. Besides this, a successful initial public offering (IPO) and/or trade sale meant that the key managers of an Internet company had no real need any more to stay, as they would be financially covered. Although difficult to generalize, there seem to be a few best practices which help Internet companies achieve the best of both worlds as much as possible:

- *Maintain the entrepreneurial feel/culture:* The feel of entrepreneurialism is upheld partly through symbolic actions, such as 'fun' premises with provisions to step away from the daily grind and get fresh inspiration through games, sports and relaxed interchanges, an informal dress code and communications structure, etc. and partly through giving the employees the freedom to spend part of their time on developing new initiatives.
- *Close cooperation:* Not only are there fewer traditional functional barriers between content, marketing, technical and advertising sales, there is also an intensive network build-up with other companies and service providers, either through open platforms,

revenue-sharing models or other mechanisms, which helps provide a continuous flow of innovative ideas.

- *Professional ad sales:* The ad-sales function tends to be run along the most traditional lines, with a strong focus on achieving short-term goals and ad-sales effectiveness.
- *Presence of the founder:* For many Internet companies, the presence of (one or some of) the founders in the board is seen as a guarantee that the original mission and culture of the company will be safeguarded. It also serves a strong symbolic function. The arrival of the critical point when the founder is no longer the right person to take the company to the next level has to be handled with extreme care, as it can throw the company back significantly.
- *Ownership:* Often key employees hold a small amount of shares or options, which makes them identify more closely with the company.

People Management at Google

The people management processes at Google are managed with the same care and scientific approach as the company's core search business. As the company grew significantly its number of employees, the management came to the conclusion that the quality of the people was at least as important or even more important to the success of the company as the quality of its search algorithms. Recruitment processes were carefully analysed and research was performed to identify the type of people who were most likely to succeed within, and contribute to, the company. This was done by comparing profiles of recruits and looking at their later success. The recruitment process became a top management priority and for a while every professional recruit had to be approved individually by the top management at Mountain View headquarters. Once the management felt comfortable with the process, it was delegated back to the regions, but still with a strong emphasis on maintaining the right approach.

The Google organization itself can be divided into roughly three groups: the engineers, the regions and the new business developers. The groups are bound together by a strong company culture ('do no evil') and mission (organize the world's information and make it universally accessible and useful). The engineers in Google are for Google what the creatives are for media companies. Their role is to come up with continuous improvements for the search and target advertising products and to develop new offerings. Based on an algorithm developed by Sergey Brin, one of Google's co-founders, their time is divided 70/20/10, that is 70% of their time is spent on improving core products, 20% on developing new products and 10% on whatever pet topics they have. According to Sergey, this time division creates the optimal balance between ensuring a continuous upgrade of existing products and developing new products at a pace the company can absorb.

The second group is the regional organizations. These groups consist mostly of highly talented business people. Their task is not only to increase the market share of Google search but also to introduce the new Google products and to ensure advertising sales. This group is managed in a fairly traditional way, with a clear focus on short-term results and a relatively strong influence from the corporate centre.

The third group is made up of the business developers, who are responsible for developing the new applications and products into businesses. Examples are Google Checkout, Google Earth, Gmail, YouTube, etc. This group has a high degree of freedom in setting its own priorities and driving projects forward. Structures are very informal as there is a strong belief that highly talented people can best set their own priorities and the best idea will survive. People working in these areas on the one hand enjoy a great deal of freedom and trust; conversely, they are sometimes over-whelmed by the chaotic environment and the high amount of interaction required, which is fundamentally different from traditional corporations where they used to work before.

Google realizes that this approach for a large, publicly quoted corporation is revolutionary and has never been tried before, and yet it is highly confident that it is the best way to get, keep and maximally profit from top talent not only in engineering but also in the business field.

Integrating on- with offline

Traditional media companies are actively building up their Internet businesses, either organically as extensions of their offline offerings or as an independent extension of their portfolio through acquisition. Initially, these businesses are managed at arm's length, for two reasons. First, companies do not want to run the risk that the 'fledglings' are squeezed out by the much more powerful traditional businesses. Second, it is felt that running an Internet business requires fundamentally different skills, which should have the opportunity to develop and establish themselves in a protected environment.

However, as Internet businesses blossom, they often have as many consumers as traditional businesses, and these consumers can become content generators, for example OhmyNews's citizen journalist model. User-generated content (UGC) is changing the way companies do business.

360° media

Companies need to structure their business around the consumer rather than around the product, and they will need to integrate traditional and new media in order to create a seamless offering for the consumer. This evokes often significant resistance, especially from the side of the traditional media. Print journalists, especially, often feel that the Internet is a completely different media that is not suitable for in-depth quality journalism. Nevertheless, more and more newspapers and magazines are actively integrating on- and offline newsrooms and editorial boards. Some media companies go even further, such as the Danish regional newspaper group Nordjyske, which has integrated its editorial desk across TV, newspaper, radio and the Internet.

Integrated newsroom at Nordjyske

The regional newspaper group Nordjyske in the north of Denmark was a frontrunner in the integration of its various media businesses. Early on, the company noticed the warning signs of decline in its core regional newspaper businesses and actively diversified in a number of other businesses, such as a regional, 24/7 TV news channel, websites and two radio stations. In the beginning of 2001 the company became convinced that the only way of offering a true multimedia offering to its consumers was to integrate the newsroom fully. It started by integrating its newsroom in Frederikshavn in 2001, followed by a new group structure in January 2002. The ad-sales department was integrated in November 2002. In September 2003 the 24-hour cable news channel 24NORDJYSKE was launched.

To achieve true integration in the newsroom the organization structure, the rules of the game, employee skills and the physical layout of the company were transformed. The organization was changed into a matrix structure where, on the one hand, there would be multimedia content groups focused around business, lifestyle, sports, politics and two regions. On the other hand, there would be media editors responsible for one of the specific medias: TV, radio, daily newspaper and Internet. The matrix as a whole was overseen by a few general editors, who functioned as 'media maestros'. The media editors would be seated together with the maestro in the centre of the newsroom at the 'superdesk', and the content departments were grouped around this desk. Work processes were changed fundamentally. Much more time was spent on idea generation and planning and less time on production and control. The whole newsroom was centred on the 'storyteller concept': who could tell the story in the most suitable media and think in the flow between the media?

For this to happen, the people involved were expected to share ideas, research, sources and stories and only then would it be decided which story would be communicated and in what media; hence, not all stories would appear in all media. All employees would know how to work with all media, although not everybody was supposed to be multiskilled all of the time. Judging when this was appropriate was also a key skill. The sales department also functioned as a fully multimedia entity: one customer had one contact in the sales department, which was divided into four divisions: key account, business to business, classifieds and business development.

Implementation of this new approach was not easy. Nordjyske approached this by first making the vision and the reason behind it very clear. This was followed by a phase of involvement, where individual workgroups could influence the concept. Then the new format was introduced in small stages, during which people would participate in a 'learn through doing' approach. Once this worked, it was scaled up quite quickly. It took quite a bit of time and patience to make it work. And yet, in the end, it was a resounding success: the readership increased and the TV channel acquired new viewers and became the main gain of the integration. This integration was the basis for further diversifications into telemarketing, events and advertising, and magazine publishing.

Integration at Die Welt

The Welt Group was also an early mover in the integration of its newsroom. It started in early 2000 with the joint production of four newspapers with a very different editorial concept: the daily quality broadsheet *Die Welt*, the Sunday paper *Welt am Sonntag*, the regional newspaper *Berliner Morgenpost* and, later, the tabloid newspaper *Welt Kompakt*.

In 2005 it was decided to transform the newsroom into a fully integrated newsroom that produced the news for the newspaper websites and mobile offerings as well as video content. Again a fundamental shift in the organization was needed. Over 400 journalists had to be trained to create articles for all channels and media. 'Online first' was established as an overarching principle, meaning that all articles and photos had to be published online first, followed up in some cases by more in-depth print articles in some of the newspapers, with everyone using the same Web-to-print workflows. A large integrated newsroom was created, where all journalists from one department shared one desk, and the chief editors also shared one desk.

Not surprisingly, there was initially great resistance both against the integration of the newspapers and later on against the multimedia approach with its online priority. However, once the journalists started to experience the new approach most of them grew more and more appreciative of the possibilities and productivity improvements it offered. Print journalists appreciated the direct feedback they would get on their Internet articles. A big print screen was put on the wall where journalists could see in real time (through colour coding) how intensively their online articles were being read. This direct feedback loop was very helpful for the journalist trying to fashion their articles around readers' interests.

As the examples above show, a 360° media paradigm requires a very careful organizational approach. The right balance has to be found between pushes from above with a clear vision and guidelines and input from the workfloor, enabling the creative talent to take an active role in the redesign. Organization structures have to be aligned more around content than around media, journalists have to be trained to become multimedia storytellers, physical locations have to be changed to a much more integrative work floor.

Open organization

With the rise of UGC, some companies are also relaxing their policy of closed creation and editing environments. A fully open model is rarely seen, even in pure Internet environments (even YouTube retains the editing rights to exclude unfit videos), and a pioneer, UGC site like OhmyNews in South Korea still maintains a closed editorial door, and takes responsibility for quality of the input news on its site. Allowing for more openness, like accepting deeper user feedback, comments, etc. is now becoming common practice. The evolution towards much more open creative models with crowd-sourced content is still minimal, and requires in any case much stronger editing and interactive

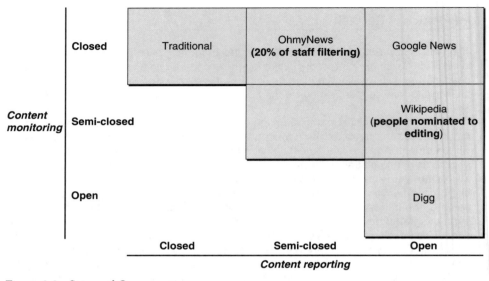

Figure 9.9   Stages of Open creation

Source: McKinsey analysis based on data from Wolf Richter; Oxford Internet Institute; Mimeo

skills. In some cases, people have solved the problem by self-selecting the best contributors to do part of the editing job, like on Wikipedia (Figure 9.9).

Vertically integrating content generation businesses

As content bundlers, such as TV channels, and content distributors, such as cable and telecoms operators, are integrating backwards into content generation, they are facing a double organizational challenge. First, they have to develop the skills to manage a company which differs fundamentally from their core business and, second, they have to take extreme care not to lose the key talent, as that would decimate the value of the company. Successful examples, such as RTL and Fremantle, amply demonstrate that there is a fine line between a hands-off approach, where the production company is treated as an independent profit centre, and careful integration, mostly based on soft factors. By bringing both companies together and letting personal relationships develop, the willingness to listen to each other and respects each other's vision is slowly nurtured. This can be enhanced by some non-intrusive privileges, such as the right of first sight and last refusal. Also designing the right incentive system for the content company is of crucial importance. Mediaset introduced an elaborate share programme for the key management of Endemol after its acquisition. Management was rewarded with vested shares, and the upside potential of the shares depended both on the time the management would stay with Endemol and a set of multidimensional performance criteria, which not only included financial parameters but also strategic KPIs, such as a number of high-margin formats to be launched and growth in digital revenues to be pursued.

'Enterprise 2.0'

Knowledge sharing to ensure fluidity of creativity and enable integrated control has been shown to be crucial for human resources management in media. The digital revolution brings about the possibility to use some of its tools, like blogs, Wikis and social networks, as ways of exchanging information within the organization.

Two challenges remain for the pervasive use of social media tools in media companies. First, it requires a clear and conscious model of adoption by employees, where they are incentivized or rewarded to share; second, the jury is still out as to the true value of those technologies. Nevertheless, successful cases have already emerged. No one knows whether they are exceptions or clear-cut examples of how to scale social Web technologies for better human resources management in media companies (Figure 9.10).

As early on as 2003, Google implemented an internal Web log system behind its firewall, after acquiring the blogging service Blogger, in order to have people take notes of meetings, exchange ideas and create new knowledge flows. A major media content production company invested in Wiki platforms to ensure that creative ideas were posted and improved by the various creatives of its organizations – about 40% of the creatives are using the platforms, and two pilot shows have come from those social media tools.

Another cable company used Wikis to motivate the codification of best practice for home wiring and modem installation among its installers. This codification replaced the

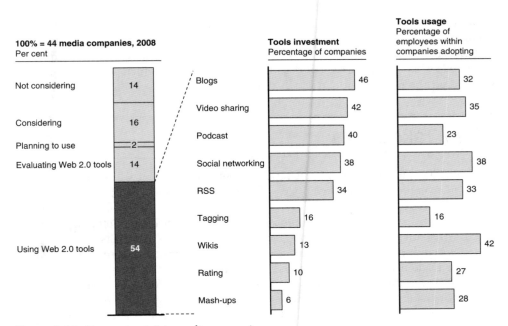

Figure 9.10   Enterprise 2.0 in media companies

Source: McKinsey Web 2.0 global enterprise survey, 2008

old guide of best practices, and improved the proportion of home wiring and installations which went right the first time by 10–15%. The payback is great for the installer, as they receive a bonus for each new well-installed product, while their time spent per installation can be improved significantly if they know the right tip: who else than peers can give those tips and improve upon them by sharing the experience of all peers?

Outlook and Open Questions

If the media industry is to cope with both today's and tomorrow's challenges, it must improve its people management processes substantially. The problem is made more acute by the digitization accompanied by the continuing consolidation of media companies (which often turns family-owned businesses into publicly managed enterprises, accompanied by the departure of the traditional patriarch). Another major people management issue is motivation, especially for those employees who are driven by success stories, such as advertising sales staff or music promotion managers. When successes are harder to come by, such people can quickly become demotivated. Indeed, a lack of vibrancy and vanishing courage and motivation can already be observed and has to be turned into digital success stories.

Irrespective of the media industry sector, HR departments are often viewed as lower-level administrative functions, rather than as top-level strategic ones. Some people management processes are rated too important to be left to HR, such as recruiting talent. Meanwhile, other processes are often rated too unimportant to be conducted at all, or they are merely paid lip service, such as systematic people development. Overall, HR departments today do not have a lot of clout within the senior management of media companies, which would be a prerequisite to changing their role. Only a few companies, such as Bertelsmann, have strategically built up their HR function. Companies need to ask themselves what the role of the HR department should be, and which processes should be kept within the department and which should not.

Key Takeaways

1. Media is a people business. Effective people management will become even more important in the digital age, as fundamental new skills and behaviours will be required.
2. Current people management processes in media companies are often not very systematic and depend on the quality of the individual managers.
3. When thinking of people management processes in media, a distinction has to be made between the creator and the transformer.
4. However, there are HR processes which apply to both groups; key examples are systematic talent development and clear performance evaluation.
5. Media companies should install highly professional HR processes for transformers. Hiring top talent in functional areas, including from other industries, should become a top priority.

6. Creators should be managed systematically throughout the job cycle:
   - Attracting the right talent should be a key element of the top management agenda.
   - Tailor-made development programmes are needed, giving the creatives the opportunity to either transition into effective managers or develop more in their creative field.
   - Careful attention should be paid to create a motivational environment.
   - Creatives should be transitioned out in a timely fashion, so they do not pass their prime.
7. Key elements to create a motivational environment for creators are the entrepreneurial freedom to pursue ideas, a great brand to work for, opportunity for peer recognition and having inspirational leaders.
8. Media companies can channel creative energy to increase effectiveness and efficiency, by involving creatives actively in creating a joint vision and strategy for the company, breaking the strategy down into concrete goals and KPIs and giving the creatives the freedom to decide how they are going to achieve these goals.
9. Transitioning to the digital era, media companies face three types of challenge:
   - Internet companies have to master the transition from an entrepreneurial to a corporate environment without losing the entrepreneurial spirit.
   - Traditional media companies will have to integrate their on- and offline businesses; this will require a fundamental redesign of the editorial organization on multiple dimensions.
   - Content packagers and bundlers integrating backwards into content generation will have to handle this very carefully through a combination of an arms' length approach and financial incentives in order not to 'kill' the creative talent.
10. The role of the HR department should be upgraded from an administrative, labour-focused unit to a strategic people development role.

BBC: Adapting the Organization to the Digital World[1]

For many in both the media industry and the technology sector, the BBC's iPlayer was the most impressive new online TV offering of 2007. The iPlayer allows UK licence holders to view a selection of BBC TV and radio programmes on the Internet, through their iPhone or iPod, or through the Nintendo Wii. The plans are to follow this successful introduction with the launch of Project Kangaroo, a joint venture by the BBC, ITV and Channel 4, which offers access to the combined content archive of these channels on the Internet.

But the introduction of new digital offerings also makes continual organizational changes necessary. For example, the Director of the BBC's Future Media & Technology Group, Ashley Highfield, who headed the launch of the iPlayer, has departed, first to become the CEO of Project Kangaroo and from there on to join Microsoft as its UK managing director. Getting and keeping digital talent poses its own challenge, especially in an organization which is funded by public money and has less freedom with, for example, remuneration policies than commercial broadcasters have, as recent criticism by the public of some of the BBC's salary practices shows. As a publicly funded company, the BBC must manage the public's expectations, in addition to being innovative and competitive with other broadcasters. The company went through some fundamental organizational changes in the early 2000s, which centred on creativity and collaboration, in order to prepare it for the new cross-media world. Will this new organization together with the BBC's current focus on new media and technology suffice to attract and retain top talent and foster an organizational culture that is innovative in both content production and technology?

Company History

The BBC is a corporation under royal charter (i.e. an institution serving public interest), dating back to the 1920s. BBC Company Limited, a private limited radio consortium, was founded on 8th October 1922 and broadcast first in November 1922.

Initially set up by radio manufacturers as a broadcasting vehicle to further their business interests, the BBC quickly made a name because of its quality programming. On 1st January 1927, the BBC was awarded its royal charter. The BBC started experimenting with low-definition TV transmissions in 1929; the first experimental transmission from BBC Broadcasting House was in August 1932. It introduced high-definition television broadcasting in 1936, initially using the 'Baird' hdtv system, which was replaced in 1937 in favour of the superior EMI–Marconi system. Television services were suspended for security reasons from September 1939 until June 1946. The company reached a first peak of over 20 million viewers watching the coronation of Elizabeth II in 1953. The

---

[1]This case is developed solely as the basis for class discussion. Cases are not intended to serve as endorsement sources of primary data or illustration of effective or ineffective management.

BBC's TV monopoly was deconstructed in 1955, when ITV was launched as the first commercial network in the United Kingdom.

On 20th April 1964, its second TV channel – BBC2 – was launched. Shortly thereafter, in 1967, Radio 1 was introduced, which offered a new service to young listeners. The previous radio services – Light, Third and Home – were renamed Two, Three and Four. The BBC was again an early adopter of cutting-edge technology when its channel BBC2 began broadcasting in colour in 1967 and BBC radio started broadcasting in FM stereo in the same year. Only five years later, the BBC introduced its teletext service CEEFAX. The BBC also opened its first local radio station in Leicester in 1967.

Organizational restructuring

In the early 1990s, a period of reforms began for the BBC. At that time there was a widespread sense that the organizational performance of the BBC had declined, both editorially – in terms of quality and reliability – and operationally. There was a belief that the BBC's traditional 'bureaucratic' style had outlived itself and had effectively led to far too high costs. In terms of creativity and cultural aspirations, however, the BBC was still perceived as a major force in the United Kingdom.

In the early 1990s, the BBC employed some 25 000 people, and there was a significant lack of performance transparency and no shared purpose or strategy. More urgently, news programmes in particular were perceived to be deteriorating and in need of reform. The new director general (DG), John Birt (Deputy DG from 1987 to 1992 and DG until 2000), decided to embark on a major decade-long organizational transformation designed to change the BBC.

Cornerstones of the change process included creating transparency and accountability, for example by making producers aware of and responsible for the cost of internal and external services, introducing a divisional set-up to minimize organizational redundancy, 'flattening' the organizational structure and making sure all departments were sufficiently represented in the top management group. At the same time, the producers had more freedom to optimize their resources, as they were allowed to choose between BBC suppliers and the external market for their facilities (producer choice programme).

Over the ten-year change period, the BBC's costs were cut by almost 40%, which was achieved, among many other things, through the introduction of internal marketplaces. The transition from a public monopoly to a market-driven company, however, continued to be challenging, leaving top management no choice but to pull a whole range of levers to effect fundamental cultural change. These levers included introducing a divisional structure and creating further budget transparency and individual responsibility.

Fostering a culture of creativity and collaboration

In 2000 Greg Dyke took over as DG from John Birt. Noticing that the organization had become very weary after the long change process, he started a company-wide process called the 'Making it Happen' initiative. The objective of this initiative was to realize the potential of the BBC's staff as a creative resource. The intended cultural change should make the BBC 'the most creative organization in the world'. A first result showed problems in trust and collaboration between divisions. To improve cross-divisional communication, the One-BBC initiative was launched in 2003. Problems in programme commissioning, the lack of leadership on all levels, low staff morale and a poor feedback process were also identified in those change initiatives.

In 2003 the BBC faced a difficult period in its history around the programming of news related to the Iraq war. The episode led to recognition of editorial weaknesses and the departure of the two top executives running the BBC. Mark Thompson, previously CEO of Channel 4, took over as DG and Michael Grade, also a BBC veteran, was hired as the new chairman.

Commercial activities

The BBC has been charged by the UK government to raise funds through commercial activities in order to keep the licence payments as low as possible. These activities should be kept strictly separate from the public services of the BBC. To this end, the BBC has set up two wholly owned subsidiary companies: BBC Worldwide and BBC Ventures Group. BBC Worldwide is Europe's largest TV distribution company and the United Kingdom's biggest TV programme exporter. It creates, markets and sells BBC brands and programmes across all platforms. It is also one of the United Kingdom's largest magazine publishers and licenses tie-in merchandise around the world. In addition, the BBC enters, from time to time, into a strategic alliance or partnership with a commercial agency, such as its 50/50 joint venture with Flextech in a suite of UK TV channels.

Digital TV and expanding online

Back on track after a period of restructuring in the early 2000s, the BBC started preparing for the advent of the digital world by launching BBC News 24. News 24 was the first of a series of six thematic channels to be carried on various digital platforms including cable, satellite and, eventually, digital terrestrial TV (DTT). In 2002, after the terrestrial ON-digital service ran into difficulties, the BBC established a consortium with BSkyB and Crown Castle to operate the new and free DTT platform, Freeview.

The BBC also has several online initiatives, including the website bbc.co.uk, the portal BBCi and the mobile phone branch BBC Mobile. In 2007 the bbc.co.uk site attracted 33 million unique users each week. The Internet portal, BBCi, which is one of Europe's most popular content sites, reached an average of 15.9 million users in 2007. Additionally, BBC Mobile is a news, sport and weather service that is accessible through mobile phones.

However, the BBC's greatest digital success to date was the launch of its iPlayer service in 2007. The iPlayer allows licence holders to access BBC content for free via the Internet. It is estimated that 100 million[2] videos were downloaded in its first 6 months of operation. The second version of iPlayer was launched in June 2008 and now supports BBC radio, and includes several design improvements. Only publicly available, free content is available through iPlayer.

---

[2]http://www.ft.com/cms/s/0/08d0f506-42dc-11dd-81d0-0000779fd2ac.html

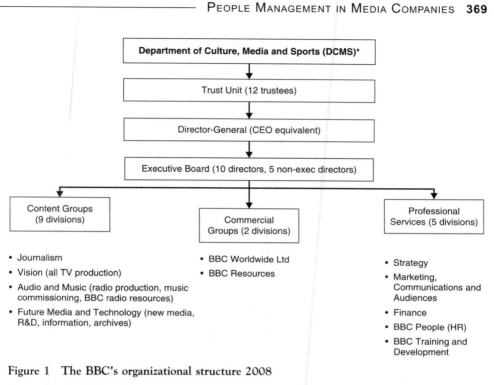

Figure 1   The BBC's organizational structure 2008

Source: data from Wikipedia

Current Situation

Industry dynamics

Public versus private broadcasters in the United Kingdom

As a public broadcaster, the revenue stream of the BBC is very different from that of the commercial players in broadcasting such as ITV, Channel 4 and BSkyB. The BBC has a stable cash flow generated from a TV licence paid by TV-viewing households in the United Kingdom.

There is a strong expectation from the UK public that, given the stable cash flow of the BBC from its licence fee, and therefore its independence from economic market conditions, it should produce innovative and high-quality content, which is readily available to the UK public. Therefore, the BBC invests heavily in producing home-grown content. Typically, commercial subscription channels in the United Kingdom only use 3% of their revenues on new UK content, focusing instead on areas like feature films and premium sport, which increase revenue per head.

But with stable cash flow comes restrictions: the BBC is not permitted to carry advertising or sponsorship on its public services. This keeps it independent of commercial interests and ensures that it can fulfil its mandate to serve the public's interest. While other broadcasters derive the majority of their revenue from advertising and subscriptions, around 75% of the revenues of the BBC come from the licence fee. The majority of the remainder comes from its international commercial arm, BBC Worldwide. The profits from this division are used to help keep the licence fee low.

For commercial TV broadcasters, both changes in the advertising market and the Internet have had a significant negative impact on their bottom line. The year 2008 was particularly tough for TV broadcasters, as advertising revenue shifted to online offerings, and the advertising market in the United Kingdom and worldwide slowed its growth. Furthermore, the BBC became a strong competitor on the Internet, through the launch of its iPlayer programme. With the iPlayer, the BBC has a more advanced digital offering than the majority of commercial broadcasters. As a result, Channel 4 is lobbying the UK government for a share of the licence fee to help make up for the tough economic conditions of the year. Early in 2008 their request was starting to be considered by the UK government.

The BBC

In 2004, a new charter for the BBC was drafted, and as of 2007 it has been officially adopted. The charter outlines the role of the BBC in its second phase of digitization, which involves creating a 'digital Britain'. It also clarifies the funding structure of the BBC (i.e. concerning the licence fee, how commercial activities can be carried out), and its governance and accountability mandate, which will be implemented by the BBC Trust and the BBC Executive Board. Furthermore, it describes the scale and scope of the BBC with respect to programme production within London and the United Kingdom, and internationally.

Based on the charter, the strategy of the BBC focuses on its role to 'inform, educate and entertain'. This is more clearly defined through six public purposes:

1. Sustaining citizenship and civil society: this focuses on providing high-quality, trusted and independent journalism.
2. Promoting education and learning: this involves education for children, teenagers and adults through children's radio and TV shows, online revision programmes for older students and adult learning of Welsh, Gaelic and Irish.
3. Stimulating creativity and cultural excellence: this addresses the need to generate creative and innovative content.
4. Representing the United Kingdom, its nations, regions and communities: this focuses on BBC broadcasts in different regions in the world.
5. Bringing the United Kingdom to the world, and the world to the United Kingdom: this involves promoting BBC-produced content worldwide.
6. Taking a leading role in the switchover to digital television: this centres on being a leader in new technologies, and adopting its programming and products to emerging telecommunications services, such as Freeview and freesat.

Given the charter, and its six public purposes, a plan to ensure that the BBC remains creative and at the cutting edge of technology was devised in 2006. This plan was intended to address the challenges the BBC faces in balancing investments in technology and new media with investments in creative talent, and in fostering a creative and innovative work environment.

From strategy to execution: implementing the creative future initiative

Inspired by the results of the 'Making it Happen' and the 'One-BBC' initiatives of the early 2000s, the 'Creative Future' proposal was created in 2006. This plan focused on delivering public service content to audiences in any media format and on any device, whether the audience is at home or on the move.

To implement this 'anywhere anytime' approach to media, the BBC gave priority to ensuring it was organizationally and culturally prepared to realize the Creative Future mandate. This involved putting technology and its potential uses at the heart of creative thinking, and creativity at the heart of its training strategy. A new Creativity and Audiences Training Board was established. Additionally, an initiative to help teams develop a more disciplined approach to creative development was implemented. Furthermore, the BBC's organizational structure, which had become flatter and less hierarchical over the years, was adapted to include a new technology division called Future Media and Technology (FMT). The goal of this division is to help audiences find and use BBC content with a focus on technical innovations in search, navigation and metadata, in addition to on-demand, mobile and Web 2.0.

Another key aspect of the Creative Future initiative is the collaboration of technology teams with content production teams. It is expected that technology teams work and interact closely with content production groups. To facilitate this, in some cases technologists sit right next to the content production staff.

Digital focus

Through the FMT division, the BBC has built up its technical expertise, as was illustrated through the launch of the iPlayer. The iPlayer has been widely popular and has reached on average 1.1 million users each week. Besides this, in order to maintain and build up technical competencies within the BBC, several senior staff members have been added to the FMT and the BBC Vision strategy divisions. Erik Huggers, previously of Microsoft, and before that Endemol, will replace Ashley Highfield as the head of the FMT as he leaves to run Project Kangaroo. Roo Reynolds, who is an expert in social networking, will be involved in developing and executing BBC Vision's strategy in social media. Also, Ayesha Mohidden will lead BBC Vision's multiplatform delivery strategy, which will focus on commissioning activities for all digital platforms.

Financial performance

Both 2008 and 2007 proved to be strong years for the BBC. Total income reached £4 415.8 million in 2007. Of this, £3 369 million came from licence fee collection, representing a 3% increase in the cost of the TV licence. However, the BBC strives to keep licence fee

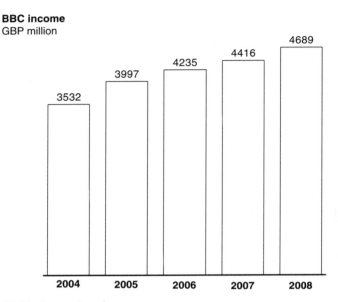

Figure 2 The BBC's financial performance

Source: McKinsey analyses based on BBC Annual reports 2004, 2005/06, 2007/08

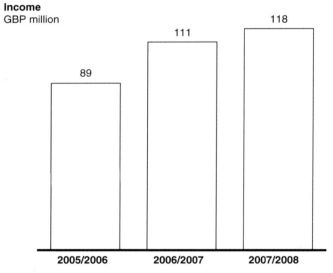

Figure 3 BBC Worldwide's financial performance

Source: McKinsey analyses based on Annual reports 2007/2008

costs to a minimum and in early 2008 was able to reduce collection costs to £123 million, down from £134 million in 2007.

Of the BBC's total income in 2007, £810 million came from BBC Worldwide's commercial activities. Early 2008 figures indicate that BBC Worldwide provided £916 million. The division's strategy of focusing on online and overseas sales resulted in growth in online sales of 10% and the division earning a record profit in 2008. BBC Worldwide earned profits of £118 million in 2008, up from £111 million in 2007.

Strategic Challenges

Retaining and attracting top talent

The BBC is often referred to as one of the best-managed public organizations in the United Kingdom. In order to retain its reputation of excellence in terms of management, content production and technical innovation, it needs top managerial, creative and technical talent. Yet to attract and retain quality staff it needs to remain competitive with the commercial broadcasters and Internet players that are also vying for top talent. That thus is difficult shows the loss of Ashley Highfield, the former head of the FMT division to Microsoft in November 2008. How the BBC can attract and retain top talent is not always obvious. Salaries are important, and the BBC has felt the pressure to become more competitive with salaries. But it must always balance this with the public's expectations of how it spends public funds. Work environment and opportunities to work on innovative projects are also important. The BBC has a history of innovative content development, and is building a reputation for technological innovation. But is this enough? What else can the BBC offer to keep quality talent within the organization?

Managing creativity

What approaches can be taken to motivate the people at the BBC to stay creative and give their best in an environment where the rules of the game change at an unprecedented speed, for example with regard to the use of different platforms and the rise of interactivity and user-generated content? Additionally, how can the BBC create an environment where creative individuals collaborate well with technical individuals? How can both groups be convinced to use their creativity not only to produce exceptional programmes and technical innovations but also to produce them as efficiently as possible? How should initiatives such as the Creative Future be further developed? Does the BBC need to further reorganize or flatten the organization to achieve greater collaboration amongst creative and technical staff?

INDEX

20 Minutes 24
8020 Publishing 142
access to online services 308–10
accountability 189–92
acquisition efficiency 137–8
Action Capital Partners 66
ad-based models 133–5
Adjug 66
advertisers, impact of online advertising on 216–22
advertising
       33, 211–58
    demand-side
      market 214–22
    direct marketing 213
    dynamics 223–5
    impact 9, 23
    reach 9, 23
    inventory provision 225–6
    new capabilities 226–47
    sales force management 242–6
    Schibsted SCA case study 248–58
    spend 3, 4, 6, 10
    strategically designed products 233–4
    supply-side market 222–6
    traditional 211–12
    value chain 235–7
    see also
        B2B marketing, *and under* marketing strategies
advertising ecosystem 217–18
advertising sales 18–19
  online 356–7
Aftenposten 249, 253, 256
Albacom 70
Amazon 6, 28, 261, 306
ancillary revenues 88
Antenne Bayern 61
AOL 224, 262, 269
AOL Time Warner
  cross-sector synergies 270
  customer value 233
Apollo project 237
Apple 26

iPod 24, 192
iTunes 24
apprenticeship model 342
aQuantive 224, 269
Arvato, vertical integration 271
attract 346
audience, impact of digital advertising on 214–16
auFeminin.com 43, 49, 261, 263
Auto Bild 41, 42
average revenue per user (ARPU) 2
Axel Springer AG 5, 38–40, 40, 43, 49, 261
  competitive advantage 270
  management as core competency 268
  niche and thematic offerings 141
Axel Springer Digital TV GmbH 42

B2B marketing 16, 29, 62, 227–8, 273, 303
  segment definition 228–33
B2C 62, 303, 304
BAA 346
Ball, Tony 354
Bauer Magazine Group 90
BBC 25, 266, 346
  budgetary responsibility 354
  talent development 348
BBC case study 366–73
  charter 370–1
  commercial activities 368
  company history 366–8
  creative future initiative 371
  creativity management 373
  digital TV and online expansion 368, 371
  financial performance 371–3
  industry dynamics 369
  iPlayer 371
  organizational structure 2008
  public vs private broadcaster 369–70
  strategic challenges 373
BBC Worldwide 346
BBradio 61
Bebo 33, 36, 308
Belo Interactive 193

Berliner Morgenpost 38, 44
Berlusconi, Silvio 69
Bertelsmann 199, 200–1, 260, 261, 262, 342
  content generation 351
  corporate university 348
  creatives 346
  cross-sector synergies 270
  image building 349
  marketers and content creators 356
  talent attraction 346
  talent development 342–3, 348
  vertical integration 271
beta factors 5
Big Brother 69, 84, 85, 86, 87, 105, 204
Bild 24, 31, 268
Bild & Funk 58
Bild am Sonntag 41
Bild brand 41, 44
  extension 141
Bild der Frau 41
Bildwoche 41
Bild-Zeitung 41, 44
Birt, John 367
blockbuster content 83–9
blockbuster lifecycle 87–9
  ancillary revenues 88
  content syndication for distribution platforms 88
  content/brand leveraging and extension 88
  original content merchandising 88
Blogger 363
blogs 22, 363
BlueLithium 224
Boing 71
Bonnier 261
book clubs 19
book industry 28–9
  electronic 28–9
  talent development 348
brainstorming 96
brand 349
  and packagers 31
  evolution 98
  importance 230
  positioning 129
  relaunch 131–2
  repositioning 130–1
  see also strategic brand management
branded content 224
branded pre-selector 35
bread and butter products 89–90
Brigitte 31
broadband 7, 306–8
  access 308–10
  rebalanced, media value chain 312–14

BSkyB 28, 260, 263
  leadership 354
Bunte Illustrierte 58
Bunte Online 61
Burda *see* Hubert Burda Media
Burda Community Network 66
Burda Digital 61, 66
Burda Group 187
Burda Moden 58, 59
Burda, Anne 58
Burda, Franz 58
Burda, Franz junior 58
Burda, Hubert 57
BurdaYukom GmbH 62
business models, required 34–6
  branded pre-selector 35
  'hit' exploiter 35
  ultimate marketing machine 35

C/Net 225
cable operators 19, 25, 26
Callahan, Richard J. 170
Canal+ Group 202, 261
Canal+ Group case study 144–55
  company history 144–7
  content costs and bidding wars 146
  current situation 147–53
  industry dynamics 147–50
  international expansion 146
  satellite technology 145
  strategic challenges 153–5
Canale 5 69
cascade rights to multiple products 30–1
case studies
  BBC 366–73
  Canal+ Group 144–55
  EMI Group 156–66
  Endemol 107–11
  Hubert Burda Media 57–68
  Lagardère Media 284–92
  Libert Global 277–83
  Mediaset Group 69–81
  OhmyNews 112–19
  RTL Group 198–210
  Schibsted ASA 248–58
  Second Life 322–9
  Telenet 167–77
  Welt Group 38–56
  YouTube 330–8
CDs 15, 23–4, 25
Cellular 61
Channel 4 25
Channel 5 25

Chellomedia 277–83
Chinese walls 3
Chip 61
churn 2
  behavioural factors 139
  event-related factors 139
  management 20, 137
  structural factors 139
  subscriber 137–9
  successful programmes 140
co-creation 101–2
Comcast Cable Company, vertical integration 271
compensation practices 353
computerbild.de 42
Confalonieri, Fedele 69
consumer opinion 121–8
  format-driven content 121
  fragmentation 122–5
  niche offerings 126–8
consumption patterns 7, 8
content
  brand leveraging and extension 88
  creators 342–5
  free 9, 22
  paid 9, 22
  transformers 345–6
  type of 2–3
content consumption 7–9, 22
content cost 22
content creation 30–1
  brands and packagers 31
  cascade rights to multiple products 30–1
  customer needs 30
  value-based pricing strategies 31
  content creation and leverage 83–119
  blockbuster content 83–9
  content generation process management 92–101
  content redefinition 89–92
  RTL Group case study 198–210
content creators and content transformers
    cooperation 355–6
  finance and product management 355–6
  marketers and content creators 356
content delivery 16–17
  process 31–3
content generation process 13–16, 20, 351–5
  creatives 14
  management 92–101
  marketing 16
  packaging 15
  pricing 15
  rights 14–15
content generation process management 92–101
  content generation 92–4

content innovation process management
    93–4
  filtering/portfolio management 97–101
  idea generation 94–6
  market research 96–7
content innovation process management 93–4
content redefinition 89–92
  beyond content 90–2
  non-blockbuster segments diversification
    89–90
  talent 90–2
content syndication for distribution platforms 88
core competencies and multi-local strategy 267–9
  analytics 269
  customer access and service 269
  superior management 268–9
core process changes 29–34
  B2B marketing 33
  content creation 30–1
  content delivery process 31–2
  customer lifetime funnel 33
  integration and rebalance 34
core processes 13, 14
corporate governance model 274–5
corporate strategy 259–301
  Lagardère Media case study 284–92
  media landscape 259–66
  portfolio logic 266–76
cost-plus deal 14
CPC 238
creating/leveraging innovative content see content
    creation and leverage
creatives 14
creatives management 346–56
  attract 346
  brand yourself 349
  compensation practices 353
  content generation processes 351–5
  entrepreneurial freedom 349
  job lifecycle processes 346–51
  leadership 354–5
  motivation 348–50
  people-development programmes 348
  rewards 352–4
  strategic goals 354
  talent development 346–45
  talent identification 347
  transition 350–1
  value proposition 348
creators and transformers 341–6
  content creators 342–5
  content transformers 345–6
cross-functional business programme 197
cross-sector synergies 270–1

current practices 13–20
  advertising sales 18–19
  content delivery 16–17
  content generation process 13–16
  end-customer interaction 19–20
  focus of media companies 20
customer
  access and service 269
  needs 30
  see also consumer opinion
customer-centric model 264–5
customer focus, sales force 242–3
customer intimacy 2
customer lifetime funnel 33
customer lifetime management (CLM) 139–41
customer lifetime value (CLV) approach 137–8
customer relationship management (CRM) 35, 138,
  166
customer-segment dominance 273
customer segmentation 228
Cyrte Investments 69, 77
Cyworld 308, 313

de Mol, John 77, 80, 354
Deal or No Deal 69, 84, 85, 105, 109
demand shifts 22
Desperate Housewives 88, 128
Deutsche Bank 188
Deutsche Post AG 43
development *see* filtering/portfolio management
DieWelt Publishing 44
differentiated service needs 232
digital asset management (DAM) 197
digital marketing 33
digital platform transition 192–7
digital rights management (DRM) 24, 160
digital skills 356–7
digital technology 214–26
digital terrestrial TV (DTT) 75, 148, 149
digital TV 6, 368, 371
Discovery Channel 142
  brand expansion 142
Discovery Tours 88
Disney 96, 267–8
  Gong Show 96
  leadership 351, 354
Disney Channel 71, 76
distribution efficiency 17
Dogan Burda Rizzoli 59
Dogan TV 42
Donau 3FM 61
Double Click 224, 269
DSF 193
Dyke, Greg 367

eBay 6, 261, 306
editorial skills, online 356
Eisner, Michael 351
electronic data interchange (EDI) 303–4
electronic programme guide (EPG) 31
Elitemedianet GmbH 61
Elle 3, 59, 84, 88, 292
Elle Decoration 88
Elsevier *see* Reed Elsevier
EMI 261, 264
  content generation 351
EMI Group case study 156–66
  adaptation to Internet 158
  digital threats and digital opportunities 160–1
  history 156–8
  situation in 2007 159–64
  strategic challenges 164–6
  technology 157–8
end-consumer segment target 231–2
end-customer interaction 19–20
Endemol 25, 69, 77, 79, 80, 81, 84, 93, 264, 267, 354
  Dutch market 100
Endemol case study 104–11
  challenges 107–11
  company history 105–7
end-to-end supply chain management *see* supply
  chain management
Enterprise 2.0 363–4
entrepreneurial freedom 349
Everywhere 226

Facebook 22, 36, 308, 310, 311
fast mover consumer goods (FMCG) 213
FastWeb 26, 76, 81
FAZ.net. 52
Fear Factor 84, 105
field trips 96
filtering/portfolio management 97–101
Financial Times 84, 348
Finding Nemo 267
Fininvest 69, 261
Finn 262, 346
Focus 58, 61
Focus brand 58
Focus Digital AG 61
Focus Gesundheit 61
focus of media companies 20
Focus Online 61
Focus TV 61
fragmentation 122–5
Frankfurter Allgemeine 44
Free 26, 269, 307
free TV 24–6
free-to-air TV 133, 239–41

FremantleMedia 25, 86, 271
funnel 94–5
  customer lifetime 33
  customer relationship 136

Gamekillers, The 224–5
GDP 4, 211–12
Giordani, Marco 69
Glam Media 66
global content 5
Goldman Sachs 77
Goldman Sachs Capital Partners 69
Google 6, 28, 35, 36, 46, 48, 49, 55, 128, 224–6, 237, 238, 261, 269, 272, 346, 363
  people management 358–9
Google Analytics 237
GoTVNetworks 316
GQ/Details 292
Grade, Michael 368
Grupo Media Capital 261
Gruppo Mediaset *see* Mediaset Group
Guardian online site 49
Gute Zeiten, schlechte Zeiten (RTL Group) 3, 100

H3G 71
Hachette 59
Hachette, Louis 285
Hallmark 350
Hamburg1 42
HBO 84
  brand repositioning 130–1
  entrepreneurial freedom 349
Heureka Growth 66
hit exploiter 35
HolidayCheck AG 61
Home Edition 105
Horzu 38
Hubert Burda Media 263
  brand yourself 349
  management as core competency 268
  niche and thematic offerings 142
  sector process skill 268
  talent recruitment 347
Hubert Burda Media case study 57–68
  central online content pool 66
  company history 57–63
  cross-media marketing 66
  current position 63
  diversification into other media and the internet 61–2
  glam media 66
  internationalization 59
  investments and acquisitions 66
  online advertising and e-commerce 66

  online content presence 66
  service businesses 62–3
  strategic challenges and opportunities 64–8
  vertical markets 66
  video 66
Huerguec 59
Hulu.com 25, 320

idea generation 94–6
idealo.de 43
Ilsemedia 346
immonet.de 42
improvement levers for non-standardized processes 189–92
  accountability 189–92
  transparency 189
Incredibles, The 267
industry trends by media sector 23–9
  book industry 28
  cable operators 26–7
  digital satellite pay TV 27
  magazine industry 28
  music industry 23–4
  newspaper industry 24
  other sectors 29
  TV 24–6
innovation *see* content creation and leverage
integration, and rebalance 34
Interactive Advertising Bureau 48
Internet 6
  broadband 6
  businesses, pure 357–8
  diversification to 262–3
  see also broadband
IPTV 42, 75, 81
ISTAT 79
Italia 1 69
ITV 25

J.P. Morgan 188
Jackass 92
job lifecycle processes 346–51
Jobs, Steve 267
Joost 154
JPG 226

key performance indicators (KPIs) 100, 344–5
  financial indicator 344
  operating indicator 344
  strategic indicator 344
Kindle 192
Kinnevik 261

Kirch Media Group 70, 263
Kreiz, Ynon 77

Lagardère, Jean-Luc 286
Lagardère 259, 262, 264
Lagardère Media case study 284–92
    company history 285–90
    strategic challenges 290–2
Last.fm 29
leadership 354–5
lean production 181, 183
Legge Gasparri 73
Lego 323
levers *see* improvement levers
Libelle 88
Liberty Global 260, 261
Liberty Global, Inc (LGI) case study 277–83
    company history 177–83
    strategic challenges 281–3
Linden Lab 322–9
LinkedIn 310, 311
Lion King 267
local content 5
Lucas Digital, KPIs 345
Lucasfilm 345

M6 25
magazine industry 28, 29
    fragmentation 122–3
    leadership 355
    moderators 97
    segment according to value orientation 232
Malone, John 260
Manchester United 346
market research 96–7
market structure 3
marketing 16
marketing and niche strategy 121–43
    Canal+ Group case study 144–55
    consumer opinion 121–8
    marketing strategies for subscription-based players
        136–41
    marketing strategy for niche and thematic offerings
        141–3
    Telenet case study 167–77
marketing needs, advertising and 230
marketing strategies for subscription-based players
    136–41
    churn 137–9
    customer relationship funnel 136
    customer relationship management (CRM) 139–41
marketing strategy for niche and thematic offerings
    141–3
    brand extension 141

Discovery Channel 142
Marktwort, Helmut 349
Maxis 102
McCann-Erickson, motivation 348
McClatchy 52
McGraw-Hill 193
    supply chain digitization 195
Mecon 264
media agency cooperation 246–7
media artefacts 90–2
Media Capital Group 261
media company management 29–34
    core process changes 29–34
    organizational challenges 34
media industry 1–10
    challenges 3–5
    content type 2–3
    core processes 11–12
    current state 5–10
    customer intimacy 2
    focus and scope of book 11–12
    revenue model 2
    value chain position 3
media landscape 253–66
    challenges and opportunities 266
    customer-centric model 264–5
    diversification to Internet 262–3
    family-owned corporate governance 263–4
    market concentration 261–2
    private equity investors 264
    regulator role 265–6
media value chain rebalancing 13–37
    business models required 34
    current practices 13–20
    EMI Group case study 156–66
    fundamental changes ahead 20–9
    Gruppo Mediaset case study 69–81
    media company management 29–34
Mediamatics initiative 237
Mediaset Group case study 25, 69–81
    advertising 72
    company history 69–71
    current situation 71–9
    digital threats and opportunities 81
    diversification through content production 77
    financial performance in 2007 79
    impact of regulation 73–5
    industry dynamics 71–6
    international expansion 70, 77
    internet and digital age 70–1
    platforms 75–6
    recent years 71
    strategic challenges 79–81
Mediaset Online 70

MediaVideo 71
Medusa 77
Medusa Film 77
mergers and acquisitions 274
Metro 24
Microsoft 224, 261
mobile phones 7
moderators 97
Mondadori 69
Monster 6, 38, 48, 49
motivation 348–50
MPEG-2 7
MPEG-4 7
MSN 238, 261, 269
MTV 92
    customer-segment dominance 273
multilocal sector dominance 272
Murdoch, James 354
Murdoch, Rupert 76
music industry 22, 23–4
    compensation practices 353
    digital right management (DRM) 24
    finance and product management 355–6
    fragmentation 122–4
    leadership 355
    music mail order business 91
    rewards 353
    transformers 344
MySpace 224, 263, 310, 311
MyVideo 135, 263

Napster 158
National Geographic 88
national multisector dominance 272
NBC Universal 25
Nessma TV 77
net present value (NPV) 99
Netflix 319
Netlog 261
new play options 272–3
    customer-segment dominance 273
    multi-local sector dominance 272
    national multisector dominance 272
    radical transformation 273
New York Times 48
New Yorker 292
News Corporation 25, 76, 262, 263
newspaper industry 24
    increasing acquisition efficiency 137–8
    leadership 354
    readers' preferences 135
Next New Networks (NNN) 142, 226, 316
niche offerings 126–8
Nike 96

Nike Inspiration Trips 96
NOB 187
Nokia 26
non-blockbuster segments diversification
    89–90
non-standardized processes/levers 189–92
Norddjske 359, 360
Nordwestdeutsche Hefte 38
NOS 187

OFCOM 276
offshoring 187–8
OhmyNews 30, 84, 101, 112–19
    company history 113–15
    current position 115–19
online advertising 217–18
online business opportunities 313–18
online co-creation 319
online communities for offline 320
online distribution 319–20
online integration 359–62
online marketing 318–19
online media
    1995–2001 303–6
    2002–2008 306–11
    business models 312–20
online media value chain 312–14
Orange TV 153
original content merchandizing 88
Orkut 310
outsourcing 187–8
Ozzy Osbournes, The 92

P2P 158
packaging 15, 31
Paramount Pictures 192
Paris Match magazine 3
pay-TV 21, 27–8
PC-TV media centres 7
Pearson 200, 259
    multi-local sector dominance 272
    company values 350
peer production 101–2
peer recognition 353
people-development programmes 348
people management 339–73
    BBC case study 366–73
    cooperation of content creators and content
        transformers 355–6
    creatives management 346–56
    creators and transformers 341–5
    media industry practices 339–40
    outlook and open questions 364
    processes 342–5

people management (*Continued*)
  transformers management 345–6
  in digital media era 356–64
performance evaluation 342–5
  key performance indicators (KPIs) 344–5
performance-based portfolio optimization 272
performance-based pricing 238–42
perishability of commodity 3
personal video recorder (PVR) 7, 25
Pin 43
Pixar 84, 267
Playboy 61
Polly, Allison 348
Pop Idol 86, 87, 204
portfolio logic 266–76
  core competencies and multi-local strategy 267–9
  corporate governance model 272–3
  new play options 272–3
  performance-based portfolio optimization 272
  portfolio and cross-sector synergies 270–1
  portfolio and scale 270
  regulatory alignments 276
  vertical integration 271
Premium Calcio 76
Prentice Hall 193
price differentiation 15
prices 15
  see also value-based prices
private equity investors 264
Pro7 61
Pro7Sat1 263, 264, 272
Pro7SatSBS 135
process changes 197
Procter & Gamble 346
Prodi government (2006–2007) 74
Project Kangaroo 366
ProSiebenSAT1 Media 42
public sector broadcasting (PSB), regulator role 265–6
Publitalia 76
purchase funnel bottleneck 230–1

Quillot, Didier 284, 290
Quinta Communication 77

Radical Media 110, 224
radical transformation 273
radio 29, 204
Radio 107.7 61
Radio Hamburg 42
Radio NRW 42
Radio PSR and PSR2 42
RAI 69, 72, 74, 76
Random House 261
  sector process skill 269

Real Madrid 346
Reckitt Benckiser 346
Reed Elsevier 99, 259, 261, 273
  competitive advantage 270
  customer-segment dominance 273
  in-house consumer panel testing centre 99
  multi-local sector dominance 272
regulator role 265–6
  public sector broadcasting (PSB) 265–6
regulatory alignments 276
  OFCOM 276
  Telenet 276
Rete 4 69, 74
revenue inventory ratio 243
revenue model 2
revenue sharing deals 15
rewards 352–3
rights 14–15
Ring Deutsche Makler 43
Rizzoli 59
RTI InteractiveMedia 70–1
RTL Group 25, 31, 86, 93, 100, 104–8, 260
RTL Group case study 198–210
  2007 situation 203–4
  company history 199–201
  digital presence 207
  digital TV and Internet 202
  diversification 202
  diversification 206
  financial performance 207
  industry dynamics 203–4
  international presence 206
  profitable growth 209
  radio 201–2
  recent years 201–2
  sector process skill 269
  strategic challenges 209
  synergies across profit centres 209–10
  television 201–2
  traditional TV and radio 201–2
RTL-TVI, digitization 195–6

sales force management 242–6
  media agency cooperation 246–7
  sales force trimming 242–6
sales force structure
  farmers 245
  hunters 245
sales force trimming 242–6
  customer focus 242–3
  incentives 245
  sales force structure 243–5
  time use 245
  integration 245–6

Sanoma group 260, 263, 346
Sanoma group case study 293–301
    company history 293–5
    current situation 295–300
    international expansion 301
    strategic challenges 300–1
SAT1 42
scarcity, management of 21–2
Schibsted, Christian 249
Schibsted 49, 260, 261, 262, 263, 342, 346
    radical transformation 273
    talent development 342–3
    vision creation 349–50
Schibsted ASA case study 248–58
    broadcasting and film production 253
    classifieds online 255–8
    company history 248–58
    free newspapers 253
    online diversification 251–2
    print classified 253
    print paid newspapers 252–3
    strategic challenges 254–8
Schouwenaar, Aat 77
Second Life 311
Second Life case study 322–9
    challenges 328–9
    company history 324–8
sector process skill 268–9
segment definition 228–33
    brand importance 230
    differentiated service needs 232
    end-consumer segment target 231–2
    purchase funnel bottleneck 230–1
    value orientation 232
Seinfeld 3
Sevenload 61
Sex and the City 86, 130
Sims, The 102, 111
single-media approach, advertising and 228–30
six-sigma principles 181
Sky Italia 71, 75, 76
Sony 26, 261
Sony Entertainment 155
Sony/BMG merger 24
Sopranos, The 86, 130
Spanish Telefonica 69
Spiegel, Der 58
Sport Bild 41
SPORTFIVE 202
Springer, Axel 38, 44
Springer, Friede 44
Springer, Heinrich 38
Star Academy 105
Star TV 263

Star Wars 345
strategic brand management 128–32
strategic goals 354
subscription-based players see marketing strategies
Süddeutsche Zeitung 24, 44
Sueddeutsche.de 52
supply chain digitization 193–6
supply chain management 179–210
    digital platform transition 192–7
    distribution efficiency 184–5
    improvement levers for nonstandardized processes
        189–92
    operational excellence 179–81
    outsourcing and offshoring 187–8
    production process efficiency 181–4
    purchasing effectiveness 185
    shared services 185–7
    supply chain processes 181–8
Swarm of Angels, A 102
Swisscom 76

Tacoda 224, 269
talent 90–2
    apprenticeship model 342
    development 342–3, 347–8
    identification 347
Taodue 77
Taylor, Jeff 38
Telecinco 69, 70, 79
Telecom Italia 76, 81
Telecom Italia Media (TIM) 71, 74
Telefonica 77
Telemilano 69
Telenet 121–2, 269, 276, 313
Telenet case study 167–77
    cable TV 171
    company history 169–70
    current situation and market position 170–4
    multiplay 173–4
    residential broadband internet 171
    residential telephony 173
    strategic challenges 174–7
television 24–6, 203–4
    chum 138–9
    digital 6, 368, 371
    digital satellite pay 27
    digital terrestrial (DTT) 75, 148, 149
    fragmentation 124–5
    free 24–6
    free-to-air 133, 239–41
    leadership 355
    pay-TV 21, 27–8
    production benchmarking 189
Terminator 84

terrafirma 345
test-tube formats 31
TF1 25, 260
TheNerve 84, 101
Thompson, Mark 368
Thomson Regional Newspapers
    talent attraction 346
    talent development 347
Titanic 84
TiVo 237
Tomorrow Focus AG 61, 63, 66
Touchstone project 237
Toy Story 267
TPS 153, 260
transformers management 345–6
transition 350–1
transparency 189–90
Tribune Interactive 193
Tributes.com 38
TV Berlin 42
TV *see* television
TV Spielfilm Online 61
TVI 134–5

UGC 359, 361
Ullstein AG 44
Ulrich & Partners 52
ultimate marketing machine 35
unique value proposition 233–8
Universal 261
usage 9, 10
usage and attitude (U&A) based criteria 228
user-generated content (UGC) 22, 30, 101–2, 209, 316, 353

value
    orientation 232
    proposition 348
value-based prices 31
value chain 3, 235–7
Vanity Fair 292
vertical integration 271, 362
Viacom 233
video-on-demand (VoD) 25
Viktklubben.se 49
Virgin 31
Virtual Me 110
Vivendi 145, 261
    content generation 351
VNU 261
    radical transformation 273
Vodafone 71
Vogue 84, 292
voice-over-Internet protocol (VoIP) 27

volatility, industry 3

wallstreet:online 43
WallStreetJournal 84
warehousing 17
Warner Music 261
WAZ, sector process skill 269
Web 2.0 22, 132, 140–2, 263, 310–11
Welt, Die 38, 44, 52, 361
Welt am Sonntag 38, 44
Welt brand 44–6
    Welt Group case study 38–56
    advertising and readership 47–8
    attracting visitors 55
    brand relaunch 131–2
    broadband penetration 38
    challenges of the transition to online 49–52
    company history 38–46
    competition for a share of online advertising 55
    convergence 55–6
    current situation 47–54
    diversification and international expansion 41–3
    early missteps 48–9
    future revenue model 55
    increased competition from web 2.0 55
    industry dynamics 47–52
    strategic challenges 55–6
Welt Klasse 45
Welt Kompakt 38, 44, 52
Welt Mobil 38, 44, 52
Welt Newsroom 44
Welt Online 38, 44
Welt TV 38, 44
Welt/Beliner Morgenpost group 46
Wheel of Fortune, The 3
white spots, idea generation 95, 96
Who Wants to be a Millionaire? 69, 86
WHSmith 285
Wikipedia 101, 310, 317, 353
Wikis 363
Wuertenberger, Peter 38

Yahoo! 6, 55, 224, 261
    broadband 307
Yellow Pages 40
YouTube 22, 30, 101, 102, 128, 132, 154, 272, 310, 316, 318, 319, 353
YouTube case study 330–8
    company history 334–8
    online video market 334–8
    strategic challenges 338

Zanox 43
Zeit, Die 24, 44